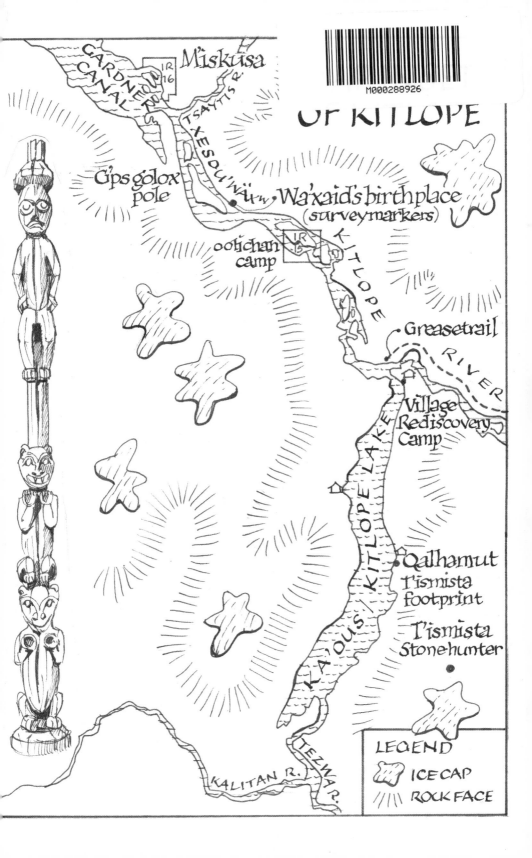

... of KITLOPE

Gardner Canal

M'iskusa

IR 16

Tsaytis R.

Txesdui wä tw

G'psgólox pole

Wa'xaid's birthplace
(survey markers)

oolichan camp

IR 15

Kitlope

Greasetrail

River

Village Rediscovery Camp

Kaous/Kitlope Lake

Qalhamut
T'ismista footprint

T'ismista
Stonehunter

Kalitan R.

Tezwa R.

LEGEND

ICE CAP

ROCK FACE

FOLLOWING THE GOOD RIVER

FOLLOWING THE GOOD RIVER

The Life and Times of Wa'xaid

by BRIONY PENN, with CECIL PAUL

For information on purchasing bulk quantities of this book, or to obtain media excerpts or invite the author to speak at an event, please visit rmbooks.com and select
the "Contact" tab.

RMB | Rocky Mountain Books Ltd.
rmbooks.com
@rmbooks
facebook.com/rmbooks

Cataloguing data available from Library and Archives Canada
ISBN 9781771603218 (hardcover)
ISBN 9781771604826 (softcover)
ISBN 9781771603225 (electronic)

Front cover photo: "Lä göläs'. Put your canoe ashore and rest." Cecil Paul. Lax
Kw'alaams. 2018. Courtesy Callum Gunn.
Jacket flap photo: "Signs say 'No Indians' except for the café." Cecil Paul and Briony
Penn at West End Café. Prince Rupert. 2017. Courtesy Callum Gunn.

Printed and bound in Canada

We would like to also take this opportunity to acknowledge the traditional territories upon which we live and work. In Calgary, Alberta, we acknowledge the Niitsitapi
(Blackfoot) and the people of the Treaty 7 region in Southern Alberta, which includes
the Siksika, the Piikuni, the Kainai, the Tsuut'ina and the Stoney Nakoda First Nations, including Chiniki, Bearpaw, and Wesley First Nations. The City of Calgary is also
home to Métis Nation of Alberta, Region III. In Victoria, British Columbia, we acknowledge the traditional territories of the Lkwungen (Esquimalt, and Songhees), Malahat,
Pacheedaht, Scia'new, T'Sou-ke and W̱SÁNEĆ (Pauquachin, Tsartlip, Tsawout, Tsey-
cum) peoples.

We acknowledge the financial support of the Government of Canada through the Canada Book Fund and the Canada Council for the Arts, and of the province of British Columbia through the British Columbia Arts Council and the Book Publishing Tax Credit.

CONTENTS

PREFACE

The Tributaries

Wa'xaid, whose name translates as Good River, invited many of us into the magic canoe to protect Mother Earth. He was never taught to read and write by the residential school system, so my job in the magic canoe seemed clear enough. I could record and transcribe his stories, as well as dig up the historical and scientific documentation that my Western education prepared me for – dates, names, court decisions, ecological concepts that correlate with Traditional Ecological Knowledge. Wa'xaid felt these written records would provide the dates and facts to form a framework for Western readers, should they need one. He is the master of engaging heart and mind together, so his *Stories from the Magic Canoe* form the main artery of the river, in half the space and with an elegance that only a gifted orator can command. In this expanded companion biography, I provide three tributaries: historical essays, journal entries and interviews with fellow paddlers. All together, they should provide many routes to navigate and interpret the life and times of Wa'xaid.

Wa'xaid shared Xenaksiala words when there was no English equivalent, such as *Lä göläs'* (put your canoe ashore and rest). Louisa Smith, Wa'xaid's sister, provided the spellings of her language using the International Phonetic Alphabet. She is one of the last four fluent speakers of Xenaksiala.

The extended family tree that grows from the matriarch Annie Paul, Wa'xaid's grandmother, is included. Family trees also tell stories. The colonial practice of only making it mandatory for white people to register births and deaths means that visits to graveyards sometimes provide the only resource for Indigenous family trees, where, if you are lucky, there are dates. Anthropologist Jay Powell provided many of the missing parts. A short chronology that marks events recorded in Wa'xaid's stories has also been prepared. When Wa'xaid says "you" in his stories, he is speaking to you, to me, to all of us – we are paddling in this magic canoe together. Our survival depends on it. I hope these stories encourage you to step into the magic canoe and join the many others for what I consider to be the greatest privilege of my life – following the Good River, Wa'xaid.

INTRODUCTION

The Place of My Birth:
"They call it the Kitlope"

My name is Wa'xaid, given to me by my people. *Wa* is "the river"; *Xaid* is "good" – good river. Sometimes the river is not good. I am a Xenaksiala; I am from the Killer Whale Clan. I would like to walk with you in Xenaksiala lands. Where I will take you is the place of my birth. They call it the Kitlope. It is called *Xesdu'wäxw* (Huschduwaschdu) for the "blue, milky, glacial water." Our destination is what I would like to talk about, and a boat – I call it my Magic Canoe. It is a magical canoe because there is room for everyone who wants to come into it to paddle together. The currents against it are very strong, but I believe we can reach that destination, and this is the reason for our survival.

When you leave Kitamaat, this is Haisla Land you go out to – they call it – Gardner Canal. You go into Gardner, and Crab River is where our boundary line was before the amalgamation of the Xenaksiala and the Haisla. Haisla and Xenaksiala share the same language, with a few word differences. Our language is close to the language family of River's Inlet. You can get the Haisla history from Gordon Robinson.

When I bring the boat into Xenaksiala land, the tide will bring us through. There is a story for that. From Crab River we enter the Kitlope Valley. The Kitlope has many, many rooms, many doors – there is a lot of history going up to Kitlope Lake. Kitlope Lake, if we manage to journey that far, it is what I call the cathedral – a spiritual place. It is quiet. I think if you experience something when we get there, our people say that you will not leave that place unchanged. You cannot leave the way that you went in. Something touches you. Something grabs within you that you never identified as yours, but something in there reveals a little of who we are.

When we get to the Kitlope, I am going to ask you to wash your eyes. Our story says that though you may have 20/20 vision or glasses that improve your vision, we are still blind to lots of things. We are blind to Mother Earth. When you bathe your eyes in the artery of Mother Earth that is so pure, it will improve your vision to see things. I will also ask you to wash your ears, so you could hear what goes on around you. So, I could hear you talk. I could hear the wind, and you can hear the birds and animals. If you have the patience to listen, to hear the songs of the birds early in the morning, all these things will be open to you.

We are so busy, we don't have the time for all these beautiful things. If

11

you have the willingness and courage to do that, you will see little things that you have never seen before. You will take a better look at your children, your grandchildren, your best friend. You'll say, "Oh, I never saw that before." To get that vision back – and when you get that back – you will be more kind to whoever comes in your path on this journey. There are many legends that we talk about to our children, and above all, the people around the universe that came with their love and compassion to save something that is known around the world – the largest unlogged temperate rainforest in the world.

A few weeks after the proclamation of the colony of British Columbia, on August 2, 1858, a map was released from a printing house near Blooms-bury, London, defining the boundaries of the British Empire's latest claim on global resources. Along the convoluted western coastal boundary, shaded in the rose red of empire, were drawn a dozen of the large fjords mapped, thanks to the cartographic brilliance of Captain George Vancouver. The largest and longest of these was Gardner Canal, a 320-kilometre inlet splitting off of Douglas Channel, giving the appearance of a crooked finger pointing to her majesty's anticipated riches penetrating deep into what would become British Columbia. The blank portions of the map allude to the polite fiction of *terra nullius*.[1] *Terra nullius* is a doctrine of international law that Europeans used to assert sovereignty over lands. It means literally "empty land" and declares that no one owned the land before European claims. Riding along the upper part of the digit was the name Gardner, an easily read label given the length and horizontal orientation of that reach of the inlet, before its lazy southeastward turn to the heart of the colony.

Joseph Whidbey, who accompanied Vancouver on the HMS *Discovery*, explored the canal in one of the ship's smaller boats. Vancouver describes BC's longest inlet as "almost an entirely barren waste nearly destitute of wood and verdure and presenting to the eye one rude mass of almost naked rocks, rising into rugged mountains."[2] He names it after his former commander, Baron Alan Gardner, as a tribute, or not, given his lackluster review of the "canal." Besides "Gardner" being an absentee namesake, "canal" was also a curious word to describe the largest fjord in the world. The sides of the canal are sheer granite rising 1829 metres from the sea bottom, piled there by shifting tectonic plates, far removed from the more familiar colonial canal being dug by indentured Panamanian slaves into their own mud.

As Wa'xaid explains, the Xenaksiala and Haisla who have occupied and owned this land for millennia have always had their own maps – visual ones. The system of land ownership of their huge territory falls into logical units of mountain watersheds, or wa'wais, that need no survey instruments, just a fine eye for topography. Boundaries follow the tops of mountains around the different drainage basins of the rivers that flow into the Gardner. Every watershed has a name that corresponds to its steward. The owners have both control and responsibility handed down through their mother's lineage. Each owner is bound by the *nuyem*, a code of stewardship that has detailed prescriptions for how the land, waters and wildlife are to be harvested, shared and respected. A *bagwaiyas* is a special place of abundance that is open to any Xenaksiala/Haisla person to harvest without special permission.

On the colonial map of British Columbia, there was no indication of the 54 wa'waises that occupy "the pointed finger."[3] Of the 14 wa'waises that pour into the Gardner, the first is Crab River, which demarcates the beginning of the territory of the Xenaksiala people and the end of the Haisla wa'waises. Halfway along Gardner is the Kemano River, which is the wa'wais owned by Cecil Paul himself. It was also the official "reserve" of the Kitlope Band until 1948. At the tip of the finger on the colonial map is a river called Kitlope, where Cecil was born in 1931 and mostly hidden until 1941, when, as he explains, the Indian agent rounded him up for residential school. That river flows into a lake, oval and luminescent with its milky-blue glacial water. Ice-capped mountains tower above this lake and for that reason the Xenaksiala call it Ka'ous. The closest Cecil can come to translating that word into English is "cathedral"; it gives people a sense of the beauty, peace and awe you feel when you first enter the lake from the river.

One of those who got into the magic canoe, Brian Falconer, recounts his first trip to the Kitlope with Cecil in May 1993:

> It is a stunning spring day on Gardner Canal; incredible granite monoliths covered with snow come down to the water. Every time you think it can't get more beautiful, you turn a corner and there is another spectacular scene. We get up to the mouth of the river, and it is like a place I could never have imagined. The next day, we set out to go up to Kitlope Lake. The water is crystal clear because the glaciers haven't started to melt. Eight-inch-deep water looks the same as three-foot-deep water when it is

that clear, so Cecil prepared us for the shallow parts of the river: "The boats have to be able to plane. If they don't you are going to lose props all the way up the river." He starts to show me how to read the river. "See the river smiling at you, it is not a happy smile, it is an evil grin. There is a big stick under there." So I learn to tell when there are logs just below the surface. Johnny Wilson is sitting in front of one of the boats and Cecil in the other. He doesn't say anything; just nods his head a little bit to the right or a little bit to the left. We'd been working really hard up the river avoiding the shallow spots, grinding along against the current beside a solid wall of rock – and then the curtains parted. I could almost hear the crescendo of the symphony music and we enter this unbelievable bowl of a lake with steep mountains all around it. Up on the mountain is T'ismista, the Man Who Turned to Stone. My life has just taken an incredible turn into wild beauty.

When Cecil says, "They call it Kitlope," his "they" first of all refers to European map-makers like Vancouver and the Hudson's Bay Company (HBC) or the Tsimshian with whom HBC traded. The first fort on the north coast, Fort Simpson, was set up in Tsimshian territory, so many of the names for Haisla and Xenaksiala places were mapped with Tsimshian names passed on by the traders to the map-makers. Even Kitlope Lake carries the Tsimshian place name on the maps. They called it Kitlope for "people of the stone" because of the huge granite cliffs that dominate the landscape. The Tsimshian live north and west of the Haisla and Xenaksiala, largely along the Skeena River and out into the islands. The Tsimshian language, known by its speakers as Sm'algyzx, is a completely different language. "They" also refers to Cecil's family, the Tsimshian Pauls.

HECATE STRAIT, SEPTEMBER 5, 2004

We are sailing just off of Kitkatla Village on Dolphin Island, which faces out onto Hecate Strait. It must be the most exposed village on the coast today. From the highest deck you can see the top of Tow Hill on the northern tip of Haida Gwaii. We left Prince Rupert this morning and the seas are unusually calm in Hecate Strait. Humpback whales are blowing; they are getting more and more common after their near brush with extinction. We've spotted killer whales and Dall's porpoise along the way – both members of the dolphin family – at least they got their name on the chart. Cecil shares with us that some of his Paul ancestors, from whom he inherited his Killer Whale Clan title, were originally from Kitkatla. He muses, "Where did these mysterious, beautiful men come from and why?" He tells us his family traded with Bella Bella, Klemtu, Hartley Bay, Port Simpson and Kitkatla. "Not only did my family, different families, trade too. Now no more. In my lifetime, that's all."

A PRIMER ON WA'XAID'S INTERWOVEN TSIMSHIAN/HAISLA LINEAGES

The Tsimshian connection is interwoven through Wa'xaid's family tree like the braids of the Kitlope River. His Great-Uncle Abraham (also known as Abel/Abil) Paul, from whom he received the name Wa'xaid of the Killer Whale Clan, has Kitkatla/Gitxaala roots. Gitxaala is a Tsimshian village and means "people of the open sea." Abraham's brother Charles was Cecil's grandfather through adoption. Charles adopted Cecil's birth father, Tom Paul, Gwä nax nood, from Annie Morrison (Cecil's granny) and her first husband, Samuel Wilson, because Charles and his wife (Samuel's sister), Esther, had no surviving children. The adoption ensured that another Killer Whale Clan name of Gwä nax nood could be passed down. Both Charles and Esther died of influenza when Tom was 11. When Samuel Wilson, Tom's birth father, also died of influenza, Annie married Johnny Paul, Chief Humzeed/Hemzid, making Johnny Cecil's grandfather by adoption. On Johnny Paul's death certificate, Abil [sic] Paul is cited as his father. Abel Paul could, therefore, be both Cecil's great-uncle and great-grandfather through adoption. Chief Paul (Sheaks) of the Kitlope is referred to in many early documents at the end of the 19th century. Chief Paul was possibly the father of Abel and Charles. The two smaller islands just northwest of Kitkatla are called Shakes Island (also written as Sheaks and Saex), named after the Gitxaala Chief Saex. The name Wa'xaid comes from the House of Hale (also written as Hail and Hael), which also includes the name Saex. Wa'xaid's grannie, Annie Paul, had a sister Alice who married Gitxaala Chief Hale. Cecil refers to his Great-Uncle Chief Hale in the "Grandson" story later, as Chief Hale bestowed both a totem pole and name in Kemano.

According to Dr. Charles Menzies, the Gitxaala scholar who is related to the Pauls through his late grandfather, the same Chief Hale (Edward Gamble who married Alice as his second wife), names are sometimes passed on to other people in other communities to strengthen alliances, without the associated land and rights. The late Chief Hale told his grandson Charles Menzies that Johnny Paul spoke Sm'algyzx fluently and was believed to have come originally from a Gitxaala family.

So when Cecil says, "They call it Kitlope," he also means the Pauls who came from Kitkatla. They would have first known their adopted community as the Kitlope. The complexity of adoptions and remarriages in Wa'xaid's family reflects the lineages and alliances needed for survival, but also the chaos they faced in the aftermath of disease and forced migrations, when entire clans and trading partners were dying out with their specialized knowledge of resources and wa'waises.

KITAMAAT, JULY 16, 2016

Cecil Paul's driver's licence has the usual information: address – 221 Kitlope Road, Kitamaat, BC; birthdate – November 28, 1931; photograph – distinguished older man with brush cut. It doesn't tell you that Kitamaat means Kitamaat Indian Reserve No. 1, which is 38 acres of mostly rock, and that there is really only room for three blocks of five roads to drive around on. The village overlooks their territory, the Kitimat River estuary, half of it now underneath the Kitimat townsite on the other side. Cecil doesn't need his licence anymore anyway. He has given up driving because he has had one too many health setbacks – heart bypasses, diabetes, cancer and now pneumonia that put him into intensive care at the Terrace Hospital.

He's back home in his house and is feeling good today, so we decide to do a road trip in his little black Honda. We have to sidestep the salmonberry shoots that took advantage of his sojourn in the hospital. Parked next to the car is his seven-metre aluminum fishing boat, *Miss Sophia* (named after his eldest granddaughter), hidden under salmonberries since he hasn't been able to fish since last summer. It is a tough, made-in-Kitimat aluminum special that can weather any number of winter storms and spring fevers. Aluminum was selected hands-down over wood as a material for a boat/canoe – a choice that is part of the paradox of being Cecil Paul. It is the aluminum industry that sent his people a lot of arrows. He hardly pauses on his journey to the car, sure as ever on his longshoreman legs over uneven ground. You can't work on boats and docks for 30 years and not have unerring balance. "A few hours for an outing only," his doctor recommended. He doesn't know Cecil Paul. He can survive everything.

Cecil wants to go to Kitimat town for brunch to fatten up at his favourite restaurant. I drive while he lights up a forbidden cigarette, rolls down the window and smiles at the bush as we wind our way around the shoreline of the estuary from Kitamaat reserve to Kitimat town – 10,000 years, 10,000 white people and two extra a's divide the two places. Young alder and hemlock push up through log dumps, rusting industrial sculptures and now the stalled subdivision clearings just out of town, called appropriately Bear Country (I suggest "Bare"). As we descend down the hill, Cecil points out the re-scarred Sand Hill, which curiously resembles his brush cut. A retreating glacier left 100 million tonnes of sand behind in the Kitimat estuary shortly before his ancestors paddled in here. That sand pile was one of the big attractions for the Aluminum Company of Canada (Alcan) back in 1952. They had a good kick at their proverbial aluminum can of shovelling it into the concrete mixers to build the plant and town on top of a rich productive delta full of salmon and oolichan. Now the remains of that sand pile have been bought by an American company carting it away, barge by barge, to service another glacial-like event, the paving over of California.

Kitimat – as bland as only a 1950s company town can be – has its own paving issues. Built in the middle of an oxbow bend of the Kitimat River estuary, it feels like a flooding event waiting to happen. Bolstered by the engineering optimism of the day, with its unlimited supply of sand, the city fathers rolled out the concrete, bank to bank, to create a town centre. The welcome signs at the gateway to the town still call it a city of "humans taking charge of their surroundings," where men "surmount the wild landscape" and "insert an urban utopian environment into the middle of the wilderness." This is the language of the 21st century. If you go back to the booster material from the 1950s, like the *National Geographic* and the *Saturday Evening Post*, they bill Kitimat as "Tomorrow's City Today," "Canada's Aluminum Titan" and the "Incredible Frontier." Whenever I read this stuff out to Cecil and ask him if it bugs him that nothing changes, he just smiles.

Cecil directs me on a slalom course between a drive-in fast food outlet, an abandoned motel and a travel agency that has cheap winter deals to Thailand fluttering from its door as the gusts of wind funnel through the concrete City Centre Mall. Cecil tells me the original owner of the travel agency was highly regarded by the Haisla, as she helped them onto flights to see doctors in Vancouver. The Honda comes to a natural stop at a wrinkled piece of concrete at the back of his regular diner. Four alders have broken through the tarmac and created a vestigial forest in the sump. We are in an old creek course that once fed the Kitimat River, into which the restaurant and its foundations are slowly slumping. Cecil knows a watering hole when he sees one.

Back at the diner, we have reached what feels like the town centre, if there is one in Kitimat. Random plaza malls and the few aging civic amenities are thrown here and there, but nothing – not even the children's playground, a mock savannah with a plastic hippo and elephant for toddlers to ride – could really be described as a heart of this glorified parking lot. The Kitimat Economic Development Association boasts that Kitimat "delivered" 15 billion dollars of manufactured products to world markets in the last decade, but there are precious few civic amenities to show for it. Probably the City Centre Mall could be described as the heart of the town, which doesn't bode well for the health of the rest of the body.

The young waitress's eyes light up when Cecil enters. He's been a regular for a good chunk of the diner's existence. The diner proudly boasts that it has served Kitimat since 1989, which for Kitimat is almost history. The menu is the most permanent piece of this town, after the concrete. He orders mashed potatoes "with as much gravy as you can find." She returns a few minutes later and apologizes for having run out of potatoes, but asks "Can you wait until we get some?" In the summer of 1899, his great-grandfather, Chief Paul, is recorded as telling the Indian Reserve Commissioner that his people "had made several fruitless attempts to grow potatoes, but have become discouraged by repeated failures." That same commissioner describes their reserves as "worthless...the soil being rocky or swampy."

Before they were confined to the reserves, they would dig up their carbs in the estuary: Indian riceroot, which mashes up nicely after a long bake. Instead of gravy, you drizzle oolichan grease. It is delicious if you like oolichan grease. Today, the foraging is done next door in the big box franchise that covers an acre of estuary. The oligarch Jimmy Pattison, who owns all the salmon and herring processing companies and most of everything else in BC, owns it. The story of scarcity would include a few chapters on Pattison's stranglehold on anything free that turns a profit. His stores are ironically called Save-on-Foods; the estuary used to feed thousands with salmon and carbs for free. "That's fine, we'll wait," Cecil says and tells me a story.

The mashed potatoes arrive and Cecil finishes off more than he has eaten in a week. Fuelled and ready, he wants to defy more doctor's orders and show me around the old haunts of his working life, the Eurocan mill, nestled up to its neighbour Aluminum Company of Canada. It was booming in Cecil's day, employing a large workforce from around the world. Today, the second-largest mining company in the world, Rio Tinto, owns Alcan. Cecil asks me about Rio Tinto. I tell him I'm not impressed with its record. It has been consorting with fascist regimes since the '30s, when it provided the ore for Nazi rearmament and sided with Franco when he ordered its striking workers shot, which solved its "labour problems." The latest human and environmental rights violations have been in California, Papua New Guinea, Indonesia and Madagascar. The list goes on.

We head out of town along Haisla Boulevard, another tip of the hat to Le Corbusier. The road name fits right into the weird blend of Euro-Canadiana worlds we inhabit. "Boulevard" evokes a wide, tree-lined Parisian avenue atmosphere; and sure enough, the trees are planted, the road is wide and, if we squint at each other, we can almost believe that I'm Audrey Hepburn to Cecil's Maurice Chevalier, speeding along Haisla Boulevard without a care in the world.

Haisla is the "Indian name" tagged on to give it the local touch. "Haisla" comes from the word "Haisu'," which means the end of the (Kitimat) river and "sla," which refers to the people. Naming the boulevard Haisla by the city planners is an improvement on Kitimat – or the reserve name Kita-maat – which is a Tsimshian name meaning "people of the snow." Cecil is not Haisla, he is Xenaksiala, but he lives in Haisla territory on a Haisla reserve called Kitamaat as a result of the 1948 amalgamation agreement. It is all very confusing, but that is part of Cecil's story – how confusing it all was.

A PRIMER ON THE CONFUSING GEOGRAPHY OF HAISLA/XENAKSIALA/TSIMSHIAN TERRITORIES

Imagine you are in a boat drifting on Gardner Canal, at the second knuckle of the "pointing-finger-on-the-map" metaphor. Crab River demarcates the boundary between Gardner Canal (upper part of finger) and Douglas Channel (the lower part). On a flooding tide, you would drift up Gard-ner to the head of the Kitlope – all Xenaksiala territory. Conversely, on an ebbing tide, you would float back into Haisla territory that stretches along Douglas Channel between Kitimat to the northeast and Gribbell Island to the southwest – the third knuckle.

West of Gribbell Island, you are moving into Tsimshian territory and the outer shores of the coast where another hand metaphor is useful. This time, think of an outstretched hand, five channels representing five fingers in an expression of alarm. "Alarmed" is a good way to remember this geography because it is a navigational nightmare of narrow chan-nels, islands, rocks, currents, tides and winds. The evidence lies in the shipwrecks. Gil Island is where the latest casualty – the northern ferry *Queen of the North* – rammed into the island and sank. These islands have been sinking ships for centuries. They also grabbed international attention when the pipeline company Enbridge – trying to sell the virtues of Kitimat as a northern gateway for oil tankers – airbrushed them out to make the route look a little safer.

The five channels/fingers of the hand are Grenville to the northwest, Douglas to the northeast, Ursula to the east, Graham to the southeast and Whale Channel like a fat thumb reaching into the open Pacific Ocean. Confused? Imagine navigating this place in a canoe with no GPS in a fog, or in an ultra-large crude carrier (ULCC) in a high wind. Along each channel is a good and bad journey that Cecil has a story about.

A PRIMER ON KITIMAT/KITAMAAT AND FORT/PORT SIMPSON

So why Kitimat/Kitamaat? The long answer is buried in the convoluted Western origin story of the north coast, which begins – like all Western histories – with the Hudson's Bay Company (HBC). HBC set up its first big box store at the Tsimshian village of Lax Kw'alaams. The company men called it Fort Simpson (later becoming Port Simpson). To picture in your mind where Fort Simpson is, in relation to Kitimat and the Kitlope, imagine again the alarmed hand. The first finger is Grenville Channel. Grenville Channel is Tsimshian territory, which, after crossing the mouth of the Skeena River, opens out to Lax Kw'alaams, the last village before the Alaskan border.

A quiver full of arrows came Cecil's way because of Fort Simpson. The Kitlope first traded with Hudson's Bay men here in 1835. Christianity first took root here by the Anglicans in 1857. In 1862 it was the point from which smallpox was allowed to spread through the North. It was also the place in which the seeds of residential school were planted a few years later. That is when Cecil's fate was set in stone, prompted by the historic frustrations of Reverend William Duncan, the Anglican vicar, and mitigated by the excesses of Thomas Crosby, the Methodist missionary, and his wife, Emma.

Rev. Duncan had set up a mission at Fort Simpson but fled with his converts when the ravages of alcohol and smallpox had left his flock vulnerable. He went west to Metlakatla and built a quarantined, Anglo-utopian society encircled by a white picket fence. Meanwhile, the Methodist Crosbys were invited to take over his vacated ministry by a Tsimshian matriarch, Kate Duoward, who quickly regretted her invitation. You get a sense of Crosby from his book, *Up and Down the Northwest Coast*, in which he describes the locals as "violent and dangerous" and in dire need of some calming Christianity. Elizabeth Anderson Varley, daughter of one of the later missionaries (who went on to marry Frank Varley of the Group of Seven and has, I believe, a fair take on her forebears) writes: "His [Crosby's] writing gives the impression that he regarded them as heathen and fanatical, and greeted force with force, meeting them head on with his own kind of fanaticism."[4] Crosby's fanaticism extended to all who traded there, including the Kitlope people. In an effort to improve the welfare of the children of the heathens, Emma Crosby founded the first girls' home there in 1874. Thus began a century-long policy of "good intentions gone awry" that led to the abduction of Cecil at the age of 10½.

Meanwhile, around the time Sir John A. Macdonald was rehearsing his Confederation speech, the Company's Captain Pender sailed HMS *Beaver* up Douglas Channel to check out the trade at a place he knew as "Kitamaat." He had heard the Tsimshian traders at Fort Simpson call it that. According to Cecil, Tsimshian families had paddled down there from Lax Kw'alaams one winter for a big Haisla wedding and found the big houses buried under snow. The hosts had come out to greet them at the shoreline through snow tunnels. Thereafter, the Tsimshian called the Haisla Kit-a-maat, "people of the snow."

All of these historic events contribute to some kind of fuzzy context as to why the spelling of the modern town of Kitimat is with one *a*, and the Indian reserve where Cecil lives has three *aaa*'s. Elizabeth Varley regarded the Kitimat naming issue a schemozzle – even by her own charitable standards. She leaves the impression that dropping two *a*'s to name the modern town of Kitimat was a case of newcomers distancing themselves, however they could, from the heathens. Historically, there is more evidence in placing the name change to 1897, when a sale of shares of a fledgling railway company, the Kitamaat & Omineca (to connect the Yukon goldfields), switched to Kitimat & Omineca, "so that it could be found by Bankers on a map."[5] It all amounts to the same thing: Christianity was always the precursor to corporations.

That original railway venture never materialized but modern Kitimat did. To understand the city, you have to get inside the head of the American planner Clarence Stein, who was hired by Alcan to design the company town. He was part of the cosmopolitan visionaries who wanted to bring alive Le Corbusier's postwar European dreams of smooth, glistening factories surrounded by clean, modern houses with lawns on which smiling families played, inoculated from war and history. At best you could call it another case of good intentions gone awry.

The Haisla's own origin story of Kitamaat goes back nine millennia before that. Haisla orator Gordon Robinson (whom Cecil refers to) wrote down the stories he heard from his mother for his 1956 book *Tales of the Kitamaat*.[6] The story starts with a man, Waa-mis, and his family, who had to flee from Oweekeno, or River's Inlet. River's Inlet lies at least a good week's paddle to the south. Waa-mis names the valley Kak-la-lee-sala, "gravel banks." Robinson explains, "There were no giant six to eight foot spruce trees such as are commonly found there now." The place name gives the clue for the date of settlement; the Kitimat River valley last looked like that when the glacier was pulling out 10,000 years ago, leaving the terminal moraine and outflow of a giant glacial river. Waa-mis had only ventured far down the channel because he was under duress as a fugitive. Earlier travellers had avoided it because of the perception of a white "monster" with a huge mouth at the estuary. Waa-mis had nothing to lose so pushed on, only to discover that the white monster was a cloud of gulls rising up and down off the untold riches of spawning oolichan.

A PRIMER ON OOLICHAN

Oolichan (eulachon, ooligan, candlefish) are a small forage fish that, like salmon, bring the energy of a life at sea to the rivers during the great boiling hiatus of a spawn before they die. In their reproductive state, they have packed on so much oil that the surface of the water develops a slick when they die. They are in high demand in the spring from most of the inhabitants of the coast and interior. The oil was so valuable to the coastal people that the trails between oolichan rivers and interior villages became major transport corridors, with elaborate bridges engineered to bear the weight of the transported oil and their carriers. The Kitimat River was one of the richest wa'wais of the Haisla, with its legendary oolichan runs.

Corridors for moving oil are nothing new on the coast, and it was the grease trails that led the first Scotsman, Alexander Mackenzie, to the coast in July of 1793, two weeks after Captain Vancouver cruised through. For Mackenzie, it was a stroll along a major trade route, hardly bushwhacking. Ironically, the route of the modern oil and gas pipelines – proposed twice so far in the last 30 years to link the oilfields with what oilmen call "tidewater" – lies along one of the traditional grease trails. Oil has always been a player in the history of this region.

Today, the oolichan are gone from Kitamat. The only active oolichan run is in the Kemano River watershed that pours into Gardner Canal, the wa'wais owned by Wa'xaid himself. And those fish were affected after the

Kenney Dam went in upriver in the 1950s. Waters that have gone through 16 kilometres of tunnel and eight turbines, and even minor fluctuations in water levels caused by dam flow changes, are significant in the lives of small fish. To bring the oolichan back has been one of Cecil's family's Herculean labours.

A PRIMER ON COASTAL TEMPERATE RAINFOREST

Until the 1980s, the term "temperate rainforest" wasn't really in popular usage; people had only just got their heads around "tropical rainforests" and their importance. The Kitlope campaign coincided with the birth of a meme – the last of the great temperate rainforests – and the other catchy slogan for British Columbia, "Brazil of the North." The commonly accepted scientific definition for a coastal temperate rainforest is a forested area lying between 32 and 63 degrees latitude, with over 2000 mm of precipitation (rain, fog or snow) per year. Typically, these forests share two geographic characteristics: they are mountainous and close to the sea, which is why they are so wet. Oceanic clouds, laden with moisture, hit the shores and ride up the cooling slopes of the mountains, causing the water vapour in them to condense and dump its watery load. The exquisite marriage of mountains meeting sea is a rare union – temperate rainforests only constitute one-fifth of 1 per cent of the Earth's surface.[7]

Of the 41 million hectares (100 million acres) of temperate rainforest that once grew upon the earth, much less than half is left. Most of it has been cut down by humans and replaced with agriculture, industrial forestry plantations or other forms of industrialization. When you look at a satellite image of the world, the temperate rainforests appear like delicate green embroidery binding the bumpy edges of the flatter continental blankets. These forests, in their earlier magnificence, used to lavishly trim the oceanic edges of Norway, Scotland, Ireland, Georgia, Turkey and California but are now largely ghost forests. Threads of their former selves still cling to the mountainous shorelines of Japan, Oregon, Washington, New Zealand, Tasmania and Argentina, but virtually nothing is left of the original forest. Chile retains the largest area of intact coastal temperate rainforest in the southern hemisphere, and British Columbia has that honour in the North, beating out Alaska, which got scalped by some lousy agreements. The Kitlope, at one million acres of intact temperate rainforest, represents 2 per cent of what was left in the world in 1991.

These forests might be scarce, but they are heavy global providers for every gift that rains down upon us. Without temperate rainforests, fresh water would not reach so far into the continents, as the trees act like transmitting stations of rain for their families inland. When it comes to pulling carbon out of the atmosphere, there is no terrestrial parallel. Old-growth temperate rainforests sequester more carbon per hectare than any other ecosystem or forest on Earth. Up to 1000 tonnes of carbon can be stored in the trunks, needles, leaves, lichens, mosses, soil and canopy of these forests.[8] Forests absorb nearly a third of all the atmospheric carbon and our rainforests are a vital part of that carbon sink – way out of proportion to the area they occupy. When Cecil refers to his gratitude to "all of the people around the universe that came with their love and compassion to save something that is known around the world – the largest, unlogged temperate rainforest in the world," it was for good reason and for the good of all of us – all forms of life that need fresh air, fresh water, diverse forms of life and a cooler climate.

A PRIMER ON THE WAKASHAN LANGUAGES

The linguistic group described by linguists as Northern Wakashan has four related languages, each of which has dialects: Haisla with two dialects of X̌a'islak̓ala (Haisla) and X̌enaksialak̓ala (Xenaksiala); Wuikinuxv/Oweek-eno, who speak Oowekyala (River's Inlet is the English name); Heiltsuk (Bella Bella region); and Kwakw'ala (Northern Vancouver Island). There are probably fewer than 500 speakers left in all the Northern Wakashan languages.

Cecil introduces his introductory story as one of gratitude to those who came to help. But first it is useful to understand that welcoming white people hadn't been too successful in the past.

PART ONE

So Many Arrows Came Our Way, 1792 – 1941

So Many Arrows Came Our Way

I bring my children and grandchildren to the Kitlope every year, starting when I was well. I try to teach them where I was born and teach them about the beauty of the place. Much of what I say was taught to me by my grandmother, my grandfather and my uncles. My late grandmother, Annie Paul, was the leader of our people. She was the matriarch of our family. We were dying off so fast due to foreign diseases that when industry came in there was only a few of us left.

Granny was the first to speak in the negotiation with the chief and council of the Haisla [Kitamaat Band] to amalgamate with the Kitlope Band. The Kitamaat Band welcomed us for amalgamation on March 10, 1948. Amalgamation took place four years before Alcan moved into Kemano territory. We tried to protect our homeland the best way we know how. My people have done it for 10,000 years. With the power of our Creator, we can guard it and keep it the way it is today.

On amalgamation, there was only a few Xenaksiala left. It was Granny who feared that we'd lose everything. The amalgamation was done by the Indian agent. He was stationed in Bella Coola. The document states: "This was a proposal that had been under discussion for considerable time. The only opposition was from the Chief of the Kitlope, who did not want to relinquish his somewhat imaginary authority." How do you trust this Indian agent who wrote that? For him to say the "somewhat imaginary authority" was wrong. The Chief of the Kitlope had the authority to serve not himself but the people. The opposite of the Canadian government's way of thinking.

My brother, Joe, is on the amalgamation document. He signed it the day we amalgamated – 1948. Gerald, Bruce and I were born a few years too late. It was my friend Charlie Shaw that got the papers from the archives. When I got really sick, I burned a lot of papers, and I had those papers on the census and amalgamation in my hand, and something tells me, *Hang on to this one*. I hang on without knowing and waiting. I had it in my hand, and I thought I wasn't going to make the year. Maybe I was waiting for you.

The story of why we amalgamated is told in the census papers, where the government said: "How many Indians left in the 'concentrations camps' at Kitlope?" How many? 30 people. What year? 1934. Kitlope Reserve. In the column "Under 7 years," it says "Male: 2." One is me; the other is my brother. When I sat down and first saw that document, my wife came down and she sees tears in my eyes. "*Doo'tii tl'sin'la*. Tell me what those tears are for?"

In our verbal history, according to my little granny and all the chiefs, each one of them said: "We numbered over 700." I heard some stories. When I close my eyes, I go back to the teaching of my three Elders. I asked them: "*G'in c'äquëlas?* How many of us Xenaksiala?" And they all came out to – not the same number – but close, eh. "*G'in c'äquëlas?* How many?"

When you begin to hear this story...the three of them told me, "*Lä'k'äi*. It's past...seven."

"Oh, seven hundred?" I say.

"*K'ew xʷenoxʷ gai'pen'xiidii kä*. No, my child, it is more than that." They mentioned all their villages. They didn't live in one village like today – a reserve here and there.

"In those days," my uncle told me, "just around Kitlope Lake alone there's four villages, five clans: the Raven, Killer Whale, Eagle, and the Beaver." Used to be Salmon and Wolf too. Look at what they are telling me: "*Aqua'ain goam sü wiixäi*. White man has come."

I believe it was the Indian agent who came and distributed blankets to the chiefs and people, and they were contaminated. Our stories said that they gave away infected blankets. They called them "ugly" blankets: *Ya'yak'sta*. At that time the government had a chemical warfare to get rid of the Indians. When I found that out years later in Bella Bella, I went to Winnipeg; I asked the chiefs. What happened? In Queen Charlottes, that chief – who was in Alberni too and a really good friend of mine – he brought me to Skedans. That whole village was wiped out. Not one person left. But when he brought me there, there was a lot of totem poles. Some standing, lots on the ground. All die of this disease. So, it went right across Canada, this chemical warfare on how to kill an Indian.

When they were mapping out the reservations, the government sent a guy out to tell the Haisla what their reservation is going to be. Our big chief told him, "*Wa'wais*" – the mountaintops where the first little stream starts from the mountain and comes down to our valley, to the hot spring. All the way down the channel as far as Butedale and all the way up to the headwaters of the Kitimat. As big chief, he knew all the boundary lands of different *wa'wais*, down the coast and further back. "That's home. That's all our place."

And the chiefs try to tell this guy [the surveyor], they ask: "Who was speaking for the Haisla?"

And that guy didn't listen. He wrote to the Indian agent: "The Haisla had 35 acres," and he described this village. "This place here, you can't cultivate it. Couldn't plant nothing, it's all rocks. There's a little stream coming down, that's the one you cross and either side of the river is rows of wild crab apples, *which the Indians like*. Your obedient servant."

That whole valley of people, the Haisla people with the oolichan fishing, only got a small little portion of Haisla land where they grew up, but that whole valley was Haisla. The chief asked: "What is this 35 acres of rocky soil? Concentration camp for Haisla people?" This was just a summer camp; they didn't understand that. Kitlope was no different. That was when you start to mistrust. I've often wondered what would have happened if some guy had written back: "Nobody's going to educate the Indian. We got a few crab apples. Your obedient servant."

There was a bad friction between the Indian agent and the chiefs. They told him, "You can't have that, that's our home. Why are they putting this reservation there?" But our people didn't know what was happening. They had a sense that these people were bad. There was an argument. And from Victoria, they had a warship called *Clio*, which came and anchored there. Now it is Clio Bay. Was it to quiet the Natives down? I don't really know.

Annie Paul, the queen of my family, 96 years old when she died. Her husband is Chief Johnny Paul, Chief Humzeed. My mother, Clara, who holds the title of the great chief lady, which my brother Dan held, Chief G'psgolox. And that is her husband who is the Killer Whale Clan chief, Thomas Paul, my father. He was only 42 years old when he died of tuberculosis. Very young. My auntie, his sister, died too, only 40. My brother, Leonard – they talk about the Miller Bay Hospital – that is where my brother died in the TB hospital in Prince Rupert, only 20 years old.

A year and a half later, after Leonard passed away, the miracle drug they called streptomycin came in. All the hospitals were filled with my people – Miller Bay, Coqualeetza, Nanaimo – all army and air force hospitals, were filled with Indian people with tuberculosis. Inside one year when streptomycin came in to hospitals, a miracle happened. Wish my brother had lived long enough to see the miracle happen. I praise society for coming up with something to penetrate that thing that tuberculosis has – the germ. No other drug would penetrate that to arrest what took my people.

Now only four of us left – four full-blooded Xenaksiala people. Three ladies: my little sisters Louisa and Vietta, and Lillian Henry, my cousin. Now, out of 700 or more, you're sitting across from the only male left from Kitlope. Kemano cemetery is where I am going to be when I go to sleep. So many arrows came our way.

KITAMAAT, JUNE 26, 2015

Cecil pulls out a faded copy of the *1934 Census of Indians* that documents the Haisla/Xenaksiala story. He has had it stashed for years on a shelf in his bedroom. One of his best friends, Charlie Shaw, brought it back from Ottawa after digging through the archives in the 1980s. Cecil can't read words, but he sure can read numbers. We go over the census numbers. In one column is the Kitimat (Haisla) 323 people and in another the Kitlope (Xenaksiala) 30 people. Beside the total numbers of Indians in each band, there is a breakdown according to age and gender. For Kitlope males under 7 years, there were just two in 1934. Cecil was one of them; he was born in 1931. His brother Douglas was the other, born in 1933. A visit to Cecil's family's graveyard in Kemano is the only record of the epidemics – besides the oral accounts from survivors who remember them. Cecil's grandmother Annie witnessed a century of diseased arrows that came her family's way: smallpox, influenza and tuberculosis. There were other arrows, though, that she didn't even know about.

Annie Morrison, Wii'deałh, was born in the Kitlope in 1870 into the Salmon Clan. She died at the age of 96. The family called her affectionately Muk'waxdi, which means "constantly following close behind." Longevity was common in Xenaksiala people before colonization. The name itself, "Xenaksiala," means "people who die off slowly," referring to their ripe old ages, not lingering diseases. The diseases came later, but they weren't lingering. They hit the shores of Douglas Channel and Gardner Canal like tsunamis.

SMALLPOX

From all oral accounts, the smallpox epidemic of 1862 – 1863 was germ warfare. Stories of the "ugly blanket," in which germs were placed and distributed, were passed down to Cecil from his grandparents but also found all over British Columbia – as were stories of their own quarantines being threatened, military raids that opened up potential for infection and the use of false vaccinations with "the knife." These vaccinations, instead of being cowpox, were actually inoculations of the live smallpox virus that made the person contagious.

Western historians are less unanimous in their analysis of how smallpox spread. There appears to be a continuum in the academic community from treating the epidemic as a largely natural disaster to defining it as premeditated genocide. Historians do not agree on what happened. One brave researcher, Tom Swanky, has looked at the relationships between the spread of smallpox, corporate interests and the colonial government. Swanky, a retired news editor with a law degree, wrote *The True Story of Canada's "War" of Extermination on the Pacific*.[9] He exhaustively reconstructs the events of the day, including the arrival of the disease at the Hudson's Bay Company's Fort Simpson, the closest trading post for the Haisla/Xenaksiala. Swanky links the journal entries of fort managers and corporate documents with the movements of land speculators and developers, colonial ships, doctors and delegations with plans to expand control over regions for national railways, mines and real estate. The first outbreak of smallpox at Fort Simpson recorded in the chief factor's journal was on May 25, 1862. By the following year, according to accounts from both Native and non-Native sources, between 75 per cent and 100 per cent, depending on the village, of all Native people were dead.

Swanky hasn't yet looked specifically at the outbreaks in Gardner Canal but states emphatically it was "either through the gross expulsion of the northern Natives from Victoria – which is how the disease got to Fort Simpson – or through carriers distributing the disease intentionally, like Poole's party at Bella Coola, or with criminal negligence in violation of English law as in some of the boats that took miners up into that area."[10] He noted, "In any discussion of smallpox up the coast, it is important to stress that Natives did not leave Victoria to carry the disease north willingly: wherever it went up there, the Douglas government was the original agent."

The journal accounts of Chief Factor William Henry McNeill at Fort Simpson leave little doubt that McNeill was not just indifferent to, but negligent in, a mounting crisis. McNeill was an American – a Boston man exposed to a merchant seafaring life. He was hired by the Hudson's Bay Company in Oahu late on in his career and came to Fort Simpson, first in the winter of 1851 as the chief trader, and returned as chief factor in 1861 for two years, which coincidentally spanned the smallpox epidemic. It was his pre-retirement junket before settling on 250 acres of prime real estate ready for subdivision in Victoria, conveniently cleared of Indians by smallpox. The real estate he bought is the Lekwungen village of Chickawick, which today is called McNeill Bay. His parting gift to Canada before he died at a ripe old age was a petition to US President Ulysses S. Grant asking for annexation of British Columbia to the United States. His career is described in the *Dictionary of Canadian Biography* as "long and distinguished." His annotated journal accounts of the two weeks between the reports of smallpox and the Tsimshian evacuating the fort expose his far-from-distinguished reaction:

Sunday, May 18, 1862
Weather cool and overcast. Wind SE A Canoe arrived from Victoria with letters to Mr. Duncan from the "Bishop" who wrote that the Indian Pox is raging among the Indians, "mostly Chimsheans" [Tsimshian] and that 30 had died, [not] one case has recovered. A number had died on the way to this place. One canoe was abandoned with all that was in her. We may expect soon to have many deaths at this place as a few cases have arrived.

Monday, May 19, 1862
Overcast, dull, cool weather. Wind SE to south. Home with Indian woman planting potatoes in garden. Antoine and Hans with 3 Indian women packing Labouchere Deer Skins. Camp very quiet no drink for the first time for many days. The Indians being frightened as so many deaths down south among their people, the Small Pox having proved to [be] stronger than "Tangle Leg" [whisky]. Trade good for the times.

Tuesday, May 20, 1862
The same splendid weather. Wind West. One man with 25 Indian women planting potatoes. Two men and four Indian women packing Furs and Laboucher Deer Skins. Many Indians moving away from the camp in fear of Small Pox. Trade fair in Martens. No bears are seen nowadays.

Wednesday, May 21, 1862
Splendid weather. Wind, West + S.W. Finished planting potatoes in the garden. It has taken us 8 and a half days with one White man and 25 Indian woman to do the Garden. One man with 8 Indian women cleaning Labouchere Seal Skins. Antoine x lashing deer skin packs. We hear of no cases as yet in camp of Small Pox. Trade fair from Chimsheans. Therm. 50° in shade.

Friday, May 23, 1862

Wind and weather the same. Still packing Laboucher Deer and Seal Skins + lashing etc. Howe with 2 Indians cleaning drains in Garden. Indians making Medicine to keep off the Small Pox. Now that we have no Schooners here to trade "Tangle" we obtain a fair trade of Furs daily.

Saturday, May 24, 1862

No alteration in wind or weather. A great many canoes arrived from Nass with Grease. Men and Indian women as yesterday. Howe [?] and Indians finished cleaning drains in Garden.

Medicine work going on all over the camp, and a [?] of stick with red medicine on it stuck on top of every house. This of course will keep the Small Pox from entering the house. Trade fair for the times.

Sunday, May 25, 1862

Wind SE AT 8 AM it commenced to rain the first we have had since 8th inst. At noon cleared off and became fair. At 5 PM a very dense fog which lasted for an hour when it cleared away and became clear. Lots of medicine work going on all over the camp. The Indians are very much alarmed and frightened respecting the Small Pox. We hear that two [?] cases are in the camp.

Friday, May 30, 1862

About 4 PM an Indian of the "Kil-o-char" tribe came into the Fort, and threw a stone at our Pigeons. Mr. Dobbs being at hand, took hold of the fellow and pulled his hair for "so doing". Shortly after three of his gang came close to the Gate and fired three shots into the tops of our houses and decamped. We require a Man o War here to call these Chimsheans to an account, for all the indignities and insults that have put upon us for years gone by. Three or four dozen lashes well laid on would have a wonderful effect. And a shell or two pitched into the "Kilo-o-char" camp would also be remembered by them. Traded a few furs.

Friday, June 6 [1862]

The sloop started for Stikeen about 10 am. The men that came here in a Canoe had it taken from them by the Indians "I-Marsh."

They have written Victoria about it. Trade good. Indians moving away daily and fast the camp is looking deserted.

> Wednesday, June 11 [1862]
> Beautiful weather. Wind west. The Stikeens traded 20 Bear and 5 Martens. They also traded four Guns for Cash. Several Chimsheans [Tsimshians] have died lately of Small Pox most of them are now away to the hunting grounds...One half of our Apple Trees are <u>dead</u> not of Small Pox, but on account of Mrs. Missionary Tugwell's Goats eating the bark from them!!! This is a great shame I should say.[11]

Swanky suggests that McNeill could have made a move to quarantine or to vaccinate (both of which the Anglican missionary, William Duncan, did by leaving for Metlakatla). According to the *Victoria Daily Chronicle*,[12] there was a medical doctor, Dr. Deschenes, at Fort Simpson at the time with vaccines. McNeill doesn't mention it in his post, and his presence "had the classic appearance of a selective inoculation program,"[13] which would spread the disease, not curtail it. Swanky asks, "Why did both the Ft. Simpson and Ft. Rupert managers each fail to disclose French doctors conducting smallpox related activity at their posts? If these had been actual vaccination programs to save natives, the H.B.C. would have trumpeted it."[14] McNeill was a paradox; he had two "country" wives, Matilda, daughter of a Kaiganai Haida chief, with whom he had 12 children before she died in childbirth, and his second wife Neshaki (Martha), a high-born Nisga'a woman. What is clear is that he had no love for the Tsimshian, to which Swanky attributes the business venture Fort Simpson Land Syndicate, "which would have benefitted directly from a targeted reduction in the native population."[15]

LAX KW'ALAAMS, JANUARY 21, 2018

Cecil and I have just circumnavigated the burial island at Lax Kw'alaams and are resting on a bench overlooking the west bay. A pod of Dall's porpoise are punching the air with their exhalations offshore. I'm interested in what Cecil thinks about a place to which so much of what he endured is tied: Hudson's Bay Company, alcohol trade, smallpox, residential school and where his first daughter, Cecelia, was adopted by John and Sharon Cashore. It is one of my stupid questions.

He closes his eyes and sits there for a while, thinking about what I asked, soaking up the thin winter sun. The oystercatchers are chatting away to one another in Xenaksiala: *kadiskadisai* – their name. Wild roses surround the bench we are sitting on. They are so plentiful that it is almost impossible to get to the bench without being snagged by their thorny stalks. Eventually, he talks about Lax Kw'alaams. In Tsimshian, it means "place of the wild roses," and he tells me what roses meant to the health of the coastal people. The delicate pink petals and bright red rose hips are an essential medicine and source of vitamin C. Cecil gets around to answering my question in a roundabout way. He talks about the story of the last canoe and how his granny warned him that he would get weak without the paddling; then the memory of a young woman in his village who died because the hospital was too far away when their medicines didn't work. Somewhere in this rose patch is an answer to my stupid question, I think.

To the missionaries and company men, it was called Port Simpson, named after the HBC man, Captain Aemilius Simpson, whose claim to fame was planting the "first" apple seeds on the coast. His assertion was somewhat ironic, as wild crabapples, from the same genus, *Malus*, as orchard apples, have been cultivated on the coast by families for millennia. Estuaries are orchards. It is doubly ironic because the *Malus* genus is part of the rose family. So, in both languages, this is still a place of wild roses.

According to Cecil's Elders, at the very least 700 people lived around Kitlope Lake and river prior to the 1862 smallpox. This figure is undoubtedly modest and was probably in the thousands. From the oral tradition and evidence of the mortuary poles, Cecil relates the conditions under which his maternal great-grandfather Chief G'psgolox (also spelled Gps'golox) (Paddy Macdonald) of the Eagle Clan, commissioned the pole – he had lost all his children and many members of his clan to smallpox and was in extreme grief. Three landslides had also occurred at M'iskusa (Wa'xaid's birthplace also spelled Misquize and Misk'usa), so what was left of the village had moved a kilometre up the Kitlope River. The pole was a mortuary pole. Cecil's ancestor, Chief Humzeed (also spelled Hemzid) of the Raven Clan, was a carver with Solomon Robertson, Wakas, in 1872.[16]

In 1890, when Peter O'Reilly came to the Kitlope and met with Chief Paul (Sheaks) of the Kitlope (probably Cecil's great-great-grandfather), he was informed by the local Indian agent, Mr. Todd, "that the population of this tribe is 103."[17] A Canadian census of the post-smallpox time was taken on July 18, 1891 (28 years after the smallpox), at Price's Cannery at the mouth of the Kitlope. Thirty-three "Indians" are listed (mostly first names only) with their home as Kitlope, BC, ranging in age from 1 to 65. This census only reflects those working at, for or around the cannery; their occupations were listed as either cannery hand or fisherman. One Kitlope family name, Wilson, occurs in this census, but the owner of that watershed, the Wakasu wa'wais, Solomon Robertson, doesn't appear to be on the document. Nor are any recognizable members of Cecil's immediate family (e.g., Pauls, Annie Morrison or Samuel Wilson). The assumption is that only those at the cannery on July 18 were recorded. The 1912 *Handbook of Indians of Canada* lists the Kitlope population at 84 for 1901, 71 in 1904 and 68 in 1911. From existing records, it is probably safe to say that one generation after the smallpox outbreak, the number of people that survived in the Kitlope would be consistent with the survival rate of other regions of BC – less than 5 per cent.

WHISKY AND GUNBOATS

The arrival in 1865 of a 61-metre, steam-powered naval vessel bristling with 21 guns in Haisla territory would have been a formidable sight at the time. HMS *Clio* was one of many British corvettes sent out to protect Britain's colonial interests around the world. She was sent on two missions to the west coast: between 1859 and 1862, ostensibly to patrol the illegal trafficking in alcohol (whisky or "tangle leg," as it was known) by schooners from Alaska, and assert sovereignty; and between 1864 and 1868, just after smallpox was introduced. McNeill, the HBC agent, provides some insight on the Company's take on American schooners trafficking at Fort Simpson and their impact on trade.

> [Thursday,] May 8, 1862
> Pleasant but cool. Wind NE to NW the Schr. [space left for name of boat] arrived from Nass where she has been trading lots of "Tangle" [short for "Tangle Leg"] got the Indians drunk and was the cause of their having a fight which continues but few Indians will be alive in a few years. These schooners are doing away [?] or exterminating [?] them just so fast as possible.

> Monday, June 16, [1862]
> Skidegate, Tongass, Nass and Chimsheans [Tsimshians] Trading Furs. The trade was good and we should do well constantly if the Schooners would away with the Whisky. The camp still appears nearly deserted.[18]

Clio Bay (the Haisla name is Gwaxsdlis) is where HMS *Clio* captured three American schooners selling whisky during her patrols. The captains came under the unforgiving judgment of the missionary and lay magistrate William Duncan, who had no patience for the alcohol trade. Duncan's heavy sentence on the men was appealed and Judge Matthew Baillie Begbie reduced the severity of the fine. Characterized later as a hanging judge, Begbie was quite the opposite in this sentencing, but it reflected the deeply ambivalent mind of the governors of the day on alcohol sales to Indigenous people.

In the early days of the colony, the effect of alcohol had dampened trade and Governor James Douglas had passed a law "prohibiting the Gift or Sale of Spirituous Liquors to Indians"[19] But the colony's coffers were increasingly dependent on the rising tide of alcohol as the fur seals ebbed. Twice bills were put forward in 1861 and 1866 to make the sale of alcohol legal to Indians. The equally alcohol-averse missionary at Kitamaat, Rev. George Raley, muses in his letter to the Methodist fathers, "It [the Dominion] pays the Province to sell licences to men to sell liquor, and again it pays the Province to fine the Indian for buying and drinking the liquor that it licensed these men to sell. To jail the white liquor seller or the Indian buyer would be expensive to the Province. Between the loss and the gain the decision is easy. It is the dollars not the Indian that counts."[20]

The gunboats apparently were being used to control any further losses in trade that ensued after smallpox had left villages virtually abandoned and survivors desperate. Earlier that year, Captain Turnour had turned *Clio*'s guns on Ku-kultz, a Kwakwaka'wakw village near Fort Rupert, for harbouring the men suspected of an inter-tribal murder. The village and 60 canoes were destroyed before *Clio* headed north to Fort Simpson. The American schooners were trading with Indigenous middlemen, and villages like Fort Simpson were divided over engagement with the whisky trade.

Bruce Alistair McKelvie, a newspaperman and historian who wrote a plethora of articles on BC in the 1920s, wrote, "Kitimat was famous for many secret societies, ritualistic cults and savage practices...HMS *Clio* was sent in to break up these practices."[21] According to Elizabeth Varley, however, "It seems that the Kitamaats, a very spirited and independent people, intelligent and content with their way of life, in earlier years refused to deal with the Hudson's Bay. They [the Haisla] wanted none of the treatment the white man had handed out to other Indians. So HMS *Clio* was sent in as a threat, with the unspoken message: 'You trade or else!'"[22]

The historians can't agree on why HMS *Clio* was there, so it is hardly surprising that Cecil doesn't know. The final footnote on HMS *Clio* was that she went off to defend empire in Australia, became a training ship off Wales, and finally was scrapped for metal in 1919. The new name of the bay still sticks.

INDIAN RESERVES

Another big arrow was the creation of the Indian reserves. The letter that Wa'xaid refers to is from Indian Reserve Commissioner Peter O'Reilly, in the spring of 1890, reporting back to the deputy superintendent general of the Department of Indian Affairs on the newly created reserves of the Kitamaat and Kitlope. The May 3 letter lists the population of the main village of Kitamaat, Reserve No. 3, at 263, Chief Solomon as their chief and that they had a church and school maintained by the Methodists.[23]

> Waw elth is situated about one mile south of reserve No. 2, and contains thirty-five acres. This is a site of an abandoned village; a number of small gardens surrounding the ruins of the old houses. A few inferior salmon are taken at the mouth of a small stream that flows through this reserve, and huckleberry and crabapples abound in the vicinity.[24]

He signs off: "I have the honour to be Sir, your obedient Servant P. O'Reilly."

The Kitlope reserves were being surveyed at the same time. They were similarly small and restricted. That story comes later.

RESIDENTIAL SCHOOLS

Diseases weren't the only Western intrusions into Kitlope life. The Society for the Propagation of the Gospel in Foreign Parts had arrived in 1892 to propagate at the Wakasu River, just around the corner from M'iskusa. Reverend Arthur D. Price started the Kitlope Mission and school at the cannery, built by his brother. Price's Cannery, financed by the Glasgow thread company Coats, hired villagers from M'iskusa as cannery workers and fishermen. This is Rev. Price's report, dated January 18, 1892, to the society after his first year of missioning the Kitlope in its entirety. He references the potlatch as being "imposed fines."

> By God's blessing my first year's labour has not been void of evident and seemingly permanent effects. Previous to my arrival, ancient superstition and weird ceremonies held full sway. The

morals of the tribe were at a low ebb. Their ignorance was piti-
ful to witness. They had a Council of their own, framed laws or
imposed fines for an infringement of the same, but these fines
were so outrageously severe that often a man or woman was de-
nuded of all his or her belongings for the most trifling offence.
The proceeds, amounting to a goodly sum per annum, were mis-
appropriated by the chief and his kith and kin. Christianity was
unknown and much less sought after.

Such was the state of affairs on my arrival one year ago. Under
these conditions was my coming not only one of difficulty, but
most opportune. From the outset my efforts to introduce a radical change have been greatly aided by the willingness of the
whole tribe, including the chief, to take advantage of my instruction. They have displayed a most unusual eagerness not only to
learn the English language, but also to imbibe the doctrines of
Christianity, laying aside their heathen practices without dissent
or trouble.

Our first improvement came with the start of a daily school.
For want of a proper building we were compelled to use a large
net-loft, kindly lent us by my brother. The average attendance,
considering the number of children of school age, has always
been good.

About two months after my arrival the Indian Agent, C.H.
Todd, Esq. of Metlakatla, visited us. He proposed the abolition
of the Indian Council, and in the place of substituting a Church
Council, having myself as President. Against this the chief and
tribe held out for some time. They were aware that such a change
meant a curtailment not only of the liberty allowed to the previous Council, but also a marked diminution in the fines and a
proper channel for their expenditure.

During the period of their indecision Christianity waned. They
did not attend church the less regularly, but on Sundays they
would publicly gamble and the like. Patiently, however, I pursued
my course, earnestly pleading and solemnly warning, trusting in
God to dispel the hovering cloud in His own good time.

You can imagine my surprise, surpassed only by my joy and
gratitude, when the Chief, on behalf of the whole tribe, spon-
taneously petitioned my brother and myself for the adoption of
the Church Council. He asked me to form it, elect its members,

draw up a code of laws with penalties. Promptly acting on his suggestion, I elected five members to assist me – the Chief and four other Indians of age and experience.

I then regulated the framing of the laws according to the evils which were most prevalent, and which needed sterner laws than entreaty. Each law in succession was read over to the members, discussed, and agreed upon. When all was arranged satisfactorily, a copy of our laws was forwarded to the Indian Agent for his ratification. His reply expressed his perfect acquiescence in our transactions. Since the change the general bearing of the tribe has improved much; and, as an instance of this, since Christmas we have had no cause to call a Council to hear one single case of misconduct. This speaks for itself.

Turning now to the church. As in the case of the school, so also for want of accommodation, our services were held in the net-loft, and during the winter and spring, in Indian houses. Owing to the coldness of the former, and the smallness of the latter, the attendance was diminished, especially notable in the older people. This spring, however, my brother Harry volunteered to erect a building to answer the double purpose of church-house and school for a time.

Calling a general meeting of the Indians, he made the following proposition: "That if they (the Indians) would make the framework of logs and poles and help in its construction, he would supply at his own expense all the lumber for the walls, flooring, seats &c., in addition to the shingles and requisite furniture." To this they willingly agreed. I am thankful to say that, owing to the generosity of my brother, aided by the willing help of the Indians, we now have a substantial structure, neat in appearance, furnished throughout.

The dimensions of the building are 30 feet long by 15 feet wide. It is built on logs, standing 2 feet 6 inches out of the ground. There are five windows, two double ones on each side and one half-window in the chancel end. Over the door is a small belfry awaiting a bell kindly given to us by the manager of my brother's cannery. The last six feet of the flooring is raised six inches, so as to form a chancel, which is finished off with match-boarding of dark redcedar boards, panelled with light spruce boards; the effect is very pretty.

For a lectern we have a large wooden eagle, a splendid piece of carving, and a good specimen of an Indian's handiwork. This has been kindly loaned to us by the chief. The chancel floor is carpeted, and Indian matting adorns the aisle. To complete the furniture, we have an organ recently purchased in Victoria. I need hardly mention my feeling of pride and gratitude at the erection and fitting-up of our church is equalled by that of the Indians. All our services are well-attended by Indians of all ages, and their hearty joining in the prayers and singing prove their appreciation. Daily my wife teaches the young children, whilst I devote my time to the older members.

It is seldom that in one year Indians have been persuaded into the erection of a church, and their readiness to fall in with the scheme, as well as their spontaneous help, provides a satisfactory state of things and holds out a great encouragement for the future. For this I say, thank God.

As regards the acquirement of the language of the Indians, I am fast making headway under the instruction of an Indian youth belonging to a neighbouring tribe. He understands English exceedingly well, and as a teacher is very clear and painstaking. By September next I hope to be able to dispense with him. I can now write sentences and converse a little in the Kitlope language. In a word, I feel justified in stating that the future prospects here are good. The seeds of Christianity now sown are germinating, and daily display their growth.[25]

Price tried to missionize for a couple of years but joined his brother in evacuating to greener pastures when the cannery and mission school slid into the Gardner after an annual spring flood of supernatural force. During that time, the steamers came to the cannery with sightseers, arriving with more frequency than cruise ships do today. The Canadian Pacific Railway (CPR) excursion ship SS *Islander*, brought poets, painters and travel writers. One such writer, Eliza Scidmore, wrote: "The Old Man, a conspicuous landmark on the canyon walls, rises perpendicularly 2000 ft from the water, and soundings at its baseline give a depth of over 1400 ft. The *Islander* has been laid alongside and passengers have gathered ferns from the scarred and overhanging wall. Irving Falls on the opposite wall, descend 2000 ft by successive leaps and there is a fine frothy fall draining the glacier above Price's Cannery."[26]

As the tourists photographed themselves in front of the waterfalls, glaciers and Indians, Sir John A. Macdonald was issuing his remarks which
were to set policy on Indian affairs for the next century: "He [the Indian]
is simply a savage who can read and write. It has been strongly pressed
on myself, as the head of the Department, that Indian children should be
withdrawn as much as possible from the parental influence, and the only
way to do that would be to put them in central training industrial schools
where they will acquire the habits and modes of thought of white men."[27]

WAKASU, MAY 2, 2000

We land on the beach at Wakasu to look around the estuary for signs of
wildlife. We find tracks of wolf, grizzly, moose and lots of birds. Cecil finds
a plastic bottle from Asia washed up on the beach with pelagic goose-
neck barnacles growing on it, looking just like exotic tulips about to burst
into bloom. He brings it for me to draw, which I do and label it "Barnacles
from Cecil." There are a few wooden stakes in the estuary, which I point
to, "What are those?"

"The dock to an old cannery, long time ago," he replies. "Everything has
gone back to Mother Earth."

Meanwhile, the Haisla matriarchs in Kitamaat, though formidable, were
hardly able to take on the indomitable fortress of matriarchs that had
colonial laws and God on their side – the Methodist Women's Missionary
Society (WMS), legislated to convert the hearts and souls of their children.
The Methodists had been sending women missionaries to Kitamaat since
Emma Crosby had set up her home for girls in 1874 at Fort Simpson.[28]
The WMS sent out an intrepid Susan Lawrence in 1883 to follow her example, running a mission home in Kitamaat. In a newspaper article by
Mrs. S. Runacres (a missionary at the subsequent Elizabeth Long Memorial Home), she recalls an "older Indian" telling her about Miss Lawrence
taking him as an interpreter to the Kitlope to "preach the gospel." It was
the same year that the federal government moved to establish three large
residential schools in western Canada, with more in the pipeline. Indian
education policies were being bandied about between government officials and the various competing churches, a pithy, turbid pool into which
the federal government started making contributions for the building
and maintenance of schools.[29] Section 138 of the Indian Act had been
amended in 1894 so that "The Governor in Council may make regulations,
which shall have the force of law, for the committal by justices or Indian

agents of children of Indian blood under the age of sixteen years, to such industrial school or boarding school, there to be kept, cared for and educated for a period not extending beyond the time at which such children shall reach the age of 18 years."[30]

Up for that task were Reverend George Henry Raley and his wife, Maude, who succeeded Susan Lawrence in 1892 and built the first mission school in Kitamaat. In Raley's collection of correspondence, there is a document dated March 23, 1896, ostensibly signed by villagers, although the handwriting is Raley's.

> Chief Jes-sea of the Kitamaat held a meeting of all his people today to ascertain, 1st the opinion of the people regarding a boys and girls "Home" at Kitamaat. 2nd What they would be willing to do towards a building and sustaining such a "Home" in this place. After a good deal of discussion upon the subject they decided to send these few lines to the Chiefs of the Methodist Church.
>
> Dear Brothers,
> About twenty years ago we were a wild blind people. But by the grace of God one of our own young men Charley [Amos] by name wandered down to Victoria and was drawn to the little Indian church there under the direction of the late Rev. Mr. Pollard. He was converted and his first thought after was for his poor blind people...
> We have seen how beneficial it is to our children already to have them in a Home and we are grateful to our Missionary Mr. Raley for what he has done so far for us. But we want something better and we are willing to help. We have over 100 children in our village of which sixty are of school age. Our children are too many to send away to be educated and that is why we are so anxious that a good "Home" be built here for our boys and girls.
> We also promise ten acres of land on our reserve and more if needed. The Kitlope promise to send their children here to school if the Home is built here.[31]

The Raleys forthwith built the school with WMS funds, and some of the Kitlope and Kemano children were schooled in Kitamaat from the 1890s on, although few records exist due to the later fire. Raley also launched the first newspaper of sorts in northern British Columbia, the *Na-na-kwa*, which ran on a quarterly basis until 1907, and in which many of the early stories and movements of the missionaries, as well as Native leaders around the coast, were recorded, including the late Chief Paul (Sheaks) of the Kitlope on the summer of 1890, as related by Andrew Smith.

> Chief Paul of Kitlope who died October 1899. He was very old when he died. He was married to a Kitlope woman and had three boys, one is dead. Chief Paul was hired by a white chief, Mr. Manson, to go with him into the interior. He saw many things. It was here that the Stick Indians dwelt.
>
> When Chief Paul returned, he found that his wife was dead, so he married Emma. He wore canoe-shoes when he came back. Not long after he called the Kitamaat people to Misquize [M'iskusa also Misk'usa] and made a great feast of mountain sheep soup and biscuits, rice, tea; and gave presents to all the people – blankets, canoes, coats, hats, pants and shoes.[32]

Chief Paul (Sheaks) was believed to have come from Kitkatla, marrying a Kitlope woman. Charles and Abraham Paul are probably the two surviving sons, making him Cecil's great-great-grandfather by adoption (see "A Primer on Wa'xaid's Interwoven Tsimshian/Haisla Lineages").

Glimpses of daily life in the home from the perspective of the missionaries are gleaned from Raley's publications, like his little souvenir booklet for New Year's in Kitamaat in 1898, which has a series of portraits/photos in the following order: George Raley, Susan Lawrence, the Mission Church, Charlie Amos, an older Haisla woman named "Alice or Pelhanixs," the Mission Home and "Home Boys at Play." There are a few landscapes, Haisla masks and houses, then another tourist attraction, an etching of the Pioneer Mineral Claim.[33] A look at a historical mining map shows solid claims around Kitamaat Reserves 1 and 2 with no land left unstaked by prospectors.

On May 20, 1906, a fire broke out in the old Mission House of Kitamaat Village, levelling the school within 20 minutes. The Women's Missionary Society rallied quickly and rebuilt a larger school with a new residence for younger boys, naming it Elizabeth Long Memorial Home after one of the women missionaries who had died shortly after the fire.[34] Margaret Butcher, who arrived in 1916 and left in 1919, wrote detailed letters to her family back home about daily life in the new home. The letters span the period of the influenza epidemic and describe a gruelling existence for the children, who were responsible for all the physical work of housekeeping.

"Floors had to be scrubbed on hands and knees; wood had to be cut and water carried."[35] The older girls were tasked with sewing their clothes and linen. There is one reference to the Kitlope children in 1919, in Butcher's letters home.

> A boat was in from Kitlope & the folks began visiting the children. Little Samuel's mother came. She had heard he was dying. I tried to make matters clear & the boy went to the Village with her...About 9, Samuel's mother came for him as they were leaving in the morning. I refused to let him go as he was asleep in bed. Once again I tried to make it clear that he was to be taken to Hospital for Miss Alton thinks he will recover if he has proper treatment. I may mention here that he lost weight during the last month & I was glad to have him go. That sounds so heartless but the Indians are so illogical, they do not consider the number of children who are brought through delicacy & sickness to strength & fitness, they only look at & count the children who are sick & "are killed by the Home" and one knows the animosity they shew towards the Home at times. Then too there are the other children to consider & if a child shews definite signs of T.B. he must go. I am so sorry that the dear kiddie is sick because he is bright, intelligent boy with a sweet disposition.[36]

With the influenza epidemic barely past, Deputy Minister of Indian Affairs Duncan Campbell Scott told a parliamentary committee in 1920 that "our object is to continue until there is not a single Indian in Canada that has not been absorbed into the body politic."[37] The policy to not absorb but eradicate a culture was obvious as "the mere presence of indigenous people in these newly colonized lands blocked settler access to the land."[38] Subsection 10(1) of the Indian Act was further amended to make it illegal to withhold children between 7 and 15 from attending the residential schools: "Every Indian child between the ages of seven and fifteen years who is physically able shall attend such day, industrial or boarding school as may be designated by the Superintendent General for the full periods during which such school is open each year."[39]

INFLUENZA

The influenza epidemic of 1917 – 1919 took Annie Paul's first husband, Samuel Wilson, her sister-in-law Esther Wilson and her brother-in-law Charles

Paul, who had adopted her son Tom (Cecil's dad). The "Spanish flu" was a global epidemic that killed 20 million worldwide. It was a new flu strain that took a wide swath through the population, but there is ample evidence that the colonial government had not improved its level of interest in the health of Indigenous communities, with the rate of deaths eight times that of non-Indigenous people.[40] The colonial census approach to the flu in the villages was to underreport it, although Indian agents' reports were more accurate. By 1934 the population of the Kitlope Nation was 30 people.

TUBERCULOSIS

The tuberculosis epidemic in 1947 took Annie's second husband, Johnny Paul, and three of her six children, Lizzie, Agnes and Tom (Cecil's father). His aunt and uncle, Esther and Charles Paul, who were childless and wanted to pass on the name and territory of Gwä nax nood, had actually adopted Tom. They subsequently died in the influenza epidemic. Only the two youngest daughters survived the epidemics, Minnie and Louisa. Minnie went on to marry Guy Williams, who became the second Native senator of Canada and a leader in the Native Brotherhood movement. That story comes later.

In her recent book *Miller Bay Hospital: Life and Work in a TB Sanatorium*, Carol Harrison uncovers another bleak history of this converted military hospital near Prince Rupert, at which Cecil worked and in which his brother died. Harrison builds on the argument posited by medical researcher Maureen Lux that this disease, like smallpox, was not just a natural disaster. Lux argues there were military, cultural and economic factors behind the slow-to-treat-Indians policy of TB. Lux sources the federal policy to Director of Indian Affairs Harold McGill, who, in 1937, "inexplicably, 'instructed agents to drastically reduce medical care. They were to remove from hospitals all Native people with chronic conditions. There would be no more funds for tuberculosis surveys or for treatment in sanatoria or hospitals of chronic tuberculosis.'"[41]

During that year, Dr. J. J. McCann, Liberal MP for South Renfrew, had made a plea to Parliament for action, as 43 per cent of all Native TB patients were left unattended by a physician. He showed the accelerating rates of infection in Native populations, while the overall rate for Canadians was declining. He drew attention to the inexperienced doctors who "were appointed because of their political affiliations."[42] The experienced United Church doctor Douglas Galbraith, working in Bella Coola, had passionately lobbied Prime Minister King about the appalling conditions at the outbreak of the war. The first Indian hospital and TB sanatorium did get built at Coqualeetza in 1941, but this was far from the coast on the southern mainland. Various nurses and staff employed at the schools, like Miss Aimee Mackay at Coqualeetza, and earlier Miss Elizabeth Shaw in Port Simpson, had drawn attention to the inadequate care of children over the years but had at best been ignored and at worst fired and discredited.[43]

By 1944, in Prince Rupert alone there were already 50-plus cases requiring treatment. Venereal disease in Native women was treated but only because of the risk of infection to the military personnel. Military personnel got priority. Indigenous mortality had now reached ten times that of white people in the region. It wasn't until after the war, on September 16, 1946, that the Indigenous population received treatment when Miller Bay was converted to a TB sanatorium and streptomycin became available. What Cecil didn't know at the time was that the federal government could have done more to get the drug to patients from the northern villages earlier. Tragically, the hospitals became another institution in which federal policy continued the agenda of genocide – people being sterilized, starved, experimented on without consent and socially isolated from family.[44]

RECORDS OF BIRTH AND DEATH
It is very difficult to get documentation on the births and deaths of Cecil's family for various reasons. Any church records of births and deaths recorded for Kitamaat up to 1906 were lost in the Kitamaat Mission fire. But that isn't the entire story. It wasn't until 1943 that it became a legal requirement to record Indian births, deaths or marriages. A thorough search through the Vital Events Index of BC uncovers few death certificates for most of the Paul family before 1943 and even afterwards, like the brother who died at Miller Bay Hospital. Johnny Paul's death certificate is the first one to appear, in 1947, when he died at Butedale during the TB epidemic, then Annie Paul's when she died at Kitimat Hospital in 1966. The Kemano graveyard becomes not only a place to gain strength from his ancestors to survive but the only physical evidence of most of the Paul family's existence.

PRINCE RUPERT, MAY 27, 2017
We are on another trip to Prince Rupert to visit Cecil's sister Louisa. As we cross the bridge onto Kaien Island, 16 kilometres out of Rupert, Cecil waves to a road that peels off into the forest from the right side of the road. "That is Miller Bay Hospital down there," he tells me, "where I used

to work and where Leonard died." I've known Cecil now for 20 years and this is the first mention he's made of working in an Indian hospital. He was an orderly for a year. He pushed a broom around and didn't like it. "Should we go see it?" I ask. "Nothing to see," he said. "Just the trees growing back." I asked him where he got the courage to keep going. He said, "The graveyard."

AMALGAMATION

The discussions for amalgamation appear to start officially, by the government's reckoning, in a document written by Jas. Coleman, Inspector of Indian Agencies, Bella Coola, in October of 1941. The document is labelled "Kitimat Indian Reserve No. 2 <u>Trespass</u>." Kitlope families had been taking up residence on the reserve and the document captures his sentiments that burned into Cecil's memory:

> I informed the Indians that it was contrary to the Department's regulations and the Indian Act for any one, other than a member of the Band, to reside on the reserve, suggesting that the best thing to do under the circumstances was to amalgamate. The Indians stated that this was a proposal that had been under discussion by them for a considerable time, the only opposition apparently coming from the Chief of the Kitlop [sic] Band, *who did not wish to relinquish his somewhat imaginary authority* [emphasis added].[45]

The final amalgamation agreement dated March 10, 1948, is a standard form from the old Dominion Department of Indian Affairs. Indian agents used these forms to record their "resolutions" with different bands. The boilerplate preamble is in italic typeface, while the blank sections are typed in by the agent, Mr. W.P. Pruden, with a typewriter that lifts the capital *B* up half a line higher than the rest of the type and puts a line through the middle of the capital *K*.

> In ᴮutedale, ᴮ.C. *We the undersigned, Chief and Councillors of the* Kitlope *Band of Indians owning the reserve situated at* Kitlope and Kemano...certify that the following resolution was passed by unanimous vote of the meeting of the Kitlope band. Resolved: That for the future welfare of the Kitlope people, union with the Kitamaat ᴮand of Indians be sought...[It is signed and sealed] *in the presence of the Indian Agent for the said reserve*

representing thereat the Minister of Mines and Resources for the Dominion of Canada.[46]

KITAMAAT, JUNE 26, 2015

Stapled to the census document is a tattered copy of the amalgamation agreement. I read out the document to Cecil as he lies in his bed. When I read, he always closes his eyes and listens: *"Nos'ta"* (I am listening). Signing for the Kitlope are Chief Simon Hall and Councillors Gordon Robertson and Joseph Paul, Cecil's older brother (who shortly after drowned in the Kemano River). He tells me his granny and brother believed banding together with the neighbouring Haisla was the best way to improve their chances of survival faced with only a handful of children left of their next generation.

ALCAN

When Annie spoke to the Haisla chief and council about amalgamation in 1948, she had just lost her second husband, Johnny, three more of her children, Lizzie, Agnes and Tom (Cecil's dad), and her grandson (Cecil's brother) Leonard to tuberculosis. She could never have anticipated the next arrow coming their way. It wasn't just more discriminatory federal policies or the resource interests of Canadian industry but world security interests arriving at their family wa'wais at Kemano. The Cold War was raging and Western superpowers wanted a secure supply of aluminum for weaponry and planes, which required cheap electricity – lots of it. Of all the places in the world, the Paul family wa'wais was the place the superpowers picked.

Almost exactly one year after signing the amalgamation agreement, BC Minister of Lands & Forests (and hydro booster) Edward Kenney and the coalition government of Conservatives and Liberals rammed Bill 66, An Act to Promote the Industrial Development of the Province, through first and second readings in a single day, March 17, 1949. The act would greenlight the building of the Kenney Dam, flooding the lands above the Kemano River and altering its natural outflow by diverting waters into a tunnel blasted through a mountain into Cecil's wa'wais.

John Kendrick, one of the chief engineers hired for the Alcan project back in the 1940s and 1950s, who wrote *People of the Snow: The Story of Kitimat*, doesn't mention the Xenaksiala. In his preface he writes, "Kitimat is a town at the head of the one of the many fjords that indent the coast

49

of British Columbia. It exists solely because it was chosen in 1951 as the site of an industry. It was chosen for one reason, the potential for the development of water power in the nearby mountains. In 1951 there was nothing at Kitimat but trees, rocks and swamps. No habitation, no road, no wharf, no people. The nearest settlement was the village of the Xaisla Indians a few kilometres away."[47] It is hard not to draw the conclusion that the greenlighting of Alcan rode conveniently on the decision to consolidate the villages of Kitlope, Kemano and Kitamaat.

Opposition MLAs, father and son, Ernest and Harold Winch, of the Co-operative Commonwealth Federation (CCF), managed to get an adjournment of the third reading but only for six days, during which time there was an attempt to amend the bill so that at least legislators had some final say on the terms of the agreement. Public opinions weren't really part of the equation. This was a slam-dunk project being watched by national security councils in the Western world. The Cold War was upon the West and it wanted a secure, cheap supply of aluminum for weaponry and planes. A huge tunnel through Cecil's family's mountain provided a seemingly bombproof spot for the turbines in the eyes of Western superpowers and Alcan shareholders.

The CCF and the newly formed BC Social Credit Association (BCSCA) attempted to oppose the project,[48] but they were fighting a $300 million dollar juggernaut (which, according to the Bank of Canada Inflation Calculator, would have been today's equivalent of a three billion dollar project) that ended up nearly doubling by the time it was built in the early 1950s. The confirmation that this was a bill tailor-made for Alcan came when the attorney general let slip: "The Aluminum Company wants this bill before it spends $1 million in further surveys."[49] The newspaper then reported, "Up jumped Mr. Winch. 'You let the cat out of the bag that time,' he shot back at the Attorney-General. 'So it is the aluminum company that wants the bill.'" The Winches must have known that they had no hope when they put forward a motion asking for a six-month adjournment. It was defeated 34 to 10, so at 8:30 that night the 1949 Industrial Development Act received its final reading with no further discussion. It is still in the statutes today, Chapter 220.[50]

The act gave blanket powers that would enable the government to override any other law to establish the industry. Surprisingly, it made one concession, that Alcan had to apply for water rights "in the ordinary way." This meant John Kendrick was directed to thumbtack notices on trees at the points where the water was to either be diverted or used. If there were any complaints they would be addressed. As one federal senator, Tom Reid, an opponent of the dam since he was a supporter of the salmon industry, noted – only a bear could see these notices. Government biologists with both the federal fisheries and the provincial Game Commission appealed on grounds of the fishing resources at an emergency public hearing in October that year, but the energy project was unstoppable.

The constitutional right of the Xenaksiala (or the Cheslatta) under the Royal Proclamation of 1763 to fish and hunt was nowhere on the minds of legislators. With a stroke of the pen, Alcan got more power than the prime minister. Lieutenant-Governor Clarence Wallace told the legislature in 1951, "During the past twelve months, the international situation has become more grave and it is apparent that every precaution should be taken to strengthen the defences of democratic countries against encroachment by those who wish to undermine and destroy our way of life."[51]

Cecil's wa'wais mountain of Yamacisa-Kemaninuxw was summarily named in Western gazeteers Mount DuBose, after John Kendrick's boss, MacNeely (Mac) Dubose, VP of Aluminum Company of Canada. An American engineer from Carolina, Dubose cut his teeth with the Aluminum Company of America (Alcoa), then, after being posted to a smelter in Quebec, moved west to pick up the reins at Alcan Kitimat. Kendrick captures the general demeanour of his boss in his description of the public hearing in Victoria that the colleagues co-chaired: "Dubose wanted all or nothing, and he wanted his licence right away... Mac reminded the meeting of the amount of money that had been spent, and the further large amounts that would be required to complete the surveys."[52] In the end, Dubose cut out nearly two million cubic metres of rock from "his" mountain to form the tunnel and a powerhouse that resembled a "mammoth rock cathedral"[53] twice the size of two sports fields, with a 36-metre arch under which the turbines sang their hymn to commerce. At least Dubose visited "his" mountain, which is more than could be said for Baron Gardner and "his" canal.

PART TWO

Journey in the Magic Canoe, 1990 – 1994

Survey Markers:
These Ribbons Are Sharper than Arrows

I will start my story during my healing journey. I took my sister Louisa, my little sister Vietta, their children and three or four of mine to the Kitlope. That's when I repeat my story to them of where I was born, what I'd done, the joy, and where to go and play. When we landed there this time, there was survey markers. Something I'd never seen there. I went to go take a look. I walked the length of our little homestead, and there was a cedar tree standing there. I saw this tree where my granny would take a little bit of the bark in May and April, when the sap is running. She made this box from the cedar bark, enough to hold 24 fish; that's how she counted the fish in the box to put away. That's what she got from that tree, and she don't touch that tree no more. She only take that much, and the tree is alive. When I got there, the tree had survey markers with black numbers. "Oh, this is bad." I went back to Kitamaat. Instead of spending five days that I promised the children, I come back here to Kitamaat on the second day. I said: "These survey markers are what I dread. These ribbons are sharper than arrows. They will cut deeper than knives." I knew logging was coming, but not this soon. They were survey markers to put a road into where? It was going to go through where I was born.

For a moment, I was hesitant, you know. I was concerned about my family. I worked for the company [Eurocan / West Fraser] in Kitimat, before they applied for a tree farm licence for the Kitlope. I want you to know I am not against all industry. It is how they take the resources out of our sacred land that is Wa'xaid's concern. I saw what happened with West Fraser, the destruction around all the clear-cut logging, and now they got approval from the government for their tree farm licence to log in Kitlope. I told my wife, "I am going to fight for this place. We might lose our house. Our kids are going to high school and need all them things for school. The company that has the tree farm licence, I am working for."

My wife Mae said, "No, you go ahead. I'll walk with you." And that is all I wanted to hear: "I'll walk with you." And that was the beginning.

Cecil puts great store in survey markers. The logic of using these symbols is that survey markers are typically the first visual clue for an oral culture – and often the only warning – that a colonial presence has arrived and laid some type of claim to your home and life. How else would you know they are there, if no one ever asks your permission to come on your land?

Survey markers arrive with astounding frequency in Haisla and Xenaksiala territory. The sign at the city gates says Kitimat enjoys "timeless competencies: natural deep sea harbour, large coastal valley, close proximity to Asia-Pacific markets and abundant hydro-electric power." The branding of the region for its "timeless competencies" comes from the century-plus-long obsession of company men looking for the perfect Pacific gateway to ship North America's resources to international markets. Survey markers have been tied to trees in Kitlope, Kitamaat and Kemano for well over a century and a half.

FIRST SURVEY MARKERS: CANADIAN PACIFIC RAILWAY, 1874

The first surveyors to arrive at Cecil's wa'wais at Kemano were Charles Horetzky and Marcus Smith in 1874 (each wrote their own account). They had been sent there by Sir Sandford Fleming, the chief engineer for the Canadian Pacific Railway tasked with finding a crossing of the coastal mountains with a reasonable descent down to a western terminal. Crossing the coastal range from low-lying François Lake to Gardner Canal was considered such an attractive option that Fleming commissioned several attempts to find a route here – expeditions that included abortive attempts up wrong routes, narrow escapes, rescues by the Haisla, suppressed reports and a follow-up investigation – a tale for another telling.

Horetzky and Smith arrived in June of 1874 aboard the Hudson's Bay Company steamship HMS *Otter*, along with passengers William Duncan, the Anglican missionary, and Judge Matthew Baillie Begbie, settling their respective spiritual and judicial issues of the day. Horetzky and Smith were dropped off at the mouth of the Kemano "with four Indians from the Kitlope Village"[54] on June 8, where the survey team made their first attempt to find a route to François Lake but ran up against a major problem – rapid elevation rise – captured in Horetzky's report to Fleming on his trip.

> The line commences on a bay at the mouth of Kemano River about 20 miles from the head of the Gardner Inlet and follows the Kemano Valley nine miles in which the rise is 175 feet. The valley is narrow and subject to overflow during the freshets from the melted snow in summer and the rains of autumn. The mountains rise precipitously from each side of the valley in masses of bare rock. At the ninth mile, the line leaves the Kemano Valley and takes a more easterly course up a lateral ravine through

which a stream flows from a small lake near the summit of the mountain. The slopes of the ravine are steep and rugged and avalanches of snow and loose rock roll down them and sometimes choke up the ravine to a great depth. The summit of the mountain is reached at the 19th mile where the latitude is 4,019 feet. At 22 miles the line reaches the head of the first lake on the eastern slope of the mountains from which the water flow to Lake Francois or the Nechacoh [Nechako] River. The line was carried along the north shore of this lake four miles; its length is estimated at from 18 – 20 miles and its altitude 2,790 above the sea. To construct a railway on this route would necessitate works of a costly character.[55]

Horetzky and Smith did a brief reconnaissance of the Kitlope estuary. Horetzky declared that "high bald mountains of frightful aspect close it in on every hand, imparting to the beholder a depressing sense of desolation and gloom."[56] They only attempted the northeast arm of the Kitlope River with a guide and asked about the other access routes to the interior. His informants were probably Cecil's surviving relatives.

Smith wrote his own account in a letter to Fleming that described rowing up the Kitlope with a local guide. He had sent the guide to ask the chief to come and visit the ship. The details of the visit were as follows:

> About eight p.m. a large canoe came down with the chief and about a dozen Indians. Mr. Duncan talked to them in their own language (Chims-ain)[Tsimshian] explained the object of our visit and enjoined them to give the exploring party all the assistance in their power and told them that the gunboat [HMS *Boxer*] would be near to punish any bad Indians to protect the surveyor. Mr. Horetzky hired two of them and Mr. Seymour made them some presents of shirts, tobacco and pipes and they departed well satisfied.[57]

Horetzky had submitted this report, but Fleming had cut it out – "a misrepresentation" about which he later testified at the Royal Commission into the CPR. In his original report, Marcus Smith, on June 22, 1874, gives a vivid portrayal of the upper Kitlope.

> At a distance of six or seven miles from the actual water-shed of the Cascade Range, the northwest branch of the Kitlope River

does really flow through a valley of moderate extent, but, unfortunately, at an elevation above sea of less than 1,100 feet: and move over that in the direction of its source, i.e., to the north west there is nothing visible but a perfect sea of glacier-capped mountains. It is possible, but very far from probable that the branch in question may lead to a pass. Such a pass, if there be one, cannot be much less than 3,000 feet above the sea, and considering the close proximity of the water-shed, or summit, to the low valley which I saw, I think the inference may be safely drawn that in this quarter no practicable route is to be looked for. The third and principal branch of the Kitlope has its origin in a glacier-fed lake situated west of the Tsatsquot Valley and in the very core of the Cascade Mountains.[58]

In February of the following year, HMS *Sir James Douglas* attempted to steam into the head of the Kitlope to discharge another party of surveyors, including C.H. Gamsby. What they met was ice.

During the months of February, March and part of April last a survey of this valley was attempted. The surveyors found the Gardner Channel or Inlet covered with fixed ice for 25 miles from its head, and the party were detained by storms of snow and rain, which partly broke up the ice, so that it was a month before they got all their baggage and supplies to the head of the Inlet and commenced work. They continued the survey 46 miles and had then struck the Chatsquot River, which flows into the Dean Inlet where they were forced to discontinue the survey as the snow was 12 to 14 feet deep and was becoming soft, and avalanches of snow were rolling down the mountain sides into the Kitlope Valley.[59]

Horetzky argued that he had proven there was no feasible route up the Kitlope, and yet Fleming had gone ahead, sending an abortive mission that ended up along a route that wasn't where they claimed it to be. Was it a case of Fleming not believing the local information? It resulted in a near disaster, but what didn't go unnoticed was the location of a suitable place for water power. The 1880s was also a time of miners wandering around, staking claims. The Ministry of Mines sent Major William Downie up Douglas Channel to report on the potential.

SURVEY MARKERS, INDIAN RESERVES, 1889

The next set of survey markers was to appear in July of 1889, wrapped around the largest spruce trees for corner pins, marking the newly minted boundaries of the three reserves allocated to the Kitlope Indians by Indian Reserve Commissioner Peter O'Reilly. He wrote to the deputy superintendent general of Indian Affairs on May 5, 1890, to describe the events of the two days that he spent in the Kitlope with Cecil's ancestor (probably great-great-grandfather), Chief Paul (Sheaks).

On the evening of the 24th July I arrived at the head of Gardner Channel, when I was waited on by Paul the Chief of the Kitlope Tribe.

In the course of the long conversation in which several of his men took part, he informed me that their principal fishery was four miles up the Kitlup [sic] river at We kel lals, where not only his people, but the neighbouring tribes assemble during the Oolachan [oolichan] fishing season.

This, with another fishing station near the mouth of the Kemano river, twenty miles distant, and the village at the head of Gardner Channel were the only places they wished for.

He stated that his people had made several fruitless attempts to grow potatoes, but have become discouraged by repeated failures.

These Indians carry on trades with the tribes of the interior, and barter oil for furs. Game, such as goats, and bears are plentiful. The young men obtain renumeration from employment at the canneries on the Skeena, and elsewhere.

On the following day (July 25th) accompanied by the Chief, I visited the village, and principal oolachan fishery, and subsequently made three reservations below described.

No. 1 We kel lals, a fishery on the banks of the Kitlup river contains two hundred and forty (240) acres, the greater portion of which is low land, partly overflowed during the freshets and at high tides. This is a very valuable fishery, for not only are oolachan taken here, as before stated, but every species of salmon frequent these waters. There is a sufficiency of timber for fuel and other purposes.

No. 2 Kitlope, on which stands the winter village, contains one hundred (100) acres, and is situated on the northern shore of Gardner channel at its head. Eleven houses have been built here.

No. 3 Kemano also on the northern shore of Gardner Channel, about twenty miles from its head, contains forty (40) acres. It is the site of an ancient village, of which but eight houses remain, and these are occupied by the Indians only when fishing. The land is worthless but for the timber upon it, the soil being rocky, or swampy.

A trail constructed by the Indians leads from this place, and affords a means of communication with the tribes of the interior.

Mr. Todd, the local Indian Agent informs me that the population of this tribe is 103. Minutes of decision, and sketches of the reserves above described are herewith enclosed.

I have the honour to be Sir,

Your obedient servant,

P. O'Reilly"[60]

His accompanying map shows the legal boundaries of the three reserves. It took a later complaint from Cecil's grandfather, Johnny Paul, and other Xenaksiala during the McKenna-McBride Royal Commission of 1913 that perhaps those weren't the "only places they wished for." Ten acres of Crab River were subsequently surveyed and added.

SURVEY MARKERS, HYDRO POWER, 1906

In 1906, Richard P. Bishop came up the Gardner on HMS *Egeria*, a Canadian Hydrographic Service ship, to chart the channel. Bishop walked up Kemano Bay to hunt and confirmed its water power potential. It wasn't long before the government of BC was on the task and had BC land surveyor Frank Swannell mapping the mountains and scoping the terrain out for hydro and timber.

Swannell was one of the most prolific and accomplished land surveyors in BC. Author Jay Sherwood, who wrote about Swannell's work, did a reconnaissance of Swannell's surveying of the Kitlope in 2005, locating many of his original survey points. Swannell's survey markers were rock cairns and blazed big trees, captured in his detailed maps and photographed in large-format black and white reference photos pasted into his journal. Those notes also captured the landscape and the people inhabiting that place – including Cecil's grandfather, Johnny Paul.

24th May, 1921 Take semi-holiday. Run up river about 3 miles to where siwashes [derogatory name for Indigenous people] are hand logging – find them with 2 launches and a canoe ready to pull out. One fellow speaks good English [probably Johnny Paul, see later reference].

27th May Up at 3:30 am – off at daylight after a cup of coffee all round. Strike tide just right and get 4 miles up the Kitlope River. Pack across bar to cache and breakfast 6 am Leave Howe? with cook to fix up camp. Go down to Gardner Canal...

28th May, 1921 Traverse toward river and get into an infernal thick swampy bottom – alder, elderberry and devil's club – blazing hot and no drinkable water. Finally got through at 3:30. Trig one mile up river past Indian houses – in camp 7 pm. Fine goat dinner.

31st May, All hands on river traverse – river now pretty swift and our keeled boat doesn't handle well. Reach lake [Kitlope Lake] at 4 pm – strong whirlpool at outlet caused by river from the east driving straight against the rock wall.

June 1 Move camp and get traverse up to lake. Line 3 times and drag boat tight through a riffle...At 5 pm I notice a man living down the river.[61]

Over the next few days, Swannell describes lugging 70 pounds of survey equipment for seven-hour stints up the surrounding mountains in order to triangulate positions, only to have the rain block their view. They end up bivouacking in small clusters of yellow cedar. When a blizzard hits, they describe hunting mountain goat for food and being tracked by wolves.

June 17, Miserable night cramped with cold. At 7:30 start up a terrible snow slope – cornice on one side and drops over crags on the riverside. Reach summit, 5300' at noon....Everywhere nothing but exceedingly precipitous sided mountains with snowcaps or immense glaciers above – nearly all absolutely inaccessible.[62]

After another 11 days of downpours they give up.

June 28th Give up waiting for Blane [fellow surveyor] and pull out – Find letter from him saying they had wrecked their boat on the 9th, losing blankets, instruments, grub and our bottle of rum. Had gone back to Rupert to re-outfit. We make down the river without difficulty – Find Blane's launch at the rancherie – go up inlet to where the siwashes are hand logging. Arrange for John Paul to run launch out for us at daylight and bring it back from Butedale – By evening the Indians have changed their mind and we pull out on our own after considerable trouble with the engine – run all night – Paul Spanbergs [logging] camp in the dark, reaching Crab River at Daylight.[63]

Swannell and company eventually get to Rupert after a boat swamping on July 2. To the Xenaksiala this was everyday life, to the surveyors this was more than they bargained for. One of the inadvertent historical contributions of Swannell's work was a photograph of Cecil's village of M'iskusa. It is the only existing photograph of this village before his remaining family members moved their winter home to Kemano in the 1930s. In the photograph, standing prominently to welcome arrivals (even surveyors) to the Kitlope, is the pole erected by his maternal great-grandfather, Chief G'psgolox, shortly before it was removed without permission and shipped to Sweden. The evidence of the location of that pole – for Western sources – lay in that photograph.

SURVEY MARKERS, EARLY LOGGING

Swannell's other task was to prepare a report for the Ministry of Forests on the forest harvest potential. The report provides the early data for consideration of her majesty's obedient servants:

Along the eight miles of valley between Gardner Canal and Kitlope Lake, the merchantable timber is scattered. A great part of the flat land along the River banks is swampy and covered with Alder, although there are some large spruce trees to be found in parts of these flats. They usually occur in small belts along the river bank, and the Indians living up here have hand-logged quite a few. The largest area of timber was near the junction of Kitlope River and Kitlope Lake. Here the valley widens out considerably, and a fairly thick stand of Spruce and Hemlock is found which deteriorates into open patches a stunted growth on the higher hill slopes, and the mountain slopes. For the few hundred acres of good timber in this region, the stand would probably run about 15,000 feet B.M. [board measure] per acre. Most of the spruce trees along the riverbank run as high as 36" D.B.H. [diameter at breast height] but the average D.B.H. of Hemlock is only around 20". Kitlope Lake is nearly surrounded with precipitous mountain slopes, and only very small patches, mostly Spruce and Hemlock occur at the mouths of the few large creeks entering it, the quality of the timber being about the same as along Kitlope River.[64]

Cecil's grandfather, Johnny Paul, had operated legitimately with his own small handlogging business on a seasonal basis, selling to local mills like Swanson Bay or other log buyers. Handlogging for the Haisla was typically seasonal small contract work to supplement the fishing. It was not the easiest work by any standards, moving big logs with simple tools down steep slopes. Douglas fir was prized, but it was rare at the northern end of its range. Less than 2 per cent of the timber was Douglas fir and most of that was in one stand in the Kitlope. Spruce was in high demand during the First World War for airplanes and propellers, but rising market prices brought in a new wave of white loggers. Swanson Bay pulp mill was expanding its sights as the spruce source ran thin, and it looked to hemlock for pulp.

When Swannell approached Johnny Paul for assistance up the Kitlope, in 1921, he already had his hands full with other troubles. Even ignoring the Native rights and titles issue, the Xenaksiala and Haisla had grounds for a grievance under the colony's own economic system. In 1921, 40 – out of a village total of 50 Haisla men – had provincial permits as handloggers. The Haisla were reknowned woodsmen. A quarter of the independent contractors on the coast were Native and one-third of those were Haisla.[65] When Swanson Bay mill closed in 1924, those numbers dropped to less than 15 and by 1930 there were only a couple left. They could still sell their logs through timber sales licences, but these were only available to loggers who were willing to "grab the few scattered trees from the rocky and extensive shoreline."[66] They were getting squeezed out by the timber-staking boom precipitated by various legislative changes, starting with the Land Act in 1907. The changes going on in the industry opened up the forests to foreign companies that consolidated licences, labour and mills. The local handloggers, like Johnny Paul, were losing their autonomy, business and trees.

KITLOPE, SEPTEMBER 8, 1998

Cecil's brought us to the place of his birth on the Kitlope River. We pulled out of the main current of the river into an eddy and pulled the Zodiac ashore on a perfect little sandy beach beneath towering Sitka spruce. A huge granite cliff cascading with ferns and moss forms the backdrop of the village site, with just enough room for a row of single houses, though just Cecil's house remains. Upriver, about 50 metres, the cliff bellies toward the river to a pinch point, beyond which you can only pass by foot on a small well-worn trail. This is the pinch point where all traffic inevitably meets: wildlife, the Xenaksiala and the West Fraser road engineers who flagged the redcedars here for the end of the road up the valley. Annie Paul had harvested the bark off these trees, and it is on one of them that Cecil found the survey markers. How anyone could have imagined destroying this place is hard to imagine. Cecil got us to wash our eyes and ears in the river to see and hear more clearly. Then he lit a fire and we brewed up some coffee for a circle around the fire. Cecil told the guests the story of the fight for the Kitlope. No one is leaving this place unchanged.

SURVEY MARKERS IN KITLOPE, 1990

The real era of big company consolidation started in 1964 for the Kitlope. The soap opera of Eurocan Pulp & Paper mill coming to Kitimat is well covered in Rick Rajala's history of logging in the North.[67] All the usual characters are there: pulp and hydro booster R.G. Williston, a.k.a. Solomon, minister of lands, forests and resources, who has his hands all over this era, carving up areas the size of the Netherlands and handing them out with a kind of Byzantine logic.

The first the public knew of a paper mill coming to Kitimat was the summer of 1965 when they held the tree farm licence hearings there.[68] American timber and paper company Crown Zellerbach had been scouring the coast looking for fibre.[69] Then enter the Finnish government, who had cut down all its timber, and Prince George's Ben Ginter, and a royal marriage of sorts conceived the Eurocan Pulp & Paper Company in 1965 with the award of 473,000 acres of Tree Farm Licence No. 41 (TFL 41; an area-based tenure that included the lower Kitimat, the Kemano, the Kildala and the Kitlope) for the princely sum of $1. The Ootsa Lake interior forests, under a different tenure (Timber Supply Area) based on volume of timber, gave Eurocan access to 2.7 million acres of pine forest for another whopping dollar. The "somewhat imaginary authority" appears to have been the Canadian government, not the Haisla, since the right to allocate this timber to anyone was never legally theirs. The company won the tenures with the promise to be in production by 1969 – 1970. Meanwhile, MacMillan Bloedel was issued its licence to cut 125 million cubic feet annually out of the upper Kitimat River.

Despite the free wood and all the subsidies, by 1974 Eurocan was claiming disappointing financial returns. It had been primarily logging its allocation of interior timber from the flat plateaus around Ootsa Lake – the reservoir created behind the Kenney Dam. These forests were being sheared off by grapple yard operators and trucked to mills. Eurocan got into mechanization in a big way and brought everything from night shift floodlights for its harvesting machinery to state-of-the-art Finnish paper machines. It had already been heavily logging the Kitimat and Kemano regions of TFL 41 prior to the 1974 report and was about to start on Kildala. Cecil was hired during this period as the lead hand receiving hundred-tonne log bundles that came over the pass at Kemano and floated to Kitimat, where he loaded them onto the trucks going to the mill.[70]

In its 20-year plan, Eurocan was looking into a new sawmill and more access to cheaper timber. The Kitlope was described as the least attractive of its coastal forest units; the company claimed that "the climate and the mountainous topography have imposed serious constraints upon harvesting."[71] It was the last place slated for logging, with a start date of 1984.[72] By 1980, Eurocan had negotiated a lot of concessions, and profits looked good enough for the Ketcham family of West Fraser Timber Company, an American family who were then Canada's second-largest timber production company, to buy a 40 per cent interest in the company. The year 1980 is also when Cecil started working at Eurocan on the docks as a longshoreman, loading up the boats with pulp, and where he remained for the next 30 years.[73] In 1983, West Fraser bought BC Timber's Skeena Lumber Division sawmill at Terrace, with capacity for the big timber on the coast. The plans started to be put into place for logging the Kitlope. By that time, over 75 per cent of the Haisla/Xenaksiala territory had already been logged or modified by industrial projects.

According to then BC Forest Service District Manager Brian Downie, the appetite for logging the Kitlope was not big at the time. "When West Fraser took over they were essentially an interior logging company. Although it was a timber company, they weren't prepared for a coastal logging operation with a workers camp, coastal environmental factors and the machinery. I don't think they were particularly interested in it. Very likely that it was postponed through the '80s."[74] Downie also pointed to the costly engineering plans that would have to be drawn up and the more financially attractive Kitimat Valley tributaries, like the Hirsch. Journalist Ian Gill, while he was working for CBC, interviewed Skeena Woods Manager Vic Maskulak, who described what happened to their logging plans in the late 1980s. "It was planned to go. All of a sudden, things turned around, things came to a halt."[75]

The writing was already on the wall for the coastal companies that had been in a decade of frenzied overcutting. Costs were rising since all that was left was the remote timber, the companies having high-graded the easier more accessible timber. Anything left would require a costlier, less-mechanized form of logging in the most difficult and remote terrain. With larger-dimension logs, at a time when prices were declining, the company's appetite for the long trip down Gardner Canal is consistent with the fall out for other companies. Rajala writes, "By the end of the 1980s the Central Coast Economic Development Commission deplored both the absence of local manufacturing and over cutting by local licensees."[76] One of the local economic development officers, Patricia McKim-Fletcher, said, "The Central Coast has been on the over cut for many years, and most of the best wood is gone with little economic benefit to our communities."[77]

The Haisla leadership had been monitoring cutting plans for decades around Kitimat, Kemano, Kildala and Kiltuish, witnessing the devastation of different parts of their territory. At that time, there was nothing they could do legally to slow down or challenge the pace of logging. But, in 1987, the first ray of hope came through the Meech Lake Accord, with the section 35 amendments to the Canadian Constitution to enshrine the protection of "existing" Aboriginal rights. In the 1990 Ron Sparrow case, the Supreme Court of Canada held that fishing for food, social and ceremonial purposes was an existing right, following s. 35. The Court also provided a checklist for determining whether activities met the criteria, for example, if it was an "integral" part of Aboriginal culture at the time of contact, and how to define *integral*. There was no doubt oolichan fishing was an integral part of Haisla and Xenaksiala culture, as it had been practised continuously for 10,000 years at least – it opened up the first window of opportunity.

According to Downie, the Haisla "were very much concerned about oolichan. They had already lost Kitimat and Kildala Rivers and Kemano Completion was going on. Kitlope was one of the last. They saw it as a threat to their culture and historical sustenance. I don't know that we – in 1990 – had the awareness of the cultural significance, but Cecil and others tried to educate us as much as they could. I think our relationship was one of mutual respect. It wasn't acrimonious. I think it was that the Haisla were very persistent in educating the local interests there."[78] The first step the Haisla took in 1990, after Sparrow, was to issue a statement that they would be serving court injunctions on any more incursions into their territories for resource exploitation.[79] Gerald Amos, as chief councillor, knew Kitlope was in the cards, but the question was when.

In 1990 the Social Credit government was still in power but an election was looming. They were enduring a lot of criticism for their cut-and-run forest management style of the 1970s and 1980s. Eurocan had been working on its 20-year plan called a Total Chance Development Plan for the Kitlope Watershed, which it brought to the other agencies for sign-off in the summer of 1990. There may well have been a certain urgency as it currently had a government very much on the side of industry, but this political window was closing – a "Last Chance Development Plan." The plan set the cutting targets for the next 20 years, projecting a cut of over two million cubic metres of wood. It included plans for nearly 250 kilometres of roads to service a rate of logging of about 100,000 cubic metres per year. The Haisla only found out about the sign-off meeting by accident – but it became a game changer.

No notes exist for this meeting,[80] but, according to John Pritchard, Amos insisted on an invitation to the meeting and brought himself and the Haisla's environmental researcher, Josette Weir, along. Consultants' papers were presented by Eurocan that would enable the Department of Fisheries and Oceans and provincial Ministry of Environment to sign off on environmental impacts: one dealing with oolichan, and the other on the physical aspects of towing strings of log bundles downstream from the log dump to tidewater.

The proposal at the time was to remove the timber from the valleys a kilometre up the Kitlope River because Eurocan couldn't get a road round a cliff face on the north bank. It just so happened that this was the exact place that Cecil had grown up. They were proposing to run a road to the upriver side of the cliffs, then float logs down as bundles. The stakeholder meeting was to confirm that there would be no conflict between the log dump and the oolichan spawning season, as the eggs would have hatched and the fry drifted downstream and out to sea before the log-dumping season started. The consultants had extrapolated the dates from the timing of the Kemano oolichan arrivals that had been gathered for Alcan on the Kemano II project.

The study had been expensive for West Fraser but spawned many problematic fry. The consultants couldn't answer questions like: Could Kemano dates be used for a different population of oolichan? Was there damage to the oolichan spawning grounds with moving the logs? Where did you get your data that they only spawn in 2 – 6 metres of water? Where did you get the data that they spawn in the slough? In the end, the Haisla proved that the study was inadequate and that research in the river needed to take place during the spawning season, which was seven months away. That provided the Haisla with a seven-month window – seven months to mount a campaign to stop them.

For the first time, the government was faced with a legal obligation not just under fisheries legislation but constitutionally to protect the Haisla's existing oolichan fishery. It was right around the time that Cecil found the survey markers – those pink fluorescent tapes that herald the death knell of forests the world over. The survey markers, tied around Annie Paul's western redcedar tree, where she had raised her family on the Kitlope River, set in place a long chain of magical events. The ancient harvesting method for cedars allowed her to pull bark and wood off the tree without killing it, evidence so concrete that the tree has scars as personal as engraved initials on family silverware. Cecil told *Equinox* magazine writer/editor Bart Robinson in 1994 that when he saw those survey markers, he said, "These ribbons are sharper than arrows. They will cut deeper than knives."[81]

KITIMAT, JULY 16, 2016

As we cross one of the bridges of the Kitimat River, a work crew is doing some patch-ups on the aging bridge. A hard-hatted worker spots Cecil and waves, greeting him by name as we pass by. Cecil tells me there aren't too many jobs for the 535 people laid off when West Fraser Timber closed its Eurocan pulp and paper mill in the middle of the winter of 2010. Cecil had retired just before it closed, but some of his friends are among the laid off. Despite a recession in the US housing market, West Fraser still returned 9.8 per cent to their shareholders that year. West Fraser paid his salary for over 30 years and, in 1994, returned 317,500 hectares of its tree farm licence voluntarily and without compensation to protect the Kitlope. It remains the largest donation of logging rights on the continent for conservation – the equivalent of the entire forested area of the Netherlands. The "somewhat imaginary authority" to allocate this timber to West Fraser was never legally Canada's to exercise. West Fraser was just giving back to Canada – for $1 less than what was paid – what Canada had never lawfully acquired. The Xenaksiala never relinquished the ownership of the 54 wa'waises. Cecil is still the owner of Kemano. While he worked for the company, Cecil fought to stop it from logging his territory. Only he could have pulled that crazy idea off.

Launch a Supernatural Canoe

I told Gerald Amos, an elected chief who had become more of a son to me – a brother – and our hereditary chief, Simon Hall, that "I'm going to put my life on the line for this. I'm going to go fast for four days. After six to eight days, come looking for me, in case I have a [motor] breakdown."

I went up on the riverbank by the tree of my little granny. I hear my granny's spirit: "*Masi sax qasüüs?* What are you here for?"

I tell her, "Because they are going to destroy, they are going to kill the Kitlope, our valley."

"In my dream, there will be a lot of people coming to help," she says. "You launch a supernatural canoe and no matter who comes aboard to help us save the Kitlope, *gän'im łaka'tlee* – there will be lots of paddlers – that canoe would never be filled. Take a person that will guide you through uncharted waters to save the Kitlope."

I stayed another two days, and I had my answer from the tree. Gerald, sister Louisa and I in the canoe, because Louisa was there when I picked up the survey marker. She was there from day one.

In my dream, my little granny asks me, "*Un'gwai dlä lä xl łli?* Who is going to be chief at the front of the canoe?" She didn't give me an answer, but I thought about it and put it on the table.

"I would like to nominate Gerald Amos to be our leader and spokesman. He understands more about the adopted language than any of us put together. He will speak for us." Went around the table, everyone nodded their head. I said, "*Noox^w dla lä xiila.* I'll steer the boat and be in the stern to see where we are going." We were in uncharted waters and each time I always had Gerald in the front of the canoe. When you're on the river, he's the one in the front that looks after everybody's safety. Gerald was our spokesman. My sister is in the middle. Sometimes the river is so wide, and she'd instruct. We all agreed.

I went back to my hereditary chief. Our hereditary chief says, "Go on that journey, but ask the other chiefs."

I asked every one of them, "Will you walk with Wa'xaid in my journey, in the Kitlope?" I said to my sister Louisa, "*Ai'go 'la 'gliss ka'tla*. We've got to walk softly. We've been hurt and damaged so many times." I thought about my brothers in the union: What are they going to do? Am I taking their bread and butter for fighting for what I believe in? Fighting for the Kitlope? For my people?

I have three paddlers now, four with the hereditary chief. Four clans said that they were in, and the canoe was filling up. The hereditary chief asked Gerald, "Do we have any funding in the kitty to get our people together?"

Gerald said, "Yes. Pick the day inside one week from today." Gerald called all the people together. I told my grandchildren to get a few of the survey markers and then stay four or five days in Kitimat. The beginning of the battle started there.

One of the nuyem, or laws, of the Haisla is to be handsome. According to the Elders, who define what this means in the Haisla book on the nuyem, "a handsome person recognizes what is needed, whether an aspect of the social fabric or physical environment and can influence others to help fix it. A handsome person is caring and sympathetic for those who grieve or are needy. A handsome person accepts others as they are and respects everyone."[82] Cecil's story could be as much about Louisa, his little sister, and Gerald Amos, whom he calls his lieutenant. These are all handsome people by any cultural definition. They were the first in the magic canoe.

LOUISA SMITH

Louisa, Amalaxa, has always been in the canoe with Cecil, looking out for him and her family, even when she didn't know it. As she's a matriarch, everyone looks to her word, including those of us outside the family. Louisa married a Tsimshian man, Murray Smith, Algmxaa, one of the house leaders within the Gitwilgyoots Tribe – People of the Kelp – from the area known as Lelu Island. Lelu Island jumped into national prominence as the location for a huge liquified natural gas (LNG) plant proposed by the Malaysian giant Petronas. The deal fell apart in the summer of 2017. Murray and Louisa had a major role in standing up for Lelu Island (Murray went all the way to the United Nations), but that all came later.

Louisa has survived virtually everything Cecil has, in addition to several years at the Indian hospital at Coqualeetza. A child was never taken away from her at birth like Cecil's, but, unbeknownst to everyone involved, she looked after her brother's adopted child in the home of her friends, the local United Church minister John Cashore, and his wife, Sharon. They were all together in Port Simpson/Lax Kw'alaams. Her young children played with their cousin without knowing, and so she experienced one of the more unusual but happier stories of adoptions at that time – a loving white family that embraced a little adopted girl that happened to be her niece. After Port Simpson, they moved to Prince Rupert, where she still is advising, after teaching in the education system, 40 years later.

PRINCE RUPERT, MAY 28, 2017

On our road trips to Prince Rupert, we stay with Louisa and Murray. They are the busiest retired people in the town. There is a constant flow of family and friends in their warm, welcoming home that sits atop one of Rupert's escarpments. The ravens, western redcedars and the Smiths perch on the cliff. They are always busy helping somebody, fishing, preparing food, preparing for feasts and fighting industrial projects in their territory. Louisa loves to sit down in her living room and watch *Dancing with the Stars* on a big-screen TV as a little break.

Louisa is the fact-checker and proofreader of Cecil's story. With only four of them still speaking the language, Louisa is the ultimate source for phonetic spellings and the written form of her language. I sit by the kitchen table listening to the two of them speak together. It is like hearing the river moving gently over the stones. There is a Xenaksiala word for that. They have words for so many beautiful images and complex feelings.

We work on the manuscript in between cleaning the chinook Cecil caught with Murray. Murray, meanwhile, is working with relatives and environmental groups to build support against the Petronas project. It is an issue that has split clans, divided families, and the stress is showing in Murray's health. Tomorrow, Louisa gives a keynote to the Aboriginal Enhancement Schools Network. Her talk is called "From Truth to Reconciliation." She begins her talk with, "This is a Canadian issue not a First Nations one." She ends with, "We are all reconciliation actors. We act on our declaration of action to stand up to discrimination, prejudice and racism and promote respect, fairness, equality and partnership. Only then can we move forward in a good way." These two live, eat and breathe the graceful daily resistance against big money on their big land. They are the kind of people you want along on a tough journey.

GERALD AMOS

Gerald Amos is the other handsome paddler. He comes from a long lineage of Haisla leaders. The Amos and Paul families also have a paradoxical history intertwined with the colonization of the region. The Methodist minister Thomas Crosby helped convert one of Gerald's ancestors, Charlie Amos (Wahuksgumalayou, who was born in 1853) to Christianity. An entire chapter in Crosby's book is dedicated to his success with convert Amos, whom he sent to the Kitlope to build a church. According to Crosby, Amos led "some of these people to the Saviour" and told them: "My brothers, we asked God to send his servant to us and God sent Him."[83] Charlie Amos went to the Kitlope around about the time that Chief Paul (Sheaks) was the leader. In the 1900 *Na-na-kwa* article, the conversion of Chief Paul is told:

> Chief Paul soon after became Christian (that was about ten years ago) all his people began to be Christians also. He started a Council and judged true; sometimes he would shut his eye to bad words in the village because he did not want to judge hard. Last year Chief Paul began to get sick. He feared God at all times, often calling the people to his house to have prayer. After four weeks he go down dead. Bob Amos, who saw Chief Paul was buried with all due dignity, and was made his successor, but soon followed Paul to the grave. And was succeeded in turn by Matthew Ross who is present Chief of the Kitlopes.[84]

The relationship between a Christian god and Xenaksiala Great Spirits is mysterious. What is not mysterious is that the Paul and Amos families are entwined through the historical records. Gerald's father Harry Amos stood up for the protection of the Kitimat River all his life. Gerald stood by Cecil's concern for the Kitlope since his first visit there in 1966. When Cecil came to Gerald, chief councillor of the Haisla, in 1990 with the survey markers, the families had already been intertwined for millennia. Cecil has described Gerald as both his *dlä lä xl lli* (person at the front of the canoe) and *SiXtabélis* (lieutenant). Those English words don't even begin to describe Gerald's role as a political strategist, leader, orator, negotiator, kinsman, defender of Mother Earth, father, uncle, husband, friend and handsome fellow human being.

SALT SPRING ISLAND, OCTOBER 3, 2012

Gerald Amos came today for a big talk titled "Pipelines, Tankers and Civil Disobedience." The talk was at the high school and was open to the public, but it was the youth he spoke to directly. He packed the whole gymnasium. My role was his "moderator." Gerald needs no moderation. He's no longer Haisla chief councillor but working for SkeenaWild, helping Bruce Hill fight Enbridge and the Northern Gateway. He tells the kids, "Enbridge is the biggest single threat to what survives of our culture." The students are so keen to know how they can help and they fire questions at him for two hours. Gerald told them, "Say thank you to Enbridge for bringing us together. From Bella Bella to Hartley Bay, everywhere we go we see the youth coming together and taking the lead on this. I feel so empowered that there are young people like yourselves who are getting involved." It took me back 20 years to when Cecil made his call to action in Victoria. Now, in 2012, my youngest son was sitting in the audience in his final year of school, being called to action. The Haisla are indomitable. Gerald finishes up, "I think what we are developing is a credible threat. If we can't build a credible threat then nothing will stop these companies from doing what they've been doing." After the talk, he goes out for a sandwich with a dozen of the kids in their environment club. They get their photo in the local newspaper. He is standing in the middle with his characteristic checked, short-sleeved shirt with a big smile, and the kids cluster around a new hero of the 21st century.

KITAMAAT VILLAGE, OCTOBER 3, 2017

It is the last day of the trip up to Kitlope to take Bruce Hill's ashes there. Gerald's voice seemed to get stronger and stronger the closer we got to the lake. He told me his determination to encourage the youth was stronger than ever. After his illness, Gerald has taken to communicating on social media, posting the photos of his many grandchildren and friends from all over the world, and sharing what the companies and front-line resistors are up to these days. It never ends, but the "credible threat" he talked about years ago has grown exponentially. The conversation is picking up again about nature, climate change and culture, and Gerald is still looked to for his guidance. Not bad for a man who for a while lost his physical ability to speak.

Referendum: 98 per cent Said They Would Walk with Me

We had a feast; a bunch of people were there. I had one of my grandchildren bring the story of the survey markers up in front of the people. The hereditary chief told the people what these survey markers are, and I told them where they had come from. I told them, "I consider it not only my home, but it's a bank for us. It's a bank for our people. From logging this valley, they're going to destroy all the species of the Pacific salmon that come here. We are going to have nothing to eat if we let this happen. What's going to happen to the deer and the moose, the bear, the oolichan, the things we harvest from this bank? This bank is threatened. What are we going to do?" We had a little referendum in the village here: 98 per cent said they would walk with me. I don't know who the 2 per cent were. Best for me not to know.

The history of Haisla political leadership includes quite a few referendums – Haisla-style referendums. There is no better way to explain that than how they used them to try and protect the Kitimat River. Gerald's father, Harry Amos, as chief councillor, had been raising concerns (since Alcan had arrived on the scene) that the huge oolichan runs on which the Haisla economy depended had virtually disappeared due to sewage, dyking, logging and dumping of toxins. The few fish that remained were contaminated and tainted in their taste. Gordon Robinson, who succeeded him, carried on the campaign in 1964. He wrote a letter to the reeve of Kitimat, pointing out the impacts of dumping raw sewage on the oolichan and salmon runs. He attached a photograph of toilet paper caught on a salmon net.[85] In July that same year, he wrote to the provincial government to suggest that they were "still gambling" with the Kitimat River and future of the spawning stream with the impending start-up of the Eurocan pulp mill. The Haisla spent the next the three decades trying to prove it. They took Eurocan to court twice and presented their claim to the BC Environmental Appeal Board.

When the final legal challenge was settled out of court in 1992, the statute of limitations would only recognize the previous six years. The final package Eurocan offered was $3.25 million to the Haisla – little compensation for the loss of one of the arteries of Mother Earth. But Eurocan was also on the hook for an additional $30 million[86] to clean the river up and $300,000 for an independent fisheries biologist specializing in water pollution to monitor the river. Eurocan's biggest tactical error in the settlement was probably the latter, because independent data was now available. The Haisla knew the power of scientific evidence in a court of law.

When the settlement was proposed in the 1990s, it was brought to the village for approval and the leadership put it to a referendum. The village voted unanimously to accept it. The settlement didn't do much for the Haisla personally, but the river quality improved a little bit, and there was now baseline data to prove any more incursions on the river.

That settlement came hot on the heels of one of the most imaginative referendums in 1990 over their fishing rights in the Kitimat River. In spring of that year, the Haisla had alerted the provincial government that they would seek court injunctions for any more industry – sparked by the Kemano 2 completion. It was substantive enough a request in the eyes of the provincial legislators to propel the premier, Bill Vander Zalm, up to Kitimat to meet with the village council, the first time in 120 years a premier had met with the Haisla Nation to talk about land claims.[87] The Haisla had done their homework and identified the evidence for "existing" Aboriginal use. The 1890 letter written by Indian Reserve Commissioner Peter O'Reilly stated, "I explained fully the benefit they would derive from having their reserves defined and that their right to hunt and fish elsewhere as of old would remain undisturbed."[88] He made specific reference to salmon and oolichan fisheries. One hundred years later, those rights were not just being disturbed but bulldozed by industry.

The Haisla wrote letters to the prime minister and the minister of fisheries and oceans and printed up T-shirts with O'Reilly's letter on it. Gerald made a public showing of burning his fishing permit, then went fishing on the Kitimat with village members, young and old.[89] Cecil and Junior were there. The fish they caught were going to be sent to an independent lab for analysis of toxins. Conservation officers arrived on the scene with dogs and cameras, asking for the name of the person who set the net. One by one, every Haisla person there stood in front of a video camera and handled the net, saying, "I set the net." All the women then took turns in the canoe at the other end of the net and said the same thing. There was well over "the 100 Haisla" reported in the newspaper there, and the conservation officers couldn't arrest everyone. That was a Haisla-style referendum.

KITIMAT RIVER, SEPTEMBER 21, 2016

Cecil and I are tramping around, trying to find the location of the Kitamaat Reserve No. 1, where the Haisla fished on the river. The Haisla haven't harvested the oolichan in the Kitimat since 1972 because of the tainting of the fish from pollution and the pulp mill. The last large run was nearly 30 years ago. We come to a fisherman's little tarp and a place to watch the river after walking a beautiful trail under huge old cedars and spruce. We sit down for a picnic with some smoked salmon that I've brought and my idea of a good complement – avocado and health juice. It is a gorgeous, crisp, autumn day and the river is alive and talking. There are spawned-out chum lying on the shores, flies are buzzing around them and mew gulls are riding the river like a conveyor belt – flying up it, diving into the water after eggs, then riding down as they eat them. Mergansers and dippers are also diving around for fish eggs and a seal surfaces right by us with a chum in his mouth. My digital recorder is running and the only conversation for an hour as we watch is the sound of the river and birds before a company helicopter flies over and sets off the squirrels with their alarm calls. I turn off the recorder. What is the use, you can't hear yourself think. He tells me, "We came up here with the canoes to the village here, eh, but I don't recognize any of it now." The river has changed its course a lot over the years. He points upstream to where they had the protest for fishing rights. "We went to go set the nets, but they didn't allow us to fish. Junior was there helping with the net. I had a couple of chiefs from that little reserve in Terrace from the Nass all supportin' us." I hand him a cracker with avocado and smoked salmon. "Not bad, good," he says. "What do you think of the avocado?" I ask. "Not bad."

This long battle over the fisheries on the Kitimat River was to set the stage and mood for the subsequent battle for the Kitlope – where the last viable oolichan runs remained. The 98 per cent referendum that Cecil speaks about was when the Haisla community stepped behind the hereditary chiefs of the Xenaksiala and got into the canoe as a group. Now it started to fill up with allies.

The Boston Men

Then I got a call from Gerald. He asked, "Are you well to travel?" At that time, I had had a massive heart attack. He said, "Some environmentalists wanted to meet with us in Vancouver."

I said, "Let's go to Vancouver."

We met two young men of Ecotrust America. These environmentalists had an office in Portland. And we met these two and a beautiful friendship developed. We called them Boston Men. Didn't know who they were, and they asked if they could be of help. "Can your canoe get a little bigger Cecil/Wa'xaid? Can you bring more people?"

I said, "Yeah, that thing will hold anybody that wants to come aboard."

One of the things that was asked: "Do we trust these Americans?"

I said, "This canoe, Gerald, we're going to teach them to paddle in rhythm. Let's not fight one another."

I got to Vancouver late that night, and we were supposed to meet with them, 8:30 in the morning. I went to sleep, and I dreamt of a cloud and there was hands coming down and the hands were almost touching but there was no connection. And there was a bang, and Gerald woke and said, "Come on partner, it's time to go. We're going to be late for these guys."

I said, "Gerald, come here. You just spoiled a beautiful dream. It should have never ended."

Gerald said, "Come on, hurry up, let's go."

That's the first time I met Spencer Beebe. I take a look at this guy and he looked at his partner [Ken Margolis] and they introduced themselves and sat down. He said, "We're on a journey to find out what's left of the rainforests in the world."

"Our satellite," they said, "stops in the Kitlope, and scientists who take these images have communicated that if no logging has started, we'll be the second largest rainforest watershed in the world that has never been logged."

Gerald called a little later. "How are you feeling, Brother? These Americans are coming. They are going to fly into the Kitlope. They gave me the date. Who should I call to come along?"

I said, "Our new member, Charlie Shaw. He's a good person when the journey is rough. When you've been standing too long without taking a step to get out of this mess we are in, he will crack a joke. He'll make us laugh a while and come back to our business." That is why Charlie was with us all through the journey.

Charlie Shaw. He married a full-blooded Kitlope girl. I told Charlie a little bit. I talk about this American we're going to meet. "I don't know them," I said, "but it's a journey to save the Kitlope."

Charlie asked, "What time do we go?" That's the fifth one in the canoe from this village, and we went there to see the Americans and some funny things happened.

The day we got to where we were supposed to rendezvous in the Kitlope, I see somebody waving on the beach. Charlie told the captain, "Pretend not to see them." We drove by in the boat where these guys were, and they turned around to watch us. None of them had dry clothes. We went on and had a big fire at the place where I was born.

Spencer looked at Gerald and me and said, "I'd like to make an apology to you. Remember I told you in Vancouver it was the second-largest untouched temperate rainforest? It's been confirmed. The scientists say it's the largest."

We were in the canoe that we were going to paddle. I told Spencer, "Your education, your science is far beyond what little I have or Gerald. If we're going to work together, I don't want nothing said to the media without our consent. We have to see what you – with your mind – think Kitlope should do to stop the logging, and we will honour you if you do the same. If we're going to be partners in this canoe, we'll have to work together. We've got to be in harmony and paddle together." There was a handshake, and that was good.

What we were fighting was big industries that have lawyers and all that. I don't understand their language very well, so we were up against something so BIG. Then the guys brought in the scientists; bird scientists, river scientists, all kinds of scientists, come help us save the Kitlope. I had a wounded spirit and sometimes I said, "I want to give up." But a little child would come to me and say, "Don't stop now. Maybe there will be a door that opens."

"Boston Men" is the coastal name for Americans that has survived in common usage for a good 200 years from the days when Boston traders, of the ilk of William Henry McNeill, plied the waters looking for trade in furs. The Boston Men, who "reached down from the cloud," actually did come down out of the clouds but differed in every way from McNeill. Spencer Beebe comes from a prominent Portland ship chandler's family who made their money off the once great salmon fishery of the Columbia. These old American well-to-do families seem to beget in equal quantities capitalists or conservationists, depending on the generation and inclination. Spencer grew up wandering and fly-fishing the last wild rivers of Oregon and practising falconry. He studied first economics then forest ecology, perhaps in an attempt to unite the two diverging points of the family moral and economic compass.

PORTLAND, OREGON, FEBRUARY 27, 2017

I meet Spencer Beebe in his beautiful restored brick warehouse, smack dab in the heart of Portland. He describes it as a "good watering hole," being the consummate fisherman/naturalist that he is. One can imagine his instant affinity for habitat with the Haisla fishermen. The similarities

78

end there. His warehouse/big house is richly appointed with organic cafes and local fooderies encircling an airy space for community gatherings. Posters for music and social justice meetings paper the industrial columns. In the mezzanine above, various non-profits perch, including the Ecotrust headquarters. As we look out over the treetops of the leafy Portland street below, he remarks on a Cooper's hawk that has been nesting within view of his desk. We are joined by a younger version of Spencer, his son Sam, who now manages communications for Ecotrust. Sam's connections to the Haisla community are deep and continue with the friends he made as a teenager. Sam is a photographer and at the meeting he projects the collection of photographs from the '90s on the screen. A much younger Cecil and Gerald smile back at us. Spencer describes his first trip to the Kitlope:

> Our first trip into the Kitlope [was] in August 1990. We had found the Kitlope in our mapping projects and thought: "Wow, can this possibly be true?" Although coastal temperate rainforests exist all over the world, the largest area of temperate rainforest left is in North America? As you start mapping in some detail the status of the temperate rainforest on a watershed basis, there is only one large, temperate rainforest left in the world, and that is the Kitlope. That instigated the phone call to the Kitamaat Village council and talking to Gerald Amos, asking him if he could show us around...
>
> It was a nice summer day, kind of hot at the mouth of the Kitlope River. The geologist was pretty freaked out and was running around in his boxer shorts. That afternoon of the day they said they were going to show up, sure enough, you could see way down the mouth of the river an aluminum skiff. As they started to get close, I turned around and that geologist was running down the shoreline in his boxing shorts, waving his arms like: "Don't miss us, we are here!!" Gerald was driving and Charlie Shaw, he was the jokester, leaned over Gerald and said: "Keep going." They pretended they didn't see us and just kept going up the river. And this guy was standing there almost in tears, "They didn't see us?" Then they came back and that was our first meeting. I think they thought: "Who are these crazy white guys? What have we got ourselves into? Maybe we have to rescue them?"[90]

Rescuing white guys is a Haisla pastime. There is another famous story still shared of Sam Robinson, Gerald's grandfather, tying up actor John Wayne's boat, which had come adrift at Butedale. The gathering in the Kitlope that ensued was reminiscent of the 1921 meeting of Swannell, the surveyor, and Johnny Paul, Cecil's grandfather. Beebe had joined forces with the Western Canada Wilderness Committee and arranged a volunteer pilot to drop the party off by a float plane three days before they were due to meet the Haisla. Some of them camped on the sand of the estuary only to wake in the night as the river swept their tent and food downstream. By day three, the party were hungry, tired and anxious, scanning the water for the arrival of the Haisla men. One of the German geologists was wandering around with his Luger pistol cocked and ready against a grizzly.

The group spent the next several days around the campfire talking. As Beebe notes, "What was interesting to the Haisla was that our data had said that this was *the* largest, intact, coastal temperate rainforest watershed in the world. When we got talking and I asked, 'What do you guys want to do?' They said, 'We don't want to see it logged. Our problem is that we aren't sure if there is going to be another generation of Haisla. We are disappearing so fast, our kids don't know who they are, how they fit in, have any pride of where they've come from and their relationship to these places, so we have to figure out what to do about that.'" The summer before, four Haisla youth had committed suicide, and the community was struggling under the grief of those deaths.

Beebe has written his autobiographical account of the story in *Cache: Creating Natural Economies*. In 1987, he had just left the Nature Conservancy of the US in Washington, DC, to found Conservation International – a conservation organization that sought to protect tropical and temperate rainforests "on the principles of local sovereignty"[91] learned from his Latin American file with revolutionary reformers. Ken Margolis, his old boss from the Nature Conservancy, joined him. It was a move that rocked the international conservation movement but was to be a gift from the clouds for the Haisla for two reasons: the Latin American revolutionary reformers, many of whom were Indigenous leaders, had taught the Boston Men a lot. They saw that to support the needs of the local communities was the only way to offset the lures of corporate capitalism. Protecting the culture protected the land.

It also marked an opportunity for Beebe to shed some light on his own temperate rainforest ecosystem stretching out from Portland, Oregon.

"In the lower 48 there is no coastal temperate rainforest of any size: private, public protected or unprotected in protected status or intact. We are running around the world telling Brazil how to save their rainforest and, in fact, we don't have a single decent example of a coastal temperate rainforest in the entire lower 48."[92] With the mapping experience and capacity of Conservation International, Beebe's team looked at the status and degree of development on a watershed basis along the whole coastline, merging databases of logging histories from the Tongass, Alaska, British Columbia, Washington, Oregon and California. They collaborated with the Sierra Club of BC, which had done detailed mapping on Vancouver Island highlighting the last six coastal temperate rainforest watersheds left out of 90. The central coast had no such data.

Beebe hired Keith Moore, a young, local forester with roots in Haida Gwaii, to fill in the data gaps. Beebe recounts, "I think we paid Keith $5,000 to bring in the data of BC and he worked his tail off. He did it watershed-by-watershed status. What we learned was that of the 25 watersheds over 100,000 hectares of coastal temperate rainforest watersheds in BC... only one was left intact."[93] According to Beebe, an entire provincial ministry of forests had been unwilling up to this point to make that fact public and the report had embarrassed the politicians. Beebe describes the "aha" moment when they looked at the final map: "We saw this great big intact area between Fjordland Provincial Park and Tweedsmuir Provincial Park, and in the middle was the Kitlope, the largest undisturbed coastal temperate rainforest watershed in the world: the only remaining example of more than 250,000 acres in size that has not been logged."[94]

Moore's career trajectory and role in the magic canoe was not unlike Spencer Beebe's. He has the same passion for rainforests tropical and temperate, with the local knowledge of the BC coast, so the meeting of the two in 1990 was another one of those fortunate parallel universes lining up. At the time, he was working on the Tropical Forestry Program in Nairobi, Kenya, for the UN Environment Program (UNEP). His boss was a famous Chilean forester, Bernardo Zentilliwo, who had headed up the national parks in Chile before being exiled by the US-backed Pinochet regime. The Chilean ended up in UNEP with Moore and they struck up a friendship as they organized projects to save tropical rainforests. The irony was not missed by the two foresters – that they were working on tropical rainforests while their own temperate rainforests were disappearing under resource-hungry regimes. Keith continues:

We knew very little about the global extent of temperate rainforests, but we knew they were way more rare than tropical –
were probably concentrated in BC and Chile and were probably
on a global scale more threatened in terms of the last great intact
blocks on that coastal temperate ecosystem. There wasn't much
written about "temperate rainforests," although it was recognized in some books as a pretty rare forest biome. I came back to
BC and spoke to provincial ecologist Hans Roemer, on the top of
a mountain on the west coast of Haida Gwaii where I told him I
wanted to look into the whole global and BC picture for coastal
temperate rainforests. He said, "Hey you should talk to Spencer
Beebe in Portland. I'll connect you." So one spring day in 1990,
I flew down to Portland, and went to meet Spencer at his new
Ecotrust office.[95]

Moore contributed a variety of key elements to the thinking behind
the project: it was his decision to use watersheds as the logical ecological
units. Within each watershed, he used the new BC classification system
that characterized forest communities into bio-geoclimatic zones. It was
a state of the art system for understanding forests developed by the ex-
Czech scientist Vladimir Krajina. Moore needed a way to compare the forests with other jurisdictions like Chile and Alaska so that global statistics
could be compared. In many places around the world, environmental and
Indigenous groups were fighting battles watershed by watershed without
any global context. Ranking individual watersheds on the planet was the
"exciting idea" that Cecil immediately tuned in to. Moore pitched the idea
to Spencer, Beebe made a call, and Moore found himself going to lunch
with the agent of actor Paul Newman. Keith remembers: "Spencer asks
the guy for $5,000 to do this great project, but the guy was reluctant – so
sitting in the restaurant, Spencer gets on the house phone and calls Paul
Newman in Hollywood. Suddenly, Spencer has $5,000 for me to deter-
mine how many watersheds over 5000 ha are in coastal BC, where are
they, how many are unlogged and what are the best three for Ecotrust to
mount campaigns on."

The first thing Moore did was take 1:20,000 contour maps for the entire coast and draw lines in pencil around the watersheds. He started at
the height of land and drew down to the estuary; he was unknowingly
drawing the Haisla wa'wais. He could determine the area using planim-
etry and recorded all those bigger than 5000 ha. With logging plans and

forest inventory maps, and a lot of phone calls to friends in coastal forest districts, he checked the logging history in each. That produced a list of the number of watersheds, the number of completely unlogged ones and the three largest candidate watersheds to work on. Moore says, "That was when I identified the Kitlope – which none of us had ever heard of – as the largest completely undeveloped watershed in the world. I sent my report to Spencer to help his campaign for Ecotrust. It was supposed to be confidential."[96]

LIMESTONE ISLAND, MAY 2015

The best place to track down Keith Moore is Limestone Island during the breeding season of the ancient and marbled murrelets. They are handsome, endangered seabirds related to the puffin who nest on this north Pacific island in Haida Gwaii. They call them the iconic birds of old-growth temperate rainforests because they need old trees to nest in and below. The ancient murrelets lay their eggs deep in the roots of old-growth trees. The marbled murrelets nest way up in the canopy on broad branches in depressions in the moss. Moore helped set up a non-profit for seabird research and environmental education for the children of Haida Gwaii; Limestone is their spring headquarters. It is the kind of community project that he and his wife, Helen, have been leading in Haida Gwaii for years. Keith brought the Haisla to many people's attention and was one of those quiet guys who got into the canoe and paddled hard. He and Cecil share lots – a love of their home, the forests, the animals and helping the local kids find their place in the world.

Beebe immediately sent the findings to journalist Mark Hume at the *Vancouver Sun* and it became a front-page story. Moore's quiet life in remote islands changed. "Next thing I know, my phone is ringing – foresters and company guys wanting to know why I am selling out to a tree-hugging US green group that is trying to shut down the BC forest industry." That first report garnered Moore $900 after expenses, but "it was the most influential piece of work that I had ever done, and I wanted to do a lot more on the subject."[97]

After the first report was printed in mid-1990, he helped Ecotrust set up an advisory panel of the scientists and foresters he had been working with to produce "a much more robust analysis of the global picture," which resulted in a second report in 1991. Ecotrust then went on to publish *The Rain Forests of Home*, a benchmark publication on the scientific knowledge on temperate rainforests. It remains a classic today.

With Moore's initial mapping results, Beebe drafted a letter in July of 1990 suggesting the provincial government defer the area under BC's Old Growth Strategy planning process. In January of 1991, the BC government granted a deferral for one year and identified it as a study area in the *Parks Plan for the 90s* a month later.[98] With so much at stake, Beebe stepped away from Conservation International to focus full-time on the temperate rainforest campaign. His first task was to start Ecotrust with Gerald Amos on the board and bring to it the full armament of research expertise in ecosystem mapping, funding and political pressure on the provincial government and the forest company.

They also raised money for the Haisla to form their own non-profit organizations. One was the Nanakila (Haisla for "watchman") Institute to help young people rediscover their culture through a Watchmen program and "promote small scale sustainable jobs without destroying the natural capital." The other was the Haisla Nation Women's Society to run the Rediscovery camps for the youth. The relationship between the Boston Men with the Haisla Men was pivotal – albeit in similarly colourful ways as the rescue mission, or what Beebe calls "their origin story." They worked together institutionally for nearly two decades through various friendships and organizations.

PORTLAND, OREGON, FEBRUARY 27, 2017

Ken Margolis arrived at our meeting halfway through, having been attending to his wife who was very ill. He started, in a very Haisla manner, with his family and their relationships in Kitamaat. "I have a daughter who was with me in the summers. She was a troubled girl at that point. I never worried about her because people looked out for her wherever she went. She had aunts and uncles all over the village. Culturally, to me these people were always my grandparents. Where I come from, where you come from, where we all come from. The Kitlope was a chance to test and live those values out. I learned how twisted everything was, but at the same time how fundamentally people like Gerald Amos and Cecil Paul were unbuyable." Margolis understood the immediate needs of the community to stem the flow of youth suicides. "There had been a string of youth suicides that summer," Margolis pointed out. "Spencer had me up there about six months after he got to know them. At that point Gerald was everything in the village. He was third term as chief of council and he was the one the kids went to, so I knew pretty much on my first visit who I was working for – Gerald was the commander, Cecil was the poet, spirit and storyteller. Gerald was the boat and Cecil was the sail. They are the ones I listened to."

Not surprisingly, Margolis could be describing himself and Beebe. He is a quiet, soulful man. He said, "In some ways, I never knew where I stood with them up until the last...we had a celebration after the Kitlope was protected and everyone who worked on it they came up and they gave away gifts. When they called me up, I got a little leather pouch with some dirt from the Kitlope in it. I thought maybe I'm not anything to these people. Then, at the end of the evening, Gerald gave us both names and adopted me into the Eagle Clan. I have never had anything more satisfying happen to me, except raising my kids. For me, it was the greatest time of my life, especially the two years that I lived up there."

Beebe commanded the Boston crew. Margolis was his muse, like Cecil, who by this time had fallen ill. Gerald was the chief and ultimately took orders from Louisa, the matriarch. Their job was only to grow, because the world was starting to arrive in earnest by 1991 and step into the magic canoe.

Dr. John: Right from the Heart

By this time of the journey, I was ill. My heart was not good then, and I'm not allowed to travel with them to meet the company that is logging. I told the both of them: "Gerald, bring your regalia along." I says, "I don't know who you are going to meet, but something tells me you'll need it." I said, "Get one for Dr. [John] Pritchard; tell my daughter to give him mine. We'll adopt him in our clan." Before that, he was the first non-Native that was adopted in Haisla land, and he was adopted into the Eagle Clan. You cannot be accepted by the Great Spirit if your own clan doesn't [accept you], but the two hereditary chiefs agreed. That was awesome. To baptize a white person that I mistrusted with that seed of hatred? I'm healing, you know. I remember in that big hall, when I gave him his name. I told him, "They will drum, and I'll knock my hand, and you'll go and dance. Dance around the place. Go to the hereditary chief – you stop and you bow to him. Don't move for a few seconds. If he gets up and they come and pat you on the shoulder you are accepted in Haisla." He bowed his head to the chief, and John got up, big smile on his face. John flew around, never danced before in his life. But he almost took off in the air. It came to him, right from the heart.

Dr. John Pritchard was already well established in the canoe when the survey markers were found. His official title with the Haisla was researcher. He had arrived in Kitamaat Village in 1972 as a young student of anthropology. His professors at University of British Columbia (UBC), David Aberle and Robin Ridington, had sent him to research the Haisla's matrilineal structures. The question puzzling academic scholars was why the Haisla were closer in social structures to the Haida and Tsimshian – who were linguistically very different – than the other Wakashan-speaking groups to the south. Pritchard changed his thesis to an analysis of "Economic Development and the Disintegration of Traditional Culture among the Haisla." From his perspective, this was a culture under a long siege of his own culture's making, and there was more meaning and work protecting the living culture.

In 1976, while Pritchard was finishing his thesis, Heber Maitland, the chief at the time, asked him to work on a comprehensive land claim which the Haisla filed in 1978. "I thought it would take three months and I stayed 25 years."[99] Pritchard then moved on to researching the illegal incursions into the band's reserves known as specific land claims, which were legion.[100] When the constitutional amendments were made, he took on the research for court challenges and injunctions. When he arrived, there was already a well-papered trail of concerns from the band for the dumping of raw sewage by the village and then toxins by Eurocan into the Kitimat River. He was the legal researcher behind the scenes for over 25 years.

The ceremony Cecil describes in this story was made prior to the first trip to Finland that the Haisla took to stop the logging of the Kitlope. Cecil was showing signs of heart disease and his doctor wasn't going to allow him to travel, so he asked his sister Louisa and John Pritchard to step into the magic canoe. Pritchard was an obvious choice, as he had been advising on British colonial law for 20 years. Alternatively, Pritchard describes Gerald as a leader with "amazing instincts." Between them all, they were a veritable war canoe of minds.

VICTORIA, SEPTEMBER 7, 2017

I'm meeting John Pritchard at Murchie's Tea & Coffee for what he calls "gossip," since it is "just from his memory." What emerges from our conversation is far from gossip but an account from his near-photographic memory of events that stretch back over 40 years ago to the time he arrived as a young anthropology graduate student to the village. He worked with Chief Councillor Heber Maitland and all the subsequent chiefs of council to advise them on the legacy of the British colonial government. He worked through an extraordinary time of change in legal remedies. When I ask him where he stayed in the village, he replies, "I slept in Art Cross's living room on his sofa." "For 25 years?" I ask. Apparently so.

I should know by now that those least effusive about their contributions play some of the most critical roles. As usual, Cecil gives me the clues about who was influential, not by what he says but what he doesn't say. If someone is mentioned, then they are important. Cecil's story of John flying during his induction into the Eagle Clan was partly metaphorical. He flew all over the world for the Haisla, helping with negotiations. Then he flew away. John now commutes between a Gulf Island and Victoria. He suggests that his Welsh lineage – that seems to carry with it a solid distrust of the colonizing English – clearly prepared him as an ally to the Haisla.

He provides me with a helpful metaphor for the Haisla's complex and heart-centred system of land stewardship and law by using a Judeo-Christian example. "*Nuyem jees* is the place where you get your ethics relating to the world, so think of the nuyem as the Ten Commandments; the *nuyem jees* the Kitlope as Mount Sinai." I ask him about his version of the naming feast.

> Before going to Sweden the first time, I was made a member of the Eagle Clan. It had to be someone from a different clan to be the speaker, so Cecil Paul (Killer Whale Clan) was picked for his oration skills. I was brought before the community in the gym. Several hundred people were there. Cecil stood by me and gave a speech in Xenaksiala. "This man has brought his skill and knowledge to work for us..." and so on. In a sense he was saying: you send a thief to catch a thief. This was a wise-crack that could be misunderstood by someone reading the bare words. My name is 'SiXtabélis (the X is a Greek chi, pronounced as "ch," as in "loch"), "the one who poles the canoe up front" because I know the river. If I lead everyone onto a rock, then I fall in first. Cecil announced it and my brothers Art Cross and Jughead [Charlie Shaw] put the blanket on me. The drums started and they started to sing and I swirled around so that I could show off the crest.[101]

Pritchard describes the events of 1990 as various parallel universes happening at the same time "with strange synchronicities and unbelievable flukes." The first to drop out of the sky were the Boston Men, literally and metaphorically. The next were the Steelhead Society.

Bruce Hill: He Put His Power Saw Away

There is a little river in the Kitlope valley called Wow'kst where only two kinds of salmon go: the steelhead in April, and September the coho. I followed the survey markers; it went right across the spawning beds for the steelhead, and I told Gerald, "You got to tell people: don't touch anywhere near the survey markers. Whoever is going to come volunteer from the Steelhead Society or sportsmen, we got to show them that this spawning bed would be no more if they log." That is why I said, "We got to invite them – they could be our greatest allies. Get them inside this Magic Canoe, Gerald. They are going to help us paddle."

And then we brought up the vice-president of the Steelhead Society, Bruce Hill. He was a logger, this guy – very sarcastic guy. We went up there to that little creek. Up there we began to talk sensibly. I said, "If you allow that logging, it is going to destroy the fish. Only two species come up this way: coho and steelhead." I brought him right up to the big hole by the waterfall. The fish don't go any further. It is the end of their journey. On the right-hand side is a big, deep hole. My Elders, years ago, had a long pole of cedar, very light, and they tied the end of the net over it and speared the fish inside the deep pool.

I try to trace back to that time when I was able to talk to Bruce as a friend without anger. He would say, "Get that damn net out of the water," and that kind of language. Now we could talk with no anger in the voice. I tell him, "We are in uncharted waters, your life and mine." I try to reach inside, that's the only way I know how. "Understand what that little creek is going to do, an artery of Mother Earth. How are we going to protect it together? It isn't just steelhead. I'm trying to give you an idea, a vision of how Wa'xaid done it."

How do I reach out and tell him that I am fighting all these years? How do I reach into Bruce's spirit and make him understand? Damaging a valley through clear-cut logging. He was a faller, vice-president of Steelhead. You got to talk softly. Talk softly with them. Let them come here and see what the valley means. Bruce put his power saw away and he came aboard the canoe, and then for a while he helped with Rediscovery camps and got the Nanakila Institute started with Spencer. They both were white men. I hear this beautiful laughter of my friend Bruce Hill. You can pick up his laughter from far away; it sounds good. I don't know where he is, but I recognize that laugh. I heard it in the Kitlope. I'll always remember this gentleman. Good journey.

The Steelhead Society of British Columbia was full of paradoxes for the Haisla, and Cecil astutely played them into the canoe like the fisherman he is: redneck hippie loggers, American philanthropists, rear admirals, movie stars and journalists among them. Steelhead fish themselves are responsible for this broad attraction. Any steelhead enthusiast will tell you that, for a sporting fish, there is no equal. They require long rods, lots of line and a lot of skill to pull in.

This threatened member of the salmon family shares all the same characteristics as the other sea-run salmonids that return to their home creeks to spawn, except the steelhead don't die after spawning – they return to spawn again. Something other than reproductive fecundity must imbue them, though, with so much veneration. The answer lies in the history of this fish as a game species. The Steelhead Society was started in 1970 by a generation of writers, romantics and businessmen inspired by the likes of angler/writer Roderick Haig-Brown. In *A River Never Sleeps*, Haig-Brown offers clues as to their lure through his initiation rites a century ago. When he was a young recent immigrant, boasting about fish back in the "auld" country, a seasoned BC fisherman stopped him in his tracks and asked, "Lad, do you know what country this is? It's the land of the free and the home of the brave." He was referring, of course, to steelhead.

Reading through the body of literature about steelheads leaves one with the impression that the anglers, predominantly white Second World War veterans, had projected some complicated desires for solitude, independence and freedom onto the fish. Maybe none of this is true, but steelhead societies attract these romantics like no other. It seems even those most responsible for endangering fish, whether it was from their resource investments or chainsaws, were also likely the first to open up their wallets and their hearts to save the rivers, the steelhead and their own souls. Such is the paradox of the steelhead.

In 1956, Lee Straight, a columnist for the *Vancouver Sun* and one of the founders of the Steelhead Society who aspired to Haig-Brown's crown of steelhead prose, wrote a loving tribute to them called *100 Steelhead Streams*. By 1970, those 100 streams had whittled down to half that number. Lee Straight and others started the Steelhead Society to save the fish – maybe themselves. They were taking on some big issues with the federal government and fisheries management. They were very effective, but some members had old ideas of what the problem was. Blaming Indigenous people for stringing nets across streams was easier than pointing the finger at their friends and colleagues in the forest industry. Bruce Hill walked straight into this controversy with his chainsaw running. He took on the leadership of an organization that "had a bit of a snarly reputation towards Natives, but," he said, "it was also an organization that got a lot done."[102]

TERRACE, JULY 16, 2016

Coming into Terrace from the west, we pass through the industrial section of town along the Yellowhead Highway. On the north side of the highway, the Skeena Sawmill is still standing, but Hank Ketcham and his West Fraser operation got out of town – wisely, according to his shareholders – a decade ago. On the south side of the road is a huge vacant industrial lot, which three sawmills used to occupy. Cecil was a labourer in one of the mills for three years, staying in the Indian dorm down the road with a shared outhouse right beside the Skeena. Wa'xaid, the Good River, lived along many rivers in his life. The mills are gone. So are the dorms. So is the outhouse. But not the Skeena. It continues its steady flow to the sea, though this year it was as high as Cecil had ever seen. Running close to the riverbank is the stretch of railway track that he worked on as a labourer in 1958 with Russell Ross, his best friend. Russell had helped him survive residential school. Never having been taught to read or write, they couldn't make more than 95 cents an hour in 1958. Along the road, Cecil points out the killer whale petroglyph on a cliff by the river. Every inch of this landscape carries a rivulet feeding into the river of his biography.

He directs me to a leafy part of the white guy's town of Terrace where his friend Bruce Hill lives. Bruce and his wife Ann greet Cecil with great hugs and invite us in for a piece of sour cherry pie that Ann has just made from their overladen tree. Bruce is a great big bear of a man the Boston Men describe as a walking unmade bed. His illness has reduced his bulk, but not his shaggy warmth. The delight of the two men – both only just out of their beds after severe illnesses – to see each other is palpable.

Bruce came to the Steelhead Society as a director and a logger, but that title is deceiving. He also describes himself as a Haight-Ashbury refugee via Alaska, so not immune to dreams of back-to-earth activism.[103] After running a sawmill in Burns Lake, he bought a fish guiding business in

Terrace and then discovered there were no fish left. That's when he took on the volunteer tenure as vice-president of the Steelhead Society, which was described by Mark Hume – the next generation of *Vancouver Sun* columnists about environment – as "one of the most important conservation organizations in North America."

Bruce teamed up with a fellow guide/conservation photographer/sailor called Myron Kozak and went looking for steelhead and found them in the Kitlope. "I grew up in New Brunswick looking at maps of the coast of BC, and there was one place where this incredibly long fjord goes with a great big lake at the end of it. I told myself that someday I'm going to go to that place. And so when I ended up in Terrace, BC, with a sailboat, I said, it's time to go there." Spring is always spectacular in the Kitlope and 1990 appears to have been no exception, but Bruce stumbled onto something he wasn't expecting: a big survey boat anchored off the estuary laying out roads and landlines. "That was when we decided we had to save the Kitlope," Bruce says, followed by his famous laugh.

One of the most publicized stories of the Kitlope is that of the apocryphal meeting between Bruce and Yvon Chouinard, the founder of Patagonia, who wrote of his involvement with the Kitlope and Haisla in his autobiography.[104] Chouinard is one of the tribe of steelhead enthusiasts who happened to come to the Bulkley River to fish in the autumn of 1990. Kozak guided on the Bulkley and tipped off Hill that Chouinard would be on the river. Hill approached Chouinard as he came off the river and asked him if he donated to environmental causes. Chouinard writes, "I'm thinking: Oh god, a redneck logger and I can't even outrun him with my waders on."[105] Hill disabused him of the situation, told him about the Kitlope, the steelhead fishing there and that he needed $4,000 to hire a helicopter to get Myron and his camera up to take pictures to launch a campaign. Two days later, Chouinard, his son Fletcher and Kozak were flying over the Kitlope in a helicopter. Kozak's photographs were to be a critical PR element, ending up in *Time* magazine. Patagonia became a major sponsor of the Haisla's campaign, awarding its largest grant ever to the Nanakila Institute. It was a big catch for the magic canoe with some key players dropping out of the clouds.

Between 1990 and 1992, four separate braids of the good river were coming together in a major river channel of power – the Haisla clan, the Terrace clan, the Portland clan and the Scientist clan – aligning under Cecil, Louisa and Gerald's careful steering of the magic canoe, which they aptly named the Haisla Steering Committee – quite a feat given the forceful characters they were dealing with. The Boston Men had moved quickly with the decision by the provincial government to defer the Kitlope. Margolis had moved up and spent the winter of 1990 fundraising and getting the spring research expeditions lined up. The Haisla and Ecotrust planned an ecological and cultural reconnaissance to guide future decision making for what they called the Greater Kitlope Ecosystem, which encapsulated all 405,000 hectares.[106]

Ten Western scientists, under the thoughtful guidance of forest ecologist O.R. (Ray) Travers, joined Cecil and other Elders in the Kitlope for the first detailed reconnaissance in May of 1991. They gathered the ecological information along with the cultural teachings of the Kitlope. They spread out throughout the watersheds collecting inventories of birds, plants, mammals, amphibians, insects and forest types. One of the scientists was Adrian Forsyth, rainforest program director for Conservation International, who picked up the baton from Beebe. One of the group, John Kelson, a young climber/birder who had first cut his teeth climbing old-growth trees on Vancouver Island to find marbled murrelet nests, continued the survey work through the summer with six Haisla youth. Alison Davis helped Elder Bea Wilson to prepare a book on the use of medicinal plants called *Salmonberry Blossoms in the New Year*. Word of their work was getting out.

Greenpeace's flagship, *Rainbow Warrior*, was scheduling a return trip for its 20th anniversary that summer along the Pacific coastline to monitor the results of the two-year attempt to clean up the 11 million gallons of crude oil spilled from the *Exxon Valdez* in Prince William Sound, Alaska, and look at clear-cut logging along the BC coast. With some rapid planning going on behind the scenes with David Peerla of Greenpeace, the international environmentalists were stepping into the magic canoe. The various groups were coordinating a detour into the Kitlope for the *Rainbow Warrior* on its way back from Alaska in September of 1991. The ship turned east down Gardner with a delegation from Finland, Sweden, the Netherlands, the Haisla and other members of the study team, bound for another opportunity of media coverage and fieldwork. The Greenpeace delegation from Finland included Native Sami activist Olaf Johansson; the leader of the Finnish Green Party caucus and MP Satu Hassi; and other Finnish scientists, environmentalists and a journalist. A full-page *Vancouver Sun* article featured a picture of Hassi and her daughter Helia ceremonially washing their eyes and ears – on Cecil's invitation – in the water of Kitlope Lake.[107] These connections were to be vital in the unfolding sequence of events with Eurocan.

Following hot on its heels to catch up, BC Parks did its own two-day ground and one-day helicopter reconnaissance in the first week of September, led by plant ecologist Hans Roemer.[108] Roemer, who had inspired Moore for the 1990 watershed report, brought his own departmental support, which just added more weight to the extensive reconnaissance of the Haisla and scientists that came out a week later.[109] In the latter, the Kitlope Declaration received its first – and certainly not last – public viewing.[110]

> We the Xenaksiala of Huduwachsdu have known, loved and guarded the Kitlope Valley for untold, uncounted centuries. Here, our people have been born, have lived out their lives and returned to the Earth, at one with the land.
>
> For we do not own this land so much as the land owns us. The land is part of us; and we are part of the land.
>
> It is given to us only as a trust; to live within its boundaries in beauty and harmony; to nourish our bodies and our spirits with its gifts; and to protect it from harm.
>
> We have a solemn sacred duty to keep faith with those that came before us, who guarded and protected this land for us; we must do no less for ourselves and for those who come after.
>
> —Haisla Nation, Kitlope Declaration

The declaration opposed "any proposals or acts that threaten the lands, waters, and living creatures of the Kitlope." It also invited anyone to step into the magic canoe to help "in wonder and respect for this place."[111] For the Haisla and Ecotrust, the rest of the autumn was spent assembling their arguments and evidence, with additional material from the Greenpeace scientific forays with lichen specialists, ornithologists and small mammal researchers.

Back in Vancouver at its head office, West Fraser was working to a December deadline of its *Five-Year Management and Working Plan for TFL 41*, in which it laid out its cutblocks, roads and timelines. Talks had started and stalled between West Fraser and the Haisla leadership, despite Ken Margolis from Ecotrust working behind the scenes with his American business compatriots. By November 1991, the connections the Haisla had made aboard the *Rainbow Warrior* with the Finns enabled them to take their concerns directly to the majority shareholder in Finland, Enso-Gutzeit.[112] Finnish MP Hassi noted to Glenn Bohn, *Vancouver Sun* environmental reporter who had also been aboard the *Rainbow Warrior*, that when she got home she was calling a press conference and heading straight for the office of Enso-Gutzeit – a Finnish state-owned corporation.[113]

Bruce Hill describes meeting Gerald for the first time en route to the airport for Finland. Josette Weir, another key researcher working for the Haisla council, had phoned Hill up and asked him if they could take Kozak's photographs to show the Finnish company. As Bruce describes the moment, "I drove to Kitamaat, gave him a set of the slides, which we had paid for out of our own pockets, and sent some to Conservation International and Greenpeace and other people. Gerald was just getting ready to go to the airport to head for Finland. I shouldn't say he was impolite, he was just harried and rushed and you know... Anyway, the photographs were being published everywhere and became a big part of the campaign. Well, I still tease him about it."[114]

The highly publicized Finnish tour, which also involved Jup Weber, one of the founders of the European Greens in 1983 and a Luxembourg Green Party MP who made the file his own personal mission, gave the Haisla leverage to invite West Fraser to a public meeting. They scheduled it for the third weekend in January of 1992. The objective for the Haisla was to hear West Fraser's plans and present their "alternate management plans and designations for the Tree Farm Licence 41."[115]

It was, by all accounts, a meeting not to miss. At the Mount Layton Hot Springs Resort, invitees crowded into the room to hear the logging company's opening bid – that they needed all the timber to keep their mills running and jobs secure. Next to speak was the Haisla Nation. Louisa rose first and spoke of her childhood in the Kitlope, the damage of residential schools and Indian hospitals, and the deep spiritual importance of the land to restore their health and spirits. According to everyone that was there, the room went very quiet and her soft voice and slight stature held the audience riveted. West Fraser countered with an offer to cut the logging by half and only hire Haisla, which, according to Hill, was "worth $125 million in wages to a community of 700 people with an employment rate of 50 per cent."[116]

When West Fraser made the offer to the Haisla, the people at the meeting said, "No." West Fraser, according to those present, countered, "But you are not talking for your people." The hereditary chiefs canvassed the families who weren't there by phone and the answer came back resound-ingly: "No." In another one of their famous referendums, the Haisla – with their overwhelming no – turned the offer of $125 million down.

VICTORIA, APRIL 30, 1992

Friends of Ecological Reserves sponsored a talk called "Kitlope: Portrait of a Temperate Rainforest," with two speakers from the Kitlope, Cecil Paul and James Robertson, and the photographer Adrian Forsyth from Conservation International, who was on the reconnaissance trip last year in the Kitlope with them. I left my son Callum with his first babysit-ter and it was strange to be without him. The two Kitlope men opened the evening in their language, which stopped everyone in their tracks. Vic-toria sure has changed; when I left a decade ago, "God Save the Queen" was what opened events. Cecil Paul spoke so poetically about the Kitlope River as the artery of Mother Earth welcoming everyone to come and leave their footprints in the sand. The photographs were stunning, espe-cially of Kitlope Lake, or Kous, which means "cathedral" in Henaksiala. I had to leave halfway through the talk because I just sensed something was wrong at home. Good thing I left. The babysitter had tripped with Callum in the backpack and scraped himself up and they were both cry-ing inconsolably when I arrived.

When I came to know Cecil better, I told him the story about how I never saw the end of his talk. It was almost inevitable that my first lesson from Cecil was about the practical necessities of caring for a child. He had been robbed of most opportunities to be a child or parented. My son's descent to earth was the first of many synchronistic events, which Cecil's presence triggers in spades with anyone who spends time with him.

The research and fundraising was unfolding under Nanakila's direc-tion, and Gerald Amos directed a wilderness planning framework to help guide the Haisla. This report was prepared by Ray Travers, grizzly spe-cialist Wayne McCrory and activist/ecologist/writer Grant Copeland and submitted before the window shut on the provincial deferral timeline. In October 1992, Minister of Forests Art Charbonneau announced that the Kitlope deferral would continue until 1995 and be included in the provin-cial protected area strategy initiated by the new New Democratic Party (NDP) government. The Haisla had another three years to prove their case. Eurocan vice-president Dave Kelly argued, "It only adds to the uncer-tainty over fibre source to keep the mill running."[117] It was a weak volley.

As Pritchard notes, "West Fraser were losing friends," and the Haisla were winning them in droves.

TERRACE, JULY 16, 2016

Ann Hill is preparing a chinook that Cecil has brought them after his fishing expedition with Murray on the Skeena. Bruce tells his origin story of Nanakila as we dig into our pie. Spencer told me a similar version down in Portland about the meeting when "something strange began to happen." His version is that Bruce came to the Haisla with tears running down his face after the January meeting when Louisa spoke, and said, "I never understood before, I want to do whatever I can for you."[118] According to Bruce, Ken Margolis asked him if he was interested in helping with the operations of the Watchman and Rediscovery programs. They needed help training the youth in ecotourism, scientific monitoring and getting the kids back and forth to the Kitlope. He jumped at the chance and stayed with the Nanakila Institute in various capacities through its formative years. They set up their office right behind Cecil's house. Cecil, now recovering from the heart operation, wandered into the office and introduced himself to Hill. Hill said it didn't take him long to "fall in love."

This is a serious love affair. Bruce recounts his favourite story of his first time with Cecil in the Kitlope to catch sockeye. "I expected when we got there that Cecil would put his net out right away. We got there and he said: 'No it isn't time yet.' We sat there for three days leaning against those big spruce trees drinking coffee, smoking and playing crib. Cecil saying: 'No it is not time yet, no use.' Then one morning he gets up and says: 'It is time now.' We went out there and...lots of sockeye. Remember that, Cecil?"

I asked him about Cecil's story of their trip to the pool. Bruce recalls, "He showed me the pool that when he was a kid they would fish in, not very far up the river from the cabin where he grew up. It was way back, the trails had all grown over. I remember we marched through the bush to this gorgeous slough and the water came out of an underground stream and it was very tranquil. He explained when he was a kid they would lay along the bank and watch the salmon swim by. It was Cecil mentoring me and showing me his world and we bonded."[119]

One of the wealthy steelhead men Hill brought up was a donor, Pete Soverel, of the Wild Salmon Trust. Hill describes him as "a rabid sport fisherman." Purported to be the naval intelligence eyes on Ronald Reagan when Oliver North was in charge of the navy, Soverel was also as close to a rear admiral as they come. Wanting to time his visit with when the salmon were running, Soverel had his own idea about salmon migrations and came sixteen days earlier than their full moon arrival of mid-July. To get that information, all he had to do was ask. He caught nothing and a grizzly ate up his supplies. Finally, on the night of the full moon, the salmon started to run and he caught a fish. As Bruce quips, "That's naval intelligence for you, but he did donate."

As we prepared to leave the Hills' home, the emotion around our departure was strong. Both men knew their time was precious. Bruce told Cecil how much his time with the Haisla had changed not just his life but his whole family, with both kids attending the culture camps. His son, Aaron, an ecologist, now works for Watershed Watch Salmon Society, an advocacy group for salmon, and his daughter, Julia, is carrying on with SkeenaWild. Cecil nicknamed her the Kitlope Princess. Bruce tells me later, "It was a really heavy learning curve for me. I had heard about Traditional Ecological Knowledge, but I didn't have a lot of experience working with First Nations people. I really got a first-hand account of just how this learning thing works."

KITAMAAT VILLAGE, SEPTEMBER 29, 2017

It is 6 a.m. at the dock in Kitamaat Village. The spiders are busy weaving their last webs around the dock lights before the winter storms catch up with them. It is drizzling as it should, and the morning light is just beginning to creep under the blanket of cloud. Cecil clambers aboard the fishboat, despite his recent broken foot. Next is Gerald, who also shows a surprising agility given his recent cardiac arrest. Gerald has his son, Trevor, and Cecil has his last surviving daughter, Cecelia, to accompany them. Ron Smith is the owner of the fishboat, Cecil the dlä lä xii la yewx. I'm the dishwasher, roles are reversed.

Cecil and Gerald are taking Bruce Hill back to the Kitlope for his last trip. Originally, all three of them were supposed to go, but the trip got postponed due to Cecil's illness and then Gerald's. There never was a window for all three of them. Bruce's cancer overtook him, so they are taking this warrior in a mason jar to be embraced by the four chiefs of Kous. Bruce died September 18, one month after the grizzly bear trophy hunt was banned on the coast. We were all glad he lived to see that day. It was more good news in a pod of good news stories of issues on the northwest coast that Bruce had helped out on – the Northern Gateway pipeline, the LNG plant at Lelu Island and the sacred headwaters of the Tahltan.

The fishboat runs at about five knots. It is a cozy space in the wheel-house around the table. There is a pot of percolating coffee on the stove as we talk, play crib – you can't beat a Haisla – and watch the rain-slicked granite cliffs slide by. Western grebes in the dozens are gathering for the winter off Costi Island where the first Haisla village was established after Waa-mis left River's Inlet 9,000 years ago. At Crab River, we stop the en-gine and drift with the tide into Xenaksiala territory. Cecil sings the com-ing home song and some of Bruce's ashes are scattered. Cecil then says: "I want to raise that person to honour, *Nuyem Jees*, I spent many hours together with him. Honour the captain for bringing us up. Take my brother to the chiefs, *Nuyem jees*."

A Haisla fisheries boat comes up and offers a pail of cooked Dungeness crab for the journey. The Haisla men sit on upturned pails on the deck eat-ing the crabs for lunch. All you can hear is the crunching of shells against the steady beat of the motor and dripping rain. We stop at some of Cecil's doors and open them up for stories along the way: waterfalls, pictographs, the place where the canoe was tied during the flood, as this is also a trip for Cecil to show Cecelia her territory for the first time. She dropped every-thing to come; when doors open in the Kitlope, you show up.

We arrive at dusk at the old village of M'iskusa, at the mouth of the Kit-lope River. The replica G'psgolox pole looks over us as we load everyone into a smaller jet boat to get up the river to the Watchman cabin before dark. A real grizzly stands up close to the supernatural one on the pole to see who has arrived in the estuary. His well-beaten stomp trail around the pole marks his territory in the estuary. Diggings for riceroot and browsed sedges are everywhere.

We all scrabble up the bank to the Watchmen's cabin. A young moose swims across the river as we arrive, getting pushed fast downstream by the current. Huge chunks of the riverbank have been washed away and it is only a matter of time before this cabin will disappear like everything else. We get inside and light a fire and it quickly overheats with us all bed-ded down as well. Cecil just curls up on his mattress with a blanket and sleeps like a child.

The next morning, we travel the rest of the way up the Kitlope River in the smaller boat, layered up in wool and rubber raingear. Getting to the lake is never guaranteed; the channels shift and get blocked with huge spruce trees and debris during the seasonal floods. Gerald's son Trevor is at the helm, Brian plays the *dlä lä xii la yewx*. We come round the huge granite cliffs, cloaked in mist, that form a portal to the lake, where the vista opens up over the lake flanked by ice-capped mountains that plunge into the milky blue water. The Eagle/Raven Clan village site is easy to pick out for the fine golden sand beach where we unload the precious cargo.

After the fire has settled down and we've had lunch, Cecil begins the ceremony, asking his ancestors to welcome and watch over his brother Bruce. His beautiful words ripple over the lake. He asks his ancestors for a sign that they will welcome a non-Xenaksiala man to the valley and at that moment the skies part, a beam of light lights us all up and a rainbow arcs over the lake. A red-necked grebe swims by too – the last little joke from Bruce – that even rednecks are welcome in this canoe.

While we are travelling, Cecil tells me about camping with Bruce during a Rediscovery camp in that very spot. "I had a campfire going, it was late. I was getting ready to go out in the boat. Bruce came down and said, 'Where are you going brother?' 'To the lake to meditate.' Bruce said, 'Can I come along with you if I'm quiet?' 'Sure,' so we go. Stopped in the middle of the lake and we sit. I wanted to make him see that the Kitlope is more than saving spruce. It is more than moose or grizzly. Little martens, little squirrels...Kous is a place of worship. The quiet distant call. There are loons up there, we hear them cry. A native duck talking. Quietness. Must be two hours. Did you get anything out of our journey Bruce? I ask. He says, 'I got more than I can ever tell you.'"

Bruce Hill's obituary describes his ability to "foster unstoppable alliances between First Nations and non-Indigenous conservationists." Those unstoppable alliances were built on the teachings of Annie Paul, born where we are anchored in 1870 – she is the unstoppable powerhouse of the story. The alliances just kept growing.

Brian Falconer: Big White Magic Canoe

The people that came aboard this canoe were something beautiful because of the love of the environment. One of them was a captain of the sailboat vessel *Maple Leaf* who was in the fight with us for years. The captain said, "I love the environment. I take people out to BC, and they are all environmentalists." He said, "Maybe we could be of help?" That was music to my ears. The offer gave me the energy to take another step. I met the captain of this boat, and his name was Brian Falconer. A journey with this man was something awesome and beautiful. My brother said he wanted to show me something – he wants to show me what the Creator wants me to enjoy. He was the first one in a big boat that brought people up to my place of birth. He told his crew, "You are going to the largest untouched rainforest in the universe." It is the first sailboat to come and help us try and save the Kitlope. The amazing part of it is, when I tell my story to the children, I am touched at how many of them were interested.

With a name like *Maple Leaf*, this century-old, 28-metre-long wooden schooner was preordained to capture an interesting chunk of Canadiana, not least of which were significant events of Cecil's life. The schooner – Cecil calls it the big white magic canoe – sailed in and out of his life in many strange and paradoxical ways. The longest continuously sailed boat on the coast, she was built in 1904 for Vancouver businessman Alex MacLaren as a luxury yacht. MacLaren came from an industrialist's family that had grown rich on lumber, which they then invested in the Canadian Pacific Railway.

This was the most expensive and sleek pleasure craft on the Pacific coast at the time, and her demise paralleled that of some of the new colony's elite. During the First World War, she was requisitioned for her lead keel, then converted into a working halibut schooner and fished by companies like Canadian Fishing Company, whom Cecil had worked for in Butedale and Prince Rupert. In 1938, Norwegian-born fisherman Harold Helland, who worked out of Prince Rupert, bought her and took her up to the Bering Sea, fishing each year until the mid-1970s. The Canadian government bought the licence as part of the buy-back program when she fell into disrepair. Then, in 1980, she was rediscovered and restored to her former glory, but this time as an ecotourism sailboat, by Brian Falconer and Susan Tweedie.

Brian Falconer, like Bruce Hill, is not your typical environmentalist. He is a prairie boy, raised on a gas station within spitting distance of the last stand of Sitting Bull in Canada (before his last stand at Standing Rock). Some of that activism must have rubbed off. Falconer left the prairie as soon he could for a life on the coast, first working as a floatplane pilot moving loggers and fishermen from camp to camp, then building and running his own fishing lodge until he tired of the drunken clientele. The fateful day at Ladner in 1980 when he saw the derelict wooden fishing schooner led to a six-year restoration project that would bring her back to the beautiful schooner she had been. By 1993, Falconer was a seasoned ecotourism owner/operator whose clients appreciated his can-do spirit and obvious skills as a coastal transport expert. He knew enough that he needed to hire locals to interpret the natural history of the place to his rapidly growing number of ecotourists.

Falconer embarked on ecotourism trips first in Haida Gwaii, and it was his naturalist friend Keith Moore, from Haida Gwaii, who tipped him off about the campaign in the Kitlope. Moore was the forest ecologist hired by the Boston Men to map the last, large, unmodified watersheds in BC and had filled Falconer in about the Haisla's call for help. Falconer recalls, "Keith's eyes would glaze over when he was talking about the Kitlope." Moore encouraged Falconer to talk to the Haisla, as they were exploring the ecotourism potential. Falconer called the band office and reached Josette Weir, who said, "Yes, they would be really keen for us to do some trips. I'll speak to some of the hereditary chiefs and arrange for a couple of the chiefs to go with you.'" Cecil and Johnny Wilson were available. Falconer phoned up his own core clients to see who would be up for an adventure and a date was set: they were to pick up Cecil and Johnny at the MK Marina in Kitamaat on May 19, 1993. The story from Falconer's perspective continues from there.

We had just finished supper, so everyone is sitting down in the galley at *Maple Leaf* when this amazing looking guy comes onto the boat. He puts his hand out right away and the first thing I notice is that part of it is missing. Good strong handshake and I introduce myself and say: "Come down and meet my guests." He said, "Well, first we should talk. I have some bad news. We have lost someone in the village, one of the Elders." He said, "I don't know if I am going to be able to come with you or not. I am going to go visit the family tonight and ask their blessing to take you to the Kitlope, the place of my birth. If they don't give it, I'll have to stay."

I was really disappointed, but I had to understand. I said, "Well come down and meet the guests." He came down into the galley and he sat at the entrance to the round table there. Everyone is very nervous and I am nervous because I hadn't had that much experience with First Nations people. Cecil sat at the table and he spotted these mini-hammocks that we had put up to hold the bread, swinging above the table. He looks up at the hammocks and says, "Gee, your bread sure looks comfortable." Everyone laughed and relaxed. He owned the room in no time flat.[120]

KITAMAAT, MAY 23, 2014

Cecil has suffered a major lung infection and ended up in the intensive care unit of the small hospital in Terrace. His family brought him home and he's recuperating with characteristic speed. Brian Falconer and I head up to Kitamaat to see him. Brian had promised Cecil he would arrange the transport down the Kitlope with all the Paul family for five days that June. Raincoast Conservation Foundation was putting up the "gas and grub" as a thank you for all his work protecting the coast. I was to tag along with my tape recorder. Instead, we spent five days sitting with Cecil in his bedroom as he recovered.

Brian and I turned his bed into the magic canoe, paddling down rivers and channels we had been on with him before. It was a sweet, storytelling time despite the disappointment of not being with his family in the Kitlope. It gave me a good opportunity to record his stories in the quiet eddy of his bedroom – an improvement over those years of using cranky mini-tape recorders that captured more blustering wind and waves than softly told stories as we travelled up the real rivers. We feel lucky in so many ways: that Cecil is still among us, and that his skill as an orator is unaffected by the illness. Photos of the places triggered stories covering the geography of the parts of life he wanted to share.

Brian tells Cecil a story about the first time they were travelling up the Kitlope on May 20, 1993. He admitted to having the same bias as Bruce and the steelhead fishermen; that First Nations would just string nets across a river and take all the fish. Brian had watched some guy in the village flipping steelhead into a herring skiff and was a little uneasy when Cecil and Johnny asked to bring their steelhead net with them.

> That evening before dark, we set some tents up and are sitting around the camp on the Kitlope River. Cecil comes to me and says, "Johnny would like to go set the steelhead net. This is [a] place that is guarded by our people. We don't want to share that with a lot of people. With your permission, Johnny will take a boat and go up and set the net." I was a little worried, but what could I say?
>
> Later, we got up into the lake and went to the beach where the Rediscovery camp was built. I left everybody there to go back to the camp to pick up those we had left behind. As I am going down the river, I see this beautiful wolf walking along the river. It had a real reddish coat – first time I noticed the distinctive

colour of the coastal wolves. I turned in the river, which isn't easy to do, because the river's running good and I'm also doing 20 knots coming down the river. I followed this wolf along the bank and into the forest. It would pop out its head every so often. It just kept going up side channels, loping along looking at me – a really stunning experience.

All of a sudden, I see in front of me Johnny and Cecil's net, and it is tied to a stump in the middle of this slough. It is straight up and down the stream, quite narrow. They could quite easily have set the net across or at more of an angle, but it is anchored straight down. When we got back down that night, we had dinner down at the camp on the river and Cecil made a fire. There is a beautiful little fire pit there. We were talking to each other and I said to Cecil, "When I was following the wolf, it led me to your steelhead net. Don't worry, I won't give out that information, but there was something I noticed that was odd. Do steelheads swim back and forth as they go up the river?" And he looked at me kind of questioningly and said, "No, we have to leave it open. We don't want to take all those fish. We just want a fish for dinner."

I was stunned by this and I confessed to having been a little bit worried because the first person I met in the village was a guy in a herring skiff and he had his net set right across the creek and he was putting all these beautiful steelhead into the boat that hadn't had a chance to spawn yet. He kind of grimaced a bit and looked at me and he said, "Like your people, not all my people are wise." It was one of the real defining moments in understanding the diversity in these communities. Pushing me out from my single view of First Nations peoples.[121]

The role of ecotourism during the pivotal years before the Kitlope was officially protected was twofold. It brought influential people into the region to see the watershed but just as importantly to meet the Haisla and Xenaksiala. Cecil, Louisa Smith, Johnny and Bea Wilson were constant fixtures on the *Maple Leaf* through the campaign years. *Maple Leaf* brought media, environmentalists and members of the public who all fell in love, according to Falconer, with the place and with the Haisla. Falconer brought trips into the Kitlope for over ten years right from the era of the West Fraser decision to the final designation of the area in 1996. The *Maple Leaf* assisted during many of Wa'xaid's battles.[122] Falconer sold the business to Kevin Smith in 2001, who continued to work with Wa'xaid until health issues slowed him down.

The other vision of ecotourism was to generate economic activity in the village through the hiring of guides, businesses and infusion of people into the region. In this regard, there is a wider story that has been virtually untold in the regional or local context. The Nanakila Institute ran its own ecotourism business and training programs through foundation grants for years, but various problems caused those funding sources for training to dry up. Cecil describes the lure of oil and gas jobs becoming the major game in town. Industry wages dwarf those of seasonal ecotourism work. Small businesses that place a high value on a tourism destination are not a friend of corporate lobbyists with Kitimat as a tanker destination. The Nanakila Institute was absorbed into the elected colonial governance system, and because donors could no longer contribute to governments, external funds slowed down. Small businesses, self-sufficiency and ecotourism are all obstacles to the economic driver for an entire continent – oil and gas.

Discovery

One day Brian Falconer says, "Cecil, I have a special guest out on the boat who I'd like you to meet."

And I say, "Yes." His special guest is an elderly man from Victoria, Dick Wells, and he is going to have Brian follow the route of Captain Vancouver surveying the ocean. I heard the story of Vancouver many times. Johnny Wilson and I, we used to go and try to learn our culture, our history. And we would go to the old lady, Louise Barbettis's granny, and she told the story three times to Johnny and I. We listened. We didn't tell her we'd heard it before – the story when we first encountered Europeans. That's what really got me. I close my eyes and I see this storyteller and her granny telling her. How many centuries ago? And then the guy, Dick Wells, who wrote the book on Captain Vancouver, brings that story. I said, "Read it to me, Brian. Read it slow." Every word in the written form was the same as the verbal history of the Haisla. Every word. Verbal culture…every word. I went to take the book to that old lady and told her granddaughter to read. "Read it really slow," I said. "*Sii lü ka'ppa?*" she asked. "Is it right?"

It is amazing. It is exactly how the white man wrote it, that the Indians traded two 80-pound fish. The Indians were sitting there, and one told his chief, "There's a bunch of ants running around." It was their hats. They had railings like Brian's sailboat and just their heads were seen from the canoe way down in the harbour. It was a bunch of ants in this new island. But it was a sailboat named *Discovery*, and that is our history – what they see.

Each chief had a lieutenant. There was this one guy called Thloxw. Not afraid of anything, he never leaves the side of his hereditary chief. He put his life in battle. And the chief told him, "See what those children are worried about." Thloxw goes to investigate what the children saw and comes back again and told the chief what he saw. "Did you go close?" he asked.

"*K'ew*," Thloxw says. "No." He wasn't afraid. He was groomed to be fearless and he noticed that the ants – what the people called them – were human beings. Their heads were black. They met at the first island after leaving Kitamaat (going out on the left-hand side), Kildala. We know exactly where that is. Must have happened in springtime? Maybe in May? They brought spring salmon, so it had to be in the springtime.

During the Second World War, a Russian transport ship called *Uzbekistan* ran into a gale, lost visibility and grounded up on the western shores of Vancouver Island, close to the Pachena Point Lighthouse. Nearly 80 vessels piled up in the stretch between San Juan and Cape Beale, leading to the construction of an access trail for rescuers – the West Coast Trail – now a national park. Watching from the lighthouse was a 15-year-old boy called Dick Wells. Wells witnessed the rescue of the 50 crew members and went on to write the classic *A Guide to Shipwrecks along the West Coast Trail*. Wells's fascination with ships, shipwrecks and early navigational stories led him on a mission to retrace the voyage of Captain George Vancouver. He sailed with Brian Falconer for several trips over the years, retracing the exact log of Vancouver and his crew. The section of the expedition up Gardner was part of his research.

Joseph Whidbey's shore party reached Devastation Channel, where Gardner Canal branches off from Douglas Channel, on the evening of June 28, 1793. The year before, the Spanish captain, Camano, had sailed as far as Gardner Canal but no farther, and Vancouver was anxious to explore further. They spent the night at Devastation (named after HMS *Devastation*) on the eastern shore opposite Dorothy Island. Vancouver writes of Whidbey's party, "Here they were visited by eight Indians in two canoes, the first that they had seen during this expedition. The natives behaved in a very civil and friendly manner, and presented the party with two fine salmon, each weighing about 70 pounds; these were the finest and largest that had been seen during our voyage, and the Indians, after being recompensed with a small piece of iron, departed very well pleased with the exchange."[123]

The next day, they travelled up to Kildala Inlet. Kildala was valuable Haisla territory, being an oolichan river.

> Here they were met by the same Indians who had furnished them with the two salmon, and who attended the party up the above-mentioned small branch...They stopped here to dine, and were visited by 10 canoes, containing about sixty Indians; the largest of these, in which was the chief and his family, had its head and stern curiously decorated with carved work, and rude and uncouth figures in painting, resembling those with which they adorn their houses. The skins of the sea otter and some land animals they readily disposed of, for copper, blue cloth and blankets, but the former seemed highest in their estimation. They all behaved very civilly and honestly and were very compliant in doing whatever they were desired. Mr. Whidbey permitted the chief to sit with him at dinner; which he considered as a great indulgence, and conducted himself very well.[124]

According to Whidbey, everyone bedded down early on opposite sides of Kildala Inlet, and the next day they headed up Kitimat Arm, where they "find the remains of an Indian village. On their moving from thence, their Indian Attendants took their leave, went up the rivulet [river] in their canoes and were seen no more."[125] Bedding down with Whidbey was a young Archibald Menzies, the botanist who was to be the namesake of the Latin name for Douglas fir (*Pseudotsuga menziesii*), among others. (*P. menziesii* is at its northernmost limit in the Kitlope and provided another argument for the forest ecologists to recommend the valley for protection.)

The account of Louise Barbetti's granny about Vancouver from the Haisla perspective is well documented. Louise Barbetti is a matriarch of Kitamaat Village. She is the editor of the book *Haisla! We Are Our History*. Her grandmother is a high-born Haisla who married George Robinson, a Methodist missionary converted by Thomas Crosby. Louise's uncle, Gordon Robinson, wrote down an account of Captain George Vancouver's encounter with Katsilanoo of the Coast Salish in English Bay in his *Tales of Kitamaat*. The term used for the white men described by Gordon Robinson is "people who can fall through boards."[126] As Cecil describes it from the deck of the *Maple Leaf*, the sailors' black hats resembled ants that slipped below the gunwales through the boards into the hold of the ship.

The Robinson family has produced storytellers adept in both cultures for generations; contemporary members of the family include carver Sammy Robinson and the writer Eden Robinson, who bases her books on contemporary Haisla life. A missionary in Kitamaat during the First World War named Margaret Butcher, who wrote a detailed set of letters to her family in England, talks about her countryman George Robinson ironically as "belonging nowhere."[127] She was only in Kitamaat between 1916 and 1919, sandwiched in between her missions in East India, Canada, China and other colony postings.

The estuary had originally been designated Kildala Arm Indian Reserve No. 10. In 1952, with the Kitimat smelter on the horizon, Canada "breached its fiduciary duty" and allowed development on the site.[128] It has been a cannery site, a log dump and an easement for hydro. The major oolichan run is long gone with the logging. In 1984 the band started research into a specific claim for this breach. Specific claims are claims against the Government of Canada for taking away what little the colonial government, in its generosity, "gave": reserve lands, timber on reserves – even totem poles. Specific claims are different from the "comprehensive" claims in which the larger overall territories are the subjects. Specific claims are like the ultimate insults upon injury; not too many Canadians will be able to tell you the difference, but it is worth thinking about. Of the 0.02 per cent of Canada that was set aside in reserves, the Canadian government has spent the last two centuries chipping away at what little remained. Those "surrenders" might be six acres here for a utility corridor, or a strip of land for an easement for a road. A lot of the time Indian agents simply drew a new line and took some land for themselves. In British Columbia alone, there are hundreds of specific claims to get the crumbs back on the table, most of them mired in legal battles. Six years later on the Kildala claim they finally made a settlement. They didn't get their land back and the oolichan haven't returned – yet.

POISON COVE, MAY 7, 2000

We are moving down Mussel Inlet past Poison Cove, aboard the *Maple Leaf*. It is Kitasoo/Xais-Xais territory to the south. The granite cliffs are the mountains from which the headwaters of the Tezwa flow north into Kitlope Lake, and the waters of Poison Cove Creek flow south to Mussel Inlet. Vancouver named it Poison Cove to mark where his crewmembers fell ill. One man, John Carter, died, and Vancouver named the bay named after him. As we travel along, Cecil points out one of the stone dogs of T'ismista that sits high up on the mountains. It defines the watershed boundary between Xenaksiala and Kitasoo territory. A northwestern crow could easily walk, let alone fly, between the respective headwaters over the western flanks of Mount Bessel.

Dick Wells reads out the accounts of the Vancouver journals and we scan the shoreline for distinguishing features that correspond to the descriptions. The landscape has changed relatively little in the last 200 years, compared to his namesake island. When we get to what is called Poison Cove on the charts, Dick concludes that it couldn't possibly be the same Poison Cove as Vancouver described. He urged us to go farther down the inlet until we came upon another little cove, which he thought was the true Poison Cove. Cecil was much impressed by Wells's attention to detail, noticing the subtle differences between the landscape and the recording of them. For most people visiting the coast, one cove begins to look like another. Not these two, or Capt. Vancouver for that matter. When you live by the sea, you learn not to die by the sea.

KLEKANE INLET, MAY 8, 2000

Looking for an old hot spring, Dick and I stumble across a bear that had died in the forest. Can't find any wound or cause. He just lay on his side as if he had fallen over into a deep sleep on the mossy forest floor. I told Cecil about it and he did what he always does on those occasions, sang a song for one of his brothers.

KILDALA INLET, MAY 11, 2016

Kildala is an industrial parking lot these days. There are always barges or other industrial equipment parked in the inlet waiting for some "show" to start or finish. The only sign of the cannery that operated until the 1930s is a sort of weariness of the shoreline. Spilt diesel and oil, pounded shoreline, rusted machinery still leave scars nearly a century later. Eventually, the moss, salmonberries and rockweed will heal everything.

Rediscovery

The world came – all these people coming to experience the uncharted waters of Kitlope. To leave their loved ones at home, to come and help us to push our cause, leaves me in awe. Without the help of these people across the border, we would be still fighting today. They all became good friends of Kitlope. My new friends said, "I will walk with you."

I replied, "You will not leave Kitlope unchanged."

There were three young ladies with two young men, and they were students from University of Toronto, and they journeyed across here when they heard about the fight. Made their own way. It was a beautiful day and the mountains were clear and they gave me coffee, and I said, "Let's go down to my land." Who are these kids who come all the way across this beautiful country to save this place?

There was the scientist Randy Stoltmann, who fell off the rock and he never lived. When the government asked me to go identify the remains for the family, I go to where he fall off, and I sat there for a while. I heard from another book that there is no greater love of man than one who laid his life down for the land. And that was what Randy was. He was a friend of the environment, a friend of the Haisla people, and my brother laid down his life for me. Lot of phone calls. Who are these kids to be swept to Haisla land? Love. It was a heavy price paid for this valley.

I had another environmental sister, Glenn Fuller. She was the Coca Cola heiress, Sweetgrass Foundation. She bought the motor for the punt. Gerald and I took her up to the Kitlope for a month when she was diagnosed for cancer. She died.

Ric Young, he came up to the Kitlope with Ian Gill, Ecotrust. Ric took the story of the Magic Canoe to a big Indigenous conference in Australia. When Ric was in Australia, he met an African chief, and he liked my story of the Magic Canoe. "My friend," he said. "I'd like you to talk to him [Cecil]." They invited me to go to Africa. I don't know why. The doctor said I couldn't go.

Dave Campeche lived near the big river not far from Seattle, and he came up. He was a cook. Owns sort of a restaurant hotel, or motel, they call it. He came and cooked with Rediscovery one year, and we became really good friends. He asked me to come down to Vancouver. He had three boys; two were in jail. I went to go visit them in jail.

One time, Gerald asks, "You got time to go to Vancouver? Americans want to meet with you."

"Okay," I say. "Let's go." It was fundraising for the Kitlope. He said there is going to be celebrities there. We go to the Vancouver Hotel.

Dr. Pritchard is with me when a guy comes. "I know that guy. He is coming to our table," he says. "Have you ever seen his movie?"

"I don't think so," I says.

"It is Harrison Ford," he says. "Movie star. Goodness sakes – don't tell him you don't know."

And the next one came. What was his name? I don't know the man, but he is with a lady who is a country western singer. I forgot him, but I remember her; I have seen parts of her body before, like Dolly Parton.

In 1982, villagers Johnny and Bea Wilson and Hank Robertson wrote a letter to the Haisla council, asking for financial assistance for summer camps with proper facilities so that they could teach young people how to harvest traditional foods. They had been raising money through bake sales but needed much more help. In the letter, they proposed three camps: Kemano, M'iskusa and Kitlope Lake. They were four years behind the same idea germinating in Haida Gwaii, where Haida Elders got together with a young draft dodger nicknamed Huckleberry to launch a program they called Rediscovery. Huckleberry, a.k.a. Thom Henley, was a charismatic Michigan kid who had hitched and sailed his way to Haida Gwaii at a pivotal time in Haida cultural resurgence. Henley was yet another braid in the widening river of white guys getting into the canoe. In his autobiography, *Raven Walks Around the World*, Thom Henley writes of the events that kick-started the Rediscovery program in Haida Gwaii, the Kitlope and throughout the coast.

The realization of the Wilsons' dream came very quickly after Spencer Beebe's subsequent visit to Kitamaat. Gerald had been sick in the hospital and Beebe went to visit him when Gerald asked, "Why don't we create our own non-profits?" Beebe went to work registering and raising the funds, and Gerald gathered the others to figure out the details. As Beebe states, "It was a way of getting around a horribly dysfunctional government." Three non-profits were created. The matriarchs were organizing the summer Rediscovery camps under the Haisla Nation Women's Society. Then a broader agenda was designed for the Nanakila Institute "dedicated to conservation, stewardship, and appropriate development of the ancestral lands of the Haisla First Nation, with particular emphasis on the Greater Kitlope Ecosystem." There was a training program for young Haisla to do research and to monitor and enforce Haisla policies in their territory.

The sustainable economic programs of the organization explored nature tourism that worked and other opportunities – like Cecil's "beautiful idea" for a local cannery run by a small hydro project – that didn't. Nanakila also provided logistical support to the Rediscovery camps. Gerald was quoted on the Nanakila brochure: "It is a huge responsibility to protect something that is the last of its kind on earth – not just for the Haisla but for everyone." Cecil's quote was: "I feel we cannot lose when I see young people come and deposit a piece of their hearts in the bank we call the Kitlope." Back in the early 1990s, an up-and-coming novelist from the village, Eden Robinson, was a young teenager attending the Rediscovery program. She wrote, "The first time I saw the Kitlope, I was ready to believe in something larger than myself."[129]

The first chair was Gerald Amos, with directors Hereditary Chief of the Kowesas Kenny Hall, Ken Margolis from Ecotrust, Cecil's friend from residential school Russell Ross, and Chief Councillor Robert Robinson. Bruce Hill left the Steelhead Society to become the first director. He had attended the Haisla / West Fraser meeting at the Mount Layton Hot Spring Resort and been deeply affected by Louisa's testimony. As Ken Margolis tells it, "At the end of it, this big blubbering bear comes up, tears are running down his face, and he says, 'I want to work with you guys.'"[130] Bruce's version is that Ken called him and said, "'Bruce, we're putting together this non-profit in Kitamaat Village and do you know of anybody locally who would be suitable for that job?' I gave him a couple names and got to thinking about it, then I called him up and said, 'What about me?' And he said, 'Oh, you're available? You'd be our first choice!'"[131] From the Portland camp's perspective, everything happened for two reasons. "There was a conservation campaign and then the real engine – the cultural campaign – to do things for the culture. The strategic purpose of Rediscovery was because one of the things the timber companies and other people in Kitimat were saying: 'Nobody is using it up there so why not go up and cut it?'"

For the Haisla, this was a much-needed cash infusion for a long-held dream to get it underway. Cecil, as he healed from his heart surgery, joined the other Haisla Elders, Johnny and Bea Wilson, as a fixture of the camps. His storytelling around the campfire was legendary for a generation of kids – Haisla and white. Most of his stories were honed around those campfires. As Hill recounts, "There was just so many lessons that he didn't even know he was teaching them sometimes. That was the beauty of it." The friendships between the Haisla and the other campaigners strengthened through the camps as they all brought their children to participate. The younger generation of several cultures was bonding with the land, the Elders and each other. The camps also included white kids from Kitimat. Eventually, the program expanded to include students from Northwest College and other universities. In the summer of 1993, Inuit children were invited through the First Nations Summit task group. Soon there were other non-profits like the Haisla Canoe Society and the Haisla Dance Society.

The revenue for the program was Beebe's fundraising for "gas and grub." All he needed to do was bring up wealthy patrons to meet the Haisla and the money flowed in. Beebe's characteristic American Boston trader brand made him a winner to back by the elite of America's philanthropists. Beebe characterized the project to his philanthropists in this way: "It took four years and we spent $600,000 dollars and we got 800,000 acres protected at about the cost of about 75 cents an acre." If ever there has been someone who can switch world views with the flick of a raven's eyebrow, it is Beebe.

In the next few years (through the Boston Men's connections), a succession of celebrities stepped into the magic canoe to protect the Kitlope, including Harrison Ford, who, having swashbuckled his way through jungles as Indiana Jones, donned his heavy-duty raingear for the temperate-rainforest cause. Ford sat on the board of the Rainforest Action Network, as did Bonnie Raitt, possibly the other singer mentioned by Wa'xaid as having been at the fundraiser. Author Paul Hawken, guru of the countercorporate non-profit movement (*Blessed Unrest*) and natural-capital economics, waded through some real natural capital.

When social entrepreneur Ric Young heard the story of the magic canoe from Cecil around the campfire, "I was moved like everybody. It resonated at a very deep level because this was a metaphor to explain stuff that I had been trying to explain on the nature of change – encouraging people to build a global canoe." He developed a lecture on social change, which spread through institutions, TEDx talks and all the way to the World Indigenous Network Conference in Darwin, Australia, in 2013, which featured Cecil's face and voice for the 1,500 Indigenous leaders from around the world. The Indigenous emissary for Cecil on the stage in Darwin with Ric Young was a young woman called Jessie Housty, a Heiltsuk member, who was to become a leader and young friend of Cecil in her own right.

There were many other prominent Canadians who stepped into the canoe. Ethnobotanist Wade Davis, who had written about canoe cultures around the world, was an ally, although rumoured to have met his Waterloo swamped by unremitting storms during his visit. Randy Stoltmann, climber and wilderness campaigner through his stories of the big trees of BC, had a much more tragic experience in the Kitlope. Best known for his *Hiking Guide to the Big Trees of British Columbia*, he fell down a crevasse on

May 22, 1994, while traversing the mountains above Kitlope, silencing a powerful voice for ancient forests in the deep snows.

Heirs of fortunes like Coca-Cola's Glenn Candler Fuller, the sons of Rockefellers, sons of Warren Buffett and a son of Gordon Moore (Moore Foundation) all camped out for periods and supported the Haisla cause. Somewhere flowing along the strange current of history, from barons of resource extraction to their philanthropic children and grandchildren, Wa'xaid's magic canoe stands ready to help a family return what an earlier generation had taken. Fuller spent some of her last days with Wa'xaid in the Kitlope. She started the Sweetgrass Foundation in 1992, dedicated to ecological health and Indigenous cultures throughout the world. Coca-Cola has taken far more from Indigenous cultures around the world than it has given back, including its role in causing diabetes among coastal First Nations, but it is symbolic that Fuller sought out the Kitlope and Wa'xaid as "the real thing" before she passed away.

KITSELAS CANYON, SEPTEMBER 26, 2017

Cecil's cast came off last week and the doctor told him to go slow on his foot, but he's keen for an outing, so we head off down the road with no destination in mind. As we get close to Terrace, he says, "Let's go to Kitselas Canyon. I've never been there before." Kitselas is a Tsimshian power place of four villages near Terrace. I'm game for anything, so we pull into the Kitselas band office to get instructions. We meet a young woman at the front desk. Cecil introduces himself and asks permission to go visit their old village. She responds as if her ancestors just stepped into the office, which I guess they did.

We head off down a gravel road to what turns out to be a National Historic Site, with a huge parking lot for tour buses, mostly shut down for the winter. A gravel track through a dappled mossy hemlock and lodgepole pine forest, groomed for tour carts, beckons us over. I park and we get out. "Do you want to walk?" I ask. "Yup," he says, so we set off like a couple of star-crossed lovers arm in arm. We overtake an elderly couple photographing purple *Cortinarius* mushrooms that are bursting through the mossy carpet at the side of the track. Cecil greets the couple and engages them in a conversation. "We never ate those things," he says. "We called them baxʷ baxʷ à hs_hziq – devil's umbrella in English." "Where are you from?" he asks. "Oregon," says the tall, smiling, bearded man. "I have a friend in Astoria," responds Cecil. Not surprisingly, they are from Astoria and know his friend – Dave Campeche, a local restaurateur and community organizer. We saunter down the track together and within a few minutes the couple have stepped into his magic canoe, covering at least a kilometre and a half before our arrival at the canyon edge, which involves well more than 87 steps down to the viewing platform.

Kitselas is a powerful place. The massive volume of water of the Skeena funnels into this narrow canyon. The villages grew up perched on the rock ledges like ferns to control food, access and trade. Forces of nature, like flash floods washing enormous spruce tree roots that could pin a full cedar canoe under in seconds, had wreaked havoc on travellers and led to a surfeit of supernatural stories and pictographs – giving the place its national profile. Cecil was exhausted after our long climb back up to the canyon top, so I left him talking with the couple while I ran back to pick up the car. When I pulled up to the threesome half an hour later, another supernatural story was being enacted. The fungi enthusiast, who was embracing Cecil, turned out to be a retired Methodist minister on a journey of absolution through the communities of the Northwest where his church had wreaked its own particular type of havoc. One of the spiritual heirs of Thomas Crosby, the first Methodist minister who wrote about "the violent and dangerous" people of the coast, this contemporary retired minister was apologizing personally to Cecil with a hand pressed firmly to his heart. He had read the entire report of the Truth and Reconciliation Commission of Canada (TRC) and was on a personal quest to bear witness and apologize. The minister's countryman Dave Campeche, who had found healing in the Kitlope, had triggered a meeting in Kitselas two decades later that healed two old men's spirits one afternoon among the devil's club and umbrella.

With One of the Rockefeller Brothers
I Go to See the White Bear

Then there was the Rockefeller Foundation – the rich people in the States. With one of the Rockefeller brothers I go to see the White Bear. He called me brother. We went up to Johnny Clifton's country in Bernard Harbour, where we anchored the boat – big sailboat. We went ashore up the creek, and he asked, "How come you don't have a camera?"

Rockefeller says, "I'll get you one."

I says, "Get me the cheapest one. Something you just push." He had one of 'em big expensive things, and that's what I got, from Rockefeller. It is still hanging on my door.

He hasn't called for over a year now, used to call all the time. I can't remember his name. Must be David. You know, for rich people to come, meet the people, eat my food, Kitlope food...he loved the [oolichan] grease. Make toast of it in the morning. He'd have toast maybe three times a day. Sometimes in the campfire, I'd take a potato and I'd put really fine sand on part of it. Oh! Take it out, eat it together with the grease. They gave us over $80,000 to buy gas and grub for our Rediscovery kids' camps. They done it with love.

Some celebrities weathered better than others. Beebe tells of a classic Kitlope moment when they had three American billionaires in a sinking boat: Steve Moore, son of philanthropist computer guru Gordon Moore; and Peter and Howard Buffett, progeny of Warren Buffett. Spencer recalls they had 50 billion dollars in family wealth represented in that boat. Bruce Hill had forgotten to put the plug back in after draining it. "We came to a stop with Howard and all his camera equipment in a foot of water in the boat and we were sinking. Bruce said, 'Whoa, we got to get ashore.' We had quite a few interesting gatherings around the campfire."

While Ken Margolis was helping to launch Nanakila from 1992 to 1994, he took Gerald and Cecil to New York to see Michael Northrop, program director for the Rockefeller Brothers Fund. "I remember walking to Times Square with Cecil," Ken recalls. "He had never seen anything like that. We went back to our hotel, then at about two in the morning my phone rang and it was Cecil: 'Can we go home now?!' He did not like New York, so we left early."[132] Beebe remembers a board meeting of Conservation International at the Empress Hotel in Victoria after the announcement of the Kitlope conservancy. "I asked Cecil to welcome people from around the world. He got up and looked at all these hotshot people from around the world sitting in the big ballroom in the Empress Hotel and quipped, 'Welcome to the white man's teepee.'"

Other prominent Americans that came to the Kitlope included Giles Mead, director of the Natural History Museum of Los Angeles County and of the Mead Foundation, Stewart Brand of the *Whole Earth Catalogue*, and Susie Tompkins, wife of Doug Tompkins, founder of the recreational clothing company North Face.

Part of the attraction of the region was a growing awareness of the white bear, also known as the Kermode and, more recently, the Spirit Bear for non-Native tourists, with their mystical ability to attract political attention. *Ursus americanus kermodei* is one of 11 different subspecies of the black bear, in which one bear in ten is white or cream-coloured. A skin was sent over a century ago by local Gitga'at hunters from Gribbell Island to Francis Kermode, curator of the then BC Provincial Museum, who sent the specimen to zoologist William T. Hornaday of the New York Zoological Society, who told Kermode that he would write up the taxonomic description and call it *Ursus alba*, white bear. Kermode wrote back, saying it should be named after him. Kermode managed to immortalize himself with a bear he had never seen and had improperly identified, which wasn't highly unusual in the colonial tradition of naming things.

The late Johnny Clifton that Wa'xaid refers to is a cherished Gitga'at Elder in Hartley Bay. The Gitga'at territory includes most of the range of the white bear, including Barnard Harbour. The Clifton family has been trading their seaweed for Kemano families' oolichan for generations.

The heady campaign years of celebrities rubbing shoulders with the Haisla, Pritchard notes, "didn't all happen smoothly." One event triggered some backlash from the matriarchs. Ecotrust had bought a new amphibious plane to get into the Kitlope and flown their board to the lake at the same time as the Nanakila kids were up there. As Pritchard recalls, "These were kids with families and the reason they were up there was to be away from substance abuse. One of the board members that flew up was a justice of the California Supreme Court and he got completely pissed in full view of the kids. He said to one of the hereditary chiefs, 'Are you a real Indian chief?' Louise Barbetti was furious and said, 'Kitlope is our home, not a playground for the rich and famous.'" Ecotrust made a public apology in the gymnasium, but the world was arriving at Kitlope's door.

The Kitlope became a poster child in the popular media – on the front pages of major newspapers and magazines around the world through the various media connections forged by Beebe, Hill and the Greenpeace contingent. Beebe's strategy was that "they [West Fraser] were going to have a fight – not just with the Indians." He points to the height of the media campaign in the summer of 1993. He had professional connections with *Time* magazine's Eugene Linden, the environmental reporter who put planet Earth on the front cover of *Time* as 1988 Man of the Year. Linden was flown up the coast for a week to meet the Haisla and other activist leaders like Guujaaw in Haida Gwaii. Linden was famously blown off by Guujaw, who passed on an interview with *Time* to go fishing, but the rainforest survived the brush-off and still made it prominently onto the newsstands.

One-time CBC reporter and Australian expat Ian Gill brought national attention to the Kitlope in the Canadian media with his mini-documentary in 1993. Gill had already built up a reputation on the coast, starting in 1988, for his documentaries on forestry, fish farms, mining and Aboriginal issues. "I chose to interview Aboriginal people in all these places because it was the right thing to do and they had more interesting stories frankly than anybody else."[133] Mainstream news reporters rarely had the airtime or inclination to get the slow, thoughtful positions of Elders over the higher-energy, media-savvy sound bites of Western environmentalists. The longer documentary style gave Gill the platform he was wanting.

Early in 1993, when United Church minister John Cashore became the minister of environment, Gill thought it would be an interesting story to do a profile of the minister-turned-minister. Cashore's ministerial assistant at the time was an environmental consultant named Bob Peart, who was also to feature prominently in the backroom decisions. Gill had asked to do interviews of the minister over the summer, but as Gill states, "I didn't want the interviews in the office, I wanted an excuse to get out in the bush."[134] The ancestors were converging when Gill called Cashore's office with the request. Peart told him Cashore was going on a five-day trip to the Kitlope. Gill had heard of the Kitlope from Peter Pearse, who was on the board of Alcan at the time. Pearse told him it was a place to watch, and to talk to "an outfit called Ecotrust," which he did. Gill joined the media junket going up with Cashore, including *Vancouver Sun* environmental reporter Mark Hume. The Kitlope became the recruiting ground for Ecotrust US, which was looking for someone with a set of broad skills to head up a new organization that could really take on the Canadian temperate rainforests full-time – Ecotrust Canada.

It was also in 1993 that Cecil first met David Suzuki, when they shared a week together aboard the MS *World Discoverer*, conducting an educational tour of the coast. Adventure Canada, an ecotourism company owned by Matt and Billy Swan, had successfully run educational adventure tours on the east coast and in the Arctic using pocket cruisers – bringing aboard scientists, activists, First Nations people, artists and musicians of the region. In 1993 they launched their first west coast educational tour, and Cecil and Suzuki were top billing. Aboard the boat were guests from across North America, and the invited speakers along the way included many of the people who were to become friends and allies: artists Roy Henry Vickers, Robert Davidson and Robert Bateman; musicians Ian Tamblyn and Rachel Gauk (Tamblyn was to write and record two songs about Cecil and the Kitlope); scientist David Suzuki; forest ecologist/authors Jim Pojar,

Andy MacKinnon and Merv Wilkinson; Masset Hereditary Chief Illjil-waas and Chief Pootlass in Bella Coola. The Swans repeated the tour in 1996 and later in 2004 on the MS *Spirit of Endeavour* under the guidance of their expedition leaders Dennis Mense and Sabina Leader-Mense. Cecil was aboard the boat in each of these tours running from Alaska to Vancouver, stopping in at places he was well familiar with, from Ketchikan to Butedale and, of course, the Kitlope.

FREDERICK SOUND, SEPTEMBER 4, 2004

We left Juneau this morning, Cecil and I, aboard the *Spirit of Endeavour*, a US pocket cruiser with guests from Adventure Canada and a pod of naturalists, scientists and environmentalists, including David Suzuki, Colleen McCrory and Ian McAllister – resource people aboard this "travelling classroom." We're in Frederick Sound, looking for humpbacks bubble-net feeding, when we come across a young dead humpback. It is floating belly up, his maleness evident. Cecil and I are the two resource people in one Zodiac, and I start chattering away about bacula (penis bones), pectoral fins and the unique barnacles that co-evolved with humpbacks. The barnacles were so prominent that I suggested we go have a closer look and collect one. Cecil waves at us to cut the motors and starts to sing for his dead brother. I shut up and we float quietly with the young whale in that vast body of water, encircled by volcanoes, whales and a pulsing sea of plankton. At the time, Cecil was fighting another health issue; we thought he wouldn't live through the year. We talked about that moment later. I apologized and told him I didn't know which hat to wear: naturalist or student. He said, "Don't worry about which hat to wear, just wear them well."

HAZELTON, MAY 28, 2018

We are at the intersection of Highway 16 and the road to Kispiox. Cecil, Cecelia and I are on a road trip and we are looking for the artist Roy Henry Vickers. Cecil had the idea to visit Roy this morning as we breakfasted in Prince Rupert. We had casually asked him who he wanted to write his foreword and he said Roy Henry Vickers. Then added, "Let's go see him." Cecil hadn't seen him in a couple of decades since the Kitlope days. None of us had any idea where he lived, but Cecil said, "somewhere near where my sisters are buried, up past Kitwanga way." So we left on a 300-kilometre journey up the Skeena to find Roy Henry Vickers. At 4:58 p.m. we had arrived in the general vicinity of where Cecil thought he might live.

The trip up was as good as it gets. I sat in the back while Cecil and Cecelia smoked, shared stories and laughed. I hung my head out the window, watched the Skeena go by and observed the dad and daughter interact as if the 30 years of separation had never happened. We stopped for picnics and walks along the river, then in Kitwanga went to visit the gravesites of his sisters Florence and Emily. Emily had married the chief Joe Daniels, and inherited the glorious fishing spot that Cecelia's husband Dave had once been invited to. It had been a memorable day for him. We found the peaceful graveyard, covered in wild strawberries and surrounded by mountains. Cecil sang a song to his sisters, then we stopped by to say hi to Cecelia's cousin who ran the band store and threw her arms around her family. She didn't know where Roy lived either.

At the Hazelton turnoff, we slowed down at the visitor centre to see if it was open and they could help us. It was 4:58 p.m. and the centre was closing. There were three people at the intersection: a herring fisherman, David Ellis, whom I knew from the coast, with a sign saying First Nation Books, and two customers. I jumped out and asked David if he knew where Roy Henry Vickers lived. He said no, but Michael here does, he works for him. Michael, a Kispiox man, turned out to be en route to Roy and invited us to follow him down the road to Roy's farm.

As we arrived, his wife was feeding their horses and waved us to a log house by the river. Roy opened the door to Cecil's knocking and the two men went silent. Tears ran down Roy's face and he welcomed us in. "How did you find me, brother?" Roy asked.

What's Left of the Fresh Water in the Universe?

Gerald phoned one day. "Good morning, brother. How you feel today?"

I says, "Not bad. Just about to go out the door when the phone rang."

"Oh, good," he says. "Could you stay another half hour? Someone's going to call you. I think you might like it. Please have patience, eh."

I wait for 45 minutes. "Let's go," I told my wife. Put my coat on, and both of us are by the door. The phone rang. Henning Hesse was on the phone, a scientist from Germany. I took my coat off. "Okay," I said. "What's on your mind?"

He says, "There's three of us. We're scientists, and the government appointed us to find out what's left of the fresh water in the universe and we're to choose three countries. We got Europe, South America...and we looked at the internet and we see the largest rainforest in the universe."

The three of us talked: "I wonder what it's like there? I wonder if our government would want to see the fresh water that's never been touched by industry? We need a guide to bring us up."

I was healthy then. I says, "Okay."

When they came, my son Cecil Jr. was working as a watchman for Nanakila in the Kitlope. Boat owners took the scientists up, me up. Explained to them everything. They had a cameraman with them, and I took him down to the river. German filmmaker asks, "What does the river mean to you?" I explained it was the artery of Mother Earth. I sang the song that they sang when we brought Granny home. And when, must be a year gone by, when they tried to invite me to Frankfurt, for the film. *Watery Visions* is the name of the documentary. Henning says, *wasser* in German. W-A-S-S-E-R. My doctor says, "too far," for my heart. And I missed the opening of that film: *What's left of the fresh water in the universe?*

The film called *Watery Visions: Is the Future Potable?*, in which Cecil was featured as a major contributor, was a production of Deutsche Welle TV, the international arm of the German public broadcaster. Henning Hesse is listed as author of the screenplay. The film crew followed Wa'xaid through the Kitlope. The promotional clip for the film is of him washing his eyes and ears in the Kitlope, which can still be seen online,[135] and his message remains more important than ever, 17 years later, about the importance of water. "We have been taught since childhood the importance of water, that it is the artery of Mother Earth, because without water, people will perish."

Merv Wilkinson: In the Wilderness He Keeps

I met this wonderful person, Merv Wilkinson, and he came up to Kitlope. He called and asked to come. He has a forest not far from Nanaimo, Wildwood. He teaches about selective logging. He wondered why none of the forestry students of the university go and study in the wilderness he keeps. Then he finds out the owners of MacMillan Bloedel are teachers of the university, and they won't allow the young ladies to go and see Merv and how to select logs.

Brian Falconer and I came to his place, and he welcomed us and we walked to a seedling. Merv says, "Cecil, try pull this one." And I couldn't budge it. We walk a little ways to another seedling, and he says, "Now try that one," and I pulled it out. He says, "That second one is man-made and that is what the foresters are doing. This first one here is our Creator's, the roots are all spread out and you couldn't pull it out. The man-made is straight down and the roots are not developing right, so when you stop and think about it – between the Creator and the man – how wrong we are."

It was amazing for me to meet a person that is educated and come up to the Kitlope. I walked with him and showed him big trees, and then I go to his place where he is trying to show the forest industry, the loggers, about select logging – no logging road, no nothing. Where I was born there was a Douglas fir still standing on the hill; showed it to Merv and how far the tree grows. It don't grow any other place as far north. It is in the book; some scientist wrote it. It is true that there are no more. For me to cross paths with that man, I am very fortunate. I was not well when he passed away. They tried to call me down to say a few words. Brian and I sat with him for hours in his home, discussing these things.

Being in the company of Merv Wilkinson and Cecil Paul together was like walking into an old-growth forest. Two big old trees festooned with lichens and stories, providing a sheltering canopy and roots that spread wide. When Merv Wilkinson died in 2011 at the age of 97, he was a local legend around his 136-acre Douglas-fir forest, Wildwood, in the Yellowpoint area near Nanaimo. He had tended and harvested his forest there for 70 years. He pioneered his own kind of forestry, which he called sustainable selection forestry, sharing the ideas and philosophy with anyone that came to Wildwood, like Cecil. He got lots of honours: Order of Canada, Order of BC, an honorary doctorate from University of Victoria, but the accolades from the University of British Columbia, his alma mater, were slower in coming. His criticism of industrial forestry with what he called "a clear-cut–and-plant policy" promoting the conversion of natural forests to industrial tree plantations had won him few converts in the Faculty of Forestry over the years. Merv's philosophy was born out of a childhood where "I grew up believing that forests are my friends."[136] He was not exactly the type of postwar industrial forester that patrons and donors to UBC's forestry department were keen on promoting. Merv described himself as a citizen forester and didn't hold back on his volleys against those who looked at the forest primarily as a short-term commodity instead of an ecosystem. "Rows of trees are not forests. They represent stupidity and a one-track mind," he wrote in *Wildwood: A Forest for the Future*, co-authored with Ruth Loomis in 1990.

His method of logging at a slower rate than the forest grows left Wildwood a showcase for teaching a different type of forestry. "I never cut over the annual growth rate, as that breaks into the 'bank account' of the tree farm."[137] Wildwood retained all the structural qualities of an old-growth, Douglas-fir forest: a diversity of different-aged trees and species with full canopies and undergrowth. Yet he had removed thousands of board feet of timber during his periodic harvests every five to ten years. His number one rule, "Work with Nature,"[138] manifested in every aspect of the forest, including the story he shared with Cecil, leaving the forest to self-seed. As he wrote, "Trees start naturally by finding their own habitat, doing it very well through a process of elimination."[139]

Not surprisingly, he and Cecil hit it off when they first met in 1993. They both knew their forests, observed deeply what was going on between the forest plants and animals and had a strong practical bent. Merv himself worked occasionally in the forest industry as a thinner to supplement his income from his own forest. Merv, like Cecil, was also a born educator and orator and spent the last quarter-century of his life teaching his methods to visiting school and university groups. It was his book, *Wildwood*, that Merv gave to Cecil on their first visit, just a few years after its publication. Merv's simple prescriptions for his style of sustainable selection forestry resonate for Cecil—Xenaksiala practitioners have had their own form of sustainable selection forestry for thousands of years. Merv writes, "Nature is so determined in her regeneration that trees grow out of stumps and can be manipulated to do so. This is called coppicing. A tree stump is kept alive by leaving its root system intact in order to produce more trees. A tree is cut high enough to leave intact one or two good limbs, preferably on the north side of the stump."[140]

Merv came up twice to visit Cecil with Brian in 1994 and 1995. Cecil came to Wildwood with the Adventure Canada tour in 1996. Cecil also had another reason to connect with Merv. Merv had adopted two Indigenous kids during the '60s with his first wife. The '60s were a particularly egregious time for First Nations adoptions, known as the '60s Scoop. Indigenous children were scooped up and placed in foster homes or put up for adoption. It was an extension of the Canadian government's continuing program to assimilate Indigenous people but enacted through provincial welfare authorities. Contracting out the care to white families was undoubtedly cheaper and even more effective in eradicating culture than residential schools. Thousands of children were scooped from the 1950s to the 1980s. Cecil's first daughter, Cecelia, herself was not technically a

'60s Scoop child, but the basis for her adoption was rooted in the same deep systemic prejudice that wouldn't allow a young white woman to be with an Indigenous man, and certainly not keep a child fathered by an Indigenous man. Merv had founded the Foster Parents Association of Nanaimo and could empathize about the heartaches and joys of adoption, whichever way you looked at the issue.

WILDWOOD, SEPTEMBER 1994

It is a day trip from Victoria up to Wildwood to visit Merv Wilkinson's ecoforest. I'm teaching a course in forest biodiversity with ethnobotanist Nancy Turner. We have over 100 students coming for the tour. We wind down the shady lane and come to rest under some towering old Douglas fir for the students' first encounter with the legend—Merv. Merv welcomes them to Wildwood. His first station is at a spot in the forest where there is a big healthy tree and a recent stump next to it. He explains how he decided to harvest that single tree: "It was losing the race for light and moisture to the older one and was starting to die." He points to another adjacent dead tree that is full of pileated woodpecker holes providing food and habitat for cavity nesters like red squirrels and owls. "This wildlife tree is going to be left, so I selected the other tree to harvest, to keep the changes to a minimum for the animals and the forest." The students see the logic and the heart. Merv talked about his trips up to the Kitlope with Cecil Paul and the class went quiet.

Grizzly Bear: He Holds Up Everything

I brought three scientists up to see what I was shown by my Xenaksiala teachers. Grizzly bear, all kinds of grizzly bears and different colours: orange and yellow. They spot at age. Some of them are pitch black; some of them are light brown with white faces. It is very unusual. My people never touch a grizzly bear. They drilled into us when we were young, that he's our friend in the bush. He is my brother; he is a guardian of the forest. All Xenaksialas hold this. The totem, you study the images of what is put down, and always at the bottom is the grizzly bear. He is strong; he holds up everything. What is on the top? The majority of the poles will have the eagle on top. The vision the eagle has is sharp. He's guiding everything above, and you often see that in the Kitlope.

One day, a grizzly hunter guide comes looking for grizzlies, and I heard him say that he would shoot through the Indian children at the camp to kill a grizzly bear. I say to him, "These are not only Haisla children but children from around the world, and you threaten to shoot through the children?" I talked to him by the little creek, "Say to me please, 'I'm sorry.'"

He said, "Wa'xaid, I'm sorry."

But what is he sorry about? He didn't elaborate on that word. Sorry to shoot through that child? Sorry because I met with him? Maybe because I didn't accept the apology? I never met him again after that. We have a word for a type of grizzly that is angry or a killer; it is called *gil dee spa*.

A time-in-motion study on coastal grizzlies might surprise many as it would be more reminiscent of a grazing cow or a foraging pig than a ferocious predator. They spend most of their lives browsing on the tips of Lyngbye's sedge in the estuary. They also love digging for riceroot and rhizomes of silverweed and skunk cabbage. In berry season, they browse in the sun-soaked avalanche paths. Much of the day is spent snoozing in their day beds under the crabapples, and a good half of the year is spent hibernating in their snow holes up in the mountains. They are largely herbivores, with seasonal exceptions. They have predictable migrations around the Kitlope watersheds as they fish the rivers with the arrivals of different salmon species. The Haisla rarely have problems with grizzlies, the guardians of the forest. They are not typically hunted for food, and wisely so, as humans are known to get trichinosis from the roundworm that infests their flesh. Far more dangerous than grizzlies, or even the roundworm, are the two-legged trophy hunters Cecil describes.

One of the early victories for the Haisla was stopping grizzly trophy hunting. The impetus for the moratorium started with the Elders in the late 1980s. The late Kenny Hall came to the Kitamaat Village Council with reports that the grizzlies of the Kitlope were disappearing; the reason was probably trophy hunting and poaching. There was little the Haisla could do until the legal opportunities opened up in 1990. Just around that time, the regional district had approved a permit for an operator to run trophy hunting lodges in the Kitlope.[141] The regional board was clearly unacquainted with Haisla concerns. A tipping point came when Cecil encountered the grizzly hunting guide in the middle of a Rediscovery camp. The guide, angered at the presence of children in prime grizzly area, threatened to shoot through the kids if he saw a grizzly. It was time for the Haisla to shut down the trophy hunt.

One of the objectives of the 1992 Haisla/Ecotrust Wilderness Planning Framework was to identify the potential for grizzly viewing in the

Kitlope – a far more lucrative, sustainable activity. Bear scientist Wayne McCrory identified the need for research on the population and the opportunities for ecotourism but highlighted the incompatibility of ecotourism with trophy hunting. According to John Pritchard, it was Bruce Hill who acted as the catalyst for their success because he lent the Haisla his deep understanding of how the trophy hunting lobby thought and worked. In early correspondence to the BC Wildlife Branch, the Haisla crafted some critical questions: How many grizzlies are there in this watershed? How do you measure how many there are? What is the quota for kills? How many have been poached? How do you monitor the population? How do you enforce the regulations? At the time, there was a handful of conservation officers for an area the size of Great Britain. There was no accurate, on-the-ground data, no monitoring or enforcement. Government wildlife biologists were modelling habitat capability on maps, but the maps told you nothing about how many bears were actually there. Models were adapted to take into account "step-downs" from quotas, based on the quality of data, but applying these step-downs was vulnerable to political interference. The Haisla argued that, given so many unknowns, the step-downs should take the grizzly quota to zero.

Meanwhile, the Nanakila Institute generated its own data by hiring McCrory to oversee an inventory with Haisla Watchmen. The inventory provided the Western evidence to convince the provincial government to ban trophy hunting in the Kitlope in 1994, which met with international support on one hand and threats of litigation from the trophy hunting lobby on the other. The Kitlope was one of the first places in BC to have trophy hunting banned, and it helped precipitate the first-ever provincial grizzly management strategy. It took another 23 years to shut down all trophy hunting of grizzly in the Great Bear region, but the Haisla did it first. On December of 2017, the government closed the final loophole for trophy hunting of grizzlies in BC with the placing of a moratorium.

Wildlife biologists like Wayne McCrory formed lifetime friendships with field observers like Cecil. Braiding the oral history of grizzlies into Western scientific data isn't a mystery or a stretch of imagination; it is two good databases getting together and merging their data to enhance our understanding.

KITLOPE RIVER, JUNE 6, 2006

We are going down the Kitlope River with guests and Cecil says, "I have a hunch there is a grizzly there, pull over at the bank." I get out and look over the lip of the bank and come face to face with a young grizzly. I greet the young bear in the way that Cecil teaches: treat them like your grandfather. With the ban on trophy hunting now a decade old, the young grizzly is not that alarmed at a boatful of visitors. He goes back to his mom but quickly resumes browsing on the sedges. I climb back down to the boat. He and his mom eventually follow me over the bank on their way to a new browsing location. We sit and watch from the boats as the pair move effortlessly from water to land to water, their lean and rangy spring bodies delineated by their now glistening, wet coats.

Many Doors Opened for Wa'xaid

Many doors opened for Wa'xaid. In my journey, I think the beauty of it was – and I tell this to the children, and to Elders – I said, "I trust them, I trust them, and that's where the trust begins. We're going to save the Kitlope with a race I hated and distrusted."

Andy MacKinnon, a mycologist by training, who was on both the early Adventure Canada trips, shared a cabin with Cecil and formed a friendship, one that was also to take the form of an important scientific alliance with government. MacKinnon was a research forest ecologist with the BC Forest Service, and he and colleague Jim Pojar threw their weight behind a project started by their US Forest Service counterparts Paul Alaback and Jerry Franklin and SFU forest ecologist Ken Lertzman, in setting up long-term, old-growth forest monitoring plots along the whole coast. It was called the Coastal Old Growth Dynamics Project, which looked at how these old-growth forests grew and functioned over time.[142] This information would allow the scientists to assess how these forest species fared in comparison to industrially planted forests, and how they responded to climate change. MacKinnon and Pojar returned to the Kitlope one month after getting off the boat with Cecil to set up two plots with the Americans and Lertzman. They also brought along forest canopy specialist Neville Winchester, who was doing pioneering studies on the diversity of life at the top of the canopy, where few people had ever looked. It was a landscape less studied than Mars but with a lot more interesting life. The selection of these plots along the coast happened to coincide with future protected areas. As MacKinnon says, "It was intentional on our part."[143] Putting in a long-term monitoring station doesn't quite make sense if you're going to log it in a few years. It was another fortuitous relationship that furthered the case for the Kitlope.

A long-time senior editor of *Monday Magazine*, Sid Tafler, went up to the Kitlope and wrote a special seven-full-page story on Cecil and the Rediscovery camps.[144] He went up during sockeye season, helping alongside everyone catching and preparing the sockeye, interviewing Cecil, the kids and some of the other visitors who had arrived that summer. Tafler wrote, "If you had to pick one person to travel with on the five-hour trip from Kitimat to the Kitlope River, you'd probably pick Xenaksiala elder Cecil Paul."[145]

Equinox magazine sent an expedition of scientists, a photographer and an artist to document the first Western attempt at rafting down the entire Kitlope River, starting five kilometres below the headwaters glacier – a feat that was discouraged by the Xenaksiala. Bart Robinson, the editor, had reached out to the River League guides anxious to do the first ascent by raft, Ian Kean and Sebastian Wade. As Robinson later wrote in his article, "To avoid 'big trouble' here, I suspect, demands a type and measure of respect we have yet to show. The Henaksiala occupied the lower river for up to 9,000 years and in all that time, not one of them ever imagined trying to do what we are."[146] They only narrowly avoided losing some of their fellow expedition members: photographer Graham Osborne; artist Wesley Clark; botanists Marc Bell and Patricia North; ornithologist John Cooper; archaeologist Don Abbott; provincial forest ecologist Allen Banner; and river geomorphologist Dan Hogan. After some swampings, they were heliportaged around the most unforgiving part of the river. What the expedition did succeed in doing was providing more national attention and beautiful images of the area and the people. Cecil, Johnny Wilson, John Pritchard and Bruce Hill met them at Cecil's cabin in the lower Kitlope. Robinson writes of one of Cecil's famous evenings around the campfire:

> In Haisla tradition, a cedar bough is passed from hand to hand, and each of us, accepting it, speaks of our individual experience. There are maybe 25 people in the circle and it takes a long time to round it. The fire draws us in and the speeches have a remarkable openness and intimacy. Among our own group, the common declaration is of gratitude for a great gift: being able to travel day after day through a land in which the cloth of nature remains whole...As the last to speak, Cecil warns us that anyone who has seen the Kitlope will someday wish to return.[147]

The final political decision on the Kitlope was hanging in the balance in 1994 and, during those many campfire conversations, Cecil shared with the paddlers the deepening story of his life as the relationships and trust strengthened. Of all the arrows that came his way, his abduction to residential schools penetrated the deepest.

PART THREE

Journey of Hell, 1941 – 1971

Wawa lumgila: *There Is No Stopping Death When It Comes to Your Door*

In Kemano, when you sit in a point across the bay, there is a mountain – there are no trees growing on it. That mountain our people call Ł'lox^w (Thok): Strong. In the middle of the highest point is one little tree still standing today, and I was brought up there by my uncle. When the world flood came, that mountain was supernatural, *yüü'xm*. The water didn't cover the whole rock, and that little tree is where our people anchored or tied the rope of their canoe around. The canoe was moving back and forth; that is the way the little tree looked. The boy in the bow of the canoe was so weak from not enough to eat that he missed his fish when he speared it. Then out came the hawk, *'tä'ta'kwa*, took the fish by the neck and put it in the canoe. It was the dogfish. It saved the people. That was the first animal that the Creator has given the Xenaksiala people from the ocean. "*Q^w'a äits*," my uncle says. "Sit down." When the water went down, they see the treetops of Kemano.

My little granny told us that when there was an earthquake there would be a big wave that would raise the canoes. *Wawa lumgila* – there is no stopping death when it comes to your door.

Ways of adapting and being resilient to change are central to the Haisla nuyem. The magic canoe would not have attracted such a range of paddlers without the Haisla formulas for survival – a deep engagement of mind and heart with the land. The flood stories are lessons in survival: some refer to the rapid flooding caused by tsunamis triggered by periodic earthquakes; others refer to the relatively slow, sea-level changes due to the rebounds of the land when the weight of the glaciers came off. The tsunami floods can occur quickly and at a height sufficient to drown an unprepared village on a roughly seven-generation rotation. Glacial shoreline changes are more dramatic in scale but slower to enact, taking seven generations to rise or fall.

Post-glacial sea level changes can be simplified to a see-saw, with the outer coast like the upside of the see-saw, and the inner coast, the lower side. On the outer coast, like Haida Gwaii, sea levels rose over 150 metres to where they are at today, and on the inner coast, sea levels fell around 80 metres. The hinge of this see-saw is hypothesized to be around Calvert and Triquet islands, Heiltsuk territory, where sea levels have remained relatively unchanged for the last 15,000 years. Gardner Canal experienced higher sea levels, which have now fallen. Both types of floods are recorded in the oral histories of coastal people.

The Kitlope is a graduate school in glacial, hydrological and sea level dynamics. Nowhere is safe from flooding under a certain elevation, and there are stories with strategies for dealing with tsunami hazard zones, seasonal floods and long-term sea level changes. It isn't any surprise, therefore, that Cecil would observe and worry about the implications of climate change on sea levels. His ancestors have been through volatile periods of sea level changes for millennia. It is life and death when you live by the sea. There is nowhere to go but up or out.

The place he describes on the mountain called Ł'loxʷ (Thok) is about 100 metres above the existing sea level and is directly across the canal from Kemano, where he lived as a child. At the peak of the post-glacial flood – before the land bounced back – the sea could well have been lapping at the top of the cliff. The 'tä'ta'kwa is an osprey, and the dogfish makes total sense for food in a time of glacial upheaval. It is a shark infinitely well adapted to take advantage during floods. They are drawn to carnage and they tolerate a wide variety of habitats with big ranges of salinity and depths. Dogfish do well in brackish waters, but they can't tolerate over-fishing. The northern spiny dogfish takes up to 35 years to mature, has the longest gestation of any invertebrate (up to two years) and produces small litters of maybe half a dozen pups. Humans are their biggest predator, especially the type of industrial fishing that wipes out schools of an entire age class. They are protected internationally, but Canada has failed to respect those standards. The flood story and Kemano pole elevate the dogfish to a place on a totem pole that reminds us all to be mindful.

PRINCE RUPERT, JANUARY 23, 2016

It is around three in the morning and we all awaken to phones ringing through the house. I answer mine and it is Junior. "Have you guys heard that there has been a major earthquake off Alaska and there is a tsunami warning? You are in Zone A, so stay alert." Junior is an emergency coordinator in Kitamaat Village and is busy getting his own neighbours up to high ground, just in case a tsunami hits. He still has time to phone us. We are high above Rupert, so we are safe and just sit and wait in the darkness for news. The night has a surreal quality to it, but these northern villages are so well connected you feel safe. A lot safer than all those "world-class safety measures" that federal governments have provided for oil spills.

In the last 20 years, the study of paleotsunamis has thrown some Western scientific light on cycles well known to coastal people. When you dig a pit in a bog that has a soil profile stretching back in time, you see slim layers of light tsunami-deposited sands interspersed between the thick, dark, organic soils. Tsunamis turn the bogs into striped storybooks. We know that tsunamis have likely occurred dozens of times since the glaciers retreated.[148] The most recent tsunami was an eight-metre wave in Douglas Channel causing severe damage to port facilities in Kitimat on April 27, 1975.[149] The flood stories all point to getting to high ground or being out at sea for safety – advice that is still essential today.

The rivers also flood seasonally after deluges, rising metres within hours. Being caught on a river in a flood event can be terrifying, and drowning is an ever-present fear on the river. The teaching about the arrival of death coming to the door was one of the teachings that prepared Cecil for when the Indian agent came knocking at the door of his family home the first time in 1937.

Elizabeth Long Memorial School: I Felt So Alone

I was six years old when I was at this residential school in Kitamaat Village. Elizabeth Long Memorial School. Elizabeth Long was, I guess, the principal or the preacher – United Church. Young as I was, they had a little window, and I looked out at the channel. I remember lying down there, looking and hoping my dad will come around the point with his boat and pick me up. I am Xenaksiala, and these boys are Haisla, and we didn't get along too well. I felt so alone. I remember that. Later, when I lived and worked in Butedale, steamboats come in. Before the boats come in they blow the whistle, and when they took me to Alberni, I could hear the train whistles just like the ships coming into Butedale. I remember I had tears of loneliness listening to the train whistles, like the steamboats, coming to take me home. It never happened. Same way here when I was six or seven years old, looking at the point: "Come on, Dad. Come, Dad, I am lonesome for you." Never come. Never came.

We had that little football [soccer] team. I am the only one alive now from that picture. Lawrence King, Percy King and Percy Mack in the picture. I think the teaching I got from all that suffering was, I say to all my grandchildren, my children: "I will never leave you. I'll fight for you if I believe you are right."

Alberni, Kitamaat and Port Simpson schools all became the responsibility of the United Church of Canada under the care of the Women's Missionary Society in the early 1920s, when they started receiving grants per student from the federal government. By 1930, there were 80 residential schools across the country and any parent withholding a child from going to school would be sent to jail. This was the world that Cecil was born into in 1931. When he was 6, his father was forced to bring him down from Kemano to his first compulsory residential school, the Elizabeth Long Memorial Home in Kitamaat. Cecil had no idea that his family would be jailed if they didn't.

The only published account of life at the school during Cecil's time is in the *Missionary Monthly*, which describes a Christmas at the home: "At bedtime the staircases are hung with stockings. When the lights go on in the morning, the stockings are examined before it is time to dress. After breakfast the usual necessary duties are hurried through and everyone gets ready for church."[150] Sometime around 1938, his grandfather took him away and hid him back up in the Kitlope.

KITAMAAT, MAY 20, 2017

I have just spent over a month in various federal and provincial archives looking for material on Cecil's time in the two residential schools. Cecil's friends Charlie Shaw and John Pritchard had done a lot of groundwork, but still, it was a bit like being a grizzly looking for salmon eggs after a massive flood event. There are a few jewels that you find under a torrent of mud and debris. I have come up to Kitamaat to share some of my findings with him. One of the things I have been looking for is a photograph of Cecil as a child at either Elizabeth Long or Alberni. Blair Galston at the United Church's Bob Stewart Archives in Vancouver has patiently scoured every possible source and followed every lead for photos. He comes up with just one photograph. In the 1938 article in *Missionary Monthly* called "Christmas in Kitamaat" is a photo captioned "Some of the Indian Boys of Kitamaat." Cecil could well be among them, but his eyesight today is too far gone to pick out either himself or any of the boys in the photograph, which isn't the best quality reproduction to start with. The photo he had of himself with the boys playing soccer is all that he has of his entire childhood.

Elizabeth Long Memorial Home used to sit up high on a bench just behind his house, next to the graveyard above the village. Today, it is a massive thicket of salmonberries, elderberries and alder. Not a trace of the school remains. Nothing has been built in its place. In Cecil's time, there was the residence, the day school, a nurses residence/dispensary and the minister's house, all enclosed behind a high white picket fence. There was also the temple of the Royal Templars of Temperance put up by Rev. Raley's Temperance Society. A sidewalk connected the school to the rest of the village. The graveyard is full of children's gravestones under a lush canopy of cedar and hemlock. Little angels, Victorian motifs of Christian grief, alternate with Haisla grave markers of frogs, beavers and killer whales. The view today out his window is almost exactly the same as his view at 6 and 7 years old. All that is different is that, instead of a small settlement of farmers and mining prospectors across the bay, he is looking at the massive industrial plant of Rio Tinto/Alcan and the expanding footprint of LNG.

KITAMAAT, SEPTEMBER 26, 2017

It is early, dark and misty in Kitamaat. The fog bank has obliterated Kitimat across the water and for once the view to Kitimat town is beautiful. All I can hear are the haunting calls of mew gulls and the blow of a humpback offshore. I skulk around the docks like the missionary Margaret Butcher did 100 years ago, scribbling away about the village. I watch spiders building webs around the dock lights, imprisoning any moth that has ventured through their barricades. The rain has filled up the boats again. Junior will walk down soon to check and bail *Miss Sophia* and the oolichan punt. One certainty is that spiders have been building their webs and people have been bailing their boats here for close to 14,000 years.

Everybody Hid Their Children

I talked about the gift of memory, and I think that's the most wonderful thing in my life. Memory was something to hang on to; that there's a good life on the other side of bad. No one can ever steal that from you at any time. It is yours, to hold the beauty of what happened, and somehow the ugliness of things disappears, but the beauty of it remains with you till the end of the day, end of your life.

I went to my uncle, James Henry, a canoe builder – learned visually without going to school and self-taught – and that is where I was directed to go by my father. My uncle said, "I'll take him." Same as the young ladies who went to their aunties to learn how to cut fish and get things from the trees and cedar and what roots to take to make baskets, that kind of schooling. That was our system in the Kitlope until my grandfather took me [from Elizabeth Long], and I never went back and kept hiding from the missionaries in the Kitlope. It was a truth that everybody hid their children and didn't know what to expect.

Dr. Peter Kelly came up to Kitlope a whole lot of times before I went to Alberni. I told my little granny: the chief's [Dr. Kelly's] wife is beautiful. He used Chinook language and little granny didn't speak English, and how at ease they were with my grandfather and grandmother, and I remember him. He was well respected.

It was 1937 or 38 because after that we went to Kemano and Kitlope and stayed there. Kitlope is where my grandfather hid me from that residential school. I used to pack his bait to the trapline. I'd make a little fire by the river. "*Kä kwa däs* – Listen," Grandfather says. "The river is singing a song to us." You could hear one river go over a rock like this, and it will make a different sound, smaller one that is bass, alto and soprano. "The river is singing to us, if you stop and listen," he says. I remember hearing that. If it weren't for him, I wouldn't know that the river talks to us, making the different sounds. It has been a long time since I have been out quietly sitting by a river.

The stories I received, at maybe eight and nine, I remember well. At that age, I travelled with my grandfather, looking over his trapline. I saw him at that age bring down a deer with a bow and arrow. In my short life on this earth, I also see footprints in the moon. Humans went far beyond our land, Mother Earth. And it goes too fast for Wa'xaid, this life. What did I do? I did a lot of many things. I was taught how to trap, how to respect the bear and other animals. I was taught that we live together in this wilderness with the animals. Take what we need.

It was at that time when I was first told the importance of water. They told us when we go hunting to bathe in the water, and my grandfather would add devil's club that I would wash myself in. I would smell of the wilderness, and if I didn't bathe I wouldn't have the pleasure of going with them on a hunting trip. When you smell of the devil's club it has an odour that's beautiful. When you walk around the bush you could smell this same odour. If the wind is not in your favour and it blows towards the animal, it will run away if you don't bathe in it.

These little teachings I got from him endured for me in my life. The joy of a sunrise and the sunset. I remember asking my mother about the four seasons: winter, spring, summer, fall – each one of the four seasons is a time to harvest, a time to prepare for the winter months when you can't travel too much. Prepare for the winter. But then with the residential schools, if no leader is prepared to defend the nation, they laid down: "Do whatever you want." That is when the death of the culture could come. We died slowly; we were conquered.

Hiding Cecil from 1938 to 1941 was probably only possible because of the shortage of available government representatives with the onset of the war. It was illegal to hide him. His grandparents, Johnny and Annie Paul, were obviously able to keep one of their small grandsons out of the eye of the Indian agent for a few years, moving between their trapline and oolichan house in the Kemano area, their house on the Kitlope River and seasonal camps. It must have been a welcome respite to have industry and churches somewhat diverted by a war. Cecil tells of spending lots of time in the mountains to hunt mountain goats and just "see the place."

One of the Methodist ministers welcomed to the Kitlope by the Paul family was Dr. Peter Kelly, a Haida leader who was an ardent activist for First Nations. He is described as a "humble diplomat and stood fast by his beliefs, even at times setting himself against the very church that employed him."[151] Kelly led the first organization, Allied Tribes of BC, in 1916 to "take the land claims through the court system to the Judicial Committee."[152] He later led the Native Brotherhood, starting the year Cecil was born.

Cecil's story of his childhood is understandably linked to devil's club and its beautiful fragrance. His memory would be the equivalent of a European child's memory of lavender or rose water. Devil's club, ʼwiʼʼqas, grows throughout the wetter lowland areas of the valleys. It was well named by the Christians because when you walk through the bush in the winter, it looks like a gnarly, devilish-looking club on a long, spiny handle. What was missed by the missionaries was its heavenly properties. The bark easily peels off the stem, exposing a fragrant green inner bark, or cambium, against the white pithy wood. You can boil the cambium for a tincture or just chew it raw. The taste of devil's club is like a Swedish bitter, an appetite-stimulant; it is also the taste and smell of the forest. In the spring, the gnarly club explodes into a profusion of sprawling branches and huge leaves, forming thickets that are difficult to walk through because even the huge maple-like leaves are spined with tiny barbs that lodge in the skin like fishhooks. The white spikes of flowers ripen into deep red berries by the late summer, just like its cousin ginseng – both highly important medicinal plants embraced by the East and the West. Every part of the plant has some medicinal or ceremonial purpose, a first aid kit growing in the forest pointing to life-giving water and immune-boosting properties. It may well have been the tonic that kept Cecil alive through a century of epidemics.

PRINCE RUPERT, MAY 22, 2017

Cecil, Louisa and I are in Prince Rupert going over the draft of Cecil's stories. I wish I were a linguist, as I have no capacity to document the subtle nuance in pronunciation, meaning and phonetical spelling that the siblings are discussing around particular words. I know that I am listening to a conversation that no other human being except two other relatives can comprehend. I can't grasp the meaning of words as they relate to this place, river, ocean, animals and human experience over millennia. I say *nosda*, I am listening, but my ears don't even know how to hear. They are master linguists. Their father and grandfather spoke many languages: Tsimshian, Chinook, Haisla, Xenakisala and English. I wish the whole nation was listening too.

Alberni: The Journey of Hell Begins

That was a joyous time in my life on the Kitlope; it was beautiful. I never knew when I was nine years old that one day I would lose the teachings of my Elders. At age ten and a half, my friends and I were playing on the hillside, and we went to an opening and looked down on the riverbank, see the boat come in. I heard a new motor coming, stopped on my beach. There was three of them on the boat. I learned years later it was the Indian agent representing Canada. Another one with a uniform was the provincial police. They came to pick me up. Someone told the Indian agent where I was, and they came up and picked me up in the Kitlope. Came right up the Kitlope River. Children at that age are kind of curious. Wondering what happened to my grandfather and grandmother, I went right down to the beach, looked out, and there was some strangers who stayed in the background and watched. He was instructed to remove children and take them to a residential school. My little granny said: *"Waa daa nox^w!* Don't look back, my son. Don't look back." Why did little Granny say "Don't look back?" I think it was because she was powerless to help. Those words are what was said when people had no choice, if they were captured in warfare. I could hear my mum crying sometimes...lonesome.

It happened to me with a few other children. At the age of ten and a half, I journeyed from the Kitlope, leaving my things, my granny, my mum and grandfather. It was years later I learned where we ended up at. It was a residential school in a place that was Port Alberni, Vancouver Island. The journey of hell begins when I was ten, when they took me away from my family. That was the beginning of hell for a ten-year-old that didn't understand a word of English. I stayed four years in this Port Alberni. I never went home. I had a lot of good friends, especially one, Russell Ross. He's a Haisla and we speak the same language: Xenaksiala and Haisla. My friend just passed away last Christmas. He was 89, four years older than me. There were signs all over – I learned later of the rules – and the one with the most big letters, that YOU ARE NOT TO TALK YOUR MOTHER TONGUE. Russell and I didn't know how to read and were talking in our language.

A big guy came, he had a whistle in his mouth, blowing his whistle. He took me by the collar and my friend, whistling until he got to what they called the playroom. One hundred and seventeen boys. They lined up the boys and circled right around and took me and Russell, took us in the middle of this playroom and asked to remove our trousers. We did. I remember I can still see the weapon they used for me not to talk my mother tongue: a black leather strap. Three feet long maybe, and it was double. One was about an inch, the other was inch and a half. One would hit and the other one would follow. They made an example of us, I learned later. They did the same with each reserve who spoke a different language. We happened to be the ones to be made an example of, my friend and I.

When I knew what was coming I spoke to my friend. I said, "*Kéc'gʷäsa. Don't cry, brother. Don't cry.*" We are talking in our language in front of them, my tormentor. I got five more hits. The third one that hit my rear end, I glanced up at my tormentor and he had a smile, I could still see. And with that smile a seed was planted in my heart. A seed of hatred. A seed of mistrust to my tormentor. My tormentor, I learned later, was run by the United Church of Canada, a white man. They cultivated this hatred so well. Cultivated this mistrust. The hate. What I mean by cultivate is planting hatred in my heart. My friend Russell and I went underground with our mother tongue. I think it is when I first began to defy authority. I think it was at that moment when I knew, there's something wrong.

I stayed in Alberni four years. I didn't know my father had passed away. When I got home my grandfather had gone. There is hatred something awful. My people didn't write, couldn't...it was a long journey. They take me away from the place of my birth and teachings of my Elders. I have a very dear friend who when he came home, there was no communication with his parents. Government almost won their battle of Canadianizing the "savage," as they called us. It says on the legal paper: a child can't communicate with his mom and dad – only in English. There was no communication.

Russell and I had the power and will to hang on through something that I didn't understand at that time, but knew something was going to happen. We never lost our mother tongue. That defying authority at that age came to play in my life very bad. For it is something that the residential school has taught people that resisted against it. My friend went on the same journey, a no-good journey. I think it really bothered his mind. Not long after that, I joined the same path he went. I didn't know that so many of us went in that direction, to hide the pain, hide the shame, and we drowned it in alcohol.

Cecil was transported more than 1,000 kilometres to the head of Alberni Inlet in central Vancouver Island. He arrived at an imposing new brick building on the Somass River, which had just been built to replace a previous school that had burned down. It was the third to burn down, probably not an accident. He described it as a prison, which it indeed resembled with its square fortress appearance and small windows. Today, there is nothing left of the school, just a patch of forest near the Tseshaht reserve. Upon his arrival, Cecil was registered as #126 in the Quarterly Returns, the official documents sent to Ottawa with the children's attendance that triggered their annual fee per student. The Returns record his arrival in September of 1941, that he is from the Kemano tribe and 11 years old. He is placed into Grade 4 for F & G (farming and gardening) trade. His attendance is the maximum number of days for the quarter. Since he never left the school for four years, his attendance was 100 per cent. The remarks about him on the far column of the report state, "Satisfactory progress," which also didn't change until the administrator just stopped making remarks on the children altogether. The only exception at the end to "no comment" was if they had been sent to Coqualeetza Hospital with TB. Above Cecil on the list is #125, Leonard Paul, his older brother, who was shortly moved to Coqualeetza.[153]

The residential school was very different from its original concept as a mission home for girls that had been started by the Presbyterian missionary, Reverend John MacDonald. It grew in scale with the funding assistance of the Presbyterian matriarchs, the Women's Foreign Mission Society and the Department of Indian Affairs. Much of the history of Alberni is documented in the United Church's online history, *The Children*

Remembered – an awful history of mistreatment from 1918 onwards.[154] A report documented severe physical abuse by an employee of the school.

Andrew Paull, a Native leader of the Allied Tribes of BC and later the Native Brotherhood, was an early critic of the schools. He drew attention to the abuse by a staff member at Alberni who "'unmercifully whips the boys on their back' as well as kicking them, hitting them with fists, and choking them."[155] Just prior to Cecil arriving, a school inspector for Ahousat, Gerald H. Barry, complained that "Children have come here from Alberni Indian Residential School, where every member of the Staff carried a strap... These children have never learned how to work without punishments."[156] The period during the Second World War is scarce in documentation.

The new school was designed for 200 students to get "the most up to date and the best equipped Indian residential school in the Dominion."[157] In the Quarterly Returns, four "Trades" are listed: Chores, F & G (farming and gardening), M.T. (manual training) and NAV. (navigation). A detailed report by H.M. Morrison, inspector of schools, in January 2 – 5, 1945, paints a graphic picture of the desperate conditions: the school is "overcrowded" with 280 students (e.g., 40 Grade 1 children are crowded into a converted sewing room); children above Grade 1 are only receiving "half time education"; the vocational training program is "weak"; there is no gymnasium and play space is "limited"; "library materials are meagre"; the industrial education shop is "inadequate"; the grounds are "unsuitable for farm produce as it is high and rocky"; there is an "infirmary with an unqualified nurse in charge"; qualifications of staff "are inadequate"; and the school's administration "has a certain inertia." Morrison found, however, the food to be adequate.[158]

The Indian commissioner for British Columbia, D.M. MacKay, Department of Mines and Resources, emphasized some "improvements" in his report to Ottawa of March that same year, although he still bemoaned that "It is always a most disheartening and discouraging experience for me on visits to this institution to invariably find most of the rooms used by the children in a dirty and untidy state and despite earnest efforts on our part to have the principal improve matters to see the same condition continue year after year."[159] MacKay attributes the improvements to the new principal, Reverend A.E. Caldwell, who took over from Robert Clyde Scott a year earlier.

R.C. Scott was a Methodist minister who was the principal of Alberni during Cecil's time there. Like all staff, he was appointed by the United Church but paid by the Department of Indian Affairs. He wrote about his experiences in *My Captain Oliver: A Story of Two Missionaries on the British Columbia Coast.*[160] In the chapter "New and Old Fight for Old Souls," he writes, "After I went to Alberni Residential School as principal in 1940, I had within a year or two a better idea of what was actually wrong with these people."[161] What is wrong, apparently, is, "There is another very powerful reason why such people do not make any outward objection to the carrying on of old customs. These old people who have taken over the direction of affairs in the life of the Reserves have their own way of forcing compliance and cooperation. Sometimes their methods are heartless and cruel."[162] Scott's private journals reveal a deeply compromised man, as evident in these two consecutive entries starting April 29, 1941, the spring that Cecil arrives, and one from August 1942.

> April 29th, 1941
> This has been a trying time, but I cannot feel that a mistake has been made in my coming here. I do seem to be out of place in my methods perhaps, and I shall have to overhaul them, and perhaps revise them. But it must be in the spirit of faith, and in confidence in the hopes I have had for this school and for this people.
>
> It looks to me as though my forerunner, Mr. P. [Pitt] had done the best job he could, but was forced to adopt a "play safe" method, and while he did a good job perhaps in the field of education, so far as class room work etc. is concerned, still he left untouched the real heart life of the people, and that is what is wrong, to my mind.
>
> This is evident by the fact that the little old church lies a ruin on the River road: the people, many of them carry on Ha 'lal games at every opportunity: The attendance at church at the school is sporadic and unsatisfactory and can only mean that the people are not interested. The young men are perhaps an exception to this. Here again perhaps the credit is due to the former school for these young men are all graduates. However, they are "loose" and without much sense of responsibility.
>
> They are perhaps becoming a problem in that they are so much at and around the play grounds with our senior boys. Within the school, upon the staff are those who do not seem to have any vision of the end to which we ought to be working. Some are fine and co-operative, but others are not wholly in that category.
>
> One staff member on the boys' side has got into a fight with

one of the senior boys. This is the crucial situation which I must face – but how? And from what standpoint?

It was as I faced this question that I came upon the words with which this sheet began: Am I to be driven to hysterical, angry action – or must I now, and always "hold fast the beginning of my confidence, stedfast [sic] unto the end.?? I think this I must do.

In the Upper Room protion [sic] for today it says ///---

"It is no easy matter ---. Our faith, our hope, our courage, are being daily and nightly subjected to terrific bombings.

---Imperceptibly, at first, by none the less surely, we feel the urge to break with an apparently losing cause. The "philosophy of escape lures us ---.

It has been helpful, and while the problems still remain to be faced, and I seem to be alone, with no one to whom I can turn, still[163]

At Alberni, Apl. 29/41.

I know that around me is "the great cloud of witnesses" among whom I am not worthy to be numbered, and too, nearer or at least more visible, are those who will follow my leadership, and Christ will be with me. It is His cause, and it can not [sic] fail. He will keep me that "my faith fail not" and perhaps as He did for Peter long ago, He has prayed for me to that end. That seems almost a sacrilegious thought, but like may [sic] of them it may only be "seeming" arising out of a lack of faith. Anyway, I trust Him for strength and grace and to lead me in a "plain path, because of my enemies" – enemies, potential, and perhaps unknowing ...

August 3rd, 1942 –

Once again it is a long time since I have written anything along the above lines. Yesterday, I had a talk with some of the village boys who seem to interfere with the younger boys, making it hard for Mr. Grantham, our boys' overseer for the summer, to handle the boys as he ought. Saturday afternoon, previous to this, Buddy Hamilton came to the office and said he wanted to see Mr. Grantham before me. His plaint was that the boy in question, Arthur Pearson, had been crying and Buddy took this as an evidence of his being unkindly treated. The fact was that money had been given the boy, and he wanted to go to the store without permission. I felt "riled" at Buddy, and told him what he and the other boys were doing in making it hard to enforce discipline and that unless they changed and fell in line with me, and the school programme, they would have to stay away together.

This incident shows the "uppishness" and insolence of these youth fellows. To think they have the right to come to the office and interfere, or criticize the member of staff!, well, that seems the limit. I am tempted to just shut down, and keep them out for good, but here again, that would mean that these boys would stay on their own side of the fence and make as much, if not more trouble than ever. So, it looks as though the conclusion researched in my last observation, still holds, and I must carry on, "looking unto Jesus – " and be true to my own convictions.[164]

Scott's journals contain philosophical musings, prayers and sporadic entries. He is clearly preoccupied with a world at war, and he is in an environment and job for which he has no great love or control. No mention is made of any other staff or Peter Allan.

Behind the scenes, in Victoria, the presbytery was corresponding on issues of federal fees for students per annum and staff salaries. Internally, they were looking at the competing demands of their staff to run schools and continue their evangelistic work. Reverend W. Percy Bunt, superintendent of missions, had visited Alberni and come back with the central recommendation to hire one vice-principal to free R.C. Scott from some school duties "to visit as many small tribes...and give evangelical services to them."[165] With a shortage of men, the dual duties of Mr. Scott had pushed him to "exhaustion"[166] and he retired.

Bunt remained on as superintendent of home missions from 1939 to 1958. He also oversaw the Japanese Canadian missions. He was educated at McGill and Wesleyan Theological College. Reverend R. Grant Bracewell, a minister in Bella Coola during the late 1960s who knew Bunt, stated that Bunt had told him, "The Church may have nominated teachers but they were appointed and employed by the federal government. When there was a problem staff member, the federal government said, 'oh, the church looks after them,' but the church couldn't fire them. The federal government weren't accountable."[167]

Stories of abuse at Alberni during the war years only came to light during the TRC in 2013, with the testimony of ex-students like Cecil Paul. The postwar years were exposed in 1995 with the testimonies presented in the Willie Blackwater civil court case. Willie Blackwater was a student at Alberni a few years after Cecil had left. The benchmark Blackwater case was to reveal levels of abuse that prompted BC Supreme Court Justice Douglas Hogarth to declare during the sentencing phase that the Indian residential school system was "nothing but a form of institutionalized pedophilia."[168] An investigation of the schools by the RCMP was initiated across BC, but by then there was already a long institutional foundation for the violence.

According to Reverend Brian Thorpe, minister emeritus of Ryerson United Church, who worked on the residential school file from 1994 onwards, there was a marked difference in the day-to-day involvement of the federal government in the management of the schools before and after the war. A detailed analysis of where the responsibility lay for the abuses of the residential schools was put before the courts in the Willie Blackwater civil court case against the federal government, which, according to Thorpe, became "a debate around the question of apportion of responsibility."[169] At the end of the Blackwater trial, the case having gone through two courts of appeal, the Supreme Court of Canada concluded that the federal government had 75 per cent of the responsibility, and 25 per cent for the United Church. Thorpe states, "There are still those in the United Church who argue that we had no real act to play...but the reality is that the United Church still attached its name to the school. It still took incredible pride in the history of the school and did nothing to challenge the existence of the school. For those reasons alone the church has to bear a responsibility."[170]

UNITED CHURCH, VANCOUVER,
BOB STEWART ARCHIVES, NOVEMBER 29, 2016

The Bob Stewart Archives in the basement of Ryerson United Church in Vancouver is in the process of being moved to more accessible premises, but I'm still made welcome by archivist Blair Galston. The United Church could not be more accommodating to help dig out records of Cecil at both Elizabeth Long and Alberni residential schools. Galston first introduces me to Reverend Richard Bracewell, a frequent visitor to the archive, who was personally acquainted with both Percy Bunt and missionary George Raley. He recalls some of his perceptions of the both of them from his conversations with them when they were elderly men. Bracewell himself is elderly. He remembers Raley as a moderate man, allowing his students to speak in their own language.

I have an interview with Reverend Dr. Brian Thorpe upstairs from the archive today. In preparation for the meeting, he has sent me an unpublished manuscript he wrote in September of 2014. It is called *A Loss of Innocence* about the involvement and culpability of the United Church in the federal government's residential school experiment.

Loss of Innocence starts with a circle of survivors of residential schools in which Thorpe is sitting and bearing witness to their accounts. He reflects back on the start of his own path to understanding the nature and scale of the problem:

> After a long day in the circle – a day marked by both the judgment pronounced upon my church and my nation by the story which was told that day and by the courage and grace of the story teller – I made my way back to my hotel. In the middle of the night I was awakened by a vision rooted in my childhood. We were visiting my grandparents in Portage la Prairie. On Sunday morning we made our way to Trinity United Church where my grandparents were respected elders in the congregation. A few minutes before the service was to begin, a large number of children were paraded into a vacant section of the sanctuary. In my childhood memory of this event, what I recall most about these children is that they were all dressed alike.[171]

I pass drawings of snowflakes from the church daycare as I make my way to his office. Thorpe has a warm manner and an encyclopedic mind. He also has a Ph.D. from McGill, and his scholarship is evident as we dive right away into his manuscript, which I find moving and insightful. He has also served different congregations, guided the church as executive secretary, worked on dispute resolution with the Gitxsan and is currently chair of a society in Vancouver's Downtown Eastside. It is easy to understand why he was the one selected to take on the legacy of the United Church's involvement with residential schools. I ask him why he hasn't published his manuscript. He tells me it isn't the right time.

In 1945, the same year Cecil is discharged, Ottawa debates a grant to upgrade institutional facilities for First Nations across Canada. In the national newspaper, a reporter cites the prevailing view: "If Parliament approves the government's reconstruction program the citizens of this nation are going to give $12,000,000 worth of the country's substance 'back to the Indians.'"[172]

Reggie Wilson: Keeping Us Down Underneath Their Feet

In Alberni a nice guy named Reggie Wilson, called him "Dusty," kind of took me under his wing. He'd done more of teaching me English than any teacher. He was quite a bit older than me; he must have been maybe 17, 16. Anyway, he graduated and asked the principal if he could go to high school. After eight days, they kicked him out of the residential school, Grade 8. I think at that time, if I remember right, the principal of that school was Caldwell. And he heard Reggie's plea that he wanted to continue his education. There's two high schools in two little towns close together, Alberni and Port Alberni. Both little towns had high school and both of them refused. The government said that there's no Indians could be educated. When you think back of what the government done of keeping us down underneath their feet. I look and admire my ladies, all of the Native people across Canada. Maybe one person... don't know, graduated from high school. He didn't understand English well. None of us do.

I tried to put words together to say how proud I am of my little niece, Dr. Jackie Green, high degree in education. In my lifetime of over 80 years, with the flashback to Reggie, I said to my niece, "Dr. Green, a breakthrough. Something's happening."

Reggie Wilson appears in the Quarterly Returns as student #2. On June 30, 1943, the remarks are uncharacteristically effusive: "Excellent pupil. Passed first in High School Entrance Class." According to Isobel McFadden's accounts of life in the schools, the local Indian agents and school inspectors had blocked promising students from even taking the entrance exams during Pitt's era at the school. The inspector was said to have claimed, "Most Indians want to go back to their reserves anyway."[173] Reggie Wilson appears to have broken through one glass ceiling – an opportunity to take the exam. There still lay ahead the challenge of getting into high school, which Cecil recalls was not offered.

Four Chiefs: Became Leaders of Our
People to Give Them Hope

I was in Port Alberni with Bella Coola's Chief Pootlass. At Alberni his name was Lawrence King. And when he came out he was, like me, a chronic alcoholic. Somewhere along the line something changed, and his grandfather said, "He is changed." He grew into a chief. There was the hereditary chief of Masset, Art Pearson; I was in Port Alberni with him too. And

Hereditary Chief Jacob Nyce in Canyon City, Nass River, big chief. All of us were at residential school. I sat down sometimes, I gave them a call and talked to them: "Can you share your story of how you changed your life? How did you correct your life? How did you manage to swim out of that river of alcoholism and make it ashore? Share with me how you done your journey." Every one of us survived. Every one of us had the same story. They almost killed me for talking in my mother tongue. Now it is alive. It is amazing, when I see so many of us – four of us – all suffered in Port Alberni, became leaders of our people to give them hope. The government failed...hearing me talk my language – my mother tongue.

No photographs of Cecil or the other boys at Alberni survive. The closest is one small book of less than a dozen photographs of Alberni children by Kay How from 1936, which portrays groups of children mostly dressed up for various Christmas parties. Particularly striking is the group of young girls dressed as angels and a group of young boys dressed as "Brownies" with little elfin caps on.[174] Perhaps these are the family members and friends he describes.

All that appears in the Returns are their names, numbers and attendance, with very limited comments on progress: Reggie Wilson, #2; Art Pearson, #134; Larry King, #146; Percy Mack, #149; brother Douglas Paul, #150; cousin Charlie Shaw, #165; Russell Ross, #169; cousin Crosby Smith, #192; brother Vincent Paul, #311. Many of these were the men who were to become leaders in their communities and share the same arrows. The list of leaders from this intake extends well beyond Cecil's connections too. Isobel McFadden writes about an evening spent with Jim Manly, a United Church minister who has been at the forefront of collecting testimonies from survivors of the schools. One of the voices Manly had recorded McFadden paraphrases in her book: "When Indians named the men and women and young people who were leaders in the communities and leaders in the current Indian movements, almost all had been students in these same church schools. In spite of the miseries, the education had prepared them to devise their ideas for the betterment of their people and to deal with problems." McFadden and Cecil might disagree on what "education" refers to, but there is no doubt that those who survived were educated in certain types of survival and resilience.

Who Is this Person Torturing Us?

Peter Allan is the name I heard, Mr. Allan. He hurt the boys bad, but wasn't just me – there was a bunch of us. I don't know what year it was, I may have been home maybe five, six years and I stole my grandfather's revolver. I came down to Vancouver Island, went to Alberni but couldn't find Mr. Allan. I was going to shoot him. I met Lawrence King and I told him afterwards what I tried to do. He says: "It's not worth it, Brother. He is not worth it." Going back in the Queen Charlotte Strait, I throwed the revolver overboard. Maybe I was blessed not to meet my tormentor, as I was determined to kill him.

Vincent, my little brother, is the only one who ran away from Alberni and they never found him or captured him to bring him back. He ran away with three others from Alberni. The others got caught by the police. He worked for a fisherman towards the end. They found his body under a wharf in the cannery in Port Edward. He was decomposed, no idea who he was, so the Sally Anne [Salvation Army] buried him in an unknown grave in Rupert. That fall my mum said, "Go look for him." Sister Louisa was already in Rupert and married. I stayed in a little hotel.

I met a policeman. Oh, he was a gentleman: "Can I help you, Cecil?"

"Yes," I said. "I think he had partial dental plates but no clue where he had it made."

"That is a good start," the policeman said. So, he went through all the dentists in Rupert, and one morning, came a knock on the door.

"Hey, get dressed," he says. "I think we have broke through something." We went to the dentist.

"Does your brother have a middle name?" dentist asked.

I said "Yes, Vincent Harry Paul."

There was a partial plate that they took from his decomposed body and that is how we found his grave. I phoned Sister Louisa: "I'm going home to tell the family."

I wanted to dig him up and take him home but my auntie Louise [not to be confused with sister Louisa] said: "Q'uu xʷenoxʷ q'uu. No, my child, no. Let him be. He suffered too much and too long. Cousin Frances's son was buried in the Prince Rupert cemetery too. He needs family to keep him company." I think Vincent went to Alberni the same time as Mr. Plint was there.

When they took that school down in Alberni, I got one brick. It really bothered me, so I took it outside and put it in the smokehouse. Quite a while afterward, I told a friend about it. He says, "I got one too. I brought a witness from my council and went up the hill and I shot it to pieces."

I says, "I took mine and took it to the middle of the Douglas Channel and throwed it overboard." Who is this person torturing us to do such a thing like that? They didn't understand what has happened to us, eh? That friend had a very difficult time with that Mr. Plint – very bad.

Reverend A.E. Caldwell took over the school in 1944 and one important improvement he may have engineered (it only receives a footnote by the commissioner) is the resignation of a Mr. R.E. Allen, possibly the same man named by Cecil as "his tormentor." No other reference to him in any United Church or government documents could be found, nor what happened to him. Cecil remembers one staff member who was "a good guy," Edward Peak.

Two years after Cecil left Alberni, Arthur Henry Plint took over as the boys' night supervisor at Alberni, a position of power that he abused for the next 20 years. Vincent Paul was incarcerated in the school in September of 1948, the start of the period for which Plint was convicted of his sexual assaults. Vincent ran away with three others from Alberni, all of whom got caught by the police. He was one of the first students to escape recapture by the RCMP. He was essentially an outlaw for his teenage years then worked for a fisherman. He was only 26 when he died. Cause of death is not known. Some Alberni survivors were able to testify about the physical and sexual abuse during the late 1990s civil court case. If Vincent had lived, he might have been one of them. Arthur Henry Plint pleaded guilty in 1995 to 18 counts of sexual assault between 1948 and 1968 and was jailed for 11 years. In the follow-up civil trial that lasted over three years, with 92 days of hearings between 1998 and 2000, the principal respondents, the Government of Canada and the United Church of Canada, were found guilty of negligence. In 2003, Donald Bruce Haddock, another member of staff, pleaded guilty to four counts of indecent assault between 1948 and 1954.[175]

UNITED CHURCH, VANCOUVER,
BOB STEWART ARCHIVES, JANUARY 17, 2017

Reverend Dr. Brian Thorpe explains how he ended up becoming the senior staff person for the United Church in BC dealing with the Blackwater civil court case. He was assigned to the matter after the criminal trial for Plint, which was dropped when Plint pleaded guilty. Thorpe heard from survivors that the dropping of the criminal trial robbed them of an opportunity to tell their stories in a court of law. "In the wider public realm it obviously did not get a lot of publicity and there was about a year when I think there was an expectation that the church would do something. And the church did nothing."[176] He pauses and then tells me, "This is when I became involved."

Three years of court cases ensued in which, Thorpe states, "Once again, First Nations survivors basically became bystanders in their own story." Court time was taken up with the church and the nation duking it out over culpability. Thorpe's conclusion at the end of the process was that "this was the worst possible way to address historical wrongs. Damages from a legal point of view were very narrow" and based on low anticipated wages in a money economy, ignoring the subsistence economy. In his opinion, "there was no recognition of loss of language, loss of culture, loss of spirituality, loss of family – none of those were compensated." Only six plaintiffs of the original 22 were still involved in the final phase. Many pulled out, some died during the process.

Thorpe mentioned an added ordeal for survivors during the trial: "lawyers would ask these men, in their 50s and 60s, to describe their Grade 2 teacher and their name. You could see them struggling to provide this kind of information. We [court attendees] had a break and we were talking about this, so I asked, 'Just out of curiosity, how many of you remember the name of your Grade 2 teacher?' These were federal colleagues, church people, and the majority of them couldn't remember. It spoke volumes."

At the end of the trial, the United Church made an official apology and then worked with the federal government to start some exploratory dialogues. They set up a trial project with the Gitxsan, but when the participants in that project had wanted language and cultural loss included in the process, the federal government said no. Thorpe had this to say about the experience:

> From the government's perspective, their hope was that the church could shoulder the responsibility, which from a purely political point of view you can understand. The problem is that it separates the residential school process from colonization. Sadly, in the public mind, I think it is still a very strong dimension that somehow the residential schools are a stand-alone experience – a tragic period in history – but people don't make the connection with all the other processes of colonization; the loss

of land, the loss of resources and all of those that are integrally tied together. That is why it is important that the whole notion of residential schools is understood as a Canadian project. The problem is when the churches say that, it can be easily seen as trying to shuffle off your responsibility. I think it is still such a dominant unexamined thread throughout the Canadian psyche and through the Christian church psyche. People can understand sexual abuse and be horrified by it, but the racism that lies at the centre of it is still unacknowledged.[177]

The Blackwater case has never been properly written up. Justice Brenner has died. In an Alberni school newsletter called the *Western Eagle*, written a few years after Cecil had gone, a story opens: "The first weeks of school saw forty little folks pass into Grade One room. Some felt very shy and some had a very strange feeling in their throats. Soon however everyone was so busy getting to know his new friends, there was no time to be lonely."[178] When the school finally closed in 1965, the Port Alberni newspaper interviewed Caldwell, and "He told of the achievements of the former students and told the youngsters that Indian children in Canada had the best opportunity for education of any people in the whole world."[179]

PORT EDWARD, MAY 23, 2017

Cecil and I are on another road trip, this time to Port Edward. We are going to see where Vincent's body was found. Port Ed is really off the beaten track; you turn south before the bridge to Rupert onto a windy coastal road. You arrive at a natural harbour on the great river Skeena. The canneries once formed an industrial strip, but today it is just a string of rotting docks and the restored North Pacific cannery interspersed between salmonberry bushes. Cecil points to underneath the government dock, "That's where they found what was left of him." The Salvation Army buried him. Cecil wanted to bring back Vincent's body after they linked the dental records to the body, but two other cousins are buried there and their mother, Agnes (who became the oldest matriarch in the extended family after Annie Paul had died), wanted her sons to have company in the graveyard.

That evening, we return to Louisa's. I sit with her, helping clean salmon eggs. She talks about her experiences at residential school and how she got over her depression as a young adult. She went to an art therapy session and drew a tree with eight branches laden down from snow to represent her burdens. That started her on her recovery. It is deluging rain as we speak. Rivulets are running down the road. Louisa talks about the importance of metaphor. "We use a lot of metaphors to get a vivid understanding. There is a canoe word in Haisla, *kew no*, it means 'nearly reached our destination.'"

The next morning on our way out of town, Cecil and I stop at Fairview Cemetery just outside Rupert, where Vincent is buried. It is still pouring rain. When you get to the check-in office, you continue straight until you reach the last tree on the left. It is less than five graves in, marked Vincent Harry Paul 1936 – 1962. Louisa had put flowers on it and Cecil sang a Xenaksiala song to him. I made a small cedar basket from cedar in the Kitlope, which we put on the grave. Cecil said, "Thank you for taking me to see my brother."

Butedale: Beginning of a Bad Journey

After Alberni Residential School, I went to a little place called Butedale, and I worked in the cannery for a little while. When I first got to Butedale I was 14 years old. It was a segregated place: Indians in one place, Chinese another, white people close to the store. I was in the Indian place. I was fishing, 14 years old. You get a share of the catch, but because I was so young and green, captain gave me a half-share. I was a dishwasher. Then after that I worked in that cannery for quite a number of years. At age 14 I was offered a drink, and I took it. That was the beginning of a bad journey. I became a chronic alcoholic. I got drunk and I never sobered up for well over 30 years. That part of my life was awful.

Sometime after Cecil was released from Alberni Indian Residential School, he got a job washing dishes on a fish boat. The boat arrived at the southernmost wa'wais of the Haisla people, Butedale, or Cedixs. Cedixs refers in the Haisla language to the state of your stomach after eating too many thimble and salmonberries, a bounty of which Cedixs offered. These berries are members of the rose family, a widely diverse family of species which have sustained humans since our arrival in the temperate latitudes.

The cannery was officially named Butedale on the maps in 1946, just around Cecil's arrival on the fish boat as dishwasher. Butedale was named after the third Earl of Bute, John Stuart, of Scotland, who was a passionate botanist and a lousy prime minister of Britain for all the right reasons. His interest in the *Rubus* genus of the berries would undoubtedly have been greater than his interest in the cannery business, as he had knowledge and interest in the former but not the latter. He died in 1792, the year before his fellow countryman Alex Mackenzie became the first European to cross the continent to the coast, finishing his journey along the grease highway.

In 1946, Cecil was 15 years old. Many of his family were dead, dying, in residential school or Indian hospitals or escaping them. He never heard from or spoke to any member of his family in those four years. They didn't even know where he was. Some sense of the isolation of Kitamaat Village that year is captured in an article written by Rev. Bunt during his tour of the Indian missions: "By the next evening we had reached Kitamaat, which is without a missionary, without a telephone or telegraph, and without a nurse. The nearest doctor is over 150 miles distant and the nearest telephone 75 miles away."[180] Bunt disbursed some $300 in alms, met with a lay preacher and the Evanses, who ran the day school. It may well have been a letter from the Evanses that prompted the visit, as they had written Bunt in May of 1945, commenting on the state of evangelical affairs and attendance in church: "the former strong leadership [for the church] is gone. And even if it were not, it is doubtful if the old authority would prevail against the changing temper of the times."[181]

KITAMAAT, OCTOBER 31, 2017

Whenever I phone up Cecil, I say, "Hello Kitamaat," and he says back, "Hello Your Place." Our territory defines us. Today, I have a very specific question: "Did your parents go to residential school?" I don't like springing questions on him. It is sort of like the lawyers asking survivors: What was the name of your Grade 2 teacher? This time he did reply: "I don't think so, they never talked about it. When once they are conquered and no leader is prepared to defend our nation, they laid down: Do whatever you want. That is when the death of the culture [came]. We died slowly; we were conquered." It is the first time I have heard him use that kind of language. I don't know why it came as a surprise to hear that Cecil once felt conquered. He seems unconquerable to me now.

BUTEDALE, JULY 5, 1999

Today, as we headed south from Khutze Inlet to Butedale, we spotted A8 and A12, northern resident killer whales. They were feeding before heading off in the same direction as us, toward Butedale. Cecil and Brian were more excited than the guests to see them. We stopped in Butedale for a walk up to the lake and a visit to the old cannery buildings. A storm warning has been issued and we have to stay here for the next 24 hours.

Cecil is a good guide to Butedale, since he worked on and off there for years, like many Haisla, in whatever work needed doing: processing halibut, shovelling pinks in the cannery, loading ice.

You wouldn't know it now, but Butedale was once one of the largest canneries on the coast, with its own small hydroelectric generating plant. The turbines and the concrete slab that was poured for them are about the only things still working. Everything else slid into the bay or remains temporarily perched on the edge of Princess Royal Island, looking out over the channel of that name. The packing house, the ice house, the herring oil reduction plant and tanks, the general store and school have mostly fallen into the sea or the skunk cabbage swamp. All that is left of the cannery is a moss-covered dock on old pilings, which are too dangerous to even tie up to. Barn swallows nest under the crumbling pier, darting in and out of the cross ties. The old guesthouse has a substantial Sitka spruce growing out of the roof. A fire hydrant sticking out of a meadow of skunk cabbage is what remains of white-picketed managers' homes and gardens. The top manager's house is the only habitable structure for humans these days. The town of 400 people is now a western ghost town with a lone caretaker and his dog. Every scheme imaginable has been envisioned since Canadian Fishing Company pulled out in the 1950s. The cost of the cleanup in spiritual terms is infinite.

Little waders are poking around in the tidal flats. Rufous hummingbirds are bombing us as we wade up through the paths cut through the salmonberry. Cecil points to a patch of mature alder over by the creek. The Indian bunkhouses were just above the little creek that turns into a roaring torrent in the winter. They were the first to get washed out into the ocean. Each ethnic group – Chinese, Japanese and Indian – lived in different bunkhouses. The closer to the white manager's home, the higher the status. The Indians were always the farthest away, he says. They were the lowest on the totem pole, which is a joke on white people because the lowest figure is typically done by the best carver and is closest to the earth.

Frogs: The Indian Way of Teaching

One of my Elders took us out, close to Butedale. He got us into the right position for this canoe, then he took a paddle and hit the side of the canoe. There was this little creek that trickled out to the ocean, and when he banged on the canoe, the little creek got bigger. Everyone was in awe. We thought he was magic, but he is telling us, "I'm not. Okay. Pick your paddles up." We didn't go far, tide was falling, so he told us to anchor the canoe out so we don't have to drag it down. We went for a hike, and we went up to a little lake there. It was summertime and the outfall was just a little trickle. Went by the river. "Walk softly," he said, "and don't make noise." We went to this little lake. Then we make noise, frogs all jump in the water and it made the river come up. The lake was just full of them frogs and little things what we seen. He had to show us that for us to believe. The Indian way of teaching – visual, not behind a desk with a piece of paper and writing and don't know how to spell. Outdoors is our classroom – visual teaching. What a benefit it has done me, our Native way, and that method of teaching of the children of visual teaching. But that has gone now too. Now they are going to classroom, inside eight hours a day; our classroom was open 24 hours a day. Got to be there to see. How he would put it together, that bang would penetrate or echo up to the lake. I just came out from Alberni. I was 14, I guess. I left him later, I drink and never look back. He was my teacher. Too bad I didn't listen, eh?

There are lots of important Xenaksiala and Haisla stories about the perils of mistreating frogs. Death is the usual consequence of disrespecting nature. The story that belongs to the Hall family is about a girl who married a frog. It all takes place in a village on an island in the Kitlope River just upstream from where Cecil grew up. She was very respectful of the frogs, then one day she went missing. A year later, two handsome little boys turned up at their grandparents' bighouse, helping them before hopping back into the river. The grandparents recognized their grandchildren and celebrated with a feast. Contemporary Western attitudes are predominantly indifferent to amphibious relatives, some are ambivalent and a few – naturalists, scientists – hold them up as highly valued members of the Earth's family.

John Kelson is a Western scientist who holds them up as relatives. In 1992, he was helping Nanakila do a survey of the amphibians in the area. It turns out that Haisla territory is one of the few places in the world where amphibians don't appear to be dying out. There are scientific records for western toads from Kitimat to Kitlope. Ensatina salamanders are a strange anomaly because they were only known in southwestern BC until John collected an Ensatina in the Kitlope in 1992. The epicentre of the Pacific tailed frog population is around Kitimat. The Kitimat watershed provides a unique gathering place for amphibians because it marks a northern limit for some, like the Columbia spotted frog; a western limit for others, like the wood frog; and an eastern limit for still others, like the northwestern salamander. Currently, 64 per cent of frog and toad species in British Columbia are listed as species of concern. Even the western toad is experiencing sharp population declines in the south, both from habitat destruction and deadly fungal diseases brought in by humans. Not surprisingly, the Kitlope watershed is vitally important globally, not only because of the large unmodified area but because the frogs' remoteness provides less chance of the deadly fungal diseases being moved in by humans.

Interestingly, Enbridge Inc.'s submission to construct its Northern Gateway pipeline, stated that Canadian toad and northern leopard frogs also dwelt in the area, which seems counterintuitive for a pipeline company wanting access, since these two species don't occur anywhere within 500 kilometres. It is no wonder the Haisla's cross-examination of their biologists' findings was successful. The Western scientists were lacking in accuracy.[182]

KITIMAT RIVER, SEPTEMBER 21, 2016

Cecil and I are on a ramble through the mud and devil's club, along a trail he remembers used to lead to the old reserve and oolichan fishing camp of the Haisla on a sidestream of the Kitimat River. Eventually, we get stopped by a creek that has adopted the trail. Cecil hardly misses a beat and bends down to remove his shoes and wade through. The water runs almost clear over the pebbles. "Gee, that cool water sure feels nice on my feet," he says. I look down at his feet. I have never seen such a healthy pair on an 85-year-old man. We cross it, then sit down to put our shoes back on, and as we do Cecil notices his brothers moving around. Small, brown western toadlets on their migration out of their summer breeding grounds. The toadlets are perfectly camouflaged against the muddy, leaf-strewn bank. Their beautiful hands and small belly tapering down to long legs have the look of distant kin. We would never have noticed them from our lofty positions in the sky. Sitting down on the bank, they start to come into sharp focus. It unleashes a story from Cecil, a story that only a toadlet could unleash.

Baptism of Jail

After leaving Butedale the first time, I got on the Union Steamship Line. I learned later was called *Cardena*, the name of the passenger boat. There were three boats, *Catala* and *Chehalis*. They called it second class. Second-class Indians. We were put way down at the bottom of the boat. We experienced a lot of bad things. I lived in Rupert in the harbour, in summer at fishing time. They had a Canadian Fish Cannery right there, close to Cow Bay. It was what Butedale was too, Canadian Fish Company. I seen a war story movie is on, and I go into see it with Russell Ross. We went into this beautiful theatre, and we sat down and soon an usher came: "You're not supposed to sit here. Over there is where the Indians sit."

I asked, "Do we pay less than those that are entitled for this seat?" And I didn't move. Before the start, two big officers come. They took me away, didn't take my friend. I managed somehow to get in deeper trouble, maybe because I'm not going to move. That was our journey.

I stayed two nights in jail because I didn't want to leave a seat that belong to a different race and go to where the Indians sit. It was a baptism of jails after that; I come to know many in my life. And that jail hurt me more and maybe just as much as what Alberni done. It went beyond the walls of Alberni now. The segregation was outside; as I'm not free, I don't feel free as to where this Indian can move. For my journey for refusing to leave, I stayed two days in the Rupert jail. At times I'd stay awake, thinking how much of my life was behind bars. How much, how long did I stay? It wasn't that young girl's [usher's] fault; she was following orders, eh? For a while, I blamed her. Until I learned the little ladies were just following orders. I never did see that war movie; they took me out before the show started. I had a show in the jail cell.

In Rupert everywhere you go signs say *No Indians* except for the Grand Café, run by a Chinese guy, Mr. Chan. He served everyone there: Chinese, Japanese, Indian. I come in and ask him, "Can I work for you for a meal?" He says sure, and serves me a T-bone steak. Washed dishes for six hours for that T-bone steak. Always had a pack of cigarettes for me too. My tormentors put up signs that say *No Indians*. They are from far away. Mr. Chan is from far away and invites the Indian in. What is different in the mind of this person, who sees everyone as a human being?

I remember a platform that was going down towards a dock in Prince Rupert, and the place was called Cow Bay. I was going down a ramp and there was a little tap above me, and there was an elevator going up, and from that it was not far that the big ships come, and I was just waking up. During that night somebody opened the water and I was lying in the gutter... lying in water. I felt the vibration where I was lying, and I heard one person say, "Look at that drunken Indian." I heard footsteps disappear and managed to get the strength to get up. Why did them words stay with Wa'xaid? Why did them words stay – "You are a drunken Indian"? Dried myself off, looked for friends to go get drunk again, and hide the shame. I heard the words that I heard, not knowing what it meant. I didn't accept it, I guess, the pain was too thick to penetrate with words like that. I believe I was not sick enough to hear words like that. "Look at that drunken Indian."

I think the worst thing I seen was a young woman, and she was going to school in Lejac Residential School. It is closed. Just this side of Prince George to Vanderhoof. There is a Catholic school there called Lejac, and my wife would come with me when I go to meetings sometimes, and I went to one in Houston and there was a young girl in there who got talking to my wife and they really got along. My wife invited her to go have lunch with her, and she was telling my wife that when she "first was a lady and first had my period, they took me to the infirmary like a first aid station. Doctors came in, put me to sleep to take my tonsils out." Here they tied her tubes because she was an Indian. Fourteen years old, 15 – whenever the period starts – and she was crying when she tell my wife. "How many grandchildren do you have?" she asks. "I will never hold a child." That woman died sad. I went to her funeral. I cried. I cried for that lady. Longing for a child. Wicked people who do that. Catholic. When I heard that, I thought, what I went through was nothing compared to what that lady went through. How she survived. I admired her courage. Lot of other people get drunk, commit suicide, couldn't cope with what happened. Look at that drunken Indian lying in the gutter. I was there. I was in the gutter. When you mentioned Cow Bay, I try to remember… a bunch of boats there tied up, notice a tap, and I was lying on that thing and somebody put the water over me. I was passed out. Lucky I didn't drown.

I got a teaching from the Kitlope that stuck with me. One day, a killer whale was trying to get back to his house and he gets sucked up by the tide, gets stranded. I was from the Killer Whale Clan. There is a grizzly bear by him and a bunch of wolves also nearby. The grizzly was protecting the killer whale from the wolves. One from the ocean and one is from the land and they trust each other. The grizzly was the protector of the killer whale, and I was from the Killer Whale Clan. The wolf was government, and the grizzly was my protector against the government. I thought about this teaching from the Kitlope, and it changed me inside. It helped me to understand what happened to Wa'xaid. I got all my teachings from the Kitlope.

In 1947, Cecil's uncle Guy Williams, Haida leader and Methodist minister Dr. Peter Kelly, and Chief William Scow (then president of the Native Brotherhood of BC) travelled to Ottawa on their own money, representing the "unaffiliated First Nations people of the province"[183] to speak to a Special Joint Committee of the House of Commons and Senate looking into revisions to the Indian Act. They came with optimism and brought arguments on bringing equity, whether it was residential schools, medical care, band membership and, as always, treaty rights. At that meeting, Peter Kelly spoke about segregation and used the example of Prince Rupert's movie theatre in which "the effect, psychologically, is damaging. Treatment such as that breeds an inferiority complex... They have been browbeaten to a point where they simply accept those things. I mean to say that personal dignity, somehow, can be just beaten down until it is broken down."[184] It may well have been Cecil's experience among others that precipitated Kelly using this example, or Haida member Jane Adams, daughter of the founder of the Native Brotherhood of BC, Alfred Adams, who was asked to move and refused. She wasn't jailed but expressed deep humiliation. The concerns raised by the BC delegates were ignored once again.

PRINCE RUPERT, MAY 25, 2017

Today, Cecil is showing me the sights of Prince Rupert. It isn't the usual tour that the cruise shippers get. We walk down to Cow Bay to the wharf where he nearly drowned in a pool of water. He told me they weren't allowed to drink in a bar so they had to swig it down out of sight. It is across from an old net loft, now called Eagle Bluff Bed & Breakfast, and tourists step cautiously across the worn, creosoted planks in bright white running shoes. We pop into the little dock store to buy lures, a tide table and a coffee, then lean over the rails as he points out the different seiners, gill netters and trawlers – boats that he worked on. He bumps into one of the Clifton family coming off a boat from Hartley Bay and they exchange news.

The families have traded seaweed for oolichan for 10,000 years. We wind up in the town to get lunch at the West End Café Chinese-Canadian Restaurant. It was his regular, and before we go in he tells me about Pansy, an old friend who waited tables for years. A blast of steamy air and clattering of plates hits us as we walk in. The West End hasn't changed too much since he fished out of here; the counter still has the same red swivel stools around it and the booths on the outside have matching red vinyl seats. The china still has the orange and brown checks around the rim and the customers seem immortal as well. We sit down in a booth, and a tiny woman comes bustling up with a big smile and says, "Cecil, coffee with three sugars right?" Her name is Angela; she is Pansy's sister. They catch up and I take a picture of them. Cecil gets a beef dip and I go for fish and chips. Cecil's fortune cookie says: "You will be united with old friends."

We are bolstered for more visits around the town. He points out the jail and the movie theatre where he was arrested for sitting in the white section. He hasn't been back. "I'll treat you to a movie," I say. We have a date and we'll take Louisa as well. The only show on is *King Arthur* in 3-D. None of us have ever been to a 3-D movie before, so we have a lot of fun with the glasses and getting the popcorn and pop. No one warned us we were about to see three hours of unrelenting warfare in 3-D. We should have suspected the plot was weak, as we were the only people in the cinema. Louisa and I hid behind our coats for most of it and Cecil just sat there smiling the whole time. He can't really see or hear what is going on, so every 20 minutes or so he would lean over and ask us if Sir George was dead yet. Didn't seem like there were too many survivors, but Cecil had a great time sitting in the theatre eating popcorn undisturbed.

They Fought So Well for Us

Guy Williams was married to my auntie, my father's sister. He and Dr. Peter Kelly worked together a lot with the Native Brotherhood. He and Guy, on the first trip to Ottawa, they had to use their own money. He told me himself: "Just us paid for that." Think of that, the urge to fight for his people; fought for us to be able to vote. Mothers of babies never received nothing until Guy and Dr. Kelly fought for those things, which other people got. They fought so well for us.

Two people had a vision, and they cut that vision off. Our community could have been self-sufficient with a small hydroelectricity. The government told Heber [Maitland], "You can't put a small dam back there." A second round came with a new leader of the Haisla Nation. Harry Amos [Gerald Amos's father] didn't believe the Indian agent. Harry went up the hill and said, "What do you see? When you have a chance go up above that waterfall on the left-hand side. Take a look at that valley. It is impossible to miss."

I said, "*Wii sii o 'tla*. That means 'go ahead and challenge it.'" That is all I said to my friend. "Challenge the Indian agent, challenge the government, challenge our people if you can't persuade them to put in the hydro-electric." We are going to try again. We could do it. If we could bring the people together and support 100 per cent, we could do it. We could have our own electricity.

The summer before Cecil was born, a group of Haida and Tsimshian fishers gathered around a fire, waiting out a storm on Langara Island. They were sheltered by their clinker-built rowboats pulled up on the beach as the storm set in. Salmon prices were so low and gas so high that these fishermen had abandoned motors and returned to hand trolling to make ends meet. Visiting them that night was a respected Haida Elder, lay minister for the Anglican Church and shopkeeper in Masset, Alfred Adams, Nangittlagadaa. Adams had been educated at the Ridley School for Boys in Metlakatla – William Duncan's dry Anglican community.

Adams was coming to the men with an idea he had picked up in Sitka, Alaska, the idea of a Native Brotherhood that would tackle "grievances that included requests for better schooling, for increased recognition of aboriginal rights in hunting, fishing, trapping and timber harvesting in off-reserve traditional lands, and for a meeting with Ottawa officials."[185] A Canadian Tsimshian man, Peter Simpson, who was also a Metlakatla man, had started the Alaska Native Brotherhood 20 years earlier.

The person who wrote up the story of that first meeting on the beach was Cecil's uncle, Guy Williams, who went on to become Canada's first Indigenous senator. He wrote in the newsletter of the Native Brotherhood, the *Native Voice*: "The men listened long into the night, no one noticing that the fire had gone completely out and the great rollers were still pounding the beaches heavily from the grey cloud wall at the edge of the world."[186] Williams spent most of his life as a fisherman and knew intimately the concerns of the coastal communities. He brought them to the ears of the politicians back in Ottawa.

> The efforts and the cause of a once noble race seemed altogether lost until one day a Haida chief and Tsimshian noblemen gathered together in the embers and coals of the fires of the beaten Allied Tribes of BC. Then was born the Native Brotherhood of BC. Now, after 17 years, this organization is recognized as the largest and most democratic Native organization in Canada and has continually strived for a change of status and for the betterment of existing conditions among the natives.[187]

The brotherhood (and the Native Sisterhood) has had powerful leadership over its nearly 90-year history and has grown out of its earlier efforts with the Allied Tribes of BC. The first leaders were thoughtful men educated in both cultures, like Rev. Peter Kelly of the Haida Nations, Chief Andy Paull (Xwechtáal) of the Squamish Nation and Chief William Scow (Gla-Whay-Agliss) of the Kwie-kwa-su-tineuk Nation. They sent delegation after delegation to Ottawa and were consistently ignored. They fought in so many ways for the betterment of the nations and were handsome in all ways by Haisla nuyem. Cecil also mentions Heber Maitland, whose contributions are legion. One of the many letters Maitland penned over the years is an example of his many contributions.

In 1978, Premier Bill Vander Zalm came up with a "solution to the problem of young Natives living in the slums of Vancouver": "Ship Indians to Reserve."[188] Mr. Vander Zalm was also the creator of an amusement park called "Fantasy Gardens." Here is part of Heber's response to that proposal:

> Unfortunately, Mr. Vander Zalm's quick and easy solution will change nothing for the Minister has been poorly advised and has mistaken cause and effect. Native people are not drawn to the city simply for "bright lights and excitement" that is casually insulting and shows a deep ignorance of Indians and conditions that afflict them...What draws Native people south is desperation, lack of opportunity and lack of hope...We have been asserting for a century now, that we cannot live on resources and lands set aside for us. In Kitamaat, for example, our reserves are scattered and absurdly small – it was submitted three quarters of a century ago, that they were too small and too poor a quality to support us besides our population has grown four times since then. To break out of the grip of poverty and unemployment, we need a number of things an Aboriginal Rights Settlement would provide...we need an economy that does not discriminate against the small producer in favour of Giant Corporations...If Mr. Vander Zalm is sincerely interested in solving the problems of the young Natives on welfare in Vancouver, he should encourage his colleagues to come to grips with conditions that drove them there in the first place.[189]

Maitland's voice stood out for political leaders that year and he was invited to present his ideas to the NDP caucus. His speech is still cited and is as relevant today as it was in 1978.

We are looked on as a cheap source of labour, and nothing more. We who are the true owners of this land are reduced to on-lookers while all around us this development is going on, making fortunes for the few investors while destroying the environment and our way of life…If you drove down from Terrace during the daylight hours, you will undoubtedly have observed what has happened to Kitimat Valley. In recent years, clear cutting has stripped the vegetation from the valley floor and from the sur-rounding hillsides. The result is serious erosion in some places. The consequences are inevitable – in the past several years we have had a number of floods that have played havoc with the salmon stocks of the river.[190]

Last Canoe

Talking about the last carved canoe, the last one that is Xenaksiala-built, is lying in the graveyard in Kemano. I tell Johnny Wilson, "I'm going to burn it, Brother."

He says, "No. Let's put it into the grave. Let Mother Nature look after it. Don't burn it; it has so much memories. Crab River is how far we go with this canoe to get the clams and the cockles. We go up to the Kitlope with it. We harvest the salmon and the mountain goat. The transporta-tion back and forth to Kitamaat. How many people would it take? Eight. It was a beautiful canoe."

One year I got lucky fishing and bought a little 5½ Evinrude. "John," I says, "let's try it. Okay." I cut the end off a beautiful canoe and spoiled it by putting the 5½ horsepower on there, but I look at him smiling: "No more paddling, John. We are getting modernized. From here to there, what took us a week, we got there in one day. "But now I pay the price, John. I don't get the paddling exercise anymore. 'Round the corner, the deer and bear will run away with our noise. Paddling allowed us near." So, there was good and bad from manual labour to a gas motor. If you ask me which one I like best, I'd say, at that time, the motor. So that is the story of the last Xenaksiala canoe.

Kitlope's cliffs are sheer, straight down to the water, so the only way out of the Kitlope is by boat or over the mountains to the interior on the grease trails. Canoes were an essential part of the culture. Cecil's uncle was one of the last canoe makers of the Kitlope. He never got to pass the skill on to his nephew. Just when Cecil would have been starting his training in earnest, he was taken away to school. That interruption of training, repeated in village after village, was one of the ways to kill the canoe culture. At the turn of the century, there were 10,000 canoes estimated on the coast,[191] but by 1950 most of them were rotting in the forest and few new ones were being made.

The other big factor, of course, was mechanization. Ole Evinrude, who invented the small outboard motor, was a Norwegian who knew fjords and the attraction of a motor. The outboards, which started at 1 and 2 HP, won hands-down over paddling, but the cost meant entering the cash economy. During the Depression, with low fish prices and high gas prices, paddles came back into their own. In 1954, the 5½ Evinrude CD model put the canoe into history with the price.

The final requirement for a vibrant canoe culture lies in the supply of huge western redcedars. A tree needs to be at least 500 years old and two metres in diameter at the butt before it is big enough to carve a canoe. Western redcedar was hard hit by industrial logging on the coast, especially in the last 50 years as the demand escalated. Their increasing scarcity has been a critical concern in places like Haida Gwaii, where cultural revitalization relies on enabling western redcedar to grow to the size and maturity required. The huge trees of the Kitlope were another critical factor in the decision to see the Kitlope protected from industrial logging. No trees, no canoes, no culture. One of the first projects of the Nanakila Institute was starting an offshoot organization, the Haisla Canoe Society, to build a canoe with the renaissance of canoe culture in 1986. They paddled it all the way to Haida Gwaii.

Grease Trails: Road for Trading

They had two grease trails for trading the oolichan: one behind Kemano and one from Kitlope River, Xesdu'wäx^w. Because there was a cannery way up there, people used to walk down and work in the cannery. And they'd bring smoked moose meat and mountain goat, and we'd exchange with grease. All the way up over the mountains. Our people call them *Aat'lä'sumx kalas*, road for trading. When the birth of the Native Brotherhood was happening, my grandfather – his name is Johnny Paul – he went all by himself. That river, once you pass a lake and then you go into Xesdu'wäx^w. That river is really swift. That trail begins there, and he walked over to attend the meeting of Native Brotherhood. And he was the last one to walk over that way. All by himself.

The decision by Johnny Paul to walk to a Native Brotherhood meeting sometime in the '30s over the *Xesdu'wäxw* (Huschduwaschdu) grease trail is just one of hundreds of journeys taken by different members of the brotherhood scattered over a huge province with few modern transportation routes then. To share their collective voice required a dedication that is hardly fathomable today.

The trail for Johnny Paul started at Kitlope Lake, enabling him to follow the northern side of the Lower Kitlope River and the smaller tributaries to the Gamsby River. He would have followed the Gamsby up for a couple of kilometres to Sam Hall's cabin, where there was a river crossing. From there, he skirted the southern flank of the mountain up the upper Kitlope, branched off at the Kapella River, then Tipso Creek to Kimsquit Lake, where canoes were left to travel up the lake. That was the first 50-kilometre leg for Johnny Paul, with a 1000-metre pass to ascend. From there it was another 50-kilometre leg to travel Surel Lake and down to the Eutsuk, Whitesail, Ootsa river/lake circuit, which can only be done by a multi-day canoe and portages, until you get to Wistaria reserve, where he crossed over the grassy prairie to François Lake. It was at least a week-long trip over very rugged country and difficult river crossings to make the meeting. The refusal by government to listen to the reasonable requests of the Native Brotherhood is another dismal chapter in the history of Canadian colonialism – a chapter that has not ended.

The grease trail Johnny Paul followed had been largely neglected since the 1890s. Prior to colonization, the trails formed a major transportation network – a web of trading routes leading from the half-dozen oolichan rivers of the coast to the interior. They were maintained by coastal traders moving oolichan oil east and interior traders moving obsidian, smoked moose, moose hides, sheep, goat horn, wool and furs west. The Kemano trail went over the pass to Tahtsa Lake, and the Kitlope also had a second trail that went south to the Nuxalk at Dean Inlet. The Kitlope families like the Pauls were trading just north of one of the five Nuxalk trails that Alex Mackenzie joined in July of 1793. He was travelling with a party of five Nuxalk families to Bella Coola. At that time, elaborate bridges crossed the rivers and villages marked stops along the way. Much of the trade focused on connecting to the Ulkatcho people of Anahim Lake who controlled one source of obsidian from Anahim Peak.

KOWESAS, OCTOBER 1, 2017

As we head past Kowesas, Cecil tells us that some of the students who were building the cabin there found a black stone tool. He wasn't sure if it was a basalt or obsidian, but it was one of the volcanic rocks. "Where did that rock came from?" he asked us. The students were from Montreal and had spent the week labouring on the cabin. They asked if they could go up to the lake on the last day, but the council couldn't afford the gas for them to go up. Cecil is still upset about it: "To see these young people who come from across Canada and I see the sweat in their brow, that is a big agreement. Why deny them to go up to the cathedral?"

Obsidian is a black volcanic glass that can be tooled into everything from microblades to multifaceted bifacial spear points. There are only a few places you can find obsidian in British Columbia, like Mackenzie Pass. It is an unparalleled material for producing sharp blades that are sharper and cleaner along their edge than even a modern razor blade. Obsidian is worked through percussion – striking chips off a core with an antler. They were used for everything from cleaning fish to delicate surgery. In the early 1990s, one of the first projects for the Nanakila Institute was the reopening of the lower sections of the grease trails by the Haisla youth.

KITAMAAT, SEPTEMBER 19, 2016

Cecil's room is filled with a cloud of smoke and I can just make out Cecil Jr., sitting on the bed, and Cecil Sr. in his chair watching a World Cup hockey game between Team Russia and Team North America. In the tiny room there is only one spot to sit – on the bed between the two men, where I face the screen of modern-day warriors. One team is wearing black and the other red, white and blue. I immediately assume the Russians are black. Cecil corrects me. I think he is having me on. The Cold War has been following Cecil around all his life. After all, it was the threat of the Russian invasions that gave social licence to this huge multinational company to tunnel into his family's mountain. "Who are you cheering for?" I ask. A pause and a smile: "Canada, of course."

I've come down to Kitimat from the Chilcotin plateau, following some of the modernized grease trails. Cecil calls the traders of grease "people from far away." When I was up in the Chilcotin, I met with my friend the local historian Sage Birchwater, to ask him about any stories he might have collected of oolichan trading partners from Kitimat or Kitlope. The Ulkatcho Elder Mack Squinas had left a story of Naganashas, a half-grizzly/half-supernatural being who revenged the killing by the Kitimat of his village by heading down to Kitimat and killing them all. Team Kitimat versus Team Ulkatcho, with Naganashas as team captain. Some things don't change.

EDINBURGH UNIVERSITY, JANUARY 27, 1983

My prof forwarded me the news release today on the establishment of the Alexander Mackenzie Grease Trail Management Committee, with a four-year budget to develop the heritage trail "used by Mackenzie on the first recorded crossing of the North American continent in 1793."[192] Parks Canada is suggesting I do a dissertation on the socio-economic feasibility of long-distance trails with the university's Tourism and Recreation Resource Unit. Scotland has created several long-distance trails and has developed methodologies for measuring their impacts. With tourism the number one industry now, Scotland is funding infrastructure to spread the money into regionally depressed areas. I have to say that it feels a little like business as usual in the colony, though – albeit a new angle on the "resource" – tourism and recreation. Alexander Mackenzie, Mackenzie clan of the Isle of Lewis, born in 1764, and a company man of the North West Co., was tough, but he didn't make the first recorded crossing. It all depends on the meaning of "recorded," I guess. Having spent last summer herding cattle with John Salinas from Nimpko Lake, I know John would shrug his shoulders at the news that one of the Chilcotin's 10,000-year-old trails was being named after a Scotsman who joined some of John's relatives one summer day to get over the mountains to the coast.

Wolf with One Paw

After the fishing season at Butedale, we'd go home and do some trapping and hand logging. See that right there, where my two fingers are missing, and it looks like a little ball? I was about 20. Crosby Smith, my cousin, went with me to the Kitlope to go hunting in the estuary. The geese were maybe 200 yards away. We had our raingear on in the fall time. The tidal grass is flattened down, and when the tide goes out you lay down the same way. I had a good gun. It had a pump action, and my grandfather gave me a little single shotgun when I was a little boy. I loved that gun and I took it. Then in the fall, the tidal grass was kind of slimy, slippery. With my raingear, I went down fast. I had that gun half-cocked so it was safe. It wasn't made like that to not fire, but I told him, "Crosby, run to your left."

I lost control of that little gun and it had enough weight and momentum to pull the trigger, and I am trying to push away, and I looked at what happened. Two of my fingers were shot off. I took my toque and covered my hand up and said, "I'm hurt bad, Brother."

From Kitlope to where I live in Kemano, we had a 5½ Evinrude on the canoe. I don't know how many hours it took. I remember I needed water: "Go underneath that waterfall and get me wet. I'm beginning to get tired." I don't remember reaching Kemano, but I woke up asking Crosby for a soft drink. Crosby got up and ran up there, up the highway, and finally stopped someone and they took me up to the first-aid station. Doctor took me with a helicopter to Prince Rupert. Went to this big guy, they say he carried me like a little baby. The only time I remember, they were wheeling me into the hospital. I was in there for nine months. The guy who worked on me was Dr. Mack. He was an air force doctor. He cut my hands to get them like that. He done a beautiful job. I still have movement; that is what I mean by "he did a wonderful job."

I had always had my hand in a pocket. This is the story of how I took it out. My little uncle, my dad's brother, Uncle Charlie Wilson, he gave me a c^x ux^wa (Choukwa) – you call it, a cleansing ceremony. He gathered the people, big chiefs in order: "I want to cleanse my nephew, my son. He had a bad accident. He hurt his right hand almost eight years ago. I am going to take his hand out for you, Haisla chiefs." He came and took out my hand and he lifted it up and showed it to the Haisla people. "Injured when he was young, and I now watch that he no longer should be ashamed. His new name is $k'uks$ g^xans $dlasiag^wmix$, Wolf with One Paw. Like my nephew, the wolf hid his paw." Wolf came and taught me that you could survive, so that is my other name $k'uks$ g^xans. Never had it in my pocket again after that. I tell that story sometimes. After the cleansing ceremony I was all right, 30 years as longshoreman.

When Cecil was brought, unconscious, by his cousin Crosby Smith onto Kemano's wharf in 1951, there was a full-blown paved road that went 20 kilometres up to the Kemano construction camp. Close on 2,500 single men and 44 families were living there to build the tunnel through Mount Dubose.[193] The road Crosby followed was built over Cecil's family's trapline and named Horetzky – after the surveyor – and continued on to Tahtsa Lake. Cecil was lucky Kemano had a helicopter, as he had probably lost enough blood to be close to dying when they flew him to the Prince Rupert Hospital. The chopper pilots were considered some of the most skilled in the world around mountain thermal winds. He was also lucky he got Dr. Mack.[194] He was a compassionate and skilled doctor, trained in the air force to handle war injuries, who reconstructed Cecil's badly mangled hand during a time when institutional discrimination was the norm.

It makes sense that Cecil was called Wolf with One Paw. Grey wolves on the coast are a unique breed, or haplotype, with a distinctive reddish hue to their coats and a mostly marine diet. The most common sighting of a wolf in the Kitlope is swimming in the water, either in rivers fishing for salmon, to rocky islets after seals or across channels after deer that regularly outswim them. Wolves caught in traps are known to chew off their trapped paw and adapt to a life with only one front paw. In the last 20 years, the wolves in the Great Bear Rainforest have become some of the most studied and secure populations of wolves on Earth. The Xenaksiala, their human relations, were less fortunate. After smallpox, the Wolf Clan died out, the names dying with the people.

CHIEF MATTHEWS BAY, MAY 23, 2015

In the sand bar at Kowesas, there are tracks of wolf, grizzly, marten, moose, mice, river otter, goose and a small shrew. It is a major highway. Right where we are walking is where West Fraser wanted to put another kind of highway to access the Kowesas timber. It is hard to imagine that a wildlife highway pushed out an industrial highway. Only the Haisla could win that one.

Cumshewa

We were in big Davis rafts in Aero in Cumshewa Inlet with my friend Art Pearson; there were three Pearson brothers from Queen Charlottes that I met up in Alberni. They cabled together big bundles in the boom. It was after the war. That was where I met my friend, the Frenchman, Albert Jacobs. I worked with him almost 30 years at Kitimat. He was a crane operator, big crane. Before that, he was an operator on Davis rafts at Cumshewa. I remember my superintendent, Panicky Bell. He fired me three times: "Don't let that ever happen again! Go on, get out of here! Go to work!"

The Pearson brothers from Haida Gwaii had been at Alberni with Cecil. Leonard Pearson was #133 and Art was #134. The missionary R.C. Scott mentions Art in his diaries as a boy with "upishness." Cumshewa Inlet was the name that the surveyor G.M. Dawson settled on after a period of unsuccessfully recording the Haida name of Hlḵ'inul. It is the inlet that lies between Moresby and Louise islands. The meaning of Cumshewa in Haida Gwaii is shrouded in mystery and might be related to one of the coastal names for "white man."[195] Cumshewa was the site of so many ships and companies grabbing sea otter furs, timber and gold that it makes a lot of contemporary sense.

When the Second World War hit, there was a big push on to find spruce for aeroplanes, hence the naming of the Crown corporation "Aero." The trees were so huge and numerous that the only railway ever built on Haida Gwaii was to haul timber from the camps to the inlet. After the war, Aero was bought out by the Powell River Company, who employed Cecil as a longshoreman to bundle logs into the Davis rafts – bundles of up to a million board feet of timber, 250 feet long, 60 feet wide and 30 feet deep.[196] G.G. Davis, a logger at Port Renfrew, designed this style of log boom in 1911. They were tied and secured through a system of weaving wire ropes though the logs, which made them resilient to stormy sea conditions. There aren't the trees anymore to make those kinds of Davis bundles, unless of course they open up places like the Kitlope.

CUMSHEWA, OCTOBER 16, 1982

I'm in Haida Gwaii with a friend and we decide to backpack along the coast trail that is accessible from Sandspit to Cumshewa Head. The forest has been pummelled. Not a single old tree is left on this headland after a century of logging. It isn't the Haida Gwaii of the tourist brochures, with towering spruce, totem poles and ancient cedar, that is down south in a few of the last watersheds. The north is more a thicket of young hemlock and alder that you can't penetrate.

Over the next few days we hike along the shoreline to the head and around the corner to Cumshewa Village. There are a few grave markers with salal sprouting out – all that is left of a huge thriving village. Aero down the shoreline doesn't look worth the long slog to get there. Any log sort, road or mine site is now alder healing the damage and covering the debris that was left. When we get back to Queen Charlotte City, we bump into Hibby Gren, an elderly man wandering the main street in his slippers and bathrobe. He has done a runner, so we take him back up the hill to the small community hospital. On the way, he tells us he worked at Aero and recounts one of the poems he made up to remember how to tie up a Davis raft with wire rope. It is called "Logger Splice Away Back When." His book of poems had just been published, so I bought a copy.

> Viv Williams, Art Holland and Panicky Bell,
> I logged with them as my poems tell,
> Logger splice here's how it goes,
> Tuck 1 and 2 and 3 and 4,
> Now No. 5 takes its first dive,
> Then No. 6 does its first trix,
> Followed again by No. 1,
> Continue like this and soon you're done.[197]

KITAMAAT, NOVEMBER 1, 2017

Cecil is telling me about Aero and Panicky Bell and I tell him about meeting Hibby Gren. Cecil doesn't remember Hibby, just his friend Albert Jacobs. Turns out Hibby died a few months after I saw him. The poem might be the only record of how they tied those logs. I've come to think of Cecil and Hibby as Davis rafts – bundles of rare, immense value resilient to every storm that came their way.

I Went Fishing Instead

Then there is the time I worked with the surveyors when they built that highway. They hired Albert Walker, Bill Starr and I. This was the river that changed. This was our base here. We brought the material up to the surveyors. They rented a canoe from Jimmy Henry, and I was in a canoe with Bill Starr. Bill had been in the war in Korea and just come home. Albert had a homemade riverboat. Two boats. We go all the way up to the Kitimat bridge. We go to Terrace. That was our base camp there for the surveyors. We got caught in a flood, so Bill and I walked out to get help and food to Lakelse where there was an old dirt road to Terrace. We got to Terrace and got drunk and forgot about the hungry camp. Then we remembered when we sobered up. Had to fly in an airdrop while we were hungover.

I am the only one alive now. Bill left first and then Albert.

August, we came down here and I met Crosby Smith. He asks me, "I am one man short to operate a drum on the seine boat."

I says, "I got a job."

He says, "What do you think I am offering? It is in your blood..." He says, "...fish. Ocean's in your blood, not the river."

He persuaded me. I went up, told the boss I was going to go fishing, He said, "I want you boys to consider coming with us on our next one in the Amazon River. We'll need two operators." I went fishing instead. Crazy.

I met one Amazon Native person when Ecotrust Canada, Ian Gill, gave me that award, and this big chief gave me a big fish scale. Gee, it was beautiful. He said you could wear it in ceremony. He says you could wear it any time you want. It had a red thing in the middle. They told me what it was, some kind of a jewel in the middle. Real pretty rock. Didn't know the history of it. Didn't know why I got it. I met the big chief. I still regret today that I went fishing; I could have seen the Amazon.

Kitimat to Terrace was once a 75-kilometre-long and ten-kilometre-wide glacial highway. The kilometre-high glacier ploughed a swath, then re-treated, leaving a highly productive floodplain through which the Kitimat River ran and trees grew. On May 7, 1952, federal Minister of Transport Lionel Chevrier stood up in Parliament to announce to Canadians a plan to construct a transit corridor to access the valley's "21 billion feet of accessible timber"[198] and move aluminum to the interior railway node of Terrace, where it could be dispersed across Canada. The railway came first and the highway quickly after. Cecil's job was servicing the surveyors who moved through the country by riverboat.

The flash flood of the Kitimat Valley that Cecil references was captured in a letter written by Milton Weber, superintendent and member of the management committee for Kitimat Construction, to Iona Campagnolo.

> In 1951 or 1952, a survey crew re: road or railroad and road went up the Kitimat Valley. At 9 PM the crew were bedded down in summer tents. Suddenly the temperatures of the atmosphere rose a great deal and in less than an hour the water in the river rose 19 feet or more. The crew in night attire took plotting charts etc and crawled up the trees to avoid being drowned. By morning the people at Kitimat Construction Camp observed gear and other material of the surveyors floating down the river.[199]

Cecil characteristically underplays the severity of the flood that he and Bill Starr, the Korean War veteran, ran into. They both had probably seen worse events. In provincial records, during the week of April 15, 1952, a spring runoff flooding event was recorded. Kemano's rainfall was reported at 115.8 mm in two days, while Prince Rupert had a record of 79.5 mm in 24 hours.[200] Press reports state that there were big floods and that Williams Creek, the wa'wais of Cecil's wife, Mae Williams, flooded

Lakelse Road, which Cecil eventually walked out on. Getting drunk while the surveyors sat in the trees is not something Cecil is that proud of. I think he would say that, for that particular incident, he didn't live up to his name of the good river.

KITAMAAT, SEPTEMBER 13, 2015

I'm looking at some of Cecil's awards and asking him questions about them. One of the awards that sits on his shelf next to a package of cigarettes is a crystal jaguar about the size of a baseball. On the base is inscribed "Hero of the Planet," from the Rainforest Action Network in San Francisco. When I pick it up, he says, "The Amazon people told me that if we lose this animal, we lose our culture." You don't get a lot more information than that about these awards from the recipient. He usually says, "I don't know why they gave it to me." The emphasis being on "me." He knows darn well why they gave it to the Haisla, because it was a big effort by lots of people.

Cecil prefers to be a handsome Haisla more than a hero of the Western world. I don't think too many people in the village know or care that a hero of the planet is striding in their midst. Every person who gives up a whole lot of money for a rainforest when they are dirt poor is a hero of the planet. What he likes about the award is that it reminds him that some people, all the way from the Amazon, got into the magic canoe. That is quite an achievement from Kitamaat Village, when getting a person to paddle with you from Kitimat can be a major challenge.

From the perspective of the Rainforest Action Network, Cecil Paul was an obvious figurehead for an organization that "preserves forests, protects climate and upholds human rights by challenging corporate power and systemic injustice through front line partnerships and strategic campaigns."[201] The Kitlope was one of the regions it helped on the "challenging corporate power" piece. Bruce Hill and Ian Gill both remember the gala evening at Golden Gate Park in 1994 when Cecil accepted his award, because they went with him. In Hill's words, "he was really reluctant to go." When Hill asked why, Cecil told him that he thought he was going to get stopped at the border because of his old gambling spree and jail sentence in Alaska. There weren't any problems at the border. Cecil met Indigenous leaders from Australia there, like Peter Yu, a Yaruwu leader, who later visited the Kitlope. It might have been Peter who gave Cecil the giant fish scale that was lost somewhere in the village – probably being overgrown by salmonberries.

174

Just about everything ends up in the rainforest, even the G'psgolox pole. The jaguar statue will end up there too. Someone might stumble on it in 500 years and wonder why a jaguar is buried in the rainforest when the only big cats in the Kitlope are cougars. But then again, what are the odds of humans and cougars surviving in 500 years? So here is the classic Cecil logic: If the world really wakes up to the idea of the magic canoe and we all pull together in the same direction, we can beat climate change and protect our forests. Then the Xenaksiala story of the magic canoe will offer a logical explanation of why a jaguar is sitting in a temperate rainforest. Knowing how long other Xenaksiala stories helped people survive, I am putting all my money on it. What other options do we have?

There I Met a Beautiful Girl

While I was fishing, that was when I met Cecelia's mom, Marguerite, at Butedale. That was an awful journey. Worked year-round in Butedale cannery, cold storage there. Halibut fishing was year-round. Not like it is now; you got a quota. None of our people worked in the cold storage. And I worked there for a while. And I worked in that reduction plant, preparing for the herring fishing. My first experience with segregation was our home plant, Butedale. We went by there the other day, you and me. When you experience something bad and somehow you think you'll heal, you cross where the dagger is put in your heart. I thought it was healed, I thought it would go, but each time I pass this place, it will hurt.

There I met a beautiful girl. Oh, she was beautiful. It was the second-most damaging part of my life concerning the colour of my skin, as an Indian. This young girl I fell in love with, she was not Indian. Marguerite's parents were both in the air force, and they homesteaded across from Butedale. I come, and ask Marguerite, "Can you walk with me?" And she never left her parents' side, and I walked away. Remember the theatre I talked about? Indians sit over there? I bleed inside for a long time.

We defied authority again in my life – a second time – that was really bad. When I defied authority and went underground, my journey again, has begun. Sneaking, I call it. My little girlfriend and I snuck around together, and they knew, there were eyes all over. Talked with the manager of the place, his name was Bill Malcolm, caretaker of the cannery where I worked. I was called in: "You have to leave." I had to go. It was in the month of October, and a boat was coming in the next day and I had to be on it. And Alcan had started, and they had vessels going into Kemano, and I know the boat was going to go there, the one I was on. I didn't go back to work; I went home. My brother Dan couldn't get a job too. And he says, "What are you going to do, Brother?"

I says, "I'm going to go home and trap for this winter. Springtime, we'll go looking for a job." Gee, that went well, trapping, he and I. My mum had a house here. We came out after New Year's and I told her, "I'm going to go. I'll be back in five years." Brother and I took off. Went to Rupert, sold half of our fur. Went to Vancouver. Auctioned it off. Got a lot of money. That was when my drinking really started. I didn't tell my mum why I left Butedale until when I came back after five years. I made her promise: "Don't you tell anybody. Just you and me know that you have a granddaughter, five years old now, and we don't know where she is."

SURREY, JANUARY 17, 2017

Marguerite Demers Wood and I have agreed to meet close to her home in Surrey at the White Spot. I get there early but still have a problem finding a table as it is packed with people fleeing an icy day outside. Marguerite comes into the restaurant and I easily recognize her. Cecelia has some of her features, voice and hearty laugh. I know it is going to be a difficult conversation, but I understand from the start that she is used to difficult conversations.

One of the few attractions at Butedale for Wa'xaid was a young woman, Marguerite Demers. After the Second World War, Marguerite's parents, Dorothy (Dot) and Paul Demers, had run a fish camp at Crab River in Gardner Canal and met many of the Kitlope families who stopped in to sell fish or buy gas and ice. The Paul family was one of them. When I spoke with Marguerite on January 17, 2017, she recalled, "Johnnie [Paul, Wa'xaid's grandfather] would come in, while Mom was working and Dad was out on the fish boat, and he would tell her stories about the Kitlope. It is too bad she isn't alive to ask her. It was that connection that probably led to Wa'xaid coming over to visit."

Marguerite's parents had both been cooks in the air force during the war. Her father had come out to Coal Harbour. After being discharged, they decided to make their way fishing on the coast. According to Marguerite, "My father knew nothing about fishing." She was born in 1947 and grew up first at Crab River and later at Marmot Cove, where her parents homesteaded in a bay across the channel from Butedale – 3.5 miles south. Her childhood became increasingly difficult. Her father had gone through a war and a family before his current one and he began drinking. He had trained as a lightweight spar boxer.

MARMOT COVE, MAY 9, 2017

Marmot Cove is a natural kind of place to pull out along the main channel, with an estuary, tidal flat and an island that is about ten metres off the bay forming a perfect little sheltered pullout. There are signs of a huge midden, historic ruins of a boathouse, old pilings, a boat ramp and a shed, perhaps a house – it's very difficult to determine as it is all just rotting timber covered in moss. I found a chipped china mug and lots of broken glass among the industrial debris. There is an old village site on a bench up behind the ruined boathouse. The spruce and cedar are in prime growing sites and already have the stature of old growth. In a gnarled old western redcedar, in what looks like an animal hole, I pull out an old whisky bottle.

The most common friends who dropped by the Demerses' were the Haisla women, including Annie Paul, Wa'xaid's grandmother. As Marguerite told me, "She would sit there and laugh with Mom and drink her tea." Marguerite's best friends were Haisla girls Cecelia Grant and Liza Nyce. "They were daughters number 2 and 3." The Demerses had few other visitors, except occasional missionaries aboard the *Thomas Crosby* mission boat. Marguerite helped her father trap on his trapline and could hunt and fish like any boy: "I don't think my dad thought I was a girl until I had that baby."

Wa'xaid "fell into our lives as so many young people came and went. We had a 'thing' – very short-term." By this time, Paul Demers's addiction had spread to barbiturates. Marguerite was dealing with an increasingly traumatized father. During an event involving the RCMP and firearms, her mother had a breakdown and fled by rowboat with the children to Butedale to meet the *Thomas Crosby*, which took them to refuge in a Prince Rupert safe house – the Friendship House. When they returned to Marmot Cove, her father had had her two dogs put down. Then her best friend Cecelia Grant (after whom she named the baby) was killed in a car accident. That was the environment in which 15-year-old Marguerite became pregnant in the autumn of 1962. "The last time I saw Wa'xaid, I remember there was chum salmon still going up the creek." She thought he was heading back to Kitamaat for the winter. She never told him she was pregnant.

The delivery was not straightforward; her water broke, and she went into hard labour right away. Her father had attended the delivery of his previous children, so "I remember him rolling up his sleeves. He made

177

some disparaging remarks about Wa'xaid. I wasn't getting anywhere so they got an emergency airlift the next day. It was really touch and go. I can remember Mom being called in, crying and asking if I was going to make it. The ministry was there to get the baby and the signatures for adoption." It was a forceps delivery, which caused haemorrhaging. In the medical records for the adoption, it says it was a normal birth. She was allowed no visitors. The baby was put at the back of the nursery and covered from view, as she was not permitted to see her. "I think the nurse felt sorry for me because I came out of the anaesthetic and I heard this baby crying. When I glanced over the side, the nurse showed me a baby. She made eye contact with me and she stopped crying."

SURREY, JANUARY 17, 2017

It doesn't take long to see why many mothers have felt safe in Marguerite's hands as a doula. Her specialty has been high-risk births – "the very hard ones," she calls them. "I had a lot to contribute to these women because I know where they are coming from." She had survived nine lives with her father's traumatized behaviours: near drownings, shootings, grounding their fishboat on sandbanks and his attempts to burn down the house. Before training as a doula, she worked as a volunteer in many roles. She had no further children. After ten miscarriages, probably caused by the forceps birth, she gave up. She talks very candidly about her life after the delivery of the baby, when she herself spiralled down with alcohol.

Before her mother took the family away for good in August of 1963, Marguerite believes she saw Cecil at Butedale in front of the cold storage. "I just told him that he had a daughter and she was put up for adoption. My life was so piecemeal back then, because the family was in disruption, everything was crashing the year Cecelia was born...'63 – other than her – there was nothing good about it." Her memories of Cecil being told to leave Butedale are also vague. "I didn't care about anything." Her mother took her and her brother first back to Ottawa and then to Vancouver. Marguerite started drinking and didn't stop until friends helped her back onto her feet 18 months later. She never stopped looking for her daughter.

VANCOUVER ART GALLERY, JUNE 29, 2015

My first meeting with Cecelia is in downtown Vancouver, in the art gallery cafe. We can sit outside, it's not too noisy and the starlings are the only ones listening in. There is much of Cecil in her warm smile and intuition. I've seen pictures of her in Cecil's bedroom: receiving her name in

Kitamaat with her button blanket, and another when she becomes the first Indigenous school trustee in Langley. She has taken a lunch break from her job as cultural presenter with the Langley School District's Aboriginal Program to come and talk to me. Cecelia is one of the first of a list of people Cecil wants me to meet about the project. I begin with: Are you comfortable with having your story out there? With me helping your dad? Did you want to write something yourself? Cecelia is a busy woman, gifted in oration and teaching and happy to pass off the research and written part. The documents I collect will all be useful for her curriculum in teaching children about the genocide. She was raised the daughter of a United Church minister, so her gift is to share Cecil's and her own story, to dig into the ugliness and the beauty and the possibility for healing. If ever there was someone to tell the story, it should be Cecelia. We are almost the same age, we both raised two boys, we both care for Cecil and the earth, we both want to get the story told. That is a strong basis for beginning our friendship.

Eagle Chick

I showed you that eagle's nest coming down the Kitlope, just before you touch the salt water; do you remember that? That nest has been there since my mum was a little girl. Once the north wind came and they found a little eagle chick on the ground, and she took her earring and she put it around the talon of the eagle. The grandfather went and put the chick back on the nest with the earring on there. Few years later, my mum seen this eagle and she seen the earring glitter. That eagle came back, reproduced. It was the one that Grandfather had put that thing on. My mum said, "My granddaughter flew away from my nest... and she's going to come back the way that little one came back to her nest... to reproduce. We're going to see my granddaughter." And we kept that our secret all along. And I didn't know where my grief was. And then I drank some more, and I drank and I drank.

That child was put up for adoption to a minister in the United Church. He was just ordained, and they sent him to an Indian reserve outside Rupert called Port Simpson. I have a little younger sister, Louisa, that got married to a Tsimshian, Murray Smith, and that was where their home was when this new minister came. The young people befriended them, John and Sharon Cashore. After Cecelia was adopted, Sharon gave birth to twin boys. Murray would play with Cecelia while my sister helped Sharon with the twins. They didn't know Cecelia was her niece. How many years, I don't know.

Clara Thompson, Cecil's mother, was in the Eagle Clan. Bald eagles are as much a part of the Kitlope as the huge Sitka spruce root balls upon which they perch in full view of the M'iskusa village. They are always waiting for something to swim up the river and wash up on the beach. The eagles are ever-present relatives in the Kitlope, faithful to nest sites. Clara married Thomas Paul and they had 11 children before he died of TB at the age of 40. Clara was a mother through the worst era of federal residential school/ Indian hospital policy. She herself was not taken to residential school, but ten of her children were taken away to residential schools, one to Indian hospital. There are some tapes recorded of Clara Paul, which were used by linguist Emmon Bach to record the Xenaksiala language. They are part of the handful that exist of fluent traditional Xenaksiala speakers.

JOHN AND SHARON CASHORE

In the early 1960s, newly ordained United Church minister John Cashore was eager to start his ministerial career in a rural, Native community. He had completed his undergraduate degree with a major in anthropology at the University of British Columbia and then had gone on to do three years of theological training at Union College. The final requirement for his ordination was a year's fieldwork, for which he picked Prince Rupert. Part of the attraction there was Bob Elliott, a popular minister in the small coastal community. Among many other things, Elliott had set up a short-stay hostel in Prince Rupert called the Friendship House, which expanded into all types of support programs for the people needing services who were visiting Rupert, mostly among the Native community.

Elliott's work was born out of the terrible conditions leading up to the Rupert riots in 1958. That summer, police brutality toward the Native population had escalated and the Port Days turned into a riot, with over 1,000 people in the streets. It was the second time the Riot Act was read in Canadian history. Elliott sensitized Cashore to the awful conditions and racism in the community. With Elliott, he had visited and made friends in Lax Kw'alaams and various other Tsimshian communities, so when a posting came up at Lax Kw'alaams, John jumped at it. His new wife, Sharon Cashore, also shared his interests, and the couple moved into the village of around 1,200 people. Their warm manner quickly led to a friendship with Louisa and Murray Smith, who had two small children. The Smiths took John out fishing and hunting, as well as supporting Sharon through her first pregnancy. She brought the baby to term, but it died at a day old. They looked to foster a baby and that is when Cecelia entered their lives. The friendship with the Smiths strengthened as they moved through grief to the adoption of Cecelia. Cecelia was raised for the next three years, with an Auntie Louisa who was – unbeknownst to anyone – her real blood aunt. She was also raised a stone's throw from the foundations of the Crosby Girls' Home that was to have had such a role to play in why she was there in the first place.

Tulsequah: Getting the Shame Out of Us

That's when I went north after that. I worked in Tulsequah Mine. We had to go to Juneau. That is where the boundary line is, Canadian. I worked in the mine there with the Belgian wrestler; met him in the streets. Both broken. I lied when I said I worked on the mine; I worked in rock drilling but not a mine. The first cheque was 23 dollars; it gave me a tin of tobacco and rain gear. It's going to last me for three days, and we put $5 in, me and this Belgian wrestler, got in a blackjack game, my goodness we won. We won! Ah! $4,800. We split that. I think we quit, went to Juneau and spent one week in Juneau, then we got deported to Ketchikan, both broke. That was part of the healing, getting the shame out of us.

Forming a boundary (that could only be done by high-stake gamblers) between southeast Alaska and British Columbia are a line of ancient volcanoes. With all that heat and pressure, precious elements like copper, gold, lead, silver and zinc pooled in their molten seams. Where the Tulsequah enters the Taku River, these rich seams were first exposed to prospectors who staked Tulsequah Chief mine in 1925. The company Cominco started mining there in earnest in 1951, working the mine for six years before markets and seams dried up. The timing is such that Cecil must have been at the site just after it closed to full production. Hundreds of men would have moved the rock up from the ground and then to a processing site right on the banks of the Tulsequah. The ore was crushed and mixed with water and cyanide, creating acid tailing ponds that continue to pour into the Taku today. Salmon have also been pouring into the Taku since the ice age. There is a classic divide between those mining the river for gold and those for fish. Salmon is a renewable resource, but fry cannot survive even the smallest doses of arsenic in the waste water. It is a bad gamble to think that you can do both.

If Cecil jumped on a riverboat heading down the Taku, he could be in the frontier Alaskan town of Juneau within a day to gamble. Gambling has always been a serious activity of the Xenaksiala. One of the major games of chance is *lehal*, played with two pairs of small marked bones. Western forms of gambling are simple compared to the complexity of *lehal*. It is no wonder Cecil won. He is unbeatable in any game of cards. Gordon Robertson told Emmon Bach, the linguist, a story about a Haisla gambler in the old days who gambled so much that he had lost everything: "his own house and his canoe and winter food and his freedom and the freedom of his wife and children, and he lost his little finger."[202]

The resolution for the gambler is cleansing and strengthening with devil's club. "Nobody knew that the devil's club was a powerful medicine until the plant itself came alive."[203] The story goes that devil's club comes alive and asks the man what happened to him, and then the plant instructs the gambler to go and wash himself down and chew the bark to cleanse himself. It gave him the ability to see through his hands to the bones and he won everything back. Cecil followed the instructions to a tee. Everything came back to him, too, except his two missing fingers. The BC government was not so lucky with its gamble. The Tulsequah Chief toxic leaching continues to haunt politicians, and Alaskan First Nations continue to call on the province to clean the mess up over 60 years later.

KITIMAT MUSEUM AND ARCHIVES, JULY 15, 2015

Cecil and I are at the Kitimat Museum and Archives. I'm looking at archival material and Cecil listens to the digital recording of Xenaksiala storyteller Gordon Robertson telling the gambler story in his language. We sit side by side in the room that houses the new exhibit on the oolichan fishery. The curator, Louise Avery, is always pleased to see Cecil and asks him his reaction to the new oolichan exhibit. It includes a reconstruction of the nets, tools and wooden vat for the oil, as well as old bentwood boxes and cultural treasures. Cecil wanders over to the nets and starts telling us all the names of the tools and goes through the process of reducing the fish to oil, which I record on my little phone. Many of the artifacts are from the Kemano. He tells me that his family house in Kemano burnt down and they lost everything, all their wooden tools and boxes. The last wooden vat was built in the Kitlope. He told us the aluminum vats were a real bonus: they didn't rot. While listening to the tapes, he points out Gordon Robertson's reference to washing his eyes in the river with the devil's club to see things clearly.

Kay Boas: They Gave Him a Chance

I met the Oxford Group way before I returned to my little granny teaching me about the Great Spirit. Oxford Group, it was a teaching of Christianity and spirituality. You read the book, and they call it the bible. That's why they sent someone around the coast to teach Oxford Group and Christianity. As I understand it, Ebby T. went to the Oxford Group and took it to the AA [Alcoholic Anonymous]. That was with Bill W. Ebby was the one rescued from jail by Oxford Group who were Christian people. They were going to throw the key away of the jail. His mind was pickled, and the young men gave him a chance with Your Honour: "We'll see what we can do." And the judge had compassion. I remember thinking, "Is anyone still a member of the Oxford Group?" We were on a boat somewhere with Kay Boas. She was Oxford Group.

The Oxford Group has almost been forgotten among the salal and moss, but it had – and continues to have – a profound impact on the people of the coast. The story of its formation begins in a streetside church in Philadelphia in 1908, with a young social worker called Frank Buchman. He had started a hospice for young men off the streets with a garden allotment, when the church cut his budget. After resigning, he ended up at Oxford University, where he formed a spiritual group that aimed at fellowship with the goals of love, purity, honesty and unselfishness. The movement caught on all over the world and attracted men like Bill W. (William Griffith Wilson), Ebby T. (Ebby Thacher), Rowland H. (Rowland Hazard) and Dr. Bob S. (Robert Holbrook Smith), who went on to start Alcoholics Anonymous (AA) on the same principles. Ebby T. was a chronic drunk in Vermont and had been thrown into prison. Rowland H. (who had been taught by Carl Jung) and two other Oxford Group followers bailed him out. The rescued Ebby T. went on to save his childhood friend, Bill Wilson, through the Oxford Group tenets: "We admit we were licked. We got honest with ourselves. We talked it over with one another. We made amends to those who we had harmed."[204] Bill W. is the acknowledged founder of AA and a continuing influence on Cecil's healing.

The movement swept onto the coast of British Columbia like a winter storm in 1932, and by 1934 there were mass meetings in both Victoria and Vancouver. Even Dean C.S. Quainton of the Anglican Cathedral in Victoria was "preparing the way for the movement."[205] The rationale for its success was that it had become "psychologically difficult to live in meaningless chaos."[206] The First World War and the Depression had left their share of casualties compounded by addictions.

Two of the most colourful coastal members of the Oxford Group (it later became Moral Re-Armament) were Rollo and Kay Boas. Rollo Boas was the son of the "adopted" son of the German-American anthropologist Franz Boas, also "the father of anthropology." Between Franz's two progeny, the latter "child" has much more documentation. Boas senior spent much of his life on the west coast documenting coastal cultures and also collecting artifacts with his collaborator, George Hunt, for the West Coast Indian exhibit at the American Museum of Natural History in New York. Boas certainly had wide-ranging and paradoxical impacts on the Haisla, although, in fact, his ethnographic research never stretched all the way down Gardner Canal. He did no work in either Haisla or Xenaksiala territory, although he interviewed two Haisla people he met in Waglisla.[207] It was his grandson who was to have a deep and more personal impact on Cecil's life.

Rollo, born in Manitoba around 1909, trained as an Anglican vicar but was heavily influenced by the Oxford Group. He married Kay Harrington, a nurse, and the couple joined the Columbia Coast Mission in 1944, operating the mission boat *Rendezvous* for a decade along the central coast, based during the winter on Cortes Island. The Columbia Coast Mission was started in 1904 as the Anglican presence providing floating hospitals/missions that helped with births, deaths, marriages, dentistry, sickness, delivering mail, services and advice. The Boases, through the Oxford Group principles, promoted a spiritual path of healing that wasn't exclusively Christian. They accepted that healing could come through other spiritual traditions. This was almost as radical a Western idea as his father's observation that race was not a determiner of cultural or intellectual superiority. Kay Boas's path would undoubtedly have crossed with Cecil's as they moved up and down the coast during that decade. They weren't to cross again for another half-century. Strangely, the Cashores also had strong ties to Cortes Island, and that family spent summers on the same island as the Boas family.

MANSON'S LANDING, CORTES ISLAND, SEPTEMBER 11, 2004

The *Spirit of Enterprise* is anchored off Manson's Landing on Cortes Island. The first male harlequins have arrived in the bay; they are softly whistling. All of us aboard are looking forward to hearing Kay Boas's talk about her life with husband Rollo running *Rendezvous*, one of the Columbia mission boats up the coast. The guests have just travelled the routes the *Rendezvous* would have taken, like Butedale, Prince Rupert and Kemano. They are all eagerly assembled in the front lounge, waiting as she comes aboard with the other guests from Cortes.

Kay was born in 1906 in Saskatchewan,[208] but the spry and tiny woman who clambers up from the tenders and walks to the front of the lounge could pass for someone a half-century younger. The ship's windows are framing Whaletown, where her family was based after the war and later retired to. As she approaches the audience, she spots Cecil and they embrace. Not just for a moment, but for a very long time. Everyone is struck by the embrace of this tiny, white-haired woman with the tall, sturdy frame of Cecil. They look beatific and they are. All of us get the sense of a meeting of kindred spirits. She told of her work with alcoholics during her mission years. Kay told the crowd, "My last wish was to meet with someone from the Oxford Group again. You brought him here and we have found each other again." It is not clear to me whether this is a reunion of body or spirit.

KITAMAAT, JUNE 1, 2006

Cecil and I are sitting on a dock at the MK Marina in Kitamaat, waiting to leave for the Kitlope on the *Maple Leaf*. A seal surfaces and watches us with a huge chinook in its mouth. The salmon is so big that it makes the seal look like a mermaid. I am imagining how mermaids entered Western mythology. Speaking of legends, it is Kay's 100th birthday, so we decide to call her up. Kay is doing well and enjoying her birthday celebrations as the whole of Cortes Island celebrates with the woman that brought them their health clinic in 1944. Her news is that she has posed in the nude for an island calendar to raise money for the clinic this year. Cecil shares his news. His great-grandfather's pole, which was taken away 77 years ago, has arrived back on Canadian soil – that day – and is heading north to Kitamaat. Franz Boas might have appreciated the strange paradox in all this.

When I First Came Back

When I first came back to Kitamaat, I sat with the three hereditary chiefs to try and learn Haisla ways. I was told that there was an oolichan camp down one of the small tributaries of the Kitimat River. There was a small village and even a field. One of the Haisla Elders, Samson Ross, at oolichan time of year, would come long after they stopped coming here and sit here, and I asked him, "Why?"

He tells me, "I can still hear the sounds of the river, the laughter and the oolichan. So I come here to remember." Now the laughter has been killed, like the oolichan. They raped this valley. Two nations, Haisla and

Xenaksiala, were the richest in the country, with five rivers with oolichan in them. I have witnessed the death of a river.

Going up to Terrace, you'll see Williams Creek. My wife's grandfather's, that is her family trapline. And he had a place close to Hartley Bay, where they dig clams. That is his territory too. Fin Island. Mae, my wife, was a big daughter of a big chief. And I lived... when I think about my little grandson, he's actually going to live in my footprint. But when I met her, I was a chronic alcoholic. I stopped drinkin' a little bit, but I couldn't quit completely. Made bad things. Made bad decisions. And finally, we stayed together. Four children came into the world under Williams. Not Paul because we was just living together. When the last one came, Cecil Junior, she says, "Let's get married and give him your name."

I says, "Okay." Went to her father. Proposed to her.

He looked at me, he says, "No, my brother will give you away. My brother Fred."

We went to her aunt, her uncle, and they say, "Okay."

We got married with only a few friends. When I fully changed my life and seen different things, I look at her father, and the woman that I love and of how I treated her. Here is this big chief of the Haisla, dreaming that he'd walk down the aisle with his oldest daughter. And this drunk denied him that. I denied him. I hurt this good man. When he was dying of cancer, I went up to him and I apologized for what I'd done and what I see now. When I got through apologizing of why I'd thought he'd asked his brother to give his daughter away – too ashamed to give a beautiful daughter to a drunken man like me. And when I finished (I had all the children go out), he said, "You let the children in now, my son." He'd never called me that before, "my son." Was that his way of saying: "I forgive you"?

Cecil Paul returned to Kitamaat Village permanently around 1967. It was at this time he fell in love with Patricia (Mamie or Mae) Williams, the daughter of Charles and Sadie Williams, a high-ranking Haisla family. Alcohol was an ever-present fixture in Cecil's life at the time, as it was in Mae's. Their four children, born between 1967 and 1970, Rhoda, Maudie, Joyce and Cecil Jr., were all born to parents struggling with the disease. Cecil and Mae married after the birth of their three daughters. During this period, some of the most important leaders of the Haisla were still alive: Gordon and Laura Robinson, Samson Ross, Jeffrey Legaik and others. This was also the era of the Canadian centenary, unprecedented industry booster-ism with rising environmental problems to spin a good face on. As for the unparented survivors returning to the village from residential school, they were unprepared for more arrows coming their way.

That Must Be Me in the Whirlpool

I was one of the greatest liars on the streets of my little reservation. We thought we could find an easy way, a soft way. In our drinking, I feared no man. I could tackle anything and think I am right. And a lot of times, I was wrong in my stupidity. I prove I was right even though I am wrong... and that guy's wrong. Many of us have tried to hold onto our own ideas. That is why it took me so long on such a short little road.

A few months after I stop drinking, I was hurting so much inside I went down to the side of the river. And I went there and I sat down by myself. It was in the autumn. The river was up a bit. And I see driftwood drifting down. I see one special one. I seen it come down. And it stopped right beside me in a whirlpool. It was going round in circles. Some of the other driftwood float by me and go to quiet waters. I stared at that little twig and it was talking to me. That must be me, in the whirlpool, and the friends that had drifted by, who had never drank, were in quiet waters.

There is one recorded speech from Cecil's days as a speaker for AA. It was at the Alcoholics Anonymous Round Up in Vancouver in August of 1984. It is an hour long and contains versions of many of the stories of his life that he has shared. There are two stories that have only been heard by the dozens of people attending that summer event. Both stories speak to his first four difficult years of sobriety and the importance of his sponsor, whom he refers to as Big John. The whirlpool story was followed by another story about how he attempted to find a cedar with his uncle to carve into a canoe, but the first two he tested were rotten inside:

> I could not found a human being that I could tell and clean this filthy heart out to that exact nature of my wrong. And that was my life for four years. I looked all right from the outside, but I was filthy rotten in the inside, until I felled that third one. It was solid. I had journeyed down to the shoreline, went back to Kitimat and found my sponsor, I done my big step with another human being. It took me two fallen trees to understand, this tree is standing before you and it was so rotten inside, until I found that other human being. Made me feel beautiful.

Beaver Story: You're Bragging Too Much

One day, my wife said, "Dad is coming in. He looks mad." I called my uncle – my dad – Charlie Wilson. She says, "Oh, put the tea on, he'll get happy."

"Do you want some tea, Dad?" I ask him in my language. "*Lukala?*" It means "are you hurting inside?" "What is the matter?" And he got right to the topic of what he came in for.

"Yes, I am," he said. "After we're finished oolichan fishing, I want you to go see two of your brothers, Samuel and your brother Dan." My wife poured him a cup of tea; I had coffee. And he says, "Why I say this, is that I feel myself getting weak, and I haven't showed you kids our tribal territory in the Kitlope, the names of the different places. We'll be up there for two months."

Gee, I was excited. He had me worried when he said, "I'm getting weak; I won't be able to walk far." The next day, I gathered my two brothers. Called 'em for supper and told 'em what our dad said, and amazed that they both agreed.

We left Kemano. We stop here, stop there, him telling us our names. White man name, our name all the way up. Went to Matthews Bay, Kowesas. He told us the name of the chief that owns it, then the first little river when you're going to Kemano, on the chart, it is called Wolf Creek. "We're going to trap and shoot beaver," he says, "to pay for my gas," while he's teaching us our tribal territory.

Everybody put their catch in Kowesas that night – our first hunting as the four of us. I was the only one that got a beaver, a beautiful medium-sized beaver. And I bragged to my younger brother Dan and the one younger-than-me brother Sam what a good shot I was. "What are you guys doing?" I says.

Next day, we had to travel, and my uncle took me away from my two brothers: "*Mii'łä suu xʷenoxʷ*". You are wrong, my son. You are bragging too much to your brothers. Do you think you are way up there? Such a good shot? Got to correct yourself." I never bragged to anyone again. After that month and a half, we got to the pool where I was born. The main camp house was still there. "*Gin tsaquai'lii*. How much did you get? We got 52 pelts. Did you hear what I was saying about bragging? Out of that 52, only the first one you got – no more – and the rest were all caught by the others." What a beautiful teaching. It didn't hurt me. He noticed every action; he watched his nephews.

Charlie Wilson was Cecil's uncle and – with the early death of Tom Paul, his father – was known to him as Dad. Charlie Wilson died in 1980, so those three months when he took his nephews into the Kitlope were probably in the early 1970s when Cecil first stopped drinking.

The bragging beaver story is a waterfall of stories, each one cascading over the other. One of the big clans of the Xenaksiala is the Beaver. There are obvious attractions of this animal: like their thick fur in a cold land; or that their tender meat is available all year round; or that the large incisor teeth make fine carving tools. A Xenaksiala man, the late James Robertson, told the story of the origin of the Beaver Clan. The story must be millennia old, as it is set in a treeless time, before the arrival of western redcedar on the coast, when paths run everywhere, even the length of Gardner Canal because they had no canoes. The story involves a man who came upon a redcedar that revealed its qualities, and his wife, Qulun, a Xenaksiala woman who takes the form of the first beaver to help shape the first canoe. *Qulun* is the word for beaver.

Genetic testing of northern populations of western redcedar suggest that 6,000 years ago the tree started migrating – or being moved as seed by people – from southern refugia in the Washington/Oregon area.[209] Pollen grains from these trees turn up in the mud bottoms of northern lakes in increasing densities from 5,000 years on. Not surprisingly, this corresponds with Haisla science and the archaeological evidence of canoe cultures.

The genetics of beaver also tell a story. The coastal subspecies of beaver, *Castor canadensis belugae*, isolated by the ice from their continental brethren, have been found from Cook Inlet in Alaska all the way along the coastal mainland islands of BC to Dean Inlet. In these ocean environments, they are more marine mammals than terrestrial. Beavers swim across channels and out to islands at the drop of a tail. In the big gravelly estuaries, the local beavers have become specialists in turning brackish sloughs into wetlands that turn into forests. In ecological terms, beaver are a keystone species – named after the keystone of an arch in a bridge without which the bridge collapses. In the Kitlope, the idea of beaver as a keystone species is easy to grasp. Everything from salmon to Wa'xaid relies on beaver. Typically, soil and mud only have one destination – downwards to the sea – without a barricade or roots to hold them. Once barricaded by a beaver's dam, the willow quickly establish, and then the soil builds to the point that the redcedars can root themselves, often around marooned driftwood. Once growing, a cedar has a mere 300 years before it can be carved into a canoe – using the teeth of beaver. If any being should brag about their superlative talents, it probably should be a beaver. Bragging, though, just doesn't get the bad press it should. Braggadocios exist everywhere in contemporary Western culture but rarely in the Kitlope. Those that are turn to stone – but that is another story.

KITLOPE RIVER, JUNE 4, 2006

We are all sitting around the fire circle at Cecil's cabin on the river. He is telling a story about his beaver trapping days. With each beaver he caught, he would tie it around his waist and continue up the trapline. A beaver can weigh up to 20 kilos and sometimes he would have 100 kilos around his waist. At night, he would cut off a fatty tail and throw it on the fire to cook and eat. The old stories cover the gamut of old sexual problems. Infidelity is a subject of another beaver story. The first young canoe maker, husband of Qulun, was good at making canoes but not good at getting food, so she left him for a better hunter. The lover's canoe fell apart, so she returned to her husband. On her return journey, she climbed over the cliff near Kemano, leaving a sign of her passage – a bare patch shaped like a beaver's tail. You can still see that patch today, and it gives you pause to reflect on the fleeting quality and practical disadvantages of infidelity. I think that is the idea; stories start another story and so the evening progresses, a constant weave of ancient resolutions of present-day problems.

KITIMAT, SEPTEMBER 21, 2016

Cecil Jr. told me as I walked in today, "We had a very important visitor today, a really big wig." I always fall for the tricks. It was a beaver that trundled by.

The Goose Story: Only Take One

We started out at Kowesas. We walk up the river. There was a triangle of small little trees, almost like a house. Dad [Charlie Wilson] tell us this history, and I heard it from Sam Hall too, that they see that thing [prospecting survey mark] sitting on the banks of the river. Americans finding gold up at Kowesas, and every one of them died. They just figured someone mentioned gold. Only one miner left after they killed one another. Someone else must have told another person, and that guy went and killed him too. I often think it might have been Knutson. Do you know about Knutson? He used to live in Butedale. I met Knutson up there when I was young boy and up in Kemano. How did one man winter there? Because it used to freeze up, and he stayed in Kowesas all winter long. Something about Knutson baffles me. Was he a Swede? Tough old guy. He was a prospector.

Anyway, when we got to Kowesas where the geese make their nests in the stumps along the river. Grandfather had once told Dad [Charlie] and his brother, "Only take one." He knew that the geese only produce two eggs, and he told the boys, "Take one." But no, they didn't listen. They take two eggs and the geese – Mom and Dad – attacked Dad and his brother. Grandfather came to them and asked, "How many did you take from that one nest?"

Dad says, "Two from that nest."

Grandfather says, "Go take it back right now. Go take it back." His voice was commanding, eh? Not right with these boys disobeying his teaching. His voice comes up: "When you take the one egg back the geese will settle down." They did. After that I never eat eggs. That was the first egg I had in a long time. That is why I held it. I think of that memory.

GARDNER CANAL, SEPTEMBER 28, 2017

We are in Devastation Channel on Ron Smith's fishboat. It is dark, foggy and rainy. The Haisla are all sharing halibut and basketball stories, drinking coffee. Having set off at dawn, I've brought along a dozen boiled eggs for breakfast underway. Gerald's wife, Gail, has packed up a big batch of bannock and smoked salmon and sent it with her men. It is pretty clear the eggs are losing to the salmon. I asked them what was wrong with the eggs. That prompted the Goose story.

Godfrey Knutson is listed as a miner/prospector from Butedale in 1931.[210] That year, Knutson has claims listed as Bute and Bute No. 2, which he co-owned with Albert Lund and were opposite the Butedale cannery on the south side of Butedale Bay. No record of a Kowesas claim was found in the annual reports between 1906 and 1930, but Kemano River was claimed in 1906 by Mr. Darkin and Mr. Pocklington of Victoria for its copper and molybdenite, while Kiltuish Inlet was claimed in 1920 by James Hickey for gold. The altercation in the Kowesas appears to have gone unrecorded by the Ministry of Mines – not the first time in the rush for gold.

Mountain Goats: He Was Calling Home

That same trip, my two brothers and I were all skinning beaver. Someone say, "Hey, look at all the mountain goats up there!" We all stopped and look.

Yeah, there were nine mountain goats in the opening, and our teacher Uncle Charlie says, *"Yä'ga'lum ɫloos gaida nox*ʷ*aid noox*ʷ *k'aɫid."* He says, "Look! That's what you're going to use when you cook a feast up for me when I go to sleep." After he said that, everybody start skinning again. That story stayed with me, what he said.

I don't know how many years later – quite a few years – I called my two brothers back. My uncle Charlie was very sick then; he was in the hospital. I go and see him, and he was in the spirit world already. He reaches up, picks something, and he's chewing in his mouth. I ask, *"Ma'sii hum siks Dii?* What are you eating, Dad?"

He asked, "Don't you see? Don't you see all the berries?" He tells me we're up in the Kitlope. I sat with him for a couple of hours and then I left, and I called my two brothers.

"I think we should go get four mountain goats to prepare for his feast, for when he dies." Dan was working. Samuel didn't answer. So my good friend Johnny, Johnny Wilson, came.

I phoned Sister Louisa. Her boy Tom was strong; he was a big man. He says, "I'll go with you, Uncle."

My uncle Charlie had a trapline about halfway from here to Kemano called Geltuis – means long inlet – and we see a lot of mountain goats up high, but this must have been in November. The fog came down, and the teaching of what I'm trying to get at reminds me of the *T'ismista*, the hunter that didn't listen. We didn't go up the mountain. The tide was high, so high I put my boat underneath an overhanging branch and took a few branches so we could see out. Just when we were settled there, I opened one Thermos, and we were gonna have a coffee and Pow!...a shotgun noise. Nobody else but him and I.

My nephew look at me. I said, "I think we should go back. This is your grandpa's trapline. He's sending me a message, and I don't know what it is."

Went back to the boat and Johnny was there, and he says, "I think you guys should take off now. I'll follow. Stay on the shoreline. If you break down, if it is too rough, get in the little harbour and come out to meet me."

So we took off in my little boat. When I heard that shotgun, I asked, "What time did we hear that?"

Tom says, "10 after 10, Uncle, in the morning."

"Today the old pole has been set free. It is no longer in shackles." The G'psgolox pole, taken away in 1929, returned to its final resting place in the Kitlope. 2011. Courtesy Briony Penn.

Cecil Paul and Briony Penn aboard the *Maple Leaf*. 2015.
Courtesy Greg Shea.

Cecil Paul showing visitors a pictograph in the Kitlope. 2006.
Courtesy Maple Leaf Adventures.

Cecil Paul and guests at his Kitlope River cabin, with Briony Penn recording. 2006. Courtesy Maple Leaf Adventures.

"The largest tree in Kitimat." Cecil Paul in front of sesek'as, Sitka spruce. Kitimat River. 2016.
Courtesy Briony Penn.

"Never been touched
by industry."
Gardner Canal. 2015.
Courtesy Greg Shea.

"Aiis'dllams a 'sinx.
A new season the
Creator has given us."
Northern riceroot.
Kitlope estuary. 2015.
Courtesy Greg Shea.

"What's left of the fresh water in the universe?" Kitlope. 2015.
Courtesy Greg Shea.

"Big white magic canoe." The *Maple Leaf* in the Kitlope. 2015.
Courtesy Greg Shea.

"All of you who have left a footprint in the sand, I am glad."
Grizzly prints. Kitlope River. 2015. Courtesy Greg Shea.

"Frogs: the Indian way of teaching." Western toad. Kitlope. 2015. Courtesy Greg Shea.

"Kalikula, cottonwood. You've had enough." Tezwa River as it drains into Kitlope Lake. 2015. Courtesy Greg Shea.

"My grandfather would add devil's club that I would wash myself in."
Kitlope. 2015. Courtesy Greg Shea.

Gwä nax nood name from the Killer Whale Clan given to Thomas Paul,
Cecil's father. Gardner Canal. 2015. Courtesy Nick Sinclair.

Gwiiyms Moodzill, humpback, the name given to Cecil's daughter Maudie. Douglas Channel. 2015. Courtesy Greg Shea.

"The grizzly holds up everything." Cecil Paul in front of the G'psgolox pole replica (sea grizzly at the bottom). M'iskusa. 2006. Courtesy Kevin Smith.

"I could make man and machinery work in harmony." Cecil Paul at Hospital Beach, Kitimat, overlooking old Eurocan docks. 2016. Courtesy Briony Penn.

"He put his power saw away." Bruce and Ann Hill with Cecil Paul. Terrace. 2016. Courtesy Briony Penn.

Kitlope (Kitlup) River canned salmon label: Price's Cannery. c. 1890s.

"Salmon-eating Indians," in Reverend Price's report on the Kitlope to
the Society for the Propagation of the Gospel in Foreign Parts, 1892, *The
Mission Field*, vol. 37, p. 390.

Kitlope fisherman at Price's Cannery. Wakasu. c. 1890s. Robert Wilson Reford and Family Fonds, Album 3 – West Coast of British Columbia. Courtesy Library and Archives Canada, e007914233.

Wakasu waterfall with tourists in front. c. 1890s. Robert Wilson Reford and Family Fonds, Album 3 – West Coast of British Columbia. Courtesy Library and Archives Canada, e007914228.

"One day they will come back." Cecil Paul testing the oolichan fishery in Kemano River. 2008. Courtesy Paul family.

"Who is this person torturing us?" Cecil Paul at his brother Vincent Paul's gravestone, Fairview Cemetery. Prince Rupert. 2017. He was the only child to escape Alberni. Courtesy Briony Penn.

"Baptism of jail." Cecil Paul and Louisa Smith enjoying a movie at a Prince Rupert theatre, 70 years after he was arrested there for sitting in the white section. 2015. Courtesy Briony Penn.

"There I met a beautiful girl." Marmot Cove, near Butedale, home of Marguerite Demers when she met Cecil Paul. 2016. Courtesy Briony Penn.

"Butedale, beginning of a bad journey." The Indian dorms, long washed away by floods, were farthest away from the cannery. 2017. Courtesy Briony Penn.

"Survey markers, these ribbons are sharper than arrows." Cecil Paul's cabin site on the Kitlope River, where survey markers were tied to the western redcedars, kicking off the campaign to protect the Kitlope. 2017. Courtesy Briony Penn.

"Who were these mysterious gentlemen?" Brothers Abraham and Charles Paul's gravestone at Kemano. 2015. Courtesy Briony Penn.

"There are four speakers of our language left." Louisa Smith and Cecil Paul working on *Stories from the Magic Canoe* in Louisa's kitchen. 2017. Courtesy Briony Penn.

"I went fishing instead." North Pacific Cannery in Port Edward, out of which Cecil Paul fished. 2017. Courtesy Briony Penn.

"She is not my queen." Cecil Paul recycling Coke cans for Jess Housty's
library fund. 2017. Courtesy Briony Penn.

Cecil Paul at Kemano oolichan camp. 2008. Courtesy Cecil Paul Jr.

"My people never touch a grizzly bear." Kitlope. 2019. Courtesy Alex Harris, Raincoast Conservation Foundation.

Cecil Paul and his sister Vietta Wilson at Kemano oolichan camp. 2008.
Courtesy Cecil Paul Jr.

Cecil Paul and oolichan reduction vat. Kemano. 2017.
Courtesy Cecil Paul Jr.

Cecil Paul Jr. with college students. Kitlope. c. 1994. Courtesy Paul family.

"Take me from A to B with no shame." Cecil's sisters Louisa Smith and Vietta Wilson, with Cecil Paul Jr. and Thomas Paul Jr., Cecil Paul's grandson, in their herring punt. Kemano. 2008. Courtesy Paul family.

John (Johnny) Paul, Chief Humzeed, gravestone at Kemano. 2009. Courtesy Cecil Paul Jr.

"Take me from A to B with no shame." Three generations of Paul men at the Kemano oolichan camp. 2008. Courtesy Paul family.

Cecil Paul Jr. and Thomas Paul Jr. with Killer Whale Clan grave marker. Kemano. 2008. Courtesy Paul family.

"Wolf with one paw." Kemano. 2008. Courtesy Cecil Paul Jr.

Daughter Joyce, Rod Smith, Cecil, Cecil Jr., Thomas, and Cecil's sister
Vietta Wilson. Kemano 2008. Courtesy Paul family.

"Breaking the arrow." Cecil Paul with Methodist minister Dave Kinman
and his wife Kathy. Kitselas Canyon. 2017. Courtesy Briony Penn.

"Referendum: 98 per cent
said they would walk with
me." L to R: Ken Hall,
James Robertson, Cecil
Paul, Roy Henry Vickers.
Kitlope. 1993.
Courtesy Andy
MacKinnon.

"Eighty per cent industry,
20 per cent natural causes."
Eroding burial ground
with Billy Hall's grave.
Kemano. 1993.
Courtesy Andy
MacKinnon.

"Four chiefs: became leaders of our people to give them hope." Cecil Paul in regalia visiting Bella Coola. 1996. Courtesy Andy MacKinnon.

Tues., June 1

Ship dwarfed by majestic scenery.

Haisla elders welcome us to the Kitlope...

told us tales of destruction with deep respect, courtesy and gentleness...

Moist eyes!

We zip up the deep turquoise blue inlet,
Cabin and giant sitka spruce in the forest
Hot coffee
and more tales...
Lupine and cowparsnip meadow

Kemano
Totem pole measures destruction of beach...

A myriad of plastic flowers, moss-covered killer whale carving, a sewing machine and cooking pot

mark the mystical graves

"The world came – all these people coming to experience the uncharted waters of Kitlope." Cecil Paul is in the middle. Journal entry courtesy of Robert Bateman. Kitlope, 1993.

"The tree where our people tied the rope of our canoe around."
Flood marker. 1995. Courtesy Brian Falconer.

"Kemano Completion Project: What damage is going to come of it?" The Kemano pole with blinking eyes of the eagle and blank space to denote the impacts of industry. 1995. Courtesy Brian Falconer.

The pole carrying the name *Dla la xii la yewx* that was given to Thomas, Cecil Paul's grandson. 1995. Courtesy Brian Falconer.

"No more paddling, John, we are getting modernized." Cecil Paul and Johnny Wilson. c. 1992. Courtesy Brian Falconer.

"We are all children of the Great Spirit." Haisla kids from Rediscovery camp, Nanakila Institute. Kitlope Lake. 1993. Courtesy Brian Falconer.

"You're walking in my moccasins, the father of my child." Cecelia Cashore as a child with John Cashore in Port Simpson (Lax Kw'alaams). c. 1965. Courtesy Cashore family.

Cecelia Cashore meeting sister Maudie (centre) and Prince Rupert family. Aunt Louisa (holding baby) and Uncle Murray Smith (far right) and cousins. c. 1987. Courtesy Smith family.

"Welcome home ceremony." Cecelia receiving her name, Nuyem dzeets 'iksduqʷia, with her aunt, Louisa Smith, Amalaxa, and father, Cecil Paul, Wa'xaid. Kitamaat. 1995. Courtesy Cashore family.

"She's our child." Sharon Cashore, Cecelia Reekie, Cecil Paul, Marguerite Wood (Demers) and John Cashore. Vancouver. 1991.
Courtesy Cashore family.

"I felt so alone." Cecil Paul and the Elizabeth Long Memorial Home soccer team, Kitamaat Village. Cecil is third from the left in the back row. c. 1938. Photographer unknown.

Cousins (unbeknownst to anyone). L to R: Susan Smith, Cecelia Cashore and Tom Smith. Port Simpson, Lax Kw'alaams. 1964. Courtesy Cashore family.

"Last trip with Brian." Brian Falconer and Cecil Paul in the Kitlope. 2017. Courtesy Briony Penn.

"Eagle chick." M'iskusa. 2017. Courtesy Maple Leaf Adventures.

"A gift of the new season." Salmonberry flower. Kitlope River. 2017. Courtesy Maple Leaf Adventures.

"A daughter that flew away long ago." Cecil Paul in the Kitlope with his daughter Cecelia Reekie. 2017. Courtesy Brian Falconer.

"We've got to be in harmony and paddle together." Gerald Amos, John Cashore, Spencer Beebe and Cecil Paul. Kitlope. 1993. Courtesy Spencer B. Beebe.

"The sun is kissing the mountains good night." Kitlope. 2017. Courtesy Maple Leaf Adventures.

"It was a magical canoe because there was room for everyone who wanted to come into it to paddle together." Haisla youth in a canoe in the Kitlope. 2004. Courtesy Sam Beebe.

"A good person when the journey is rough." Charlie Shaw, Gerald Amos and Cecil Paul. c. 1991. Courtesy Spencer B. Beebe.

"With one of the Rockefeller brothers I go to see the white bear." David Rockefeller Jr. and Cecil Paul. Kitlope. c. 1993. Courtesy Spencer B. Beebe.

"Watchmen: caretakers of the Kitlope." Top, L to R: Gerald Amos, Kenny Hall, Cecil Paul Jr. Bottom, L to R: Cecil Paul, Louise Barbetti, Dan Paul, Louisa Smith. Kitamaat. 1994. Courtesy Spencer B. Beebe.

"Let us take it home, we'll give you the new one." Two G'psgolox poles, one old and one new. Museum of Ethnography, Stockholm, Sweden. 2006. Courtesy Spencer B. Beebe.

"Largest protected unlogged temperate rainforest left on the planet." Upper part of the Kitlope watershed, the Tezwa. 2009. Courtesy Sam Beebe.

"Five rivers of oolichan." Oolichan pole at Kemano with Cecil Paul. 1994. Courtesy Sam Beebe.

"The canoe was filling up. My Japanese brother." Elders, Ecotrust members, and representatives of other conservation foundations, such as David Suzuki. Kitamaat. 2006. Courtesy Spencer B. Beebe.

"Lots of emotion in my journey." Gerald Amos, John Cashore, Louisa Smith and Cecil Paul. Kitlope. 1993. Courtesy Spencer B. Beebe.

"Boston Men." L to R: Spencer B. Beebe, Cecil Paul, Gerald Amos, Bruce Hill, Yvon Chouinard. Terrace. 2012. Courtesy Sam Beebe.

"We were up against something so big. Then the guys brought in the scientists..." Forest ecologists Jim Pojar, Jerry Franklin and Paul Alaback. Kitlope. 1993. Courtesy Andy MacKinnon.

Thomas (Tom) Paul, Gwä
nax nood (Cecil's father).
Location unknown.
c. 1936.
Courtesy Paul family.

Clara Paul, Hay ˣwäks
(Cecil's mother).
Courtesy Paul family.

"I will walk with you." The Paul family. L to R: Maudie, Rhoda, Sophia (Rhoda's daughter), Cecil Jr., Mamie (Mae), Cecil Sr., Joyce. Kitimat. c. 1987. Courtesy Paul family.

"Annie, the queen of my family. Ninety-six years old when she died." Annie Paul, Wii'deałh. Location unknown. c. 1960s. Courtesy Paul family.

Cecil Paul and Roy Henry Vickers at Roy's house. Kispiox. 2018.
Courtesy Briony Penn

"When you bathe your eyes in the artery of Mother Earth that is so pure,
it will improve your vision to see things." Kitlope. 2017.
Courtesy Maple Leaf Adventures.

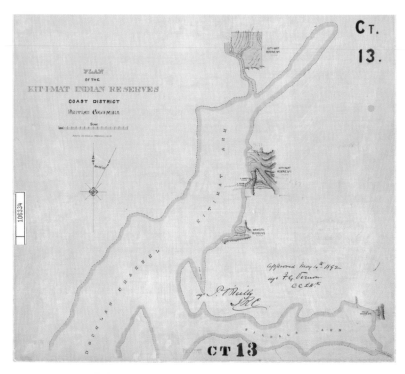

"What is this 35 acres of rocky soil? Concentration camp for the Haisla people?" Plan of the Kit-i-mat Indian Reserves, Coast District British Columbia, F.A. Devereux, 1891 – 1892. Surveyor General Division Vault, LTSABC. Plan 13 Tray IR-Coast, Indian Reserves.

"A gift that is free." Sophia Paul eating salmon and oolichan grease with her granddad, Cecil Paul. Wa'xaid's kitchen, Kitamaat. 2018. Courtesy Briony Penn.

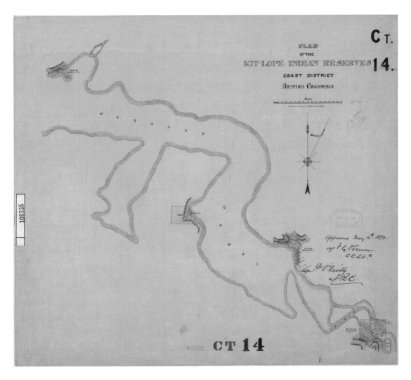

"Why are they putting this reserve there?" Plan of the Kitlope Indian Reserves, Coast District British Columbia, F.A. Devereux, 1891 – 1892. Surveyor General Division Vault, LTSABC. Plan 14 Tray IR-Coast, Indian Reserves.

"In the wilderness he keeps." Merv Wilkinson at Kitlope Lake. 1995. Courtesy Sherry Kirkvold.

Demers family ice and fish store at Crab River where Marguerite spent her early childhood and first met the Paul family. c. 1948.
Courtesy Marguerite Wood.

"The supertanker has no respect at all." *Save Our Shores* pamphlet, Kitimat Oil Coalition, 1977 (included Haisla Environmental Group). Iona Campagnolo Fonds 1972 – 1978, Northern BC Archives, UNBC Accession No. 2009.6.13.12.28-32.

April 29/4I. I have not written much of this sort of thing for a long time.
I feel I must begin again,for things are getting a bit involved.
This moring I read in Heb. IO::35 FF " Cast not away therefore
your confidence which hath great reward. For ye have heed of
patience after ye have done the will of God,that ye might
receive the promise.-------
         " Now the just shall live by faith: but if any man draw
         back,my soul shall have no pleasure in him.------
Heb. II: " now faith is the substance of things hoped for,the
         evidence of things not seen. ------
         32: " and what shall I say more----- for the time would
         fail me to tell of Gideon,et.al. who through faith
         subdued kingdoms, wrought righteousness etc etc . ---
         " out of weakness were made strong ".
I know God has not failed,but I may,and will, if I"hold not the
beginning of my confidence until the end"-- stedfast until the
end,it says.
This has been a trying time,but I cannot feel that a mistake has
been made in my coming here. I do seem to be out of place in
methods perhaps,and I shall have to overhaul them,and perhaps
revise them. But it must be in the spirit of faith,and in
confidence in the hopes I have had for this school and for this
people.
It looks to me as though my forerunner, Mr P. had done the best
job he could,but was forced to adopt a "play safe" method,and
while he did a good job perhaps in the field of education,so far
as class room work etc is concerned,still he left untouched the
real heart life of the people,and that is what is wrong,to my
mind.
This is evident by the fact that the little old church lies a
ruin on the River road: the people,many of them carry on Ha 'lal
games at every opportunity:The attendance at church at the school
is sporadic and unsatisfactory and can only mean that the people
are not interested: The young me are perhaps an exception to this.
Here again perhaps credit is due to the former school for these
young men are all graduates:However, they are "loose" and without
muchsense of responsibility:
They are perhaps becoming a problem in that they are so much at
and around the play grounds with our senior boys:
Within the school,upon the staff are those who do not seem to
have any vision of the end to which we ought to be working.Some
are fine and co-operative,but others are not wholly in that
category.
One staff member on the boys' side has got into a fight with one
of the senior boys. This is the crucial situation which I must
face-- but how? and from what standpoint?   words
It was as I faced this question that I came upon the #### with
which this sheet began: Sm I to be driven to hysterical,angry
action? -- or must I now,and always "hold fast the beginning
of my confidence,stedfast unto the end.?? I think this I must do.
In the Upper Room protion for today it says ///---
  " It is no easy matter --- .Our faith,our hope, our courage,
     are being daily and nightly subjected to terrific bombings.
     -- Imperceptibly,at first,but none the less surely,we feel the
     urge to break with an apparently losing cause. The "philosophy
     of escape lures us ----.
It has been helpful,and while the problems still remain to be
faced,and I seem to be alone, with no one to whom I can turn, st
                                                                  i
                                                                  1₁

"Who is this person torturing us?" R.C. Scott's journal entry while at
Alberni Indian Residential School, 1941. R.C. Scott Fonds, box 573, file 10.
Courtesy United Church of Canada, Pacific Mountain Region Archives.

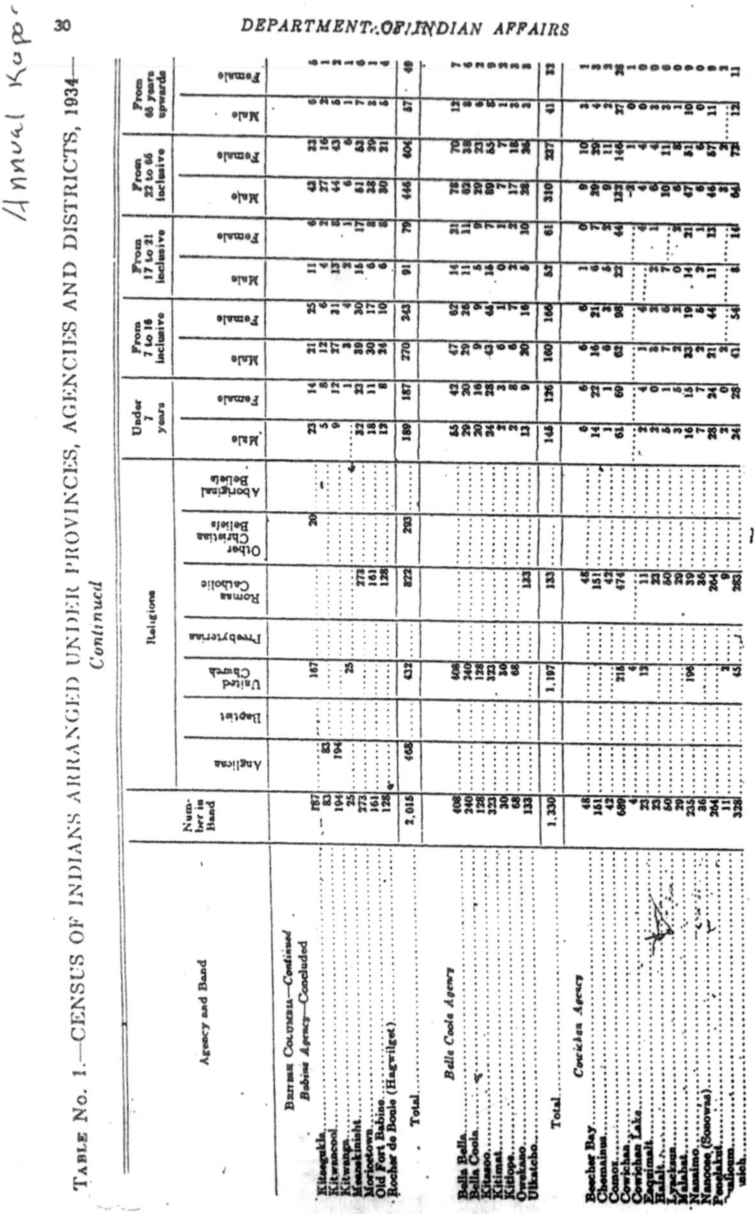

Annual Repo

TABLE No. 1.—CENSUS OF INDIANS ARRANGED UNDER PROVINCES, AGENCIES AND DISTRICTS, 1934—Continued

Agency and Band	Number in Band	Anglican	Baptist	United Church	Presbyterian	Roman Catholic	Other Christian Beliefs	Aboriginal Beliefs	Under 7 years Male	Under 7 years Female	From 7 to 16 Male	From 7 to 16 Female	From 17 to 21 Male	From 17 to 21 Female	From 22 to 65 Male	From 22 to 65 Female	From 65 years upwards Male	From 65 years upwards Female

BRITISH COLUMBIA—Continued
Babine Agency—Concluded

Kitsegukla
Kitwancool
Kitwanga
Moricetown
Old Fort Babine (Hagwilget)
Rocher de Boule (Hagwilget)

Total

Bella Coola Agency

Bella Bella
Bella Coola
Kimsquit
Kitasoo
Kitlope
Owekano
Ulkatcho

Total

Cowichan Agency

Becher Bay
Chemainus
Comiaken
Cowichan Lake
Esquimalt
Halalt
Koksilah
Malahat
Nanaimo
Nanoose (Sonowas)
Penelakut
uish.

"Hang onto this one." Table of Census of Indians arranged under Province, 1934, Department of Indian Affairs. Cecil kept this sheet of paper. He is one of the two boys under 7 for the Kitlope band.

242

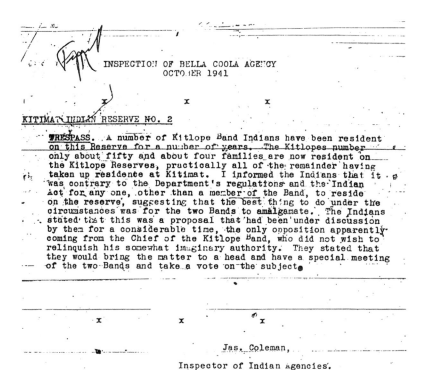

INSPECTION OF BELLA COOLA AGENCY
OCTOBER 1941

x   x   x

KITIMAT INDIAN RESERVE NO. 2

TRESPASS. A number of Kitlope Band Indians have been resident
on this Reserve for a number of years. The Kitlopes number
only about fifty and about four families are now resident on
the Kitlope Reserves, practically all of the remainder having
taken up residence at Kitimat. I informed the Indians that it
was contrary to the Department's regulations and the Indian
Act for any one, other than a member of the Band, to reside
on the reserve, suggesting that the best thing to do under the
circumstances was for the two Bands to amalgamate. The Indians
stated that this was a proposal that had been under discussion
by them for a considerable time, the only opposition apparently
coming from the Chief of the Kitlope Band, who did not wish to
relinquish his somewhat imaginary authority. They stated that
they would bring the matter to a head and have a special meeting
of the two Bands and take a vote on the subject.

x   x   x

Jas. Coleman,

Inspector of Indian Agencies.

The letter by the Inspector of Indian Agencies regarding "the imaginary authority" of the chief of the Kitlope during the amalgamation of the Kitimat and Kitlope bands, 1941. Department of Indian Affairs, RG 10, vol. 8213, file 972/1-1. Reproduced with the permission of Library and Archives Canada (2019).

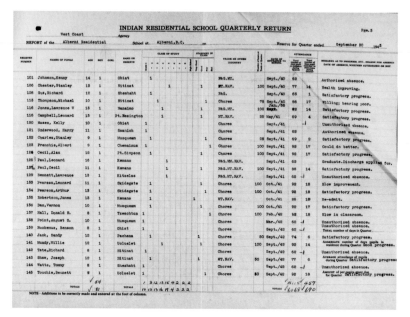

INDIAN RESIDENTIAL SCHOOL QUARTERLY RETURN Pge. 3

"The journey of hell begins." Cecil Paul is #126 in the Alberni Residential School Quarterly Return, September 30, 1943, p. 3. Department of Indian Affairs, RG 10, vol. 6432, file 877-2, pt. 1. Reproduced with the permission of Library and Archives Canada (2019).

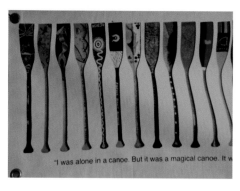

"I was alone in a canoe. But it was a magical canoe. It w

"The currents against it are very strong, but I believe we can reach that destination and this is the reason for our survival." Section of the Magic Canoe banner from the World Indigenous Network Conference. Darwin, Australia. 2013. Courtesy Briony Penn.

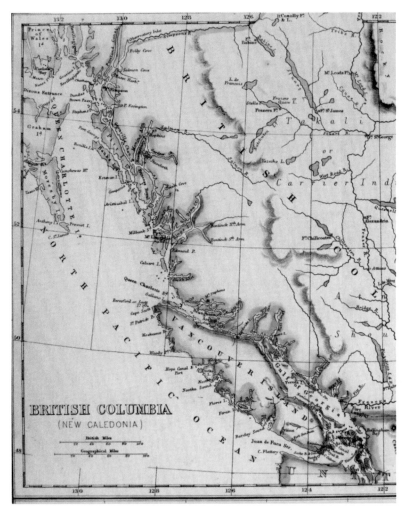

"They call it Gardner Canal." British Columbia (New Caledonia) Map, Edward Weller, 1858. Courtesy University of British Columbia Rare Books and Special Collections.

So many arrows came our way. Letter of Peter O'Reilly's Indian agent, 1890. Library and Archives Canada/Department of Indian Affairs and Northern Development Fonds/File 29858-5, vol. 6. Reproduced with the permission of Library and Archives Canada (2019).

"You must listen to your teachers." T'ismista, the Stone Hunter. Kitlope Lake. 1997. Courtesy Sherry Kirkvold.

"In my dream there will be a lot of people coming to help." L to R: Twyla Roscovitch (front), three unknown Maple Leaf guests, Heidi Krajewsky, Steven Anstee, Chris Genovali, Misty Macduffee, Brian Falconer and Sherry Kirkvold. Kowesas. 2001. Courtesy Sherry Kirkvold.

"I don't want to take away your bread and butter, but look what you are going to take away – our whole world." Cecil Paul and Murray and Louisa Smith. Prince Rupert. 2018. Courtesy Callum Gunn.

"Eighty-seven steps: forgiving the church." The United church is 87 steps from Cecil Paul's home. Kitamaat Village. 2017.
Courtesy Callum Gunn.

"LNG: it is still damage." "Visitors must Report" sign at old Eurocan site and home of LNG Canada. 2018. Courtesy Callum Gunn.

"Walk softly." Frog grave marker. Kitamaat. 2018. Courtesy Callum Gunn.

"Look at that drunken Indian." The Prince Rupert docks where Cecil nearly died. 2017. Courtesy Callum Gunn.

"Only take one." Goldeneye ducks nesting on the Kitlope. 2017.
Courtesy Maple Leaf Adventures.

"How are we going to conduct ourselves to share the beauty?"
Northern Harrier, Kitlope. 2017. Courtesy Maple Leaf Adventures.

"My little granny said, 'Look for the pole.'" The only photograph of the original G'psgolox pole before it was taken in 1929. M'iskusa. 1922. Frank Swannell Fonds, I-58649. Courtesy the Royal BC Museum and Archives.

"They fought so well for us." (L to R) Minister Iona Campagnolo, Hartley Bay Chief Johnny Clifton and Senator Guy Williams (Cecil's uncle). Location unknown. 1978. UNBC Accession no. 2009.6.13.49.1121. The Honorable Iona Campagnolo Fonds. Courtesy Northern BC Archives.

"The stem of the fern is the centre focus. You take one off and you start to see it lean to one side... That is how life is as an alcoholic." Licorice fern. Kitlope. 2019. Courtesy Greg Shea.

"The last canoe of the Kitlope." Kemano. 2019. Courtesy Alex Harris.

"Kitlope, people of the stone." Tsimshian name. 2019.
Courtesy Greg Shea.

"When you come to the Kitlope, you cannot help but change when you
leave." 2019. Courtesy Greg Shea.

"My cathedral." Ka'ous/Kitlope Lake. 2019. Courtesy Alex Harris, Raincoast Conservation Foundation.

Mamie Paul with two grandsons, both named Chris, Cecelia's son on the left and Maudie's son on the right. 1991. Courtesy Cecelia Reekie.

Bea and Johnny Wilson. Kitamaat. 2001. Courtesy Sherry Kirkvold.

"'Brownies' taken four years before Cecil arrived." Kathleen How Photo Album of Alberni Indian Residential School, 1936. Kathleen How Fonds, box P-35, file 6, item 13. Courtesy United Church of Canada, Pacific Mountain Region Archives.

We got to Kitamaat, just before dark – 3:30, 4 o'clock in the afternoon. Kitamaat at 10 o'clock they brought Charlie into the church for the funeral service. That's when we heard that shot. That was communication with my uncle to me – he was calling home. But we missed his funeral.

Mountain goats are extraordinary animals with the ability to endure the harshest of mountain winter conditions, scale cliffs along tiny ledges and survive on virtually any kind of plant food, including bark and lichens. Snowpack will drive them down to sea level in the winter, but come spring they'll retreat to safety from their many predators to alpine meadows close to their escape paths on the cliffs. Watching for goats at the Kitlope requires its own kind of stamina: holding a pair of binoculars up for hours to a tilted head as you scan the cliffs for the characteristic whitish-yellow dot against the black-grey granite. Goats are discernible from white dots of snow by the yellowish tinge, but only just. They shed their long guard hairs and thick under fur for a shorter summer coat. Picking up the wool from their trails was an important task for the weavers of the wool. Goats are a leftover from the Bering bridge, with their closest cousins being the goat-antelopes of the Himalayas and southeast Asia. British Columbia has half the world's population of mountain goats, and the Kitlope constitutes an important sanctuary for them.

KOWESAS, JUNE 3, 2006

Mountain goats are one of those strange animals that spill over the edge of the mountains down to the intertidal zone. Gardner Canal takes you deep into the heart of the province geographically but also elevationally. It is no wonder there are so many supernatural Xenaksiala animals that inhabit multiple dimensions. Today, we looked right into the eyes of a mountain goat browsing on a rocky patch of penstemon flowers at sea level. It was more typical of an alpine meadow than an intertidal zone. Cecil tells mountain goat stories and how they once dipped low in numbers but have come back. He also talks about running into marmots, flying squirrels and owls in unlikely places. Where there are so many animals to cross paths with in so many transformations, there is synchronicity. There are signs everywhere for every part of your life, if you have the time to look and make the connections.

I Could Make Man and Machinery Work in Harmony

We had worked in the booms with a Frenchman, Albert Jacobs, in the Queen Charlottes. He was operator. I worked here in Kitimat, and our boss said they were going to leave pretty soon. "Albert, you can come if you want, and you too, Cecil. Our next contract is in River's Inlet." But it was across the bay in Kitimat that they were starting a new boom. "Tomorrow, Albert's going to take half a day off and go apply for the job. Next day you go." Oh, we both got on.

I used to bring all the logs from Kemano. My job was a boom man. They towed all the way, hundred ton. They got it in a big boom. Put onto big trucks. I was a lead hand for I don't know how many years in the boom. The supervisor had to leave, and they asked if I could be a supervisor. They brought me to the head office. I told them I could work with man and machinery, but the other part, like what you do on writing, I couldn't do that. I had to decline to be the supervisor. Didn't go to school, but I could make man and machinery work in harmony.

I never experienced where they logged. I worked in the finishing part where they made paper. And my job was to fill the boats, come in and I load them up with pulp. They go all over the world. The Russians were really friendly. I was on the docks for 30 years. I don't know where that gift I got from Eurocan / West Fraser when I retired went – 31 years.

West Fraser are the ones that had the tree farm licence for the Kitlope. That's why when I seen those survey markers I talk to my wife. I said, "I might get fired if I fight for this. I am working for the one that has got such tree farm licence."

We talk for a while, and then she look at me and say, "I'll walk with you. Go ahead and fight for what you believe in." That came from the woman, from Mamie. That what makes me decide: Okay. The journey I have in the Kitlope decided by a woman that has said "I'll walk with you."

The logs Cecil loaded were mainly coming out of Kemano, Cecil's own wa'wais. Once the 100-tonne bundles got towed to the Kitimat dock, they were loaded onto trucks that drove the 75-kilometre highway he helped survey, then to the Skeena sawmills he laboured at. Finally, they were shipped down the railway line he helped build. There wasn't too much of the journey of those logs that didn't rely at some stage on the sweat equity of Cecil Paul. When Cecil worked for the Skeena mills, he met a young man called Bill Munro whom he made friends with. Munro was the person he recommended to take the supervisor position, which required the ability to read and write. His friendship with Bill Munro lasted a lifetime, and when they needed two old-growth cedars for the replica G'psgolox poles, Cecil went to his old friend, now high up in management at the Skeena mill, for two large redcedar logs.

When the Eurocan pulp mill started up in 1970, he moved to the docks loading pulp. He was there until his heart attack forced him to retire in 2001. He was never fired for his advocacy for the Kitlope. Nine years later, Eurocan closed with some very good assets to sell, a strategic dock at a deep-water port and a good chunk of real estate for the next extractive industry – LNG. Hank Ketcham, the owner of West Fraser/Eurocan, was Cecil's boss. Ketcham didn't recall that Cecil was his employee. "It was a long time ago," he apologized. Ketcham told me he remembered meeting with Cecil and Gerald Amos over the Kitlope deal.

> During the early 1990s, there was a lot of activism going on up and down the coast with regard to the environmental impact of logging, predominantly on the coast north and south but to a certain extent in the interior of British Columbia where we also had a mill. That was all going on as background to these particular discussions. We sat down with the company and said, "Look, can we run this company, fibre up our mills without the wood we have a right to harvest in the Kitlope?" So we spent some time thinking about it, following up on an investigation so that some of the things we were being told were actually correct. Collectively, we made the decision to relinquish our cutting rights in the Kitlope – an ecosystem that would remain in its natural state in perpetuity. That is the whole story from my point of view.[211]

Crab River: Is this My Mountain?

One hundred and fifty years ago, there was war amongst my people. They were raided for food and grease. The raiders slaughtered a young warrior's family, so he went for revenge. This young man couldn't believe that he survived what he went to do. It was a moonlit night, and he stopped the canoe and the canoe drifted alone. In the middle of the river, he stopped paddling and he looked, and he said, "Is this my mountain? Or am I dreaming?"

And then he heard the quietness of the evening and that little stream coming down. "You are home, my child. You are in *Xesdu'wäx*ʷ [Huchsduwachsdu]." And it is the first time he heard his homeland talk to him through the sounds of the river. He listened to the waterfall across the bay and this creek here. He could hear it all welcoming him back, and the breeze that you feel.

"Warm breeze," he said, "blows on my face. I am home, home to my mountain and I am alive."

Cecil is referring to the period over 150 years ago, when a germ war was being waged through smallpox. With so many dying during the summer of 1862, anyone left either starved or went looking for food. It is remarkable that any cultural knowledge survived the chaos. Cecil tells the story of the return of the young warrior to his home because it is the story that brought him back to his valley after a similar assault on culture – the residential schools and his struggle with alcohol. In that 150 years between smallpox and today, Crab River has been a saltery, a steamer stop, a logging camp and a fish camp, where Marguerite Demers, the mother of his child, was raised. What hasn't changed are the katabatic winds. The warm breeze he describes is a phenomenon of the inlet. Cold air spills down from the glaciated mountains and, because of its density, slides underneath the warmer, lighter air rising from the sun-baked mud and sea. One breeze follows the other in quick succession and the Creator indeed warms you with each alternate breath.

PART FOUR
Healing Journey, 1971 – 1994

Salmonberry and Riceroot:
A Gift of the New Season

Anyway, there was a journey of loneliness and stuff, and I wasn't well and I'm getting more sick with this disease of alcoholism. I try to remember the hell I was in then. I don't know if you've experienced loneliness. I knew I was sick, but I never knew where it come from. I didn't know where this illness started; I didn't know how to attack it. The thought of suicide, I remember this too, July. I remember this trip, when I go up there, somehow my drinking stopped a little bit, and I knew that something in the Kitlope – in my heart – was something there, and I go.

It was July 18, 1971. I was drifting down the river, a warm breeze would hit me, the next second it would be cold. I stopped my paddling and I drifted there. It was a breath of my Creator. I went to where I was born, and I pulled the canoe up and laid down and the words was coming: "You're in bondage; you're a prisoner." I got up and I walked around to where I remember having coffee with my dad, my granny, and this word keeps coming up: "You're in bondage to your drinking." This is now beginning to register, and I told this pickled mind that I'm here on a healing journey and the memory of my grandmother. And then the things she asked me, "What was it like in the nine years, what you remember in the Kitlope?" All the beautiful teachers, the peace I remember I had in my heart.

That memory of my little granny saying, "*Mä s'i sax ga süüs?* What do you want? What are you here for?" And I'm talking to her memory. I'm going crazy, I thought. And I sat down and told her of my journey, and the memories of her kept floating in this mind. After little Granny told me the story of that, I went to the estuary, and there's a flower, the salmonberry. I walked around.

She came to me and said, "Son, this one little flower in middle of June, it become a berry. When you take it and put it in your mouth it's sweet. It's a sugary taste." In the estuary there's a purple flower. I dug it up and she showed me the root of it. Here it was white as rice. Two flowers: the first one the Great Spirit gives us as a gift of the new season to feed our bodies; it's the spring, the salmonberry sugar. This one here's the wild riceroot. He feeds us under the ground. We take them and we combine it with the oolichan grease and we eat it together – *aiis'dllams a'sinx* – a new season the Creator has given us. All these teachings, our spirituality drowned out through all 40 years of trying to hide the pain. Hide the shame. Until I'd had enough...and I went home to the Kitlope.

I would go, especially at midnight when everything is quiet, around the lake. The four villages were guardians: the killer whale, beaver, eagle and raven [or five with salmon]. My grandmother tells me that they invite each other, and they laugh and they dance. I'm in this middle of the river and I'm the opposite – I'm not laughing, I'm not dancing. Why is that so? A quiet moment. It's so loud sometimes – stillness, opposite from how I feel. I think when I say these things that I crave so much about in my journey, since I managed to put the alcohol away was a touch of serenity, peace within.

Each journey I take I feel it will improve: the feeling of beauty, my eyes, my vision is clearing from alcohol, the sweat was almost pure, there was no poison coming out from my body, and I bathe in the artery of Mother Earth, cleansing me in a lake.

It was that one evening, as I was drifting down to where I was born and at my main camp, I sat there. I said, "Great Spirit, thank you for this land. Help me find myself, Great Spirit. Who am I? What is it you put before me? What is the destination of my life? Who am I?" I got in my boat, just before dark went back into the lake. I stayed there for two days.

I think now, when I look back, I think it was fasting because I had nothing to eat. I just reached over the side of my canoe and I drank the beautiful river water. I come out of there that day, for a moment during the evening, I was one with the universe, everything was fine, but I swear it didn't last more than a second. I had a touch of serenity in the Kitlope. I go back, I tell my wife what happened. I had the strangest experience, something came over me, and made me feel good.

When I look back on it, there was not a breath of wind, nothing, quiet. But something inside exploded. I remember I laughed out loud. I heard the echo; I'm not alone on this lake. I think the Great Spirit penetrated something, opened my eyes a little bit. I told Gerald that: him and I go. When you come to the Kitlope, I tell you, you cannot help but change when you leave. You change your thought; you change your feeling. I said, "It's a cathedral, Gerald. I think that's what changes."

He says, "Is only the lake the cathedral?"

I said, "I don't think so. I think the whole valley is a cathedral."

I began to sense that there's something here in the Kitlope. I could break the cycles of the life I'm going through, an ugly life. I called the journey a healing journey. My wife would say, "Where are you going?"

I'd say, "If I don't come back in ten days, I'll be up in the Kitlope."

She was saying, "You're on your healing journey?"

I'd say, "Yes."

She'd prepare things for me to go. She sensed a change, somebody had seen the change. She was a beautiful lady. Her father accepted me for who I was – "You could have my daughter."

Ethnographer Brian Compton spent 1988 to 1992 with Xenaksiala Elder Gordon Robertson (not to be confused with Haisla Elder Gordon Robinson), recording the rich relationship between Xenaksiala plants. There are many aspects of this relationship from which you can draw parallels to that between a child and a grandparent. Plants keep you company, they teach you of their uses, they feed you, their medicine heals your body, they hold the earth and feed the animals. One of the richest plants for stories is Indian riceroot, *xukʷm*, *Fritillaria camschatcensis*. Gordon Robertson recalled at least a dozen words and references for riceroot, including the name for the whole plant; the whole bulb, which is fleshy white and has little rice-like bulblets surrounding it (to the Xenaksiala the bulblets look like lice); just the bulblets; just the flowers; a verb to gather riceroot and another to eat it; and various names/stories that incorporate riceroot. The blooming of riceroot is as much an indicator of spring, or the rebirth of the year, to the enaksiala as daffodils are to the English and cherry blossoms are to the Japanese. They are harvested in April/May along with silverweed roots (another important member of the rose family) and mixed with oolichan grease. From a dietary perspective, the mixture of oolichan oil, riceroot and salmonberry is a perfect combination of vitamins, carbohydrates, omega oils and proteins, with all the amino acids represented. The body would be pretty receptive to this life-giving medicine flooding into it after a long cold winter – for Cecil, it was after years of an impoverished institutional diet.

The Xenaksiala traditionally celebrated the New Year with a flower dance. Gordon Robertson performed the dance around 1907 as a young child, taught by his grandfather's two sisters. The flowers of riceroot, salmonberry, Nootka rose and others in bloom were sewn into costumes and wreaths for the head. Robertson was given a ceremonial name based on the flowers and the place where they were gathered, now at the Kitlope River reserve. These names were given to children of promise in the village. Robertson was the last person to perform the dance.

Robertson's grandfather, Joshua Macdonald, shared his Kitlope teaching story of riceroot with his grandson, who in turn shared it with Brian Compton. As the story goes, a chief's daughter was digging riceroot near the Kitlope oolichan camp when a frog started jumping into the hole and interrupting her work. She threw the frog out, but he came back as a young man and took her to Frogland, where she had children. The longer version of the story suggests practical advice for harvesting the bulbs. To ensure the riceroot comes back each year, a digger must pause and leave some of the bulblets in the ground. Tending and aerating of the soil increases the productivity of the plant, as with any root crop. Protecting both the riceroot and frogs was part of the nuyem, traditional laws respecting all of nature.

All the species of *Rubus* – blackcaps, thimbleberries and salmonberries – are cultivated and harvested from the time they appear as shoots, which are picked, peeled and eaten like celery, to the harvesting of berries. Gordon Robertson recalled many words for salmonberry: the whole bush; berries in general; the dark, ruby-coloured berries, the golden berries and the regular salmon-egg-coloured berries; the young shoots; the verb to eat the young shoots; the star-shaped structure left behind when the berry is picked, which also means to tickle; to pick berries; to go off in a group to pick berries; the place where salmonberries are picked; the place where there are early shoots to pick; the Swainson's thrush whose song ripens the berries; and the small worm in salmonberries. The blossoms are full of vitamin C. There are many stories associated with salmonberries, but none more mysterious than the story of the Xenaksiala shaman Billy Hall, whose ceremonial name was salmonberry, or Gùlali. Billy Hall was able to ripen salmonberries out of season, but that is another story.

KITLOPE, MAY 15, 2017

We arrive at the Kitlope estuary with the migrating swallows – flashing white, iridescent green and blue-black. The chatter of excitement from them is infectious as barn, tree, violet-green and rough-winged swallows wheel and dive among their larger cousins, Vaux's swifts, all foraging over the water. It is a richness of swallows thicker than the emerging insects they are after, narrowly missing our heads as we make our way up the river. The wildflowers in the estuary are primed for pollinators: the bell-shaped heads of riceroot lilies with their checkerboard chocolate petals and yellow stamen; blousy magenta salmonberry flowers are bringing in the hummingbirds with their bright red throats; velvety, purple-blue lupins form a river themselves in which yellow and red bracts of paintbrush swim. The bumblebees are working the umbellifers of lacy white. Mourning cloaks and swallowtail butterflies carry the love from blossom to blossom. If this isn't a healing place then where is?

Wii sii o 'tla: *Don't Be Afraid to Speak*

They had an election with the young lady Iona Campagnolo. She was completely for the Eurocan expansion. She said that the water would be so good that you could drink a glass of fresh water after the expansion. I said, "Your Honour, let me have the honour of giving you the first glass of that water." Now there is no oolichans on the Kitimat. How far does the poison go into the riverbanks? How deep does it go? How many years will it take to purify the artery of the Mother Earth? They took away from us something so precious to our culture.

That day one of the Elders comes up to me and says, "*Wii sii o 'tla.* Don't be afraid to speak." He was telling me to have the courage to keep speaking out. They listened to industry before the Indian, and now Kitimat is still polluted. The almighty dollar.

Iona Campagnolo won the Skeena riding as a federal Liberal in 1974. Heber Maitland was the chief councillor of the Haisla during her years in office. There are newspaper accounts of the Haisla taking their concerns to the federal government through the '70s but no record of Cecil's request to Her Honour is in the public record. The only surviving letter from Haisla leadership found in Campagnolo's collection is dated May 18, 1978. It is addressed to her fellow minister the Hon. Hugh Faulkner and cc'd to her. Cecil was a band councillor at the time (the only time he served in a political capacity) under Maitland, before he stepped down that November for health reasons.[212] Cecil calls Heber Maitland "a beautiful leader – he thought about what was going to happen in 20 years time." Maitland's wife was married to Cecil's cousin, and Cecil's niece married Maitland's son. These are excerpts from Maitland's letter listing the historic concerns.

> The stability and direction that people normally find in their culture and traditions are seriously endangered in our society; our old ways have been scorned and even outlawed by Canadian society; our chiefs and elders have had their authority undermined; and instead an alien system incompatible with and often hostile to, our own ways, has been imposed on us....

The land and resource base will, we believe, enable us to maintain ourselves in some of our old occupations, re-establish ourselves in others now lost to us, and gain entry into a number of new ones. The most important of our traditional occupations covers our subsistence economy: the taking, processing, distribution and consumption of our native foods. This aspect of our way of life remains highly significant, both from a nutritional and a cultural standpoint. A study of traditional foodstuffs conducted last year at Kitimaat revealed that fishing and hunting and gathering continue to play a vital part in the diet and household economics of all elements of our society, no matter what age, occupation or social position. It is important to us that this way of life continue, yet it is under threat from a number of directions. In the past several years there has been a marked decline in the both the quantity and quality of some of the foods taken near Kitimaat. Industrial pollution, damage to habitat, severe competition from sportsmen and increasingly restrictive regulations combine to make continuation of our traditional gathering ways more and more difficult.

We wish to negotiate a settlement to our aboriginal rights claims as soon as is practicable. Before such negotiations can proceed however we will need time and resources to prepare our case.[213]

Iona Campagnolo has been widely honoured for her work on women's and human rights. She was celebrated during the 150th anniversary of the nation for her "profound passion for her province, its environment and its cultural diversity."[214] Raised as a child on the Skeena in Prince Rupert by fish cannery workers, she was the first woman to hold the minister of sports portfolio, the first female president of the federal Liberal party and the first female lieutenant-governor. She was given names by both Tsimshian and Haida families. She is credited with bringing down Conservative Prime Minister John Turner, when he casually patted her bottom and passed it off as collegial. She worked on the file to stop the first oil pipelines from northern Alberta to Kitimat. She wasn't as successful with the Eurocan expansion and her guarantee of fresh water.

The Largest Tree in Kitimat

Kitimat town council, they decide to dedicate a park to the biggest Sitka spruce left there. Sisi Kaas. It is still alive, eh? The pitch is coming down Hyda wakalla off this tree. This old tree is going back to Mother Earth. Just like humans going back to the womb of Mother Earth slowly. Pretty soon it will fall back to dust, the largest tree in Kitimat. We appreciate the beauty of Mother Earth. In many ways, if you slow down in our journey, appreciate this wilderness, stop for a moment in your fast life and relax a little bit – you see how big it is? How the north wind blows over a hundred miles an hour? All the weight... just imagine how far these roots go all over to keep it up. This root here is beginning to decay... look at how big it is. How far does it go? It has one root in the middle; that is the one that feeds it with water. That root is broken and the tree falls. Any tree will die just with that one artery breaking that will drink water. Twisted and entwined. The north wind blows well over and yet it stays.

Gerald, he got invited to when they were opening the big tree park. Gerald was the chief councillor, Kitamaat Village, and Kitimat Mayor Joanne Monaghan was a big one here. Gerald said, "I didn't go, even though I was invited." He said, "Used to be hundreds of them trees like that. They raped our land. How many houses could that big tree build? And not a penny came to our village. I am not accepting this invitation."

I said, "Good for you." He thought I was going to argue and tell him to go.

KITIMAT RIVER, APRIL 23, 2016

Cecil wants to take me on an expedition, this time to visit the Giant Spruce Tree. You can't miss the sign in Kitimat because it is one of the few outdoor tourist attractions near the city. It is described as the largest living Sitka spruce tree in BC and the oldest organism in the Kitimat Valley, at 500 years old. He told me that Gerald Amos, when he was chief of the Haisla, was asked by the city council sometime in the 1980s to come to the opening of the Giant Spruce Tree Park. Gerald refused.

We travel along a dike with Clarence Stein's garden city to our left, Cecil Paul's garden city to our right. Stein's paradise is lawns and flowerbeds. Cecil's paradise is what is left of the Kitimat floodplain of spring wildflowers, berry bushes, devil's club, alder and towering cottonwoods, western redcedar and more of the old veteran Sitka spruce. We plunge off the dike into a puddle-strewn gravel road that leads to a small parking lot. He pulls out his cigarettes and walking stick and we saunter down to the tree when he tells me a story of the spruce.

Huge trees in floodplains are like Cecil: survivors. Typically, impermanence reigns in a floodplain like the spring blush of the wild Nootka rose. The spring freshets reach velocities and forces that make Alcan's efforts to move Sand Hill seem almost puny. Sand and silt are deposited, then they are taken away. The banks are in a constant flux of wax and wane. Thickets of berries wash away and re-establish as long as there is water and bears to disperse their seeds. When a nurse log comes to rest on these shifting sands, it is like a small raft upon which trees can safely take root. The young tree anchors itself through the rotting nutrients of the log into the shifting banks, spreads its roots far and wide and taps into one of the most powerful life forces ever documented on Earth. When you grow up among 77-metre spruce, you don't get the sense that you're the greatest show on Earth.

Virgil: The Man that Broke the Arrow

One day I'm working – I'm sober maybe eight years – and a guy came up to me. He said, "How you stop drinkin', Indian?"

I said, "If you wanna stop, I'll take you to a place that helps us."

He says, "I wanna try."

"Okay. I'll pick you up tomorrow."

As Virgil walked away, every bit of my life was Virgil. He was shakin' this way, snot almost down to his knees, staggering. Walked away, and in my mouth, he says, "Brother, I love you. You walk in my moccasins. I love you, my brother."

Virgil was a white man, and he come ask an Indian, "How'd ya stop?" Virgil broke my hatred of the white man. I don't hate. It was the system, not the people. That's what I needed to learn, how to forgive the white man. To trust how to come back. But it's there, because of my little granny. First one salmonberry in June. I'll go to the estuary and pick up some wild rice. Put them together. Thanks, Great Spirit.

Virgil stayed sober for five years; he became my brother. Next thing he says, "I'm well enough to go stay close to my family in Vancouver Island." He got a job in Port McNeill.

One wintertime in January, I got a call: "Are you Cecil Paul? We found this thing [card] on a human body, the only one in the wallet, the name on it was you. Are you Cecil Paul?"

"Describe him," I said. "If it is my friend, he got family there."

Who's Virgil? He's telling me through that little piece of paper – the only name he had in his wallet – Cecil Paul and my phone number: "Don't try what I done, or you'll end up like what I did." He's one step ahead of me. He never left me, he's just giving me the courage never to take it with me. "Face the music," Virgil told me. See the way he broke the hatred and mistrust there.

I'd like to go back to this man that broke the arrow, Virgil. I dreamed of dry-out centres and all that, but there's not enough in there to try and put a sick person into society. I think there's more that could be done. When I look back at where I came from, from the gutter, and to where I am today, anyone I see, whether it be an Indian or a white man, or a black man, I will reach out my hand: come with me on my journey. It's much better where we are today because I was there, I know what it feels like. I've been in hell, and now I have a touch of serenity and I wait for my people. I dream, I could raise hell tomorrow. So that's my learning, how to forgive.

Sometime we have a picnic on the river with AA. If you walk slowly you look at this sword fern and it has a stem and every one of them leaves has the same distance. The stem of it is the centre focus. You take one leaf off and you can see it start to lean to one side. Two leaves off, lean more, and then you go all the way to the top and that is the end. That is how life is as an alcoholic. My life was not in centre focus. I lost leaves, I lost my Great Spirit, so I used the fern at the AA meetings. Walk softly when you walk around the bush to look at this artwork. How beautiful it is, and all that beauty was erased from my mind with alcohol. I try to share my experiences of what I see and what I lost all those years. But it came back when I think about my little granny's teachings.

I went to Vancouver, Prince George, Whitehorse, Winnipeg, Prince Rupert – Indigenous meetings all over the place. This guy, I travelled with him for a while, and he asked me to be a speaker at their round-up. There was a few people from Old Crow, and they invited me over there. It was awesome, see no roads or nothing up there. We went in by boat from plane. Lots of sick people there. Maybe 50 years since the Medical Association recognized alcohol as a disease, like cancer, can be cured. Majority of them, in the gutter like I was, manage to crawl out of it. I tried to share my experience of how I got sober, and it was all through going back to the teachings of my little grandmother; and that is what the government wanted, was to take away our language and our culture.

Two times I got invited in Vancouver to the Indigenous AA rally. There was a lot of non-Native people there. Saved my life. This May, the round-up in Kitimat, which I have to prepare for, things were a little hard this year. Too many layoffs at work. Forty bucks usually bought a big meal, all free coffee and food. But that is hard to come by for anyone on social assistance. We talked to cut the cost way down.

I talk about my life but don't realize what I done or said. Brian Falconer was telling when he was going across from Vancouver to Nanaimo, and he sees an Indian kid, Chris Cook, and somehow Brian asked him, "Do you know Cecil Paul over there?"

He says, "He saved my life."

I was invited to talk in Port Hardy Indigenous AA meeting, and I see that guy, Chris Cook, standing around and he asked me, "What are you doing?"

I said, "I'm going to a meeting because I was a drunk."

I made maybe five steps when he said, "Sir, can I come with you?" I stopped, and he still hasn't drunk to this day. Chris Cook.

Alcoholism is a disease that kills slowly and selectively. There are genetic, social and childhood trauma predispositions for the disease. Cecil struck bad luck on all three. The Xenaksiala adaptation to metabolize native root crops like riceroot with high insulin content is the very genetic advantage that made his body vulnerable to alcohol addiction and diabetes. There has been increasing awareness about alcohol addiction, but some would argue without enough context of the history behind the disease. In a 2009 study, alcohol-related deaths among First Nations in British Columbia were five times higher than the rate for other residents. Harold Johnson, a Cree author, calls it the "filthy stinking subject of alcohol" in his book *Firewater: How Alcohol Is Killing My People*. Wab Kinew, the Manitoba MLA and author, has written about his battle with alcohol. But alcohol started another systemic addiction; colonial governments became dependent on revenues from the sale of alcohol. Among a certain class of lawmakers and shareholders, the incidences and impacts of the disease drop for various reasons, so there is a constant internal conflict with the governors over the net value. The trade-off in a socialized health care system that relies on the revenues is that alcohol is the leading cause for hospitalizing all people of BC, especially when you add in the indirect effects of brawls, mental illness and impaired driving injuries.

Cecil has witnessed first-hand the disease among those working in isolated industrial camps where money is flush. Coined the "Gillette effect," from the oil and coal boomtown of Gillette, Wyoming, that experienced rapid resource development in the 1970s, the syndrome includes high rates of drug and alcohol addiction, violence, car accidents and sexual assaults of the vulnerable, all associated with predominantly male resource extraction camps. No country that bases its economy on large-scale exploitation of resources is going to advertise this problem. Cecil, as a speaker and a sponsor for AA, has supported hundreds of men in his life, Native and white, most in anonymity.

Support for the members was for Cecil a lifetime commitment. Cecelia speaks about one member of AA whom Cecil referred to as his brother, Tom Smith, from Sooke. Cecil was his sponsor, and Tom, who had a small plane, would pick Cecil up and take him to AA round-ups around the North where he was speaking. Cecil and Cecelia had visited Tom when he first contracted cancer, during which time she met his three daughters. Cecil encouraged Cecelia to support Tom's family because one day he would be dying and she would need the support from others. When Tom was close to dying, Cecelia went to visit him at his home, for her father. She recounts her reception: "He sat right up in his bed when he heard Cecil's name and was animated. When Dad spoke to Tom at that visit, he said, 'I will meet you on the other side of the lake one day, so have some coffee ready for me.'"[215] When Smith died shortly after that, Cecil made the long trip down for the funeral to be with the family.

Another leader who has spoken of his disease is Chris Cook from Alert Bay, a fisherman who went on to become the leader of the Native Brotherhood fighting fish farms through the '80s and early '90s. Brian Falconer tells the story of meeting Cook on the ferry. He describes sitting next to this man with a beautiful carved eagle and striking up a conversation around the carving. According to Brian, it was Chris Cook who asked him, "Do you know Cecil Paul?" Brian recounts that Cook told him, "Cecil helped me quit drinking. Now I am rich."

Indigenous leadership in the AA toward people suffering from the disease – white and Indigenous – is another undertold BC story. People looking for a strength that is bigger than their addiction have found people like Cecil to help them. Cook says of Cecil: "He speaks from his heart, he speaks from the land and he speaks for his people. When he speaks, he has such a beautiful voice that you can't help talking to him."[216]

HIRSCH CREEK PARK, SEPTEMBER 20, 2016

Today, Cecil wants to go to Hirsch Creek Park just outside of Kitimat to see if the salmon are running. It is a cool but sunny autumn day and the air is pungent with redcedar. I practise my Xenaksiala for the different parts of cedar. We wander along the well-used riverside trails near the town that have a faint unease about them, some litter and vandalism; that is when he tells me the story of the swordfern. They are everywhere, looking asymmetrical after three seasons of being browsed, nested in, stomped on and foraged. There are still a few symmetrical fronds and he picks one to demonstrate his talk.

Hirsch Creek Park is a good place to talk about going off the centre. Cecil tells me about a handyman who killed three young men and wounded another in the park over what appeared to be a dispute over loud music. I look it up and find out the 43-year-old killer Kevin Vermette disappeared and was never seen again. It was possibly a case of drinking and violence. These drive-in river parks along the highway have a reputation for being a place to drink and party. Murders in forests and in nature are a stock item in the news. Making people feel unsafe in a place is another way of colonizing land, another deadly arrow for those who call this river home.

Kemano Completion Project: What Damage Is Going to Come of It?

Up here in Kemano River, ten miles south, is a hole Alcan made in the mountain where there is about ten miles of tunnel, and it has a drop of 2,600 feet, and that is where all the turbines are to make electricity. On the other side is a new lake. It made a lot of people happy...a lot of my people happy. All the bread and clothing for people coming from all over the world. It has done a little bit for some people. I was really interested to go and see where the lake is. I went to go visit the Cheslatta people – my mother's people – took me in their rowboat. They told me, "They didn't give us enough time, and then they flooded the whole thing – families, the villages. Not only the Native people, the non-Native people too."

People from the Fraser River, Native and non-Native people, farmers, ask, "Why were we silent on the Kemano 2 completion?" All the hereditary chiefs were concerned, but I didn't know nothing about it except for the goodness of some people who told me about it. For the impact of what they were going to do with Kemano 2 completion was build another dam and send that dam and another big tunnel to come through the mountain that will raise the river. It would destroy a lot of the valley and the Fraser Valley, but what is going to happen to that outcome of where the water's going to come out after the detour? What damage is going to come of it?

I ask the advice of my people, and we send a delegation of a few young people. They went to the community where they were going to dam it and listen to their concerns. What they came back with was some very troubling things. We write down these little things, like oolichan, bear, sea life, eagles and where the project has left nothing; the uncertainty of this valley; the uncertainty of what is going to happen when industry comes and changes something what the Creator has left for us. Will there be no more oolichan? What damage will be done when the river will be raised two feet higher than what it is now? And that is what Alcan tells us. It took eight years for the Kemano oolichan to go back up again. The chiefs decided that we would build a totem pole, and we will use it as a thing for opposing Kemano 2 completion. And when Kemano 2 was finished, we hired a carver. We had it laid in state and we brought it up.

The Kemano Completion Project, known as KCP, was part of Alcan's long-term plans for expanding its production of aluminum. Aluminum is an electricity vampire, so Alcan needed to extract more water from the Nechako Reservoir, which obviously would release more down the Kemano River.[217] Both these changes in water flow would have impacts to the salmon of the Fraser (as the Nechako is a major river of the Fraser system) and the oolichan of Kemano River. The increase in flow would require a billion-dollar investment in additional infrastructure in the form of a new tunnel, powerhouse and transmission line.

There were already concerns from federal fisheries scientists about the volumes of water being taken out of the Nechako River. Chinook spawned in the river and sockeye migrated along it and DFO (Department of Fisheries and Oceans) officially expressed concerns in 1980 for those species, which it followed up with injunctions against Alcan. The battle between fisheries and Alcan went on for seven years until the 1987 Settlement Agreement was signed. No First Nations were involved in those discussions, nor were they brought into the steering committee the following year when KCP loomed on the horizon. This time, DFO, wanting to avoid another protracted battle, gathered Alcan and the provincial Ministry of Environment, Lands and Parks to "ensure environmental and fisheries protection."[218] They still forgot to invite the owners of the rivers.

It was around then that members of the Kitamaat Village, under Gerald

Amos's leadership, went to find out what was going on with the people of the Nechako, the Cheslatta – their trading partners at the end of a grease trail. The Cheslatta were as much in the dark as the Haisla had been with the 1950s Kenney Dam when the rising of the river and flooding of their homes and traplines was the first they knew of Alcan. The social cost was indefinable: another form of genocide. The settlement for the Cheslatta only came half a century later and almost all of the people affected were dead.

Back at the Kemano, the 1984 report by the consultants, Envirocon, anticipated an increase of 103 cubic metres per second, with a recommendation to lower capacity during the oolichan spawning season.[219] One million small fish were going to courageously swim between a billion dollar company and a quarterly return. The Haisla weren't buying the promises.

In the spring of 1989, Kitamaat Village Elders and councillors prepared their affidavits for an injunction to halt Alcan's KCP and any other megaprojects that threatened their way of life. Chief Maitland had filed a comprehensive land claim for the Haisla back in 1978, but nothing had happened since then. Gerald Amos told the local newspaper that the band was "using a peashooter to challenge a billion-dollar project."[220] It was a peashooter that was to have startling range and power. It kicked off a campaign to raise awareness that ultimately triggered a two-year review under the Utilities Commission Act. The three commissioners – Lorna Barr, a fisheries scientist empathetic to their cause, Peter Larkin and J. Alistair McVey – submitted their report at the end of 1994. The process was summarized by Bruce Hill in his testimony to the commission: "I don't believe the three commissioners can stop Alcan; Mayor Frank Read of Vanderhoof can't stop Alcan; Premier Harcourt can't stop Alcan; Minister Chrétien can't stop Alcan; I do believe that the people of the valley can stop KCP."[221] Cecil, Gerald Amos and other Haisla Elders took their objections to the Kemano Completion Project on the road to support the Cheslatta and brought many of the same people who were getting into the magic canoe for the Kitlope. Together, they shot the pea right out of the arena.

Five Rivers of Oolichan

Five rivers of oolichan – two for the Haisla: Kitimat and Kildala, both of which are contaminated; and three for the Xenaksiala: Kemano, Kitlope and Kowesas. Jimmy Henry built the last boiler at Kemano. I got one out of aluminum now. The oolichan don't like flooding water. We see the oolichan not do too well with big spring flood, so when Kemano flooded the river, it washed the oolichan away. They aren't strong swimmers. We were beaver hunting, and we noticed the water rises a few inches and then we know Alcan opened the floodgates. The trapline of the Kemano ran up ten miles and 40 traps or more. I could do it in a day. Now it is a road to the turbines. We asked Alcan to stop raising the waters during their breeding season, March to May, and then had to ask for longer to leave the fry longer to survive.

It took eight years for the Kemano oolichan to go back up the river, but they came back abundant. Even without oolichan, my son and his brother-in-law were the only ones to go up there, waiting in the rain every year. One day they will come back. Patience paid off.

Once the Haisla got their foot in the legal door to talk about oolichan with government and industry, a few things started to change. The timing of 1989 was good, as it coincided with the arrival of the Boston Men and their independent sources of funding for research. One of the first things the Haisla did was hire some independent fish scientists, like John Kelson, who, with Adam Lewis, worked with their members who knew the oolichan the best, like Cecil. The baseline data that was captured in the 1984 report on oolichan runs would be instrumental in arguing their case with Eurocan.

According to John Kelson, "Alcan discharges the waste water from its power plant into the Kemano, causing the triple whammy of attracting eulachon, that are attracted to flow, washing away the fine sediments needed for incubation, and increasing flows during incubation. This turned a small river with an intermittent run into an eulachon killing zone and depopulated Gardner Canal including the pristine Kowesas and Kitlope rivers."[222]

Cecil's observations were correct. Even subtle changes in river fluctuations could have profound impacts on the poor-swimming oolichan, and any siltation increases were death to the little fish. It also showed that distinct populations developed their own adaptations to their rivers. (This fact worked in the Haisla's favour for the timing of the logging plans for the Kitlope.) Over time, the communication between Alcan and the Haisla allowed the flows to be regulated to the point that the oolichan might have a chance to successfully spawn – if they managed to return. There were other arrows coming the oolichan's way. It wasn't just logging, industry and hydro causing declines; other factors were suspected, like loss from bycatch in shrimp nets, river armouring and changing water conditions from climate change.

The oolichan had plummeted in 1988, and by 1999 even Fisheries and Oceans had to pull its head out of the silt to acknowledge the decline.[223] In 2003, there was a single small return but then it sunk back down again to negligible levels for another five years. The Haisla, like Cecil Jr. and others, continued to go every year to check, waiting in the rain, as Cecil describes it, "for the river to run black."

Virtually everywhere south of them, like the Fraser and central coast, where the oolichan once spawned in 33 documented glacial rivers, the populations disappeared. In a 2011 national assessment of the oolichan population by the Committee on the Status of Endangered Wildlife in Canada (COSEWIC), that independent board of scientists evaluating the status of oolichan wrote of the contribution of local knowledge and absence of federal fisheries: "First Nations input [on their status] is pervasive, fundamental and substantial."[224] The southern oolichan were put on the watch list for an endangered species list under the federal Species at Risk Act, and the central and northern populations were raised up to the status of special concern.

In 2008, the oolichan returned that year to Kemano. Louisa said, "There was some thought that this river had fallen as well because we were in that drought for so long. When the oolichans did come, the elation was beyond words." The family pictures of the Kemano oolichan camp that year hang on the wall of Cecil's house. The whole Paul family is in those pictures, including his sisters Louisa and Vietta. Daughter Joyce is handling the nets filled with flashing silver oolichan, cousins are stirring the new aluminum vats with steam, laughter billowing into the crisp March air. Junior is driving the punt, and Joyce's son, Thomas, is never far from him. Cecil is in his waders going up the river, checking the fish. Everyone is bundled up in checkered woollen shirts, waders and boots. Oolichan aren't just about the oil, they are about the place and company where the family feels whole again.

Billy Hall and the Bek^{w}us

In Misk'uk'w is a big valley, and the guy's name is Billy Hall. This is a true story. It is not a child's story. Our people keep saying that they didn't realize that there was hunger in the 1930s. They had an abundance of food:

the moose, the deer, the fish. Anyway, Billy went up hunting here with his friend in the place where it divides into two valleys – one this way and one that way. Billy went to the right and his partner went to the left. And when they come to this place, they had one stick. "If that stick is still standing, I am still up, but if I go down before you, I will lay that stick down." That is how they can tell when they come back. Billy went up just before dark, and he seen a black bear. And he had one of them guns that you muzzle loaded, and he went, and he shot this animal. It was a *bekʷus*. And he knew he had made a mistake.

It was a long story, but when he ran down, *bekʷus* were chasing him. He made it down here. He never thought about putting down that stick. He was so scared. And here was his partner waiting for it, and he hauled out. They seen the big things right behind them. He went to Kemano and when he got there, he went to sleep. This is what amazes me, of how my people kept him alive. For one year he slept. How did his system work for one year without waking up? What did they use to feed him? They put bull kelp down his throat to feed him, and when he woke up, he had supernatural powers. He sees things that you and me could never see. He sees a death before it happens. There was this charcoal that he walked across and never got burnt.

In the wintertime, they were having dance and people celebrating a good harvest of salmon. Their cellars were full of food for the winter. And they were dancing. He hollered, and he asked three young men to pick up salmonberry bush. The bush were already asleep; there were no leaves from them. This was in January, and they came and they gave it to him and he looked at it. And there was a fire in the middle of that place and they start dancing around chanting. They went 'round three times. Now there is three salmonberry bushes coming to life. Once more and there was little flower, once more and berries. He went to the highest of chiefs and he said, "What is it?" The salmonberry that he made great. Maybe he touched the Creator. Some power came, like those places in Africa where they go through the fire without getting burned. If my people hadn't experienced that, I wouldn't have believed what I hear. For this mind to conquer fear, conquer heat and to make the salmonberry ripe in the middle of the winter. His tombstone is at home. His grandson was Kenny Hall, who fought for the Kitlope with us. The name for the valley is Misk'uk'w. Place of my birth is Misk'usa. I don't know where the "mis" comes from.

Sasquatch or *bekʷus* is the Haisla "monster" that most captures the Western imagination, as it does all through its North American range. Haisla author Eden Robinson's *Monkey Beach* brought her contemporary Haisla storytelling skills to the old story of *bekʷus*. The title of her book is named after the English local place name referring to the resemblance of *bekʷus* to a monkey. The Haisla place name is Q'waq'waqsiyas. It was an encounter at Misk'uk'w that features in Cecil's story of Billy Hall.

MISK'UK'W, OCTOBER 3, 2017

We are travelling back from the Kitlope along Gardner Canal and we are passing Misk'uk'w, just below Kemano on the south side of the canal. Cecil points out the valley where Billy Hall encountered the *bekʷus* and tells the story. It is just past Barrie Point on the chart. West Fraser is in there now with a logging camp. Misk'uk'w lies just outside of the protected area/conservancy. Too bad; if ever there was going to be an opportunity to collect evidence that keeps our Western skeptic minds at bay about the existence of a sasquatch, this would have been the place. Now there isn't a hope in hell some monster is going to venture into that clearcut and camp. Their chances of survival would be nil.

There are other Haisla monsters, like the small primates called *kwaluxw* who lived at Foch Lagoon, killer whales with two dorsal fins, a giant rat and sea monsters. The missionary George Raley reported in the *Na-na-kwa* in April 1901 that

> what we believe to be a sea-serpent or immense strange sea monster was seen from the Mission House, travelling along the opposite shore with a peculiar spiral motion at about the rate of fifteen miles an hour. In its flight it threw the spray high in air and wide in extent until the sea appeared like a boiling caldron. Some said it is an immense whale. The missionary however got his field glass and then and there noted the size of the monster, which appeared to be two hundred feet in length.

Billy Hall was a skillful Xenaksiala healer. He was born sometime around 1860 and married Susan (no last name), who gave birth to Simon Hall in 1899. Simon married Amelia Duncan, who gave birth to Kenny and Simon Hall Jr. (hereditary chiefs of the Kowesas and Kitlope, respectively, who supported the Kitlope campaign), both of the Eagle Clan. Billy Hall embodies the skills of an ancient healer: clairvoyance, walking on embers, plant husbandry, hypnosis and storytelling. Witnesses of *bekʷus* are not uncommon. Hall is one of thousands of coastal people who continue to see a primate-like being (that is not a bear) digging for clams or scavenging for food with unforgettable characteristics: a foul smell, a shrill call, a tall stature that appears neckless because of long hair and a primate-like face. Georg Steller, the famous 18th-century German naturalist who recorded species new to Western zoologists during his ill-fated voyage to Alaska in the 1730s, like Steller's sea lion, Steller's eider duck, Steller's jay, Steller's sea eagle, Steller's sea cow (now extinct), also documented Steller's sea ape. No specimen was collected, though, and it remains a cryptid – or hidden animal.

The ability to ripen the salmonflower early must be like forcing bulbs in the winter indoors. Plants measure the amount of darkness in the day to determine when to bloom. Hall might well have known how to force dormant plants in a warmed bighouse lit by fires, especially given the salmonberries' importance to health.

Eighty per cent Industry, 20 per cent Natural Causes

In my journey, I met a friend. His name was Jean-Louis LeMay. He went to visit Kitimat maybe one or two times, but Jean he was a big guy in Alcan, and his office was in Toronto. When he came here, he told me, "Cecil, I want to come and see what you guys are doing."

I says, "Jean, you know I welcome you, but my government, how would they feel? We are opposing you, my friend. We are opposing you."

Jean says, "But I want to learn. I will strip my title and come as a friend."

Okay, I go to my government and I asked for five minutes when my government had a meeting and I gave the message of my friend. And they asked me to repeat the last words: "He will strip his title and come as a friend." So my government said, "Try to get your friend. How can we penetrate Alcan? How can we deny someone that wants to come as a friend?" So my government said, "Welcome." So I told him to come and he came.

"Jean," I said, "my argument was for years that 80 per cent damage to the Kemano River was caused by your industry, 20 per cent by natural causes."

He says, "Cecil, no, 20 per cent by industry, 80 per cent by natural causes." Naturally there was some conflict there. The outcome was beautiful. They took part when I showed them a lot of things. I videoed the movement of gravel. I talk about what Kemano project was, what it meant for us. I talk about the pollution of the Great Lakes, the oil spill in Alaska.

One day I got a call. Jean said, "I looked through your videos, Cecil. Eighty per cent industry, 20 per cent natural causes."

And I went to my people and I say, "Industry is beginning to change, beginning to listen. Listen to my friend who has stripped his title of this big organization. What can we do to help? I will show you graveyards here in Kemano. A graveyard that was eroded bad by Alcan's boats." I brought my friend to see. He had to see with his eyes what I was trying to say.

Alcan have a big ferry boat, the *Nechako*, that makes big waves. We were trying to make an agreement with Alcan to slow down the boat mid-channel because the waves are so big, and that wave would bounce back off the other shoreline. One day, Jean came up. Never told me, never phoned me. He just said, "Let's go up to Kemano. Bring your friend." I brought Gerald along. We came in unannounced and put the boat around the back out of sight so there was no evidence that there was anyone in the village. Then we wait for the ferry boat to come. The water would hit the other shore and took 20 minutes to come back and giving it a double wave.

"Jean, you want to wait 20 minutes for that second wave to come." Timed it. "How many times does this come a week, Jean?"

He agrees. "Yes, Cecil it is 80 per cent industry, 20 per cent natural causes. What can we do to stop the erosion?"

Jean got on the phone to his men – they must have recognized his voice – and he told them, "Get on your boat and come to the Indian village." We all watched the boat come in. They didn't know we were observing them. They come full blast and Jean witnessed them. I met the young man who was in charge of the boat. The surprise that he had when he met the big chief of Alcan. I brought the young man to show him the erosion. They talked about all the rock that came from that tunnel. Estimated how much it will cost to truck it down, put it on a barge and what machinery we use and then we will make this breakwater. That was the gift from Jean-Louis LeMay.

The breakwater was finished in November. I asked my people, "What are we going to say to Alcan? How can we put it into words to say thank you for saving our graveyard?" The totem pole was the gift. It is called Nanakila, which in my language means the sentry or watchman. It has oolichan and other animals, and an eagle on top with mirrors in place of eyes. When the totem pole was taken up to Kemano Village, it was in September. It was foggy, and somehow the sun burned through. The tide comes close to the pole and when the totem pole was raised up, the sun's reflection in the water hit the eagle's eyes, and like an eagle it would blink.

Jean says, "It is alive, Cecil. The pole is alive." Carver of the watchman and that is what this eagle is.

The breakwater, when I sit and walk along it, I feel the gratitude for Jean-Louis LeMay. His ability to change his attitude towards environment and the people who love the environment that make some seeds for change; that in my short lifetime I have witnessed destruction and I have witnessed a change. I will never see it completely change, but the beginning has started. How do we carry it on? How do we keep telling industry, not with anger, not with roadblock? The largest untouched rainforest that we saved with no roadblock. I keep telling my people, "Negotiate in good faith, with easy language, no cursing. Got to tell them who you are. Sometimes if you go in with anger, you make an avalanche with all that noise." The change in attitude of industry was beautiful. After that we found the survey markers.

With Alcan now being at the table, Cecil was anxious to draw attention to another important issue: the burial ground at Kemano. Over the years, the graves and village reserve were being washed into the ocean, not by just the increased flow of the river but the wash and backwash of the high-powered water taxis that ferried crew back and forth to the town. One of the graves, centimetres away from being washed into the sea in 1993, was that of the healer Billy Hall. When the 1993 Adventure Canada trip took people into Kemano, it was Billy Hall's gravesite that Cecil highlighted to illustrate the backwash problem. One reason Cecil worked so hard for his ancestors is that, in most cases, the only evidence of their lineages are in this graveyard. There had been no legal requirement by the Government of Canada to record Native vital statistics until 1943, and even then it was badly done.

According to John Pritchard, Jean-Louis LeMay was a manager of the power operation at Kemano and "a reasonable human being."[225] His reasonable solution was to support Cecil's recommendation to build up a bulwark and shore up the burial ground and village site. The totem pole was an expression of thanks but also a reminder. It is a striking pole, with oolichan swimming up from the bottom chased by seal, sea lion and grizzly. Beaver and eagle are at the top – the eagle has flashing mirror eyes. In between, there is an empty part of the pole to account for the loss of wildlife due to industrial activity or the unknown future of industrial occupation – a river devoid of oolichan and the culture of life they support. Glenn Candler Fuller, the Coca-Cola heiress and friend of Wa'xaid, donated the money for the pole, as did Michael Northrop, who managed the Rockefeller Brothers Foundation. Henry Stewart carved it. Many assumed it was an assertion of sovereignty at Kemano by the Haisla, having launched their injunction against Alcan that spring. Gerald Amos speaks to the Haisla intention at the pole raising in the late fall of 1989.

> Nanakila commemorates for the first time in living memory the humble oolichan. Totems commonly celebrate more dramatic manifestation of the culture like eagle, killer whale, raven and beaver...Nanakila is one measure of our effort to challenge all concerned. It will stand as our candle, a noble and reflective expression of conscience. To ponder and judge all who approach and partake of these lands and resources.[226]

Today, the burial ground is intact. Billy Hall's grave marker is still there to trigger the story of his remarkable life, and the pole looks up to what is left of the industrial townsite of Kemano – alder rapidly filling it in. The powerhouse has been mechanized and only a skeleton crew maintains the site – hopefully still bringing their boats in slowly to prevent the backwash.

KEMANO, SEPTEMBER 7, 2004

Cecil is taking us to see the Kemano burial ground. The trail picks up in front of a row of cabins for the oolichan season, which have had a summer of salmonberry growth to hide them from the sea. It continues on toward the tip through the graveyard. There are two poles you pass in Kemano. Cecil tells us first the story of the pole commissioned by his Great-aunt Alice and her husband Chief Hail (Hale), from Kitkatla, then the Nanakila pole. Kemano isn't a burial ground so much as a library of 10,000-year-old lineages.

A Daughter that Flew Away Long Ago

One winter night, I got a call from my sister Louisa who lives in Prince Rupert. She said she had a telephone conversation with a minister, John Cashore, and his wife Sharon, who they met when he was the United Church minister in Port Simpson. The minister asked her if she knew a person by the name of Cecil Paul. She said, "There's something I'd like to share with you." John and Sharon Cashore knew that Louisa was a Haisla. They were close friends in Port Simpson.

I said, "Go ahead and share."

Cecelia was near her 30th birthday when she went on that journey in search of who she is. She knew she was adopted. She found her mother was not 50 miles away from Cecelia all these years. And she met her mom who told her that "Your father is Haisla." She told John Cashore, her adopted father, who phoned my sister, Louisa.

I told Louisa, "Make contact; I dreamt about this." I told my wife, I told her my journey: "I have a daughter that flew away long ago."

This is Cecelia Cashore Reekie's story:

> I had my first-born son, David, in 1987. Holding my son for the first time was very powerful for me as he was the first person to whom I had been biologically connected. It was then that I understood the importance of that connection and decided to search for my birth mum. I applied through Parent Finders in 1989. My birth mum had been registered with Parent Finders for a number of years and so the match was made almost immediately. They called the following day with Marguerite's phone number. I was still living in Langley and she was living in Delta. I had grown up within a half hour of my birth mother. I called her and we made arrangements for myself, Dave my husband, and baby Dave to meet her that night. We spent the evening sharing stories and pictures and at some point I asked her about my dad. I am very lucky, because she was honest and gave me his name.
>
> That night, I went home and phoned my parents, John and Sharon Cashore. I had promised that I would call them and let them know how the reunion went. In that phone call, I mentioned that my birth father's name was Cecil Paul from Kitamaat. I asked Dad if he had a connection to Kitamaat because I wanted to find out if he knew someone who might know him. My mum said, "Aunt Louisa's maiden name was Paul and she came from Kitamaat. I wonder if they are related?" She said that she was going to phone Aunt Louisa that night. We hung up the phone and Mum called Aunt Louisa and explained that I had just found my birth mum and that my birth dad was Cecil Paul of Kitamaat. Mum asked Louisa if Cecil was any relation. I don't think Aunt

Louisa said anything at first and that she would have to call my parents back. Then Aunt Louisa called Cecil that night and asked him if he had had a baby girl in 1963 and he said, "Yes." Aunt Louisa said to Cecil, "Well I know who she is and she is now looking for you." Aunt Louisa called my parents back and told them that Cecil was her older brother and, yes, he would be willing to meet Cecelia.

Cecil was scheduled to travel down for a doctor's appointment and Aunt Louisa said she would travel with Cecil. I met them in a hotel room in Vancouver. I was anxious but excited at reconnecting with Aunt Louisa and meeting my birth dad. I made my way to the hotel room, with my arms full of albums and things, and knocked on the door. Aunt Louisa answered and after greeting her I noticed that Cecil wasn't in the room. I asked her, "Where is he?" And Aunt Louisa said, "He is pretty nervous, so he went out for a walk." We were sharing pictures and chatting when there was a knock on the door. I couldn't see the door from where I was, but I heard Cecil ask Aunt Louisa in their language if I was there. She said, yes. He came around the corner and didn't say a word. He walked up, gave me a hug and then said: "Be proud of who you are and where you come from." Then I knew; I had found my way back to my family.

Cecil, Aunt Louisa and I spent the afternoon sharing pictures, stories and talking about our lives and then I took them out to Coquitlam to meet my [adopted] parents, John and Sharon, and my husband and son. We stopped en route for a bouquet of flowers for my mum. When we arrived at the house I grew up in, we gathered up in the living room. To watch my parents meet my birth father and reconnect with their dear friend Aunt Louisa is an unforgettable memory. My son was standing over on one side with his dad, when he let his hand go and went over and took Cecil's hand. It was a symbol of connection that was beyond explanation. One of the reasons I wanted to do the search was so that my sons, the next generation, would know who they are and where they come from. It was also then that I realized that I had gained three sisters and a brother. Somehow Cecil magically managed to get all of us into a circle as he spoke to my parents to assure them that "They weren't going to lose a daughter but the family was just expanding."[227]

You're Walking in My Moccasins, the Father of My Child

Amazing part was John [Cashore] became a politician. He was an Environmental minister, later an Indian Affairs minister, and that's when we first met him, fighting for the Kitlope. Gerald said that when he called the ministry up, they sent John up, Environmental minister. What it was like when I met this man that was the father of my child and holds the title, Environmental minister of BC, which includes the Kitlope? What it was like to talk to him? What it was like when I first met the man that raised my child, that hugged her, that put Band-Aids on her feet when she had a scratch?

I remember the first acquaintance when my sister and I, Louisa, went down to Vancouver to meet Cecelia, and it seemed forever we were in separate rooms and then Cecelia was ready to see me. Without hesitation I felt the blood connection, I embraced. We talked for about four hours. My sister said, "I made arrangements that her parents are there, going to meet us." We went home to where Cecelia was waiting.

I asked my sister, "What gift are we going to give to a person who raised a child? Maybe a little flower, okay, that sounds good. You bring a flower and you give it to John, and I'll bring a little flower to give to her mom, that sounds good." We didn't know how to act; we didn't know what to expect.

John and Sharon weren't sitting together, they were sitting in two chairs, and I was the first one to speak and I told to the both of them, and I stressed it too, "I come here not to take your daughter away. I come here if you will have a compassion to share your child with me." The two of them came, we embraced and we cried, a little laughter here and there through the tears. I looked at these two women, at this man and wife, you've raised my child so beautifully. And that's how I addressed John, the father of my child, and I feel comfortable with it. I asked John, "How do you feel?"

And John said, "She's our child."

Sharon says, "Ours."

That was beautiful. I needed to hear that.

And to Cecelia I say, "You are what I hungered for." I close my eyes and I said, "I think I see your father behind you. He's with you and your mom."

When I learned of her father – you know this residential school too was run by the United Church of Canada and that's where Minister Cashore was before he became the minister of the Environment – the question comes back of mistrust. Remember I talk about mistrust? That was quite a thing in my short life. The torture and abuse I got. It was the United Church of Canada who ran Port Alberni Indian Residential School. And who would I meet that raised my child? It was the United Church minister. From a person that was abused. And the hatred was planted in my heart of mistrust and hate. United Church. And I stand in front of a person who raised an Indian child. My child. Cared for her.

You try and understand and condemn a whole United Church. Not only me, but hundreds and hundreds of people went to residential school. Coqualeetza Hospital was run by United Church. I brought that up at the Truth and Reconciliation conference in Vancouver. I told my story of learning how to forgive. White person didn't want me to marry his daughter, and the father wanted to kill the Indian child, and more hatred come. I lost five years. Then we finally met, and I learned that her father and mother were the United Church minister. I close my eyes, you know. One has to live through it to try to understand. I think that was the beginning of this wounded spirit on another healing journey.

When I first went up to the Kitlope with John, there was that trust. I said, "John do you think they will save the Kitlope?" I remember asking the father of my child, and I remember the smile on his face. That was quite a question to ask a minister: "Are you leaning towards saving the Kitlope?"

I think his answer was, "I think it's an appropriate thing to do, and to gain trust." There's that word again, to gain "trust."

I looked at this man, I says, "You're walking in my moccasins, the father of my child."

I told Gerald the whole story, just him and I and Louisa. "What I'm afraid of: Is it going to hurt our cause? Is it going to hurt Cecelia's dad? Everything's going to go against him in a question period. Or if we win the battle, will this degrade him? People will say, 'He done that because Cecelia's father's a Xenaksiala,' and I don't want John to get hurt. How can we save him? He done so much for me. We could ask for another minister to come up. Not the Environmental minister. We could ask his secretary or..."

"No," they said. "Let's face it... let's talk to John. See what he says." Not a word was mentioned. Lots of emotions in my journey. I have pictures of him and me and Gerald sitting on the riverbanks of the Kitlope.

VANCOUVER ART GALLERY, SEPTEMBER 15, 2015

John Cashore arrives at the art gallery for the interview. He is a striking, silver-haired man with a warm smile and handshake. We sit at the same table where I had interviewed Cecelia, his adopted daughter, several months before. Our conversation ranges from the strange legacy of the 19th-century schism of the Methodists and Anglicans in Port Simpson to the alliances of the Native Brotherhood and the Methodists in taking land claims to Ottawa. Cashore is someone who has lived every day in the paradox of institutional life. Besides the gift of adopting Cecelia, he also speaks proudly of the young people from villages up the coast who became part of their family while getting an education in the city. He feels his most important political achievement was supporting the principle of recognition and respect while conducting treaty negotiations. During his years with the United Church as Native affairs consultant, the task of which he was most proud, he was putting himself out of a job.

After Port Simpson, the family came back down to Vancouver in 1969 and Cashore took up the position of Native affairs consultant for the BC Conferences of the United Church of Canada. In his first report, he wrote, "I consider my appointment to this job as being strictly a three year appointment and do not intend to stay on... hopefully we will be in a position to hire a native Indian to continue this work in whatever form it should be continued as of 1972."[228] In another comment in this report, he writes,

> We have often heard it said that the solution to the Indian problem is to be found in enabling him to receive an education. If this is the case, then the solution to the White Problem would be also in enabling him to receive an education. With this in mind I see it as one of my primary responsibilities to arrange for opportunities whereby non-Indian people will be able to receive adequate learning experiences.[229]

One of the big issues in 1971 impacting Native fishermen on the coast was the federal Davis Plan. The idea behind the plan was to restrict the number of licences to reduce "obsolete" boats to upgrade the fleet and as a conservation measure. The unintended or intended implications were that it prejudiced subsistence fishermen with poorer quality boats in favour of the companies. Cashore wrote, on behalf of his constituents, to Minister Jack Davis in Ottawa:

A "Just Society" will not allow its dominant economic system to further destroy the way of life of those who were making a living from the sea centuries before the coming of the white man. We believe that the present salmon fleet reduction program will result in immeasurable cost to the rich heritage of native Canadians of the North Coast. This may well break the spirit of many of the Native Indians of the North Coast.[230]

Cashore visited Kitamaat Village in March of 1971, where he met Harry Amos, Gerald's father. Cashore recorded Amos's comments as follows:

We have to get way from just being led, waiting for orders. We depend too much on outside resources... The Church in Kitimaat Village is dying, but there is still a spark, kept alive for sentimental reasons: not that we really believe anymore in the United Church – only for sentimental reasons... This is perhaps the basic approach of all the Kitimaat people to the United Church – a feeling that it has failed to meet their real needs coupled with a deep sentimental loyalty to the United Church and its Methodist forerunner.[231]

One of the last of many letters and duties that Cashore performed was writing to Minister of National Health and Welfare Marc Lalonde to endorse the BC Union of Indian Chiefs in their proposal to take over Coqualeetza residential school to create their own cultural education centre. He writes to support "this Indian Solution for Indian problems."

The unique approach of the Union's proposal, it seems to me, is that this is not a request of financial support... but rather an opportunity for the Government of Canada to participate in enabling the creative process... You will notice that the brief does not dwell on the past; it does not dwell on the injustices perpetrated by the non-Indian immigrants in this land; it does not play upon guilt feelings – instead it transcends that negative approach and deals in strictly practical terms.[232]

Before John Cashore met Wa'xaid in 1989, he was three years in as an elected NDP member of the provincial legislature. He was in the Opposition for the first couple of years as the critic for social services, then environment. He had travelled up around that time to Prince Rupert with his wife Sharon to visit their old friends, whom their kids referred to as Uncle Murray and Auntie Louisa Smith. Cashore tells the story that "Louisa and Murray had been up to the Kitlope and they had all these pictures there with her brother – this was before the connection had been made. You could just tell when they got talking about the Kitlope what a beautiful place it was, what a powerful feeling and that they just loved this place."

One of Cashore's duties as environment critic was to chair a committee on sustainable development – a heady topic for the time. The United Nations' Brundtland Commission on Sustainable Development had come out in 1987 proposing 12 per cent of the land base be set aside for conservation. With the Convention on Biological Diversity in Rio looming on the horizon, his caucus was stepping up to be the very first signatory. The leader of the Opposition and his colleagues had lots of shared personal interests in sustainability and Cashore found himself part of an exciting team. Into this busy milieu in the summer of 1989, his daughter Cecelia contacted her birth parents and John describes what happened after the dinner at his house, at which they all first met.

> In a way that I certainly recognized as traditional speeches after dinner, Cecil got up and said he had some things he wanted to say. At this point we were becoming aware of the powerful moving way he has with language and presence... he was thanking us. He didn't want us to fear that his daughter was going to be taken away, but that, in his Native tradition, the circle becomes larger, and we were all part of this circle. It was beautiful imagery and very helpful too at a time like that because it was a transition time for everyone.[233]

In 1991 the NDP won the election and Cashore was appointed minister of environment, lands and parks. He was walking into a showdown: "The lines were very clearly drawn in the NDP between the International Woodworkers of America (IWA) and environmentalists. We were having to find ways to end the wars in the woods and deal with these issues." It was the time of mass arrests in Clayoquot Sound and other hot spots around the province. Cashore's rationale was to accept the Brundtland recommendation and take BC from 6 per cent of the land in protected areas to 12 per cent. "Part of the rhetoric of arguing for it was business needs certainty." The NDP gave itself ten years to accomplish the task – then the miraculous happened. Wa'xaid, the father of his daughter, walked into Cashore's office.

> The timing was amazing because of the research that Ecotrust had done globally and then in a respectful way they connected with Cecil and Gerald [Amos] and others. One of the steps was they would come and talk to me. I can't speak for what happened, but I think Cecil had told them he had met me. The next thing I hear is that a delegation wants to meet with me and talk about the Kitlope. So my first awareness of the Kitlope was from Louisa and Murray and their photograph album, the second was in meeting Cecil for the first time, and the third was Cecil bringing a delegation to meet me to talk about the Kitlope.[234]

John Cashore first met with the Haisla delegation on January 28, 1993. He was still environment minister at the time and brought Dan Miller, the minister of forests, with him. At the meeting, they agreed to jointly sponsor two public workshops in the spring about the Kitlope.

Over the next year, Cashore transitioned from the environment ministry to his next appointment as minister of Aboriginal affairs. Moe Sihota, an ally and ambitious, was moved into minister of environment. Premier Harcourt had wanted Cashore, with his background in Aboriginal relations with the church, to take on this portfolio. Bob Peart, his ministerial assistant, pledged to keep the two offices linked with regard to protected areas as they all involved First Nations. There wasn't much not to like in the proposal. The Haisla were asking for a million acres to be protected, which would boost the provincial percentage up a whole percent in one transaction. There was strong community support, even from the sportsmen and unions. There were just two hurdles left: compensation for West Fraser's relinquishment of the vast tree farm licence worth millions, and the fact that the main spokesperson for the Haisla was the father of the minister's child.

It was that summer in 1993 that CBC journalist Ian Gill went searching around for a story on Cashore and latched onto his Haisla/Ecotrust invitation to visit the Kitlope. Gill would join journalists from the *Globe and Mail*, the *Vancouver Sun*, the *Los Angeles Times* and others as the leaders from both governments shared their thoughts over three full days in the Kitlope and many sessions around the campfire. As Cashore relates,

> It was an incredible experience. Cecil brought the eagle feather.

Sitting around the campfire, each person who held the feather would speak as an element of respect. The three evenings I was there, I put on the table that I have a background in two of the institutions that have been a problem for First Nations – church and government.[235]

Representing the Haisla were Cecil; Louisa; Alan Hall, hereditary chief of the Killer Whale Clan at Kitlope; and Gerald Amos. Spencer Beebe was there for Ecotrust. Gill filmed a 17-minute news special on the trip, which aired on August 31, 1993. It showed Canadian viewers, for the first time, the stunning landscapes of Gardner Canal and Kitlope Lake and exposed them to the "powerful language and presence" of Cecil Paul and Louisa Smith. In Gill's mini-doc, Vic Maskela speaks for West Fraser and suggests that the government needs to find them "an equivalent supply." Cashore and Cecil told the gathered media of their personal relationship and Gill included the story in his CBC piece as well as in a *Georgia Straight* article. Cashore had cleared it with the conflicts commissioner and few seemed to think it a problem, other than Social Credit politician Rafe Mair. Cashore was now confident enough to commit to meeting with Premier Harcourt and doing everything in his power to make it happen.

Meanwhile, the Haisla and the Boston Men were working behind the scenes. On February 22, 1994, the Haisla put on a big potlatch feast for the Kitlope. The *Northern Sentinel* newspaper reported, "Haisla elder Cecil Paul also spoke to an attentive audience about his willingness to do anything to protect the Kitlope from logging. Paul, who was born in the Kitlope, said he welcomes the world to come and see the Kitlope and learn from it."[236] West Fraser was still telling the press at this time that its five-year management plan included logging the Kitlope. The provincial government was still reviewing its protected area plan but would provide a decision within the year. Sometime between February 22 and August, West Fraser made its decision to donate the Kitlope allocation from TFL 41. Hank Ketcham, owner of West Fraser / Eurocan, spoke in April 2017 about his understanding of the gift.

> It is a matter of public record but [the gift was] around 125,000 cubic metres of an annual cut. We relinquished our right and did not ask for compensation. This wasn't a business transaction, but we wouldn't have done this if it had significantly eroded our timber supply for the mill. We had 100 employees.

It would have made us millions of dollars, but we felt we could run the mills without it. The public's perception was changing; our perception was changing. We were in a unique position to do something good here; it wouldn't hurt our employees. In fact, they got some benefit of the social and environmental benefits and pride in the company.[237]

Cashore says of that time: "West Fraser gave up the timber rights for the area and this wasn't something that was done lightly or without a certain amount of diplomatic toing and froing. Maybe some of the scars on my back come out of that time."[238] In August of 1994 the province and the Haisla Nation announced that the Kitlope would be fully protected and jointly managed.

Final Decision Kitlope

Twenty minutes before the announcement – the government was going to announce that the Kitlope was going to be saved – (they gave us a little room in the part of the building where we were debating who was going to talk and who was going to open) and there was a knock on the door. A young man went to go answer it and he gave me a piece of paper and on it said, "Kowesas will not be safe." They took it out of the agreement. All this, 20 minutes before the announcement. The delegation with the Xenaksiala/Haisla got up to leave. They were so disheartened by what happened.

I would not leave my chair. Everybody was at the door to walk away and tell the government to go to hell. But my little sister stayed. "Well, what is the matter with them?" I didn't answer her. Then the chiefs came, and they all got their seats back. This is a big surprise, but I knew something was going to happen today.

I said, "We should appreciate and enjoy what little time they have given us, and the people around the universe; we won a little battle. Let's accept what they offer us, and we'll rest for a year and then begin to fight again." It was a debate around the table, and then they said okay. They accepted, they took it.

Kenny Hall, hereditary chief of the Kowesas, he gave me the authority to walk on this land. He's the grandson of the fellow I told you about, Billy Hall, the man who saw the *bek*ʷ*us*, Sasquatch. This place here was part of the Kitlope that we fought for. There was only a five-year moratorium on this place. It was almost up, and they could have started logging again, but the moratorium kept adding five years. This one was done by labour and love.

In the end, it wasn't Cashore who signed the initial government-to-government agreement on the Kitlope. Moe Sihota, in his new portfolio as minister of environment, signed it in 1994. Cashore was in the Khutzemateen at the same time, announcing that valley's protection with Prince Philip and Chief of the Gitsi'is Buddy Helin. He had followed the Kitlope closely to the end, though. The decision to leave the Kowesas out of the agreement, according to Cashore, was a political compromise. "We weren't able to get the portion in the Kowesas, but what we did manage to do was really a strong step in the right direction. After that there were delegations from Kitamaat on a fairly regular basis coming down."[239] One of the Kitamaat delegation was John Pritchard, who assisted with the detailed, two-year-long negotiations on behalf of the Haisla to create a co-managed conservancy, a new designation insisted upon by the Haisla that put as a priority the cultural laws and management of the land. The final Kitlope agreement was signed on February 16, 1996.[240]

Kowesas was left out of the original agreement, but the moratorium has never come off the valley. When Hank Ketcham was asked about the Kowesas, he had no recollection of it, although he hadn't been the owner of the licence for six years.

PART FIVE

More Good Journeys in the Magic Canoe, 1995 – 2020

Welcome Home Ceremony

A year goes by after the Kitlope was saved. One day Cecelia phoned and she said, "I'm coming up, Dad. I'm coming up with my husband, one grandchild – your grandchild, my father [John Cashore] and mother [Sharon Cashore]."

I said, "Okay."

I met Cecelia when they landed. Somebody came and said, "Your daughter is over there." I waited so long for that young girl that flew away from the nest, at that moment, separated by so many feet. I embrace my daughter. "Great Spirit, thank you. Thank you, Great Spirit."

Cecelia never met her grandmother, my mum, but she knew she was going to come back. I have some pictures of when I introduced her to the Haisla people – her and John Cashore. I says to Cecelia, "If the hereditary chief gets up and touches you, means he is going to welcome you. He might not say a word."

The hereditary chief got up. I watched him with his arms around my little girl. Ah, I weep with joy. It was something. My auntie was the one who drummed and said, "Welcome home." And her daughters are two doors from here, Auntie's children. John Cashore came up to see the places where he raised the little girl and be welcomed by her people back home. All the miles he must have went through with my little girl.

Cecelia's welcome home ceremony came a year after the protection of the Kitlope at which she was given the name Nuyem dzeets 'iksduqʷia, which means Code of the Eagle. The Haisla issued an invitation to those who had worked on the Kitlope's protection, which included John Cashore, in his political capacity, many of the groups and West Fraser. Father and daughter narrate the rather dramatic ceremony. First John:

> It was in Kitamaat and there had been a huge snowstorm. There was snow 10 feet high on each side of the road out to the runway at the airport. There was an extra seat on the [government] plane and Cecelia was able to come up. There was a circle dance, and she was presented by Louisa with a button blanket, then she was given her name. When the event was over, we got back on the plane and flew back. We got in to the airport at around 2 in the morning. That was quite the event.[241]

Now Cecelia:

> I didn't understand the significance of the event at the time.
> One of the things that really stands out for me about that even-
> ing is that after Auntie Louisa introduced me and explained who
> I was to the community, everybody came up and said, "Welcome
> home." It was so moving for me because then I had a sense of be-
> longing, not to just my family members but the whole commun-
> ity. From that moment on I felt I was part of that community
> and I wanted to be part of it. I think it was the formal ceremony
> that needed to happen. Knowing that aunties had worked on my
> blanket and when it was wrapped around me and I danced with
> it, that brought it all home, the love and coming together. It was
> wonderful that Dad was being honoured as well as that was an-
> other way to understand what all our ties were. It is because of
> all those ties that I am who I am today.[242]

There was one more reunion: that between Cecil and Marguerite, which
took place a few years later in a Greek restaurant. Marguerite recalls the
reunion:

> Cecelia had come down and had asked me once before if I
> was willing to meet with Cecil and I had said, "Only publicly."
> Cecelia phoned me and left a message on the machine because
> she couldn't get hold of me: "Dad is in town, do you think you
> could come for supper tonight?" She had said, "The Cashores are
> coming and my in-laws are coming, will you come? But you don't
> have to if you don't want to." I really thought about it; talked to
> Peter, my husband. He said, "If you want to go, go. It is OK with
> me." So I thought doors can't open if you don't ever open them.
> So I went and I thought, now I am here, what do I do? Do I shake
> hands with him? Do I give him a hug? What is the protocol?
> It was really awesome, because Maud [Cecil's late daughter] came
> in ahead of him. Cecelia introduced me to Maud, and Maud threw
> her arms around me and said, "I've heard a lot about you." He was
> right behind and I said, "I guess we should hug?" I don't know if
> those were the actual words and it was a careful hug, but OK.
> So it worked really well. He gave a very slow speech and he
> honoured me for carrying her, and then honoured John and
> Sharon for adopting her, and then honoured the in-laws for their

care of her. I thought, "There is something good about you; I just couldn't find it at the time. There were times that I was really angry at him and did counselling around it, but what good is there in holding it.[243]

If Cecelia were to have gone looking for two sets of parents committed to welcoming her home, she couldn't have found better than Cecil Paul, Marguerite Wood and John and Sharon Cashore.

Eighty-seven Steps: Forgiving the Church

I think that mostly people of my age have a little difficulty of accepting things have turned 'round for them. Can you forgive everything in your journey? It might be another person. From the back of my house here to the front door of the United Church, is 87 steps. I still never stepped inside, and I never go. The United Church of Canada tormented me and hurt me bad, and the church of prayer is right here. I have still got something right here that I can't get rid of it. Some of my people are suing the United Church of Canada and the government. They ask me why I don't sue. But that is not my way. If I am going to get well, I need to forgive. Eighty-seven steps.

KITAMAAT, SEPTEMBER 23, 2017

The house has three generations of Paul men left in it. Three of Cecil's daughters are now buried. One in Kemano and two in Kitamaat. Junior is looking after his dad and his eldest sister Joyce's boy, Thomas. Cecil Jr. keeps the supply of hot coffee and all other life support systems going for his dad, including sitting up with him nights when he wakes in distress. He is uncle and aunt to all his nephews and nieces, as well as Thomas. He's been temporarily laid off with injuries and for now he is a full-time caregiver.

The Blue Jays are playing their last game of the season and Cecil Jr. is watching it with his dad. A real blue jay – a Steller's jay – pops fearlessly into the house, ferreting around the sofa for crumbs. "He knows we are Blue Jay supporters," Junior jokes. The crows stay out on the porch, loudly finishing off the leftover rice from an old dinner. Cecil comes over to pour himself a coffee and watches a red squirrel leap effortlessly from a very dead and old crabapple tree (probably one that Indian Reserve Commissioner Peter O'Reilly wrote about in 1890) to the old smokehouse, then from the old family house – all collapsing under moss and lichen – to the brand new porch on the new house. He points out what a miracle that such a small creature can leap such wide gaps so easily.

There was a big walk for Reconciliation down in Vancouver this weekend, and Cecelia was in Vancouver, where she lives, organizing one of the orange T-shirt campaigns to raise awareness. Cecil had joined her for the first Reconciliation walk in 2013. As they walked, Cecelia leaned over to her dad and said, "Dad, they are all walking for you." The photograph of the two of them says it all.

Tonight we are going to a dinner in the basement of the church hall held by Gerald and Gail Amos in honour of Bruce Hill, who died last week. When I walk to the church basement, I count out the 87 steps to the church. Bruce was all set to go on a trip with Cecil and Gerald one last time to the Kitlope, but he didn't make it. Gerald is declining rapidly too. Cecil only buried his third daughter Maudie a month ago in the Kemano. Her name, Gwiiyms Moodzill, means humpback whale. On the way back from the burial ground in Kemano, a humpback whale appeared and dove right by the boat. It was a goodbye wave.

Louisa and Murray Smith arrive from Rupert with a tray of smoked black cod for the feast tonight. The kitchen fills with steam and smells of smoked cod and carrots. Junior goes down to the basement and brings up a jar of oolichan grease. It is gold and pure. Cecil puts on his dress trousers and black fedora and walks the 87 steps over to the church basement for a memorial feast. He would do that for his white warrior brother.

Watchmen: Caretakers of the Kitlope

When we finally won the battle for the Kitlope, they were gonna start the Watchmen, Nanakila – caretakers of the Kitlope, Haisla. And my boy was one of them, Cecil Junior. It had never dawned on me, what's going to happen. None of these Haisla or us had the experience caretaking something. It was taken away from us for how many centuries? Now put it in our lap again. Here you go. We had no experience. I talked to Gerald about it: "Let's get the chiefs together."

Brian [Falconer] came to ask me what is it going to be like for him in the Kitlope. He knew that we're in a journey that we have never travelled before. Of taking responsibility that's put in our land, of how we're going to conduct ourselves to share the beauty of the most untouched rainforest in the world. We could be thinking we are above our white brothers, white sisters, or we welcome with open arms and tell 'em, "We got the law here. All we want you to do is follow it. That's all we're gonna ask." I had to prepare my boys, when they get the uniform. It's amazing, once you have been underneath the feet of the government and then they give you a uniform, the power you feel inside has to explode. And an explosion is no good.

One day, this couple came up to Kemano, they were going to the United States, so they asked me to come along for a couple of months. We went to all the parks in the states starting in Seattle, all the way down, and I met all the young people who have uniforms working for the parks. I met all nationalities, having coffee with them. That is why I took the ride around all the parks, all the nationalities; your mind and heart are not separated by race or colour. My boy was one of the first to wear a uniform, and I told them what my brother said from Haida Gwaii: "Welcome each one with grace and tell them this is our law. No alcohol, pick up all the garbage. Simple little things."

One of the underrated success stories of the coast is the Guardian Watchman Program. The program, born in Haida Gwaii, adopted by the Haisla in the 1990s and most of the coastal nations since then, became a Coastal Guardian Watchmen Network in 2006 to coordinate activities. The network's slogan is, "We are the eyes and ears of the coast," at a time when government stewardship presence on the coast is virtually nonexistent. The provincial agenda of the last two decades to deregulate and substitute the "eyes and ears" of government oversight with a system called professional reliance (referred to by critics as "the fox guarding the chicken coop") has left the seas and land vulnerable to poaching, pollution and illegal activities; it has also left the field wide open to resume traditional stewardship activities.

Watchmen duties have increased every year, monitoring for illegal activities: trophy hunting of grizzly, illegal sport fishing, oil spills, injured marine mammals, poaching, dumping of garbage, illegal logging, looting of archaeological sites, forest fires, lost tourists and natural emergencies. Watchmen are also collecting their own scientific information on wildlife, marine life and archaeological and recreational activity on behalf of their nation to help guide some agreements on land and water management. Funding for the Watchmen programs comes partially from the interest earned on the $120 million Coast Opportunities Fund, which was generated by environmental organizations and First Nations and matched by provincial and federal funds for the Great Bear Rainforest Agreement.

There are now various training programs that translate into what a fisheries officer or park warden job would require.

Fishing Licences: The Government Lowering Us Down

Fresh prawns, halibut, it is so important to go out and relax on the ocean with a beautiful fresh fish. There are only four of the prawn fishermen left from the central coast: Bella Bella, one from Hartley Bay and two from Port Simpson. Anyway, there was seven Native people had licences, and my brother Dan Paul was one of them. Instead of calling it Indian licences, they call it "grandfather," but you cannot sell those licences. They put that "grandfather" name on so that the Native people would be confused, the government lowering us down. The licence that they will sell to non-Native is quite high; Native licence is almost half. They had a real difficult journey. They had a few meetings. They called me down to Bella Bella to meet the people, and I didn't say a word. I didn't know nothing about prawn fishing. But what I heard was some painful things, the language they used, the government, concerning Native people for fishing. But that is the way it is.

When the Davis Plan was introduced in 1971, the Native fishing fleet had already declined by half in less than seven years. The commercial fleets were blowing locals out of the water at the same time that stocks were declining. It was the final nail in the coffin for small-scale Native fishermen; it favoured those with capital who could improve the efficiency of their boats to meet increased operating standards. Through the buy-back program, the Department of Fisheries and Oceans reduced the number of boats, as those who couldn't afford to upgrade had no alternative but to sell. The department also consolidated the fleet by giving larger boats the ability to obtain rights to fish in other areas.

The "grandfather clause" that Wa'xaid refers to is the special Native licence that the Department of Fisheries and Oceans created in response to the rapid decline in Native fishers. It was a token, inexpensive licence for existing boat owners which gave them the right to fish but not the ability to sell the licence – hence the "grandfather" term. Under another federal program, called the Indian Fishermen's Assistance Program, there was a bit of capital available to upgrade, but again it favoured existing boat owners who had the down payment necessary to get in on the scheme.[244]

Fishing policy did not change substantially with the Mifflin Plan in the

1990s, replacing the Davis Plan with the same results. Here Corky Evans, then minister of agriculture, fisheries and food for BC, sums up the two world views of fisheries at a standing committee for the House of Commons on fish:

> The economists argue that when the fishing fleet is too large the marginal fishers should be eliminated, and hence the Davis plan and then the Mifflin plan and the placing of huge costs on the acquisition of a licence to go fishing...For example, if you were an economist studying west coast salmon you would say that total salmon harvests are generally increasing. But if you're a resident of Bella Bella or a DFO biologist, you would say that people are starving because the ecosystem that once made them commercial fishers and processors is wounded. If you're an economist, you would say that the Mifflin plan to reduce the fleet to increase the viability of the remaining operators was a perfectly rational response to a changing technology and market conditions. If, however, you were a resident of Ahousat, or maybe a lot of the people in this room, you would say that it's the elimination of half the jobs in your community.[245]

A Gift that Is Free: My Japanese Brother

In the old days, they wouldn't catch salmon for the winter until after they spawn. The male and females loses lots of its fat and they had bent boxes – see them in the museum – where they stack them up. When you think about it, that is conservation our people are doing. Letting them reproduce. The eggs lay and then they take the fish after they have spawned when the flesh loses all of its fat. Without the fat it means it won't turn rancid in the boxes in January and February. They say in February, *Quo'xemt'swa*, when people will take the scraps of meat from the bottom of the box. It is the last time they take what they preserve from the fall before. The next fish that comes up is the steelhead. First salmon that will go up the river. Now they can take it to eat. Then oolichans come. Gift from the Creator. Spring salmon now. The flesh is still firm, but it will taste different when it is in the river. So the spring come early. Then the humps [pinks], dogs [chum] and coho. Coho is the last one that will come up. Last fish. Coho running until November. They made it so that our people never starved, always food. Our house burnt down in Kemano, with all the old bent boxes and artifacts in them.

They wanted to put a fish farm in Kitamaat. Without knowing too much about it, I opposed it. There was only the two of us, me and Russell Ross, who I was with in Alberni, opposing this fish farm. One hereditary chief of the Kitasoo – very good friend outside the political arena – he was for it 100 per cent. He seen his people with money in pocket and could bring money to put in a fish plant close by here: "What the hell is our alternative, Wa'xaid, to put a few dollars in our people's pocket?"

I tell him, "Hemas, I am not too far away from you, and I appreciate it if you lower voice when you address me." That was my opening statement. How can I penetrate to tell him how bad the fish farm is for the natural gift of the salmon? How do they interact? Is there going to be differences? I don't know. But let us find out the differences before we say okay. I am for putting money in people's pockets, but before I agree I want to find out what damage fish farming does to the natural fish – a gift that is free.

When you have a debate, you try to explain to people what happens. *K'uun qʷotla*. Did you hear? Maybe I didn't hear; I'm sitting right beside you, but it didn't go through. I told him, "There are many alternatives to keeping a foreign fish – the Atlantic salmon – in our land. Nobody knows too much about what the Atlantic salmon is going to do if it escapes and goes into the rivers. You have enough salmon from our Creator. Every year, these rivers are full. Why bring in farmed fish from the Atlantic and plant it here? What is the alternative? Build your own cannery and do Alaska black cod but not a foreign fish."

The Kitasoo invited us down to take a look. They took us out to the pens and there was a Native kid feeding the fish. I ask the kid, "When did you start working here?"

"Three days ago," he said.

"Who worked here before?"

He said, "A couple of white boys."

They hired the Native kids because they invited the Haisla and had promised that it would be all Native people working there. I went to the chief and asked, "What did the government promise? That all the Kitasoo would work?" In the plant, not one Kitasoo was working there. When I got close to the pens, I smelt something like the fur of a dog when it gets close to the fire. When I saw what the kid was feeding the salmon, the stuff smelled the same.

We went through the plant and put those white clothes on. We see all this white fish. "Why is it white fish?" I ask.

"These are for Japan. Those fish over there are red, ordered by Americans. They like the red flesh." How do they change the colour for Americans buying red fish and Japanese buying white? Playing god?

We had a little gathering, they fed us, and I said, "You taste that same dog smell from the feed in the salmon's flesh." When I got back to Kitamaat, I went and told each hereditary chief, one-to-one.

Five years, we fight the fish farms. That is when I got really close to David Suzuki. Phoned him every day. I think he got tired of me. I learned to trust him because he was my Japanese brother. No matter what colour, there is no difference. It's the feeling, once you came into the arena and see what you are facing. David sent a young Native guy from Alert Bay who had videos underwater from the farms; the bad things coming into the farms, the sea cucumbers all dead below the nets. He showed it to the people. What did the company promise? It was the turning point.

One springtime, David calls up and says, "Hey, Brother, get your regalia. We are going to go on a big trip." We flew to Juneau. He took me to his stateroom and told me, "We are going to stop in every village along the coast and I want you to ask each chief to welcome us in his land." We had to go to Masset first, then Rupert, Hartley Bay, Klemtu, last stop Bella Coola.

I told him, "You are a crazy Japanese-Canadian, my brother."

Tara his wife said, "What did you call my husband?"

I said, "Your honourable Japanese gentleman."

When we got to Bella Coola, there was a big friction in the village. There is a beautiful river and the council want to clear-cut it, but dogs [chum] go up there. The village was divided. A lot of people were unemployed. The hereditary chief said, "No, leave it the way it is. Once we clear-cut that river, how long will it take to feed our people again? The logging is going to kill our river and there will be no more fish." The hereditary chief was Lawrence King. After he came out of Alberni Residential School, his grandfather gave him that name Chief Pootlass.

I say a prayer. I talked to the chief councillor who was the hereditary chief's brother. Then they had two little girls, each carrying a spring salmon. They were Salmon Clan, and the only way you could be a Salmon Clan was to be a twin. My friend came with a knife, and they cut out the hearts of the salmon. They were facing the river and they slowly turned 'round and they sang a song and threw the hearts back into the river: "Come back to the river."

That night, they had a dance, and Lawrence told me this song came from the Kitlope and the dancer was a Haisla girl. The drums started dancing. It was the first time I heard the Kitlope song and danced with her to hear the heartbeat of the Kitlope. The rhythm was there, the Kitlope part of my heart. We witness the Bella Coola people and that's when they decide to save the river.

With ancestors so ever present in Wa'xaid's life, it wasn't surprising that he and David Suzuki sailed together down the northwest coast on the MS *World Discoverer* two weeks shy of two centuries after Captain Vancouver brought HMS *Discovery* into Gardner Canal. Those aboard and their aspirations, however, couldn't have been more different from one another. This time, a Japanese-Canadian and a Xenaksiala man, with a joint heritage of surviving white detention camps, were sailing in to share a vision of protecting a culture and landscape for which Vancouver had harboured different aspirations. The convoluted history of how the two of them ended up there is the story of the coast.

Both had their own lineages bringing them to the coast. Suzuki was first hired at UBC in 1963 by the head of the biology department, Ian McTaggart Cowan, a wildlife biologist and early conservationist known by many as the father of ecology. Cowan started the first nature television series on the CBC, in 1955, which Suzuki picked up and ran with in 1970. Cowan's *Web of Life* was the intellectual forebear of *The Nature of Things*. Cowan had conducted biological inventories of birds and mammals on the central coast starting in 1939 and was the first critic in 1949 of the Kenney Dam and the downriver impacts to wildlife in the Ootsa and Kemano watersheds. It was his colleague, fisheries scientist Peter Larkin, who did the first research on salmon and oolichan populations impacted by the Kenney Dam and Kemano tunnel and presented evidence against it. Forty years later, he was appointed utilities commissioner to consider the evidence against the Kemano Completion Project. His conclusions hadn't changed: dams were death to fish populations.

Larkin and Cowan were members of a brotherhood of scientists in the '40s and '50s who were fighting similar issues for the protection of fish and wildlife as the Native Brotherhood. The two societies became aware of one another when a young lawyer, Thomas Berger, began to bring the strands of Western and Indigenous scientific evidence together in his first legal case of 1963. A decade later, Berger was to chair the Mackenzie Pipeline Inquiry that finally accepted Indigenous testimony and turned down a pipeline. These early naturalists/scientists and leaders of the Native Brotherhood had beaten a trail to the Kitlope for Suzuki and Cecil. Travelling in that boat together in 1993, the two men could examine each other's science and find common ground, and – even more importantly – a common spirit. The struggle against corporate destruction of natural systems was not along racial lines as much as economic and world view.

Wa'xaid and Suzuki also travelled together in 1996, this time aboard the *Yorktown Clipper* to Bella Coola, where they met with Chief Pootlass, Lawrence (Larry) King, who was defending an important watershed from logging in a time of high unemployment. Larry King was one of the four chiefs (whom Cecil refers to in his "Four Chiefs" story) who survived Alberni residential school and alcoholism and came out leading the fight for survival of their land and culture.

Suzuki and Cecil have continued their friendship throughout the many issues on the coast, from fish farms to oil and gas. The fish farm issue raised its head for the Haisla Nation somewhat indirectly in the late 1980s. Atlantic salmon open-net fish farms arrived on the coast in a fairly innocuous way earlier that decade – mom-and-pop operations around Vancouver Island and the Sunshine Coast. There were just ten farms in 1984, but within a couple of years the industry had grown tenfold, although only the northern village of Klemtu, which Cecil refers to in his story, started looking into the industry. The tiny remote community of Klemtu had lost its fish boats to the Davis and Mifflin plans. They had an existing processing fish plant that was standing empty and had few economic alternatives.

A moratorium on further expansion of fish farms was put in place in October of 1986, while a commission led by David Gillespie explored some of the stickier issues of growth. That report came out in the winter of 1987 and included some Haisla input, as Gerald Amos was chief at the time. The leadership showed concern for the impact to their own fishery, the commercial fishery and environmental impacts, but many families were now without fish boats or a livelihood and this raised the hope for an alternative. The recommendation was to lift the moratorium but introduce stricter guidelines. The moratorium was lifted in 1987[246] and lasted until 1995, when the NDP once again clamped down on issuing any new licences, although production was allowed to intensify at the existing sites. Klemtu Village ramped up its operations, forging an agreement with the multinational company Marine Harvest. This caused increasing tension between the neighbouring nations, which had placed their own moratoriums on the farms, especially where there were overlapping territories, like the Heiltsuk.

With the next political cycle, fish farm expansion was once again a hot item. Suzuki was well aware of what was coming down the line and turned his foundation's sights on getting a broad review of the science and alternative views to the industry boosters. The year 2001 was a busy one for reviews of finfish aquaculture. The federal *Auditor General's Report* came out in the new year, the Standing Senate Committee report came out in June and the David Suzuki Foundation–funded Leggatt Inquiry came out in November. Stuart Leggatt, a retired judge, was given independence to hear and review the evidence. The northern villages were not on the inquiry circuit, but the Native Brotherhood spoke for the coastal fishermen. Chris Cook (whom Wa'xaid had supported to take on his battle with alcohol), of the Namgis First Nation, was an important witness as leader of the Native Brotherhood. Several of his observations were cited in the report: that Native bands were left with no choice but fish farms because of erosion of their fishing opportunities. He spoke about the divide-and-conquer tactics and his people "being used as pawns by the aquaculture industry... I'm tired of sending letters. I'm tired of talking. I hope my people stand up and start to fight."[247]

None of the three inquiries gave green lights to fish farms. Leggatt gave a definite red light and recommended a permanent moratorium and switch to closed containment, land-based operations. The Standing Senate Committee recommended the precautionary approach;[248] the auditor general reported that DFO was "not fully meeting its legislative obligations under the Fisheries Act to protect wild Pacific salmon stocks and habitat from the effects of salmon farming"[249] and recommended keeping the moratorium while more public review was conducted. The moratorium was lifted on new locations for fish farms, and the five-year battle (that Cecil refers to) was waged in the northern communities where there were still livelihoods to be made in fishing. By 2008 a total ban for the north coast (north of Klemtu) was placed on open-net fish farms.[250] Wa'xaid's "turning point for the north" refers to when the scientific studies started to show the long-term impacts to salmon populations.

Ten years later, Chris Cook was still fighting in his territory on Vancouver Island for a southern moratorium. His nation, Namgis, had led the way and set up the first closed containment, land-based fish farm.

Members of his community did stand up and start to fight, with an occupation of the farms in the summer of 2017. At 75, Cook told the press: "What happened to us, the coastal First Nations people? My words would be 'economic assassination.'"[251] In December of 2018, the first ten fish farms were decommissioned in Cook's territory to create a "farm-free migration corridor [for the salmon]."[252]

Wa'xaid's reference to the Bella Coola people was in 1995 when the Nuxalk (Bella Coola people) hereditary chiefs, led by Nuximlayc (Lawrence King, Chief Pootlass), took a stand and blockaded their most sacred valley, Ista, against the logging company Interfor. The chiefs were jailed, but they issued a declaration of Nuxalk sovereignty. They lost their last run of oolichan in 1998.

Return of the G'psgolox Pole

After we won the case for the river, I went up to Kitlope alone and I meditate. Did it really happen? I remember my little granny telling me of a totem pole that was stolen. We would gather in our little grandmother's house and very faintly I would remember her stories about the old totem pole and how it was taken against our people's will. That was when the journey of the pole begun. They weren't only going to destroy the Kitlope; they have already wounded it by taking the grave marker of a big hereditary chief from the Kitlope. And we don't know where it is. From my little granny, she said, "Look for it." I was ten years old when she told me that. Before the boat came in and they took me away and I ended up in Alberni. That was my parting thing with my little granny, "Look for the totem." And, it took me I don't know how many years to find it, and it was in Sweden.

My little sister and I talk about what I knew about it to my people, but very few people gave me help. I got a Christmas card from a friend from New York. "I have a young friend, works in New York," she says. "Maybe she could find it." She says, "I'll look." She sends me a Christmas card: "I couldn't find it." I spilled my guts out to a stranger in a coffee shop, and then I turned around and she was a beautiful young girl, Spanish, Montserrat Gonzales. I told her I was up in the mountains looking for a totem pole, and I can't go up there anymore. It's over the mountain; it's over there. I close my eyes sometimes and the green grass, and it's over there.

And she says, "Maybe I could be a help with this new technology? I'm the curator of this museum here."

Oh, this Spanish girl caught me with Spanish eyes. Took her ten years. In that ten years, when I left her in that little coffee shop, I forgot about her. But she didn't forget. Took her ten years to figure out where the totem pole is. She says to me, "I went further up the mountain," and what she found in the records was something awful. Swedish consulate was stationed in Rupert and the Indian agent that looked after my people in Kitlope was stationed in Bella Coola. What she found was the correspondence of these two men, on how to steal a totem pole. Wow. It was awful.

I said, "Itemize it down. I'm going to call two friends."

I called Sister Louisa. She was the school coordinator in Prince Rupert and I said, "It's important that you come."

And she said, "I'll be there on a certain date."

Gerald was still the chief because he was re-elected. I went looking for Gerald, I said, "I want to show you guys something."

And the day came, the three of us walked in. I remember I told the Spanish girl to itemize it down to how she found it. She had a little piece of paper. I said, "One of you read it out loud so the three of us could hear." The very first line is: "Ten years ago, Cecil and I went on a journey." I realize now that it was the mountain of waves going across the Atlantic Ocean. It was some big waves. I seen only big hills, you know why I couldn't walk on water, I couldn't go halfway. I'm in my canoe, trying to paddle, trying to look for it; I couldn't make it.

The negotiations for that totem pole to come back were something hectic. When they weren't going any place, then Gerald said, "What do you think if we offer them a replica in exchange for that pole?"

"I'm not the owner of that pole," I say. "Chief G'psgolox is, my older brother. We cannot do nothing without his consent."

So in that little room they say, "Phone your brother and tell him. See if it'll be all right."

I finally got through. I says, "We're in a dilemma here. We're standing still. Gerald suggested if we make a replica in exchange for your pole."

There was a moment silence, maybe three, four seconds. And my brother came on, "Whatever it takes. You go for it." And that was all we needed. And the next time we meet with the Swedish government, our little delegation put that on the table.

In our culture, when a big chief dies he makes two carpenters build it. And when the pole falls, it go back to womb of Mother Earth. When that thing is almost decayed and back to the womb of Mother Earth, the new chief will take G'psgolox name, and he will build another totem pole.

Now when they have taken this totem pole and cut it down, my culture believes – strongly believes – that they could never raise it up again. It's against our law, our *nuyem*, built into our mind. And we had a hard time with the Swedish government because they wanted us to make a museum. When I had our people together, I say, "Look at our land! No ships come in, this is the end of the road. And if you're gonna build a museum, it's got to have proper heat and things. We'd need a lot of people to pay a few dollars to come. No way can you keep a building to do what the Swedish government wants us to do." So I asked, "Come aboard my way of thinking and refuse those conditions." My government was still trying to raise money for a museum, but we couldn't find no funding.

Quite a debate about that, finally the Swedish museum say, "Okay, we'll let you take it back."

And when we came back, the little totem-pole committee said, "Dan and Cecil will go get the trees for the totem poles. We need two poles." I'm old; I couldn't climb around a mountain anymore. I had a friend, Bill Munro, who works for West Fraser who have the tree farm licence for the Kitlope. We had to figure out the funding to pay for the totem poles. Who's going to carve it?

Still the Swedish government didn't understand what a totem pole means to our people. "Why do you want that old pole? Why don't you keep that replica that you are going to give us and put it back where the graveyard is?"

I said, "That's the difference between a museum and our Indian culture. You have stolen this from our graveyard. Its roots are there. The people that carved it could feel the sweat, the calluses on their hands building this totem pole. It don't belong in a foreign land. Let us take it home; we'll give you the new one. In our culture what this totem pole was meant to be, is back to where Chief G'psgolox is buried." And that's why we brought it back up to Kitlope – and it's there now.

They put a replica up in Sweden, and the Swedish people came when they raised the other replica in Misk'usa. I was in the hospital here – I couldn't make it. Great-granddaughter of the consulate from Sweden came up to Kitlope. She came to visit me in the hospital, and we had a long talk. I say, "I forgave your great-grandfather long ago. I forgave long ago." And there was something else. That original totem pole I gave her permission to go and see. Today the old pole has been set free. It is no longer in shackles. Bringing cultures together. We are all one creation.

The Spanish girl who found the pole in Sweden, Montserrat Gonzalez, was at the museum for seven years then she disappeared, and no one has heard from her since. We wanted to thank her. I ask people to try and find her like the totem pole, but nothing turn up.

Can I smoke? More than half-dead and I am still smoking.

In the opening scene of the National Film Board television documentary *Totem: Return of the G'psgolox Pole*,[253] the camera pans the G'psgolox (also Gps'golox) pole from the mythical sea-dwelling grizzly at the bottom, up the body of Asoalget, half-animal/half-man, and ends with Tsooda – the magic man – at the top. Tsooda had been looking down onto visitors of the Swedish Museum of Ethnography for 77 years when Gil Cardinal trailed his camera up to Tsooda's hatted head and sad expression. The camera pauses at the steel collar holding the pole safe just below Tsooda's feet, and the commentator reflects on the "imprisoning of the spirit" that the collar evoked when Louisa first saw the pole in December of 1991. It is a powerful image. The story is told by a masterful filmmaker, who joined the masterful storytellers in the magic canoe.

The public Xenaksiala story of the G'psgolox pole starts in 1872 when it was commissioned at M'iskusa, where the remaining Kitlope people had converged after the smallpox.

> Long ago, when G'psgolox was chief of the Kitlope people, he suffered a great loss, losing all of his children and all the members of his tribe. These deaths filled him with great grief. One day, he set off into the woods where the Tsooda Spirit revealed himself, asking the Chief why he was so sad. G'psgolox told Tsooda about his woes and Tsooda showed great compassion by giving him a piece of rock crystal. He told G'psgolox to go back to his dead people and bite a piece out of the rock. G'psgolox did so and called out to his people up in the trees. The dead people returned from the trees – alive. He observed Zola among them and realized the Zola Spirit had brought his people back to life. From that day on, G'psgolox was a great medicine man. Before healing someone, he first took a bite out of the rock that the Zola Spirit had given him.[254]

Cardinal did two documentaries that aired across Canada in 2003 and 2007 about the repatriation: the first tells the story of the search, and the sequel, *Totem: Return and Renewal*,[255] tells of its final return. Cecil tells his own version of the story that is more about other people's roles than his own: his sister Louisa, Gerald Amos, John Pritchard, Louise Barbetti, and his brother Dan, the owner of the pole and of the name Chief G'psgolox. Cecil also names the central hero of the story as Annie Paul, his granny. It was one of the last things she asked her small grandson to do before he was taken away to Alberni. Annie's insistence on finding the pole had to do with providing the visual evidence for the smallpox deaths. It was also essential that the pole return to Mother Earth, as that triggered the carving of a new pole, providing a time to revitalize the history and cultural teachings.

The details of the return of the pole are in the two documentaries, as well as in a professional journal on cultural heritage.[256] The case was of interest to the museum profession because not only was it the first totem pole successfully repatriated voluntarily by a foreign museum to a First Nations community but it was notable for being such a positive experience for the European institution. Even though they were losing an artifact, the Swedes gained a window on a living culture and the chance to reconnect the public with the owners, storytellers and contemporary carvers – artists who were related to the original carvers. Museum attendance went up and renewal flowed both ways. It was a typical Haisla solution to a seemingly intractable problem of contested ownership. The teachings, of course, are attributed to the pole itself – a living being.

Montserrat Gonzalez, whom Cecil credits for finding the pole, was an archivist for the Kitimat Museum and Archives in the late 1980s and early 1990s. She had learned of the job while working in the UBC art history library with June Pritchard, John Pritchard's wife, when she was a master's student. Pritchard refers to another "parallel universe" that the pole was travelling in at the same time as the saving of the Kitlope. The pole was put into the magic canoe with the same paddlers pulling it home. Both Pritchard and Gonzalez had found the missing pole in Marius Barbeau's 1950 *Totem Poles* book, complete with photograph.[257] He had noticed it while researching government incursions into and thefts from Haisla and Xenaksiala reserves for various specific claims. As Pritchard remarks with a smile, "Cecil never asked me." The first trip to Finland that the Haisla made in the winter of 1991 to negotiate with the Finns over their trees was also a trip to see the pole for the first time next door at the Swedish Museum of Ethnography.

The colonial paper trail, uncovered by Gonzalez, Pritchard and others, was captured in a chronology prepared by the Nanakila Institute. Even Sherlock Holmes is indirectly implicated in the disappearance of the pole.

It was Holmes's creator, Sir Arthur Conan Doyle, who wrote to the Canadian Department of Indian Affairs in 1924, requesting the protection of coastal totem poles. Doyle, at that time, had lost many members of his immediate family to the war, including a son, and had taken his sorrow deep into the spiritualist movement. Like many, he was drawn to the mythological qualities of the poles brought back to Europe and popularized by anthropologists like Franz Boas and Marius Barbeau. Barbeau had spent a summer season in Port Simpson in 1914, documenting the totem poles of the Skeena. That same year, Doyle travelled to Canada on an official invitation to visit Jasper National Park. He and his family were photographed camping in a "wigwam" in the mountains of Jasper. They were apparently moved by the land and people and returned in 1921. When Doyle was penning the Department of Indian Affairs, he was also writing his novel *The Land of the Mist*, in which he delved into seances and raising spirits. One of the spirits he raised was Red Cloud. Red Cloud issued signs from a spirit world to his bereaved attendees at the seance, who greeted him: "Good day, Chief! How the squaw? How the papooses? Strange faces in wigwam to-night...Seeking knowledge, Red Cloud. Can you show us what you can do?"[258]

The Department of Indian Affairs clearly wanted to show the famous Sir Arthur what it could do and assured him that it was "commissioned to take up the matter, perhaps to buy out the totem poles of the Skeena River."[259] There were certainly no policy barriers when the Swedish consul in Prince Rupert, Olof Hansson, approached the Indian agent for the region, Ivan Fougner, to purchase a pole for his country. Fougner obliged and wrote the department, recommending the purchase since "chances are that the pole, if not removed, after some time would fall down and be destroyed."[260] On January 11, 1928, the department granted Fougner an export licence, given that "the Indian reserve was uninhabited and very isolated" and "provided that the Indian owners are willing to dispose of it."[261] Although no one was there that winter, it wasn't uninhabited, but the pole was cut down and taken away to Stockholm, where it was erected outside the Museum of Ethnography for six months. Perhaps Conan Doyle saw images of it, "seeking knowledge" before he died the following year. Cecil was born shortly afterwards, and Annie Paul impressed upon her grandson, as soon as he could understand, that no such permission to take it had been granted.

The pole then spent the next 40 years in an old storeroom in Stockholm. It was then moved to another storeroom and treated for dry rot, along with the ancient warship *Wasa*. *Wasa* was to become an important lever-age tool in the Haisla case for repatriating the pole. The Haisla argued that if they had taken away *Wasa* without permission, then the Swedes might feel the same way the Haisla did about their pole.

In 1980 the Swedes built a special climate-controlled building designed to accommodate the pole, and there it stood until the Xenaksiala/Haisla delegation arrived to see the pole for the first time in December of 1991. John Pritchard picks up the story of the visit of Louisa Smith, Gerald Amos and himself that winter to Europe for a dual purpose.

When we first went to Finland to talk to Eurocan, we dropped in to Stockholm to visit the museum. It was Sunday. The museum was closed and we wandered around and that is when we went to see *Wasa*, the ancient ship. On Monday, only the staff were there, but they let us in. No Xenaksiala had seen the pole since 1927. Louise wasn't ready and it was felt she needed to be the first to see it. When she was ready, she put on her button blanket and went into a trance. She started to keen louder and louder as she got close to the pole. Singing to her granny and aunt. Gerald and I held one another. The Sami filmed it. It was very emotional.

When we went to the meeting then, the Swedish museum folk asked if we had any identification. Gerald and Louise were in their blankets and they rose up and turned around. Gerald's father was Blackfish and mother was Beaver, Louise was Eagle Clan. That was all the identification that was needed. Thanks to Greenpeace, it was all over the 6 o'clock news. The director, Per Kaks, said, "The pole is ours legally, but morally it is theirs." I knew we had won then. When we had been on the *Rainbow War-rior* with the Sami, a man and wife that run a little video company conducted video interviews. We thought it was really important to act as if we'd won already. Queen Victoria's quote comes to mind: "We are not interested in the possibilities of defeat."[262]

Per Kaks came out to Kitamaat in 1992 to negotiate with the Haisla. They followed up with a declaration claiming ownership of the pole, and Premier Mike Harcourt sent a joint letter with the minister of Aborig-inal affairs, none other than John Cashore, to the Swedish minister of culture for its return. The pressure was mounting, with increasing public attention on the Kitlope through the rainforest campaign. The two issues were certainly linked in the international press, and the Swedes' negotiating room was narrowing. In February of 1994, the Swedish government agreed to "gift" the pole back to Kitamaat Village but directed the Kitimat Museum to ensure that the Haisla would preserve the pole. Perceptions of what a gift was, who the gift was for and why there were conditions on the gift filled the next three years of negotiation but also triggered the Haisla's "creativity of the negotiation process."[263] The Haisla were back on the plane to Sweden again in 1997 – this time with Cecil. He shared a room with Pritchard, who appeared to spend the first part of the trip on his knees begging Cecil to reconsider.

> We thought that that issue had been settled early on in the negotiations – that it would be preserved in Canada in the same manner as in Sweden was a given. Cecil wasn't involved with the Swedes at that stage – it was Gerald, Louise and me as a kind of go-between. The initial letter to the museum, written while we were in Stockholm for the first time, and after we had had our preliminary talk with the staff, stated explicitly that the pole would be kept under standard museum conditions designed to preserve it.
>
> That's why it was a problem when Cecil's first trip came after the Swedes agreed to return the pole, and the conditions were established. He didn't say a word about it publicly until he got to Heathrow, and we were sitting around a restaurant waiting for the connection to Stockholm. At that point he said that preserving the pole was white man's law, not Haisla law, and why should they let the Swedes dictate to the Haisla how they should treat their own property? He was really adamant. That's when I crouched down and said that he was right, but being right wasn't going to get the pole back. The Swedes had possession, and had agreed to give it up under certain conditions; if we now demanded to change the conditions, it would be the end of the agreement.
>
> At that point, we couldn't force the issue short of a lawsuit – given the money we were spending on a dozen other things, how could the Haisla ever fund a suit against a foreign government? And could you imagine going into a Swedish court saying that we want the pole back in order to let it rot? A big part of my job

was trying to apprehend how the Swedes were thinking and how they would react to various issues. That's why I argued that taking them head-on was a mistake, and that enlisting their sympathy and help by reassuring them that they were good people, and had been duped, was the way to go. But this one had me stumped. It was difficult enough explaining to Per Kaks why the Haisla were making a big thing of the pole at the same time as they were leaving some remarkable works to rot away at Kemano. He didn't miss the irony, and brought it up to me privately. When Per Kaks came over, I took him to a full-fledged potlatch in Alert Bay and he saw that it was a living culture.

Our obvious strategy was to play to their weakness, and their weakness was the Swedes' conception of themselves as humane people. We were offering them a carved replica with a carver, and bringing it back to a museum. Gerald said so publicly, to reporters and on Swedish national TV that "the Swedes were innocent parties; it had not been represented to them that it hadn't been purchased, and that we have the Swedish people to thank that this pole still exists and they had taken good care of it for 70 years." His frankness and honesty went a long way there. The museum jumped at the bait because they needed to up their attendance. Meanwhile, we were using the Swedish demands to use in our specific claim for compensation to leverage funds to build a museum for the pole in Kitamaat for economic development. En route to Sweden, at Heathrow airport, Cecil said, "No, I want to tell them that the pole needs to go back to Mother Earth like our traditions say." I crouched down and begged him not to say that and lose our negotiating ground.[264]

Cecil won many Swedish hearts, despite raising the expectation of an unconditional release of the pole back to its rightful owners. His determination may have lost ground for Western negotiations, but it gained ground on Haisla relations. That is when they came up with the idea of carving the replicas. When the delegation returned, Nanakila and Ecotrust Canada started raising funds for two replica poles: one for M'iskusa and one for Sweden. Cecil's friend Bill Munro at West Fraser kicked in with the logs. That is also when filmmaker Gil Cardinal started filming their efforts.

The replica pole, carved in Kitamaat, was raised in M'iskusa the summer of 2000, and the sister pole was sent to Sweden with carver Henry Robertson and his nephews Derek and Barry Wilson to do the finishing touches. They were a big hit and boosted attendance, but Per Kaks was still not ready to surrender the pole unconditionally. From his perspective, returning the pole was one thing, but "the property of mankind"[265] shouldn't just rot back to Earth. The G'psgolox pole remained tethered by its wire to the European institution and the replica lay alongside. That was when Cecil boarded another big white magic canoe.

SPIRIT OF ENTERPRISE, SEPTEMBER 8, 2004

We are anchored off M'iskusa aboard an American pocket cruise ship, the *Spirit of Enterprise*, a strange paradoxical thing to be doing. If there is any spirit here, it lies with the grizzlies, Tsooda and Asoalget, not American enterprise. Yet, from this well-heeled crowd, there couldn't be a more captivated audience for Cecil and the screening of the new documentary *Totem: Return of the Gps'golox Pole*. One hundred people are sitting transfixed in the lounge, watching the film after spending the day with him and Louisa in M'iskusa. The replica pole has a commanding presence even with its newness. The passengers are clearly moved to help the Haisla in their cause to get the original pole home. It has been four years since Henry Robertson and his two nephews carved the replicas and took one of them to Sweden. The Swedes are still demanding that the Haisla provide a climate-controlled culture centre, but fundraising has been slow for a building that needs millions. Cecil has argued that raising funds for a cultural centre is impractical given all the other competing demands. Besides, it just isn't the Haisla way to stick living culture into a static museum. The naturalists and resource people aboard the boat have contributed artwork and services for a silent auction for the centre. We've raised about $35,000, but there is a long way to go. A couple of women aboard who own an oil company in Texas decided it was a better use of their cash to pay for the Haisla to fly to Sweden where the film is premiering and argue their case one more time. Strange world when oil magnates are the vanguards of social justice. The magic canoe gets bigger and more remarkable by the day.

From start to finish, the pole negotiations between the Haisla and the Swedes lasted 15 years. In 2005, the Swedes finally conceded and dropped their conditions. The Haisla took one more delegation over in March of 2006 for the raising of the replica pole. Cecil and Cecil Jr. went for the ceremony and visited their Sami friends. Junior left quite a mark, as he entered and won the Sami reindeer sled racing contest.

That spring, the museum readied the pole, cut off the steel collar and boxed it up ready for shipping. It crossed the Atlantic, went through the Panama Canal and ended up at the UBC Museum of Anthropology on April 26 for its official welcome by Cecil's brother Dan, Chief G'psgolox. The Vancouver Foundation also had a big gala to celebrate the return for National Aboriginal Day (now called National Indigenous Peoples Day). The pole arrived in Kitamaat Village on July 1, 2006, to another village celebration, and there it lay, at first in the new school, then Kitimat City Centre Mall for five years before going to its final resting place on September 19, 2011 – the rainforest from whence it came.

KITLOPE, JUNE 3, 2006

In the centre of the largest protected intact rainforest watershed in the world is a jar of white sugar. It is not the first thing you notice in a place the size of New Brunswick that looks like a View-Master show, but it is one of the little things that helps the whole ecosystem function smoothly. The sugar sits on the shelf of a small cabin that belongs to Cecil on the Kitlope River. He stores it there for when he comes up to harvest oolichan and salmon. He needs three spoonfuls of sugar in his coffee to get him going in the morning, and keeping Cecil going is important because he is as much a part of the Kitlope as the oolichan.

Dusk, he tells us, is what his granny called "the time when the mountains are kissed goodbye by the sun." When visitors first see the huge, domed, ice-capped mountains of the Kitlope at sunset, they always comment that they look like great cones of strawberry ice cream. Sweetness features in the conversation frequently. Cecil is a little apologetic about his sweet tooth, against doctor's orders, but when you are pushing nearly 80, and you've lived through as much as he has, you can be excused for small imported vices. There are a few other imported vices he has grown fond of: the internal combustion engine that gets you from Kitamaat to his cabin in one day instead of the week it took to paddle.

A dozen of us are sitting around a fire at his cabin, drinking coffee with various degrees of sweetness. We travelled here aboard the *Maple Leaf* and our time here just happens to coincide with the arrival of the pole in the port of Vancouver. We spent the day with the guests in the estuary and saw the replica at M'iskusa. "I can tell the pole is nearly home," says Cecil, and no one doubts him for a minute.

There is one last thing Cecil wants to restore now that his pole, daughter and valley are returned, and that is the oolichan. They never turned up this March. Populations have crashed up and down the coast and even the large Fraser River run never arrived. As Cecil says, "I can live without sugar, but I can't live without oolichan oil." The reason for the collapse is a mystery because, for the Kitlope population, there is no direct industrial impact. One of the main causes for overall declines appears to be changing oceanic temperatures from climate change. Taking on the fossil fuel industry might be Cecil's Waterloo, but if anyone is up for the challenge then it's him. He can shuffle off a luxury like sugar and gas like the rain from his head, or the arrows in his heart.

PRINCE RUPERT, SEPTEMBER 2017

Louisa told me today about the language of the totem pole and the three different realms that each pole represents: water, land and sky: "The animals each take qualities and teachings of the universe and then they master them."

HAZELTON, MAY 28, 2018

We have travelled 500 kilometres on Cecil's intuition and found Roy Henry Vickers at home. But it isn't just a regular day for Roy. He has just completed carving his gift of a pole for the House of Walkus in the new Tlakwagila bighouse of Oweekeno. His assistant carvers have gathered for the final blessing, as he and the pole are heading there for the pole-raising ceremony. The pole is a replica of one stolen around the time of the G'psgolox pole and put into the provincial museum. Roy tells us he got the idea of carving a replica from Cecil and the G'psgolox pole. This replica is a present to Evelyn Windsor, a high-ranking matriarch of both Oweekeno and Bella Bella. Roy had been adopted by Evelyn into the House of Walkus.

In the Oowekyala language, which comes from the same Wakashan root as X̌enaksialak̓ala, Walkus translates as none other than Good River. There are few better qualified to bless the pole than Wa'xaid, who could sing directly to his handsome ancestors who had upheld that name of their culture. After the blessing, Roy reaches for a cane lying in his carving room that he has also just finished and presents it to Cecil. It has a white eagle head carved out of a killer whale tooth. Cecil's mother was an Eagle and he was adopted into the Killer Whale Clan to keep the name of his Tsimshian uncle alive. The ancestors were definitely pulling strings.

Last Trip with Brian

I got a phone call. I knew in his voice he was suffering inside – Brian. "I'm halfway across Hecate Strait," he says. "I'm going to put the boat down in Vancouver Island and it is the last time I'm going to sail on it."

I said, "What are you telling me?" I ask. "Are you selling the boat?"

He said, "Yes. Will you come with me?"

No hesitation. "When do I have to be in Rupert?"

He gave me the time. "I'll be waiting for you."

I stayed with Louisa. When the time was right, they drove me down. Just him and I left Rupert, sailed all the way. Talked, he cooked for me, I cooked for him. It was miles and miles of quiet, but to me it was loud. The silence was loud. I look at my brother, all that love he had for that boat. He had repaired it from the old fishing boat; all the people he took around, taking all the environmentalists all over the coast, now his last trip and I had the honour for him to call me halfway across Hecate Strait, for the last trip. And for me too. Brother, it is a beautiful battle.

Brian Falconer sold the *Maple Leaf* to Kevin Smith in 2001 and joined Raincoast Conservation Foundation to assist with its research and advocacy for the protection of the coast. He refitted and captained the research vessel *Achiever* that carried crews for studies into salmon, grizzlies, seabirds, whales and wolves. *Achiever* has travelled several hundred thousand kilometres up and down the coast, whether it is inventorying marine mammal and seabird populations in the path of the tankers or the seasonal movements of grizzlies to get a better determination of populations. Raincoast also purchased the guide and outfitting licences (that give access to mostly foreign trophy hunters) of much of the central coast, and Brian has been the de facto guide, leading "shooting" expeditions as required by the licence. To date, they have been singularly "unsuccessful" in shooting a single bear. In the spring of 2019, Raincoast purchased the guide and outfitting licence of the Kitlope. The organization also used its research to support the end of the grizzly trophy hunt, which was instituted by the BC government in the fall of 2017. Cecil's actual last trip with Brian coincided with that announcement, when they accompanied Bruce Hill's ashes to Kitlope Lake.

The Supertanker Has No Respect at All

One day, Gerald said, "You got *The Province*? Vancouver newspaper?"

"No," I say.

Gerald says, "Come over right away. It is a captain from India quoting that this channel will be the safest route to Canada. This captain never came into BC waters."

When I come I said, "Read it to me slow. What is this captain's name? Got his address? You know who could help us? Maybe Captain Brian, a person who came into our shores and can tell how the north wind can blow 100–130 miles an hour in a small funnel like that through the mountain, and if you got a big supertanker coming in with 2 million barrels of oil in it. If you got 12 big tugs trying to keep it out, there is no way you could beat Mother Nature. You got to get Brian; he knows about it. He knows the value of the wind. How can you navigate a supertanker into a narrow channel? The supertanker has no respect at all."

The Haisla have been fighting supertankers since the first proposal to bring a pipeline to Kitimat was put on the table in the mid-1970s. Trans Mountain Pipe Line Company put in a proposal to build one from Edmonton to Kitimat, with the backing of five US refining companies.[266] At that time, the federal and provincial governments were maintaining their position against west coast tankers plying their way from Alaska to southern refineries in Canadian waters. With proposals like Trans Mountain proliferating, the federal government set up the West Coast Oil Ports Inquiry, appointing Commissioner Andrew Thompson to review the policy question.[267] The proposal to move Alaskan oil by tanker to Kitimat and then pipe it to Edmonton for redistribution was made in the wake of the Mackenzie pipeline decision. The inquiry was adjourned before getting to the northern towns like Kitimat, but the northern communities mounted their own campaign in 1977. Trans Mountain pulled the proposal at the end of 1976, arguing high costs, but Kitimat Pipe Line Ltd. had submitted a new proposal to the National Energy Board. Thompson recommended a reopening of the inquiry to evaluate the big question of the public interest for oil on the north coast.

Grassroots groups sprouted up from Masset, Skidegate, Prince Rupert, Hartley Bay, Telkwa and Kitamaat Village. Lloyd Starr was the spokesperson for the Haisla group. It came at a time when Cecil was undergoing heart surgery, but he remembers the village was unified on this issue, as were the Canadian Association of Smelter and Allied Workers union from Kitimat and the Native Brotherhood of BC. The United Church of Canada passed a resolution opposing the pipeline, stating "the proposed Kitimat – Edmonton pipeline poses a serious threat to four coastal villages where the shoreline and marine life would be drastically affected in the event of a major oil spill from tankers moving to or from the Kitimat terminal."[268] Three southern environmental groups joined the fray: Greenpeace, Sierra Club and SPEC (Scientific Pollution and Environmental Control Society). All of these groups formed the Kitimat Oil Coalition. Posters with big tankers bearing down with the slogan "SUPERTANKERS THREATEN BC COAST" were posted in coastal towns, and a letter-writing campaign was launched. It was an early prototype of the magic canoe. Commissioner Thompson came down clearly on the side of concerned citizens.

> It alarms me that this opposition is so vehement. Whether they be motel operators, sport fishermen, shore workers, naturalists or just plain citizens, people are indignantly outspoken. Some have been pessimistic; they think that what the oil companies want, they get... Rather, they want the importance of Canada's Pacific Coast and marine resources recognized and taken into account. People see no reason why "national" interests should necessarily be considered more important than their "regional" ones. If the final assessment, after all the experts have been heard, is that oil spill damage may be catastrophic, British Columbians will expect other Canadians to respect their right to say NO![269]

Iona Campagnolo, MP for Skeena at the time, was caught in the crossfire between regional and international interests. Federal government documents marked "SECRET" in her portfolio give some indication of the political hot potato of the oil and gas industry of 1978.

> Already some environmental interest groups are suggesting that the NEB study is just a ploy to cover a government decision – already made – to allow an oil port. The Government might weather this story if only a fringe element of the population were involved, but a political analysis of the situation points to the formation of an adverse image of the Government in the minds of voters who are more in the "mainstream" of British Columbia society.[270]

The public pressure helped. In a letter to one of her colleagues, Minister of Indian Affairs and Northern Development Hugh Faulkner, Campagnolo shared a comment with him by their prime minister: "He stated that if the Kitimat proposal was just to meet American needs, 'then my attitude is, Why don't they just build a port on their west coast?'"[271] The only dissenter on record for scrapping the project in February of 1978 appeared to be the mayor of Kitimat.

One generation later, on May 27, 2010, Enbridge Inc. submitted its Northern Gateway Project application to the National Energy Board to bring a pipeline from Bruderheim, Alberta, to Kitimat. Markets and the resource had changed; this time it was Albertan oil financed by Chinese refineries looking to ship their bitumen west. The argument about what constituted Canadian versus British Columbian interests became the basis for a prolonged and political battle in which the Haisla were to exert the same arguments but with 30 years of honed legal precedents and scientific data to draw from. Many others with whom the Haisla had forged relationships testified. This was the *Kitimat Daily* report of the opening of the hearings in Kitamaat Village:

> These hearings began with a frenzy of media activity in Kitamaat Village, the terminus of the proposed Enbridge Northern Gateway pipeline, on Wednesday, January 11. Due to Prime Minister Stephen Harper and Minister Joe Oliver using inflammatory language, referring to radicals and protesters in the days preceding these hearings, reporters and cameramen representing every major media organization across Canada arrived in Kitamaat Village to record the demonstrations and "protesting radicals." They recorded nothing but a dignified, proud, respectful people standing together in determination and strength declaring the proposed pipeline will not proceed.[272]

The "alarmist distractions" were Minister of Natural Resources Joe Oliver's claims that "radical" environmentalists were being fuelled by "socialist billionaires" from the US intent on "demarketing" Alberta's tar sands.[273] Not surprisingly, Oliver's attempts to distract backfired spectacularly and spurred a flurry of activity among journalists to get to the bottom of the real motivation behind this "escapade." Journalist Terry Glavin wrote in the *Globe and Mail* after the opening: "If there were a global competition for the most brazen and preposterously transparent attempt by a ruling political party to change a necessary subject of national debate with alarmist distractions and hubbub, the Conservative escapade engineered in Ottawa these past few days really deserves some kind of grand prize."[274]

What didn't pass unnoticed was Oliver's failure to note that there were ten foreign oil companies registered as intervenors and not a single *foreign* environmental organization. Nor did the fact that $20 billion has been invested in the tar sands by foreign companies over the last three years, compared to the foreign donations for conservation over the last 20 years that don't even amount to a fraction of 1 per cent of that. According to Statistics Canada at the time, 35.3 per cent of the $461 billion oil and gas extraction and support industry was already foreign-owned, and foreign-owned companies received 51 per cent of all oil and gas sector revenues.

Oliver's "socialist billionaire" outburst stemmed, it appears, from the blogs and special missives to the *Financial Post* and *National Post*, of Conservative conspiracist Vivian Krause, ex–Conservative party worker and oil patch apologist,[275] and Ezra Levant's "ethical oil" rantings. Among the more puzzling of the Krause examples was the moral outrage at the $5,000 donation from an American charity to a children's summer camp for Heiltsuk First Nations. The fact that underprivileged children from Bella Bella were unlikely to be posing a national threat to economic security seemed to pass Harper's communications branch by.

KITAMAAT, JANUARY 16, 2012

The Enbridge pipeline hearings in Kitamaat are underway. Gerald Amos kicked off the proceedings and told Oliver, "The fact that our conservation leadership has attracted the support of conservation funders should be a source of pride for British Columbians. We do not follow the lead of anyone, we assume and take responsibility for our lands and lead others in that regard."[276] Jess Housty, from Bella Bella, came to Kitamaat to support the Haisla Nation and prepare for her own community engagement in February. Jess is the director of the Heiltsuk kids summer camp that was singled out for Krause's attack in 2009. The Krause spotlight on the children woke the Heiltsuk up to the strength of their voice. "I have never seen people united over an issue like this before. It is incredible seeing the energy that this has brought to our community to fight. If this pipeline were to happen – and I know it won't – it would be the greatest travesty of justice in Canada today."

The Haisla brought their final, 362-page legal argument before the federal and provincial Joint Review Panel in May of 2013. Brian Falconer, with Raincoast Conservation Foundation, presented his final written and oral argument later on marine safety. Biologist John Kelson also brought his evidence on the risk to oolichan populations. The paddlers of the magic canoe continued to bring their research skills 20 years later to the Haisla cause for cultural and ecological justice.

LNG (Liquified Natural Gas): It Is Still Damage

Two pipelines gonna go down to my country. I go to the meeting as I was concerned about the pipeline. I heard the money talk first and then the environmentalists. The hereditary chief Hemas asked me, "K'uun qʷotla? Did you hear what they said? What is your vision of what you heard?"

When I first heard about it, I tried to talk to a friend who is a really good scientist. I was very uncertain about LNG, but in my heart I knew. I phoned David Suzuki. I said, "David, explain to me little bit what is the difference between the oil and gas. On the left hand is oil. I am afraid of that. I am 100 per cent against oil pipeline. On the right hand is natural gas, and in my crazy mind it tells me it will evaporate into the air and the other will sink to the ground and the bottom of the ocean. How do I stand?"

David says, "There is less damage with natural gas but phone me back in 20 years." So, I think: less damage... less damage. They are buying us out if we allow these industries to come in, the garden is destroyed, all for that mighty dollar. And we are so blinded by the dollar. How do we tell our people to think about our garden? A lot of them opposed my way of thinking. And that was my journey.

My little sister Louisa and Murray Smith, they are fighting the LNG at Lelu Island with the other hereditary chiefs of Port Simpson. Murray said at a meeting [with] the federal government, "Chairperson, what is this meeting about? It is supposed to be us telling the government our stories in our country and it is reversed. Government thinks, *They are only Indians; they don't know what the hell they are saying.*"

My little sister calmed things down: "I know you're working for the mighty dollar, but I want you to hear our voice. We don't want to take away your bread and butter, but look what you're going to take away – our whole world."

KITIMAT, JULY 16, 2016

On our way to the old Eurocan mill, we see the only trace of Eurocan left is the road sign saying Eurocan Way. West Fraser seems positively saintly in comparison to the latest corporate tenant to rent Wa'xaid's territory for $1 (or maybe the province is paying them?). The new branding is Orwellian; the sign tells us we are approaching Shell's "LNG Canada: Opportunity for British Columbia, Energy for the World." As we drive along Eurocan Way, Burma-Shave-type signs lead us inexorably closer to the gates: "COMPLY," "INTERVENE," "RESPECT." Unless you have worked for the Royal Dutch Shell company around the world, it might not be obvious that these are the "Three Golden Lifesaving Rules." According to the VP for safety at Shell, Mr. van Dijk, who oversees these rules, "When we look back in Shell, we found that we have over the years quite a number of fatal accidents which were related to people not sticking to the rules."[277] I wonder aloud if Mr. van Dijk is referring to those 60 people resisting oil development in the Niger delta who didn't stick to Shell's rules and died at the hands of militia gangs financed by another department of his company.

We arrive at a 25-centimetre barbed wire fence encircling the complex and fluorescent stripes swaddling everything, including a young security guard. He goes to Cecil's open window. "Can I help you?" he asks politely. Cecil replies, "Just like to show my daughter here where I used to work for 30 years." The guard crouches down to hear Cecil better, then looks inside the car at me, looks at Cecil again, then slowly pulls up to his full height as he tells us he'll have to talk to his supervisor. He enunciates carefully to someone over his radio: "Do you have a minute for a little story?" Cecil and I exchange looks. "Little story" appears to be code for a "little problem" down at the north gate. "Yes, I have a gentleman from the village and his... daughter... here asking if they can tour the site." We can't hear the response, but he bends back down to face Cecil. "Sorry, sir, no one is allowed in without an escort. They require people to set up appointments to visit the site." Cecil pauses, always with good effect. "That's a good idea, we should have done that a long time ago – set up appointments to visit." Irony is lost on corporations and our friend at the gate who directs us to the supervisor's office. As I turn the car around, Cecil comments on how polite the boy had been about the "little problem."

There are three LNG projects proposed for Kitimat: the $40-billion Shell Canada LNG Canada; the $3.5-billion Chevron Corporation Kitimat LNG, just outside of Kitimat at Bish Cove; and a smaller project of floating LNG terminals, Cedar LNG, proposed by the Haisla. Ellis Ross, son of Cecil's friend Russell Ross, with whom he went through Alberni residential school, has spearheaded the Haisla's push for LNG. Ellis Ross entered political life in 2003. He ran on a platform of economic independence, first as an elected councillor, becoming chief councillor for two terms. During those terms, he signed a $50 million agreement with Kitimat LNG. In 2016, the province earned overall $129 million in LNG revenue but gave the companies back $132 million in deep drilling credits, road subsidies and other helping hands with infrastructure.[278]

Ross was hand-picked as a candidate for the 2017 election by then BC Liberal leader Christy Clark on a pro-industry platform. After winning the Skeena seat, he was briefly appointed the first Indigenous politician to hold a provincial cabinet position, minister of natural gas development, before the NDP took power as a minority government. Ross told the *Financial Post*'s business columnist, dubbed "everyone's favourite oil and gas shill,"[279] Claudia Cattaneo, "For the first time since white contact, we were ready to take our place in BC and Canada."[280] When LNG Canada decided to delay investment, he responded in a CBC interview, "To witness the wealth generation in our territory for the last six years but to not be a part of it, and now to continue to not be a part of it, is really distressing to us, because we had built up our entire future around this."[281] Not all the Haisla shared Ross's vision of their "entire future" depending on LNG, including Wa'xaid.

On October 2, 2018, LNG Canada was greenlighted by the new NDP government and the federal government. It was billed as the largest project in BC's history, exceeding even Alcan as BC's ultimate megaproject[282] – a $40 billion juggernaut that carried with it the promise of doing "less damage... less damage."

KITAMAAT VILLAGE, MAY 13, 2017

Visiting Cecil today. I just got back from a trip up the Kitlope and wanted to tell him about the thousands of scoters and western grebes that we saw at Kildala. The grebes are so striking in their elegant black and white breeding plumage, with their long slender necks. They are also plummeting in numbers. To see a flock is like a gift. Their presence means herring. Herring means chinook. Chinook means killer whales. All good news for the house of the Killer Whale. As I came in, I noticed the NDP signs for the candidate stashed behind his door. He hadn't put out NDP signs as usual, out of respect for his old friend Russell Ross. Russell's son, Ellis Ross, was running as a BC Liberal – pro-LNG. Ellis Ross won the urban ridings but not the villages. Cecil told me Nathan Cullen, the federal NDP MP, had dropped in for coffee the day before the election to see his old friend. I couldn't imagine navigating these kinds of confusing waters.

Another footnote to the chapter on LNG is the fate of the rich wa'wais in Haisla territory called Gwaxsdlis (Clio Bay).[283] Clio Bay became a major log booming and storage site, and the lush eelgrass beds were covered up by accumulating logs and wood debris up to ten metres in depth. In such huge concentrations, wood resins become toxic. Both the federal and provincial governments have avoided responsibility for cleaning up all the contaminated sites like Clio, despite endless requests from the Haisla. The jurisdictional tangle over ownership of foreshore, ocean bottom and water column kept the 50 contaminated sites in Haisla territory in a deathly limbo.

Clio Bay's recent foray into corporate boondoggles was the attempt to clean it up by capping the logs with marine clays excavated from another massive industrial project, Kitimat LNG at Bish Cove – a solution dubbed "complicated, controversial and costly."[284] When Ellis Ross was elected chief of the Haisla, he saw it as an opportunity for employment. The work was postponed in 2015 when Kitimat LNG lost one of its major financers. Clio Bay remains in limbo.

This is a list made by the Elders of the free gifts that once were available to them at the wa'wais of Clio Bay: black-tailed deer, moose, black bear, marten, mink, wolf, river otter, lynx, cougar, red squirrel, weasel, white-fronted geese, many species of ducks, grouse, harbour seals, six salmonid species (coho, spring, pink, chum, sockeye and steelhead), bullheads, halibut, red cod, herring, crab, mussels, cockles, sea cucumbers, anemone, octopus, prawns, large western redcedars, hemlock, spruce, blueberries, raspberries, red and blue huckleberries, grey currant, blackcaps, cranberries, crabapples, rosehips, salmonberries, fern, clover and silverweed roots, false hellebore, red alder, devil's club, Labrador tea, fireweed, cattails, cow parsnips, wild rhubarb and dune ryegrass.

TERRACE, JULY 14, 2016

Louisa Smith texts Cecil while we're sitting at a picnic table at Hospital Beach, getting some fresh air after our run-in with LNG Canada. Hospital Beach is the one bit of foreshore accessible to the public left in Kitimat. It is the only place to stop along Haisla Boulevard where we can even see the sea and aren't moved along by security people from either Rio

Tinto or LNG Canada. The beach was one of the public amenities selected by the employees of Alcan to commemorate the 25th anniversary of the company in 1979. It is a windy, forlorn sort of place, but at least we can see the old docks of Eurocan where Cecil used to move pulp around. We watch as a tug battles its way in, its load swinging precariously back and forth in the wind. It is only blowing 40 knots.

His sister Louisa is texting from a Terrace hotel just north of Kitimat. She is there with Murray Smith, her husband, sent by his hereditary chief, Donnie Wesley, Yahaan, to represent Gitwilgyoot – House of Kelp. The territory of the Gitwilgyoots is another massive glacial event of sand. The mapmakers called it Lelu Island. The same glacial surge that left Sand Hill created Lelu Island at the mouth of the Skeena River. It is a place of almost mythical life-nurturing properties: by virtue of unique cross-currents counteracting tide here, neither the river nor the sea can scour the sand away. Instead, the water circles around it, feeding it with nutrients from land and sea. The large flat island has extensive shallow meadows of sea grass and kelp that offer a perfect staging ground for the young salmon that hover at the mouth of the Skeena before making their way to the ocean.

The hereditary chiefs and representatives of the eight other allied tribes of the Tsimshian have gathered in a hotel in Terrace to notify the Canadian Environmental Assessment Agency (CEAA) of their unequivocal concerns and position: Lelu Island is not for sale. The giant company Petronas, owned by the state of Malaysia, has offered a billion dollars to the nine allied tribes of Lax Kw'alaams to give up their interests in Lelu so Petronas can build an $11.4 billion terminal for liquefied natural gas. The community voted no three times, unanimously, because of its impact to the river and their lifeblood of salmon, but Petronas has started work anyway.

The hereditary chiefs stand between Lelu and two of Canada's most controversial megaprojects at the moment: the $36 billion Petronas LNG and port deal and the $9 billion Site C dam in the Peace, whose political rationale is linked to the movement of LNG to eastern markets. Lelu Island, with the extensive Flora Banks around it, forms a unique estuarine sand formation that acts as the nursery for Canada's second-largest salmon river. To the east, Site C is one of the most biologically important lowland riparian areas of the northeast that has fed people for 11,000 years. The Petronas LNG project has elements from Lelu to Fort St. John and includes such things as water licences to remove from the Williston reservoir 10,000 cubic metres of water a day for fracking. These projects are proving to be

Waterloos (or "Waterlelus") for Prime Minister Trudeau, relying on the old corporatese of mitigation, compensation and consultation, because they are failing to listen to the message of Algmxaa. The CEAA had resumed a review of the project but had not yet granted its permit. The Smiths are there to remind the government of its obligation to shut Petronas down. Cecil looks at his text. "I need to go see my little sister and support her." It appears that the one great gift of the multinationals is to continue to bind these siblings together.

The nine hereditary chiefs of Lax Kw'alaams nations signed the Lelu Island Declaration on January 22, 2016. It states: "The undersigned First Nation leaders and citizens of the Nine Allied Tribes of Lax Kw'alaams hereby declare that Lelu Island, and Flora and Agnew Banks are hereby protected for all time, as a refuge for wild salmon and marine resources, and are to be held in trust for all future generations."[285] Three NDP MLAs and Nathan Cullen, federal MP, also signed it. One of the other signers was Gerald Amos, who commented publicly: "I think that the significance of this is that First Nations are coming together and exercising their right to say no to projects like Petronas on Lelu Island that are simply in the wrong spot, and it speaks loudly with respect to the Canadian Environmental Assessment Authority's process and how flawed it is."[286] The Lelu Island Declaration triggered then-Premier Christy Clark's own famous declaration of sorts: "It's not really about the science, it's not about the fish, it's just about saying no. It's about fear of change, it's about fear of the future. The world is being divided into two: the people that will say no to everything, and the people who want to find a way to get to yes, recognizing that's the way to create jobs, that's how you build a future for your kids, even sometimes when it's really hard."[287]

Lurking in the wings of Clark's government, helping "build a future" for her sizeable army of oil and gas investors, boosters and media shills, were two brothers anxious to say yes – Calvin and John Helin. Calvin is president and John is vice-president of Eagle Spirit Energy Holdings Ltd.,[288] a company described as "seeking environmentally acceptable projects with Indigenous people,"[289] founded in 2012 to establish a First Nations Energy Corridor across northern BC. Calvin is also an Indigenous lawyer, entrepreneur and self-styled "advocate of Indigenous self-reliance."[290] John Helin set up Embark Engineering out of Burnaby that same year to take on engineering works associated with the industry.

The brothers were born in Port Simpson, and were perfectly poised to throw a wrench in the seemingly solid position of the Tsimshian. Heavily promoted by pro-industry media, backed by the billionaire Luigi Aquilini, who owns the giant Vancouver construction company of his name and the Vancouver Canucks hockey team, Calvin Helin is also on the Vancouver Board of Trade, a member of Geoscience BC, whose mandate is to attract mineral and oil and gas exploration, and the Macdonald-Laurier Institute, a right-wing think tank that advocates for deregulation.

On November 20, 2015, John Helin unseated the incumbent chief councillor of Lax Kw'alaams, who didn't support Petronas. What followed in the community was described as a descent into "one of the most polarized and contentious resource development battles that Canada has witnessed in years."[291] Members of the village, interviewed by Ian Gill (now owner of an independent investigative reporting online media company), identified claims of electoral fraud, bullying tactics, discrediting of hereditary chiefs and other divide and conquer techniques.[292] Hitting home personally for Cecil were the public and unsubstantiated attacks on Donnie Wesley by other alleged leaders of the community, and Murray Smith, the husband of his sister.

TERRACE, JULY 14, 2016

Cecil and I drive up to Terrace to find Louisa and Murray. When we arrive, we sit in the lobby and order a coffee. The CEAA meeting is closed, so we wait. When the doors open, Murray and Louisa join us and Murray tells us his impression of the meeting. "One thing that is left out is the sacredness of our land; nobody talks about that; nobody says we have to protect our land and water." In his statement he said, "By turning down the false promise of a billion dollars in so-called benefits, we have told the world that you cannot buy social licence from the Lax Kw'alaams people. We will not sell our salmon future for any price. So understand this. We stand united against this project for the peoples of the world. We don't want money, we want justice."[293]

They have recently returned from New York, where they joined two up-river hereditary chiefs, Nmeexl, Christine Smith-Martin of the Gitxsan, and Nmoks, John Ridsdale of the Wetsuwet'en, to present a statement to the UN's Permanent Forum on Indigenous Issues. Murray was repeating the statement he made in New York to the CEAA, which hadn't yet green-lighted the project, but construction had already started despite no permits in place.

Murray and Louisa have low expectations. As Nmoks warned in New York that May, "Right now in our ancestral lands, everything the Trudeau government has pledged to get right with Canada's Indigenous peoples is in danger of going very, very wrong. It is 2016, and Petronas is the wrong project in the wrong place at the wrong time." No Canadian media covered the visit of the chiefs to the UN, except Smithers's *Interior News* and Nasdaq's online news service. As the Smiths explained that evening, no Canadian political leader has ever had the courage in 150 years of colonial rule to stand up and say they respect the sanctity of land and water. The question is: Are we getting close to the time when nature will have to enter the political discourse?

Although Canada is now a signatory of the United Nations Declaration on the Rights of Indigenous People, the Convention on Biological Diversity and the Paris Agreement on climate change, there "appears to be no change in the relationship" or understanding of what is at the essence of the three declarations – the duty to respect Indigenous world views of the sanctity of land and water. West Coast Environmental Law travelled to the same communities this year and heard three messages resoundingly: 1) local people are alienated from the decision making; 2) there is a lack of faith in either the provincial or the federal government to manage the cumulative impacts of multiple megaproject; and 3) people don't want reactive individual processes, they want a proactive plan. Whether you frame the message through a legal lens or an Indigenous world view, the principles of sanctity, respect, justice and survival are still at the heart of the issue.

Murray talked about the failure to listen or follow even the recommendations of the scientific community, let alone those who have the responsibility for the stewardship under ancestral laws. His also wants an end to the deliberate policy of divide and conquer, destabilizing traditional governance. "An organization called Eagle Spirit came into Port Simpson and told people: 'We can give you $46,000 a year each every man, woman and child if you just sign a letter.' There are some that believed it. What they did is try to divide and conquer. Those guys know what they are doing. My nephew is chief of the Eagle Clan and he was invited to Vancouver and offered money. He turned around and left, and told them: 'I am against the project and that is all there is to it.'"

PRINCE RUPERT, MAY 21, 2017

We arrive in Prince Rupert in a rainstorm. Murray and Louisa are busy preparing for a strengthening ceremony for the community after being ripped apart over Petronas. That means the gathering and preparing of food and gifts for many people. Murray's health is suffering; Louisa is a rock as usual. There is some good news from Haida Gwaii. Two hereditary chiefs who accepted bribes from Enbridge to sign a letter supporting the Northern Gateway pipeline were stripped of their chieftanship in a ceremony of over 500 members of the community. It makes you wonder how much one small group of people can take in a lifetime for just being good stewards of the land for all the rest of us.

Oil apologist Claudia Cattaneo wrote her column in the *Financial Post* on the failure of LNG projects to advance at the close of 2017, focusing on the reaction of Ellis Ross and the Helin brothers, headlined "'Sickening': First Nations Left Empty-Handed as Environmentalist Pressure Kills BC Energy Projects." She quotes Ross: "We were just starting to turn the tide on that opposition to everything," and Helin: "These environmentalists are happy to make a park in somebody else's backyard. Well, screw that. You are talking about people where there is 90 per cent unemployment."[294] The cancellation of Petronas, according to the company, was due to "prolonged depressed prices."[295] Art Sterritt of Coastal First Nations, the alliance of First Nations on the coast, identifies its position with regard to the "Aboriginal" pipeline company: "literally no First Nation on the coast is in favour of Eagle Spirit."[296] The divide and conquer tactics of Big Oil permeate every nation, every family and every relationship that stands in its way.

LAX KW'ALAAMS, JANUARY 21, 2018

Cecil hasn't been to Lax Kw'alaams since he attended the funeral of Chief Marvin Wesley, Donnie Wesley's brother. I want to hear some stories connected to Port Simpson that figure strongly in the history of the north coast and in his life. My son Callum has come along to film Cecil, if he lets him, and it is exciting for him to be at the last village before Alaska in the dead of winter. We've been staying with Louisa and Murray and it is Murray's home patch, so he calls Donnie to look out for us.

The village ferry *Spirit of Lax Kw'alaams* leaves Seal Cove and we travel up the sheltered inlet to the island. There is a big boat loading logs called *Forest Venture* as we leave. Men are running over the boom, guiding bundles of logs into the beaks of the cranes. Cecil stands by the frosted glass, watching his breath fogging up the window. I spot what look like buffleheads far off and he corrects me. His eyesight has deteriorated, but he can still distinguish between goldeneye and bufflehead at 100 metres from the way they sit in the water. Grebes and loons scuttle away from the ferry wake, diving at the last minute.

We share the ferry with a construction firm, a few vans and lots of boxes bound for the village. It is a 45-minute trip and at the dock Cecil tells how his grandfather used to call a new bay a door to a new house. We open the door and enter the huge house of Lax Kw'alaams, with 13,500 years of rooms to explore.

A new multimillion-dollar road takes us from the dock to the end of the village. It feels like a gesture from the oil and gas industry given the dwindling number of permanent residents, which Donnie puts at under 100. We drive over the island with spectacular views to Alaska, from whence came the whisky schooners and mining ships of the 19th century, and stop at the end of the road. Murray has told us go straight to the boardwalk, which encircles a burial island connected by a causeway. We walk around the island followed by a pod of harbour porpoise clearly hunting in the waters. In another bay, a flock of harlequin whistle gentle calls to one another. The old hemlocks are gnarled and peaceful on the island. It is hard to conjure up the chaos of the time of smallpox in this peaceful place. Looking south, you can see the channel that HMS *Clio* came up to defend Her Majesty's trade or that the *Beaver* plied, delivering furs to markets and diseased blankets to villages.

There is a seat looking west at the end of the boardwalk that is enjoying a brief patch of sunlight, and Cecil sits down to rest. Out of a neighbouring house pops Donnie, now a retired fisherman, who had spied us and came to welcome us in for a cup of coffee. When we get in, he brings out a picture of the Eagle house that once stood where he had just found us. It was the house of the Eagle Clan and his ancestors Kate and Alfred Duoward. Alfred had received his high chieftanship from his mother, the Tsimshian matriarch Dieks. They had initially welcomed the Crosbys and their Methodist ways and set up the first school themselves before growing increasingly disillusioned with the Methodists that marginalized their leadership. Alfred defected to the Salvation Army – the church in which Donnie grew up.

The Methodist Crosbys had arrived after the smallpox and Reverend Duncan's departure to Metlakatla. Donnie tells us of the chaos that prevailed during that period, the churches dividing up the members who had survived the smallpox. He shows us a photograph of the departure of some of the families to Metlakatla, then motions to the island: "There was a road going up to the grave and they had these big carts, one man pulling and two men pushing on each handle, and the bodies were piled up high and they were going on five to ten times a day and they couldn't keep up. We are still recovering from that."

When Donnie was little, they played cowboys and Indians in the cemetery. "We all wanted to be the cowboys," he says. "I started looking at the headstones and noticed they were all young, so I asked my mum what happened. 'Smallpox,' she said. That is when I really started asking questions."

The conversation between Cecil and Donnie covers everything from the Kitlope to Eagle Spirit and the toxic band politics that prompted its place in the Canadian history of resource battles. Donnie talks of the big offers Petronas lawyers were making to him if he signed his approval for the deal: "My mind about money is that if it comes out of a pipeline, it is welfare."[297]

Sesek'as, *Sitka Spruce: There Is a Story We Can Learn*

Those big spruce, *sesek'as*, are washed down the river. The river got the trees by its roots, bounce them up and down. We say the Creator is making the riverbed soft for the salmon to spawn in the spawning ground. Cultivating where the salmon swim. The roots soften up the sand, so the male salmon will go like that. Preparing for his children to come and reproduce. This tree is one of the gifts of creation, to soften up the river, even when dead.

The pitch, our people use for a wound that will not heal. The pitch you mix with the bud of the cottonwood, which is oily. You mix it together, so it will not stick on the skin when you use it for medicine to heal. Our people have experienced it and carried the grief and the stories, told a chief from the Kitlope. He had a trapline way up in the bush and there was a big spruce up there, and he had seen an animal, a sea lion, and it had a wound on the neck and putting pitch on there to heal the wound. I have shot a black bear with pitch on it and birds. All the animals use it to heal their wounds. If you have a boil, it will heal it. Now the Xenaksiala/Haisla people will use it.

There was a guy who went to granny. He had fish poison and they wanted to take his hand off, amputate his hand, and he heard about my little granny and he went all the way from Rupert to Kemano/Kitlope, and my grandmother healed it. For two weeks they change it, and all the ugly things come out. One month later, he went to the doctor. The doctor said, "How did you heal it?"

And he said, "The person who healed it told me not to share."

When I first got sick, they removed the lower lobe of my left lung; I had cancer. Johnny and Bea Wilson came. They said, "Drink this when you are thirsty." When my friends heard about it, they made a medicine, and now I am healed, by a different medicine for this cancer.

There is a tree down the path that is about love. It is a cedar and spruce joined at the roots and trunk, but they split halfway up to become spruce and cedar. There is a story we can learn.

The first long-term study by the provincial government on the effects of forestry practices on rivers and salmon was started in Carnation Creek on Vancouver Island in 1970. The government reported "This comprehensive, multi-disciplinary study has made major contributions to B.C. forestry legislation, regulations, and guidelines in the 1980s and 1990s. It continues to inform best management practices today."[298] Even gathering the data up to present day, that is still only 50 years of observation, compared to 10,000 years. Medical longitudinal studies are about the same. Perhaps there are one or two stories we can learn.

Cottonwood: Kalikula. *You've Had Enough*

In July, you know the cottonwood trees? The inner bark is ready in July. We call it *luu'kwax*ʷ. You scrape it off. You know the coleslaw we eat in the restaurant? It taste exactly like that. Sweet. Dessert. You couldn't keep it long. The watery sap is *xwä yau*. It is in July too when the sap is running good. I haven't tasted that for a long time. The last time I tasted that, my sister and first cousin made it. She got married in Klemtu, said, "Brother, I got a present for you. Here eat it, with eggs of fish." You can only harvest the bark when the sap is running and after that the tree says, "*Kalikula*. You've had enough."

TERRACE-BOUND, SEPTEMBER 20, 2016

We get back in the Honda and head for Terrace. It takes an hour to get there. It used to take much longer. Wa'xaid tells me about his job on a crew surveying the road. He was in his late 20s and he points out his camps at the rivers we cross, then the territories and their hereditary chiefs we are moving through. The family of his Haisla wife, Mae Williams, owned the large territory of what is now Williams Creek that we are passing through. The smell of cottonwood is still in the air. He tells me the story of the cottonwood and the tree that says, "*Kalikula*, you've had enough." I think Cecil is telling me he's fought enough fights. He's had enough.

Stone Hunter: T'ismista

I close my eyes and go back to T'ismista, our legend, our history of the man who turned to stone and the story behind him. It is the most important one of all the legends in the Kitlope that I use to tell the students that go up to Kitlope Lake. Like the college kids in Terrace who come up and go to the largest classroom in the universe, and I take them to this place. We are all children of the Great Spirit. No matter if you are 18 years old and have never heard the teaching of a Xenaksiala chief of how we came to be.

T'ismista is a hunter looking for mountain goats, that young guy who didn't listen. He was ambitious; he wanted to go and went against his Elder's teaching that he wasn't supposed to go up. He climbed up the mountain and got stuck on the ridge above Kitlope Lake. He whistled for his dogs. They went off. You can see one at Kemano and one at Mussel Inlet. The moral part of that story is that he did not listen. I tell my children and grandchildren that you will not turn to stone like that man, but you will go to the womb of Mother Earth before your time unless you listen to your teacher, your grandparents, your parents. Look at the newspapers of my people dying with overdose because they did not listen to their teachers.

T'ismista has a big hood that covers his eyes. In the month of June, on the longest days of the year, he reveals his face. You see his nose, his eyes and his lips. There are two mountains like that, and the sun will come down in the middle. It is the only time it is not in the shadow. Two times in my journey I have seen his face. The story of T'ismista. Where we can see T'ismista, this is where sockeye spawn, all along here. They spawn close to the shore.

When we took the college kids up the Kitlope, we take the boats and go over with the paddles. I say, "Focus on that man. Focus on T'ismista." T'ismista's footprint is on the rocks going up at Qalhamut, and there is a little place farther up, a rock on the trail where he sat down, and this rock fits every shape of bum. A big guy fits right. Young girl maybe 100 pounds fits just right. When you ask people, "How come they all fit the same?" I get a smile on my face. Then there is a hole in the ground that is never filled. Every time I go up when it rains, sand and stuff should cover it over, but it never has.

Kenny Hall went up in the helicopter to see where the Kitlope starts, and they took me up. We went from where the river starts rights down to the water. At that time there are some big amounts of snow. We were thinking about the ecotours starting at the head and going down to the Gardner. The helicopter came really close to T'ismista. Everyone had those earphones they talk to one another with, and in my language I told Kenny, "This bee is buzzing too close. Don't go too close." Everyone had their camera going and at once all them cameras stopped working, then all the cameras go on again, at the same time.

We got back to Kitamaat. Dr. Pritchard and Gerald came over carrying a big TV: "You got to see this, got to see this, Cecil."

You could hear my voice saying, "This bee is buzzing too close." Then the picture stops.

KITLOPE LAKE, SEPTEMBER 30, 2017

Trevor, Gerald's son, manoeuvres the boat just offshore between the two mountain peaks on the north side of Kitlope Lake. He knows the point where you can see T'ismista silhouetted against the horizon perfectly. It is an eerily realistic caped man with the shadow from his hood falling over his face. Cecil tells the story and points out the stretch of lakeshore where the sockeye spawn. The two images are forever intertwined. That's the idea: listen to your Elders, sockeye to eat. The ancient geographic positioning system of using your eyes, the alignment of two mountains and a summer solstice has the same effect on me that Egyptian tombs do for others. He asks me for my binoculars so he can find the white rocks, which are the mountain goats in the story and the stone dog. There are two other stone dogs in their territory: one we saw in Poison Cove with Cecil and Brian, another above the oolichan camp at Kemano. T'ismista brings him comfort that some things are timeless, like youth not being able to hear their Elders.

He shares the cautionary tales about helicopters buzzing too close to T'ismista. Besides the story of the video screen going blank when they flew too close to T'ismista, there was another helicopter that dropped into the lake. Cecil Jr. was a Watchman at the time, and he helped drag it out of the lake. The pilot and passenger were lucky to escape alive. Tales abound of aborted climbs to the top, cameras falling into the water, even shaving accidents; things just going wrong when trying to get too close to T'ismista. We all stayed at a respectful distance.

When Cecelia's father, John Cashore, came up to see the Kitlope for the first time, Kenny and Alan Hall had stumbled upon the pictograph of a face and hands on a cliff angled up toward T'ismista. Cecil had never seen that pictograph before, and neither his grandfather nor his uncle had ever pointed it out. Cecil says, "Something was falling into place there." After a half hour of stories and stone hunters, he asks Trevor to go get some of the freshest water in the universe from the little creek near where the sockeye spawn. Another survival tip.

Daughters

One day, wintertime, Cecelia called: "You better come down, Dad. I have a flight for you on the plane. Maudie is really sick." So I got on the late plane, they paid my way, waited for me. Here my daughter, Maudie, she had a heart attack and her heart stopped. But the paramedics got it going again. It's the last resort anyway, so they done it really rough and they broke one of her ribs, but the heart worked again. She was all right. I met the two nurses who helped her.

When I went down there and stayed the doctor told us that it will be okay. And then she says, "Dad, if I live three or four days, I talked to Dave. I want to get married. Right here, right now."

And her older sister says, "Well, why not?" So she got the Justice of Peace, the doctors and the nurses. They didn't know if she was going to live, but she wanted to.

She said, "Dad, I look the Creator in the eye, I have no shame in mine. The way I feel about this man."

I says, "You gonna get better, woman!"

She had a little wedding cake. Her sister, Cecelia, they look alike. How can one put them into words of how a dad feels for a young daughter they took away from me for years. Two other girls that I've lost, almost lost another in my lifetime, but she came and got me.

KITAMAAT VILLAGE, APRIL 20, 2006

This is the first time I have visited Cecil at his home. It is a modest, two-floor, four-bedroom, blue house. The first thing you notice as you climb the stairs to the living room are the photographs on the walls; lots of them and they are all family. Pictures of all his kids adorn the walls, including his four daughters, each of whom he points out lovingly: "That is my daughter Rhoda. I lost this girl few years ago. She was like me. The alcoholism she died of was through her liver and I still weep today. That is her sister Maudie you just met. This is my youngest daughter, Joyce, who you'll meet today, and that is Sophia, my granddaughter, Rhoda's daughter, who looks after me in the house."

KITAMAAT, SEPTEMBER 25, 2017

I've just arrived for a week and Junior is exhausted. He's been looking after his dad round the clock, and he's lost two sisters in the last ten months. My arrivals, I reckon, are mixed blessings for him. I kid myself that I give him a break in the cooking and cleaning department, but I have a tendency to overdo the tidy-up for the three generations of Paul men that now live in the house. I come from a long tradition of mission-izing families that sent out their women to all the corners of the globe to spread the gospel that "cleanliness is next to godliness." I'm a giant pain in the ass, so I sit on my hands, watch the Steller's jays and get skunked in crib by Cecil. They say no one can beat a Haisla in crib and basketball and they are right. The next morning we are going to go on a trip. Ori-ginally, we were going to go to Metlakatla to find some clue about the mysterious gentlemen who were his great-grandfather and great-gran-duncle from whom he got the name Wa'xaid. But he told me that, after taking his daughter Maudie back to the Kemano burial ground earlier that month for her burial, he changed his mind. He saw the killer whale grave marker of his great-uncles and it had nearly decomposed back to the earth. "Their home was Mother Earth," he told me. "I don't need to find where they are from anymore."

By 2017 Cecil had lost three daughters: Rhoda died in 2002, Joyce in 2016 and Maudie in 2017. Losing three daughters before your time requires a cathedral as big as Kitlope in which to lay your sorrows. Cecil talks about returning his girls to Mother Earth. The oldest, Cecelia, who only met her little sisters as an adult, is the only daughter left. Maudie survived three happy years after her heart attack with her husband, Dave. Her son, Chris, and Dave accompanied Maudie's ashes from Duncan to Kemano. They also witnessed Gwiiyms Moodzill, a humpback whale but also Maud-ie's Haisla name, sounding off Kemano after the ceremony.

VANCOUVER INTERNATIONAL AIRPORT, JULY 20, 2018

I'm en route to Kitamaat and have a couple of hours to kill before my flight north. The airport is packed full of sweaty, anxious travellers and I've found the quietest spot in the whole airport to do some writing. A young woman comes and sits next to me on the only other seat but looks familiar. I ask her where she is going and she says Kitamaat. She is coming from Calgary to visit her grandfather, her "Dad" she calls him. "Are you Cecil Paul's granddaughter, Sophia?" I ask. "Yes." Of course.

TERRACE, JULY 16, 2016

Cecil and I have stopped for lunch in Terrace and just after we sit down a young couple walks in. It is Chelsea, Cecil's granddaughter, and her husband, having just travelled from the North where they work. They are en route to see him. You don't need cell phones when you are with Cecil.

TRC: *The Weight Lifted from My Favourite Canoe*

There was an election for school board and Cecelia won. She's the first Aboriginal, first Native, to go on the school board in Langley, BC. And it was my daughter. Now her work is educating people about the TRC. I watched the TRC Panel all day on the TV. It will never heal this generation, maybe my great-grandchildren. I talked 30 to 40 minutes, saw old Buffy Sainte-Marie. I met a young man from Port Simpson who said that I gave him the courage to go back. Come and talk about the pain. Talked most, when I am invited to go. I always talk about residential schools. I have reached someone from the darkness.

I'd never met him, Wab Kinew, before, but he was giving a talk at the school that Cecelia works at; Cecelia asked him to go. "Okay. I'd love to go." I don't know how long we drove, but we made it to this little reserve and there was an Elder sitting by the door and children and a lot of visitors. He opened the thing with his own language then translated, introducing the young man to the crowd. He talked in his mother tongue. Then he spoke English after that. What really impressed me was the Elder sitting there, quiet, and he introduced Wab Kinew in his mother tongue. I got the weight lifted from my favourite canoe.

Hanging in Cecil's room is a framed newspaper clipping from January 2011 from the *Langley Times*. The headline reads, "Reekie Wins Trustee

Seat," and underneath is a full picture of Cecelia Cashore Reekie, John and Sharon Cashore and Cecil Paul. Cecelia became the first elected Indigenous school trustee in the Langley School District. Chief Marilyn Gabriel from the Kwantlen Nation signed her nomination papers. Cecelia relates: "I was honoured when Chief Gabriel spoke at my swearing-in ceremony of her dream to have an Indigenous person at the table, and that it was a moment to be proud of. She believes that our children are our most valuable resource."[299] Cecelia became passionate about learning the history of residential schools and participated at the Truth and Reconciliation Commission event in Vancouver. When the report was released in May of 2015, she travelled back to Ottawa with her friend Kwantlen Elder Josette Dandurand, a residential school survivor, and Josette's son, Luke Dandurand. On their return from Ottawa, Cecelia, Josette and Luke made a presentation to the Board of Education in Langley and the Langley School District made a public commitment to working toward reconciliation.

Before leaving for the Truth and Reconciliation event in Ottawa, I shared the true history of Canada in regard to residential schools with students in three Grade 6 classes from Langley. One of the teachers went out and got seed paper and cut out hearts. Each of the kids (there were 60 of them) wrote powerful and beautiful messages on them, which I took to Ottawa and handed out to survivors at the event.

I arrived Friday afternoon. The cab drivers weren't asking a lot of questions then. By Monday, managers at the cab companies were telling them what was going on in downtown Ottawa and maybe a little bit about protocol because I got into this cab Tuesday morning and he said, "I don't understand what this is all about." I thought, "How do I explain in a 20-dollar, ten-minute cab drive the history of residential schools?" So I said, "Where do you come from?" English was his second language and he said, "Lebanon." "OK, if you immigrated to Canada and you got off the plane and you had to sign off that you were never going to speak your language, never be able to practise your culture, you had to wear different clothes and eat different food, would you want to come to Canada?" He said, "No." "We, the first people here in Canada, that is what happened to us. This is what the Europeans did to First Nations." He said, "I get it, now I understand." The cab drivers were fabulous. By Wednesday, they knew who we all were. Every morning, I would ask the driver if I could put my drum under the front seat for the heater. By the time we got there, they'd ask, "Is it warm enough, or do we need to wait a few more minutes?"

On Sunday, we did the walk for Reconciliation. There were about 10,000 people that marched with us: Aboriginal people from across this country; various religious organizations; many people with different ethnic backgrounds all having their own reason for being there. The walk started in Gatineau, Quebec, and went to downtown Ottawa. There were so many drummers and singers, and as we walked we went by many churches, all different denominations. Their church bells tolled as we went past. It was very powerful to me with my background in the United Church, and signifying the coming together to continue the work. When we completed the walk, there was a group of women singing the women's warrior song, so Josette and I joined in. The energy was incredible. They called the survivors out to dance, and I have to say how proud I was to see Josette go out into the circle to dance with a beautiful smile on her face. Josette thought no one would see her, so she joined in. Little did she know that she would be on APTN that night and the whole clip would go viral with 240,000 hits.

On Monday, the staff at Delta Hotel was amazing, but they weren't sure what it was all about. People were drumming and singing all up to the lobby area and into the restaurant. Wab Kinew was there as an honorary witness, and there were some drummers drumming in the lobby. Wab went over and started drumming with them. There were three girls from the University of Winnipeg (which is where Wab works) and I was standing right beside their booth. I am watching Wab and I turn to the girls and I say, "You know, when I was young, I had Shaun and David Cassidy plastered all over my walls because I loved them. Now if I could have anybody plastered all over my walls, it would be Wab Kinew." They just burst out laughing. He is just so dynamic.

When Cecil came down to visit me last year, I asked, "Have you seen *Eighth Fire*, the CBC television show hosted by Wab Kinew?' He was going to be speaking at the University of BC Kelowna, so I asked Dad if he wanted to go. We got tickets and went. Dad wasn't feeling well and listened to Wab all day and then, at the end of the day, went up to meet him. I don't know what they shared with one another, but Wab had talked about how the Elders had kept the fire alive. Because Wab's dad had also gone to residential school, I think Cecil said, "Yes, we kept the fire alive, but we weren't doing an amazing job of keeping it alive with the next generation." I was driving the Coquihalla back down to Vancouver and my phone went off. "Dad," I said, "Wab Kinew has just tweeted that he met this amazing man – you." It was so funny.[300]

Son: Take Me Home

My boy has many years of sobriety. Him and Gerald's boy really hit it off together. They trust one another. Good to have a partner to trust. Everyone loses trust, lied to too many people. I took him out since he was six. Made a bed for him. He helped me fish. I ask him, "Do you remember the bend in the river? Remember the tree that you see on the right-hand side?" The third year, he was nine, and I didn't tell him why but said, "Make me a bed. I'm going to lie down, and take me home." He took me from Kitlope Lake back to Kitamaat.

I tried to teach him how Johnny Wilson and I were. How to be here at this point at a certain time, not ten minutes late, not half an hour late, not 20 minutes early, and then you give up or he is late and then you leave, and they come up and check. You have to program your mind when you tell anybody when you're leaving.

KITIMAT, JUNE 14, 2016

I'm sitting with Cecil and asking him what Cecil Jr. thinks about the writing project. "His day off is today. I'll see if he is home." Junior lives down the road with his wife Karen. Cecil calls him up and hands over the phone. I'm feeling a little awkward. I don't know Junior; I've only worked with Senior. I suggest we meet here, but he recommends meeting in Kitimat at a coffee shop. Cecil says, "Ask him if he'll talk about his dad. Ask him if he remembers when he was 6 years old and I first start taking him in this boat to go to Kitlope to get sockeyes... and when he was 9 years old up in the lake and I say, 'Get dad home.' I gave him the whaler. He come down the river, took me all the way to here. Nine years old. See if he could remember that, what Dad tried to teach him? See if he wants to share."

Junior and I and Brian Falconer meet for coffee that night in Kitimat town. "Are you OK with me writing down your dad's stories?" I ask. "Not really," says Junior. "I'm not sure why the old man lets you write them down, he won't let us write them down." He worked as a watchman/warden for Nanakila/BC Parks in the Kitlope conservancy for 15 years. He knows the Kitlope as well as, if not better than, his dad. "What was it like to have Cecil as a dad?" I ask. "Not easy."

KITAMAAT, JANUARY 26, 2018

Cecil Jr. has just come in through the door after seeing his students through the last part of their job-counselling program. Lots of people came to celebrate with them, family members, even the federal government, wondering what the counsellors did that worked so well. I'm making dinner with my son Callum for the three Paul men: granddad, uncle and grandson. We are a motley family for the week. I'm able to give Junior a bit of help to keep meals on the table for his dad and get him to doctor's appointments. Callum keeps us both company with his steady smile. Cecil and I are talking about our boys and then he recounts the story of how Junior drove the skiff all the way from Kitlope Lake to Kitamaat at the age of 9. Junior continues, "I learned to look back at the landmarks so I could remember what it would look like coming home. I memorized every submerged stump that was in the river. Him and I travelled a lot in the boat to the lake during the days I worked as a Watchman. Dad would say to visitors 'Junior is going to take us up because he is my teacher.' It was his way of recognition. We differed on the question of being scared. When you take people up the river, they are putting their lives in your hands, so you need to be a little fearful yourself to keep your mind sharp."

Grandson: Take His People from A to B with No Shame

The government almost succeeded in brainwashing us. They failed Russell Ross and I because we defied the order and went underground. Now, when you think about this generation, did they succeed? I'll use my household, my grandchild, as an example. I use mostly English when he comes and talks to me. Once in a while I use my language: "Go get this for me; go get that," in my language. He hears somehow, but I'm not teaching him enough of my mother tongue. I'm using half and half. Penetrating another culture, another language. "Grandpa, come back to Grandpa's language." What's in his mind? I don't know.

My granny had a sister called Alice, and Alice married a big chief, Hail from Kitkatla, and my granny married Chief Johnny Paul. The two sisters... and Granny gets lonesome for her sister and asks her husband, "I'll call her up to come oolichan fish with us?"

And the chief agrees: "Call your sister."

When she came, she brought along a little boy, his name is Russell Gamble. And my grandfather was so happy that they were coming that he made a totem pole for that nephew, his name was Dla la xii la yewx. Only him can control the direction his boat wants to go. He is the chief that will take his people from A to B with no shame, with no hunger and no battle. It will probably be a chief that will do good to his people.

I have given Dla la xii la yewx name to my grandson. His name is Thomas Paul. It was my wife who negotiated the name to transfer it, to come back to the Kitlope, Dla la xii la yewx. When people address my boy in the feast, they call him Hemas Dla la xii la yewx, Chief Dla la xii. He don't know it yet, but somebody will tell him. I addressed all the chiefs in the community: "You might see my grandson, Dla la xii, laying in the gutter, and if he don't listen, one of you have compassion; take him up. See if you could make him?" That is my wish to my people.

KEMANO BURIAL GROUND, SEPTEMBER 8, 2004

Cecil shows us an older pole of the hatted man, or Dla la xii la yewx pole, commissioned by his great-aunt Alice, Annie's sister who married Chief Hail (Hale) of Kitkatla. He told us, "I remember when I was 8 or 9 meeting Alice and Chief Hail. I never heard them speak before that of the Gwa-leet, the Tsimshian grandfathers, Paul." This is the way to keep the story of the Dla la xii la yewx name – the deep teaching of leadership from his great-grandfather from the Kitkatla side.

KITAMAAT, NOVEMBER 1, 2017

Cecil gave me the document printed for his grandson Thomas when he received his name on October 26, 2002:

> Dla la xii la yewx was placed on Chief Hail, Russell Gamble, and my great-grandfather, Thomas Paul. This name was returned to the house of Wa'xaid, by my grandfather, Cecil Paul

Senior of the Killer Whale Clan. This name was placed on me, Thomas Paul, son of Joyce Paul and Pete Smith on October 26th, 2002, at the stone moving feast of my grandmother May Paul and my aunt Rhoda Paul. Given by my uncle, Cecil Paul Junior, I am in the house of Wa'xaid. My grandfather is Cecil Paul.

With Joyce's death, Thomas is being raised by his Uncle Cecil Jr., who has moved into the house to look after both him and Cecil. Three generations of men left in the house. In the family pictures, Thomas is never far from his uncle's side – on boats, at the oolichan camp, at the gym. We joke that Thomas is a mini-me for his uncle and grandfather. Thomas has a lot riding on his shoulders, but they are broad.

The Way He Speak My Language

I was going down to the marina to check the boat a few years ago, and there is one white guy. I hear this: *"'iks nak^{w}a."*

He is the only one there. I say, "I beg your pardon?"

And he says, *"'iks nak^{w}a."*

I say, "Who are you?" I shook his hand.

He says, "I am learning about the Haisla language." He said good morning to me in Haisla. His name was Emmon Bach. That surprised me, and we became really good friends, with Louisa, my sister. Everything was beautiful the way he speak my language, that is why I didn't see him. I didn't see a Haisla Native, I saw a big white guy: *"'iks nak^{w}a."* It is amazing. Speaks so clear Haisla words. You have to dig deep down here to pronounce it.

Among the ethnographers, anthropologists and linguists that beat a trail to the Haisla's door, Emmon Bach, like John Pritchard, stands out for many of the people in the village. He was a distinguished linguist and specialist in the Haisla language, finishing a long career as professor emeritus at the University of Massachusets. What he is best known for in Kitamaat Village is helping with their goals of capturing and teaching the language. He held true to what he called the "Mike Shaw Principle," after Mike Shaw, a Haisla speaker. The principle states that time and resources for research and activities relevant to the community should equal those devoted to academic goals external to the community. In an interview before he died, Bach described his epiphanal meeting with Shaw that led to his departure from a more traditional academic practice of giving little back to the speakers themselves – in either practical support or remuneration: "Mike asked why we were there... We gave a 15-minute sketch of linguistics, talked about Universal Grammar, about figuring out what the basic structures and possibilities of human language are, about the special reasons why his language was important. When we finished, Mike said, 'Well, I can see all that but... why should we help you, what good will all that do for us?'"[301]

When Cecil met him, Bach was a visiting professor with the University of Northern British Columbia's First Nations program. He spent five years teaching the teachers in various northern villages. He also assisted with the transcriptions of traditional Haisla stories, created an archive of Haisla linguistics and acted as a resource person for the Haisla treaty work. He compiled the *English to Haisla Word List* in 2006, and one of his sources was Clara Paul (Cecil's mom), who had been recorded before she died. He translated and prepared two volumes of *Stories from Kitamaat*, by Jeffrey Legaik, a great Haisla storyteller, and other Haisla. Bach died of pneumonia in Oxford in November of 2014. Various Western linguists had worked on the Haisla language before Bach, beginning with Reverend George Raley, who wrote the first dictionary, 81 pages by hand. Dutch linguist Hein Vink worked on a draft dictionary and a first course in Haisla with other linguists and Elders in the 1970s.

The Xenaksiala dialect has typically been included with the Haisla work. When Cecil, his two sisters and their cousin go, the unique dialect of the Kitlope language spoken fluently will be only heard on the tapes of Clara Paul, Cecil's mother, and Gordon Robertson, but the tapes prepared by Emmon Bach will at least be there for another generation to discover.

She Is Your Queen

I'm watching the queen's 90th birthday. "I don't want to watch," I say.

Brian said, "Me too."

I says, "But try to go visit her. They won't allow us in their palace. Four chiefs try and go to England. I wanted to ask the queen to apologize to the Canadian Natives. They done it for Australia, apologize, and New Zealand. Two. They won't even call my chief, have a cup of tea. Well, I don't want to see her. She is your queen."

That little girl, Jess Housty in Bella Bella, is something, meeting the queen's grandson. It takes the one you trust to write a letter to the queen, to her husband. Now we're fighting for the same thing, what the chiefs are meeting of the pipeline, and they have been through this before. Why they are going to put the pipeline through? And she questions: Is this wise? How many years have they celebrated the birthday of Canada and yet so many people know very so little of Wa'xaid and his people? Very few.

The story of Native leaders petitioning the royal family for justice is a long and depressing one: mostly one of snubs and betrayals. The tradition of clan leadership speaking directly to the royal family stems back to the Royal Proclamation of 1763. Between 1904 and 1906, four BC chiefs petitioned King Edward VII. A Cowichan leader addressed a nephew of the king who was visiting their territory, and three other BC chiefs followed that visit up with a trip to London to put forward their argument. This is a newspaper account of their plea to the king, which includes the reporter's summation:

> ("We bring greetings to your majesty from thousands of true and loyal hearts"), explained briefly the way in which their land rights had been ignored ("in British Columbia the Indian title has never been extinguished, nor has sufficient land been allotted to our people for their maintenance"), threw their cause on the Crown's mercy ("We are persuaded that your majesty will not suffer us to be trodden upon or taken advantage of"), and asked for an investigation of their grievance: "We cannot tell your majesty all our difficulties, it would take too long, but we are sure that a good man, or some good men, will be sent to our country who will see, and hear, and bring back a report to your majesty."[302]

The king was out hunting when they arrived in London, but he eventually granted a brief audience to the chiefs to deliver their petition. Nothing came of it.

In 1979, over 200 leaders from the National Indian Brotherhood visited London again to petition Queen Elizabeth II. It was their last hope, as constitutional talks at the time threatened once again to leave them out of the discussion. The queen was advised not to meet with them by then Prime Minister Joe Clark. When the most recent royal visitors, Prince William and Princess Kate, came to Bella Bella, Jessie Housty placed a letter in the prince's hands. It stated:

To the Duke of Cambridge September 26, 2016

Dear Sir,

My name is 'Cúaǧiláкv (Jessie Housty). I am a Heiltsuk Nation citizen, a young mother, and a part of the elected tribal council that greeted you here in Bella Bella.

I hope your visit to our homeland impresses upon you the cultural and ecological richness of this coast, and the strength of the Indigenous peoples who have cared for this place for millennia.

Last Wednesday, I received a call from revered Haisla Nation Elder Cecil Paul, who telephoned me from Kitamaat, BC. Cecil has done a great deal of tremendously important work in his lifetime, and inspired emerging leaders of other generations – myself included – to carry on his work of protecting land and culture.

He shared with me that there is something he'd still very much like to see happen in his lifetime. And knowing that you would be visiting us in Bella Bella, our Haisla relative asked me to share a request with you.

Cecil talked to me about the Queen's apology to the Maori people in 1995, in which she personally signed the royal assent for an Act of Parliament acknowledging the injustices our Maori brothers and sisters faced under British colonialism. While these gestures cannot undo past injustices, they represent moments that we can seize to reset our relationships and move forward with clearer hearts.

I am honoured to be asked by Cecil to share this message with you: Please consider the importance of your family's role in resetting the relationship with the Indigenous peoples of Canada. It would ease our beloved Elder's heart to hear such an apology in his lifetime, and if that is not to be, I have promised to keep his request alive until the time is right for it to be acknowledged and fulfilled. This is an important step in beginning to address generations of injustice, and a beautiful and moving step it would be.

Cecil has imparted to us, through a lifetime of stories and teachings, a deep belief that we are strongest when our peoples come together in unity as has been prophesied since time before memory. With the Canadian government's recent focus on reconciliation, this spirit seems to be echoed right from the remote villages of the coast to the halls of parliament in Ottawa.

We hope that spirit catches your heart as well, and that you and your family consider the wish of our gracious and precious Elder.

With kind thanks, 'Cúagilákv (Jessie Housty)

KITAMAAT, MAY 23, 2016

Cecil is sorting out his two full shelves of books. More than one would expect for someone who doesn't read. Most of the books feature the Kitlope. He is in a lot of them – smiling, fishing, telling stories, welcoming people to the biggest unlogged, but not untouched, temperate rainforest watershed in the world. The books are gifts from the many people from across the country and around the world who interviewed or photographed the Kitlope and the Great Bear Rainforest over the years. He is sorting them for Jessie Housty in Bella Bella.

Jess walks softly in the footprints of her Elders. Besides being on the village council and raising her little boy, she leads the summer science and culture camps for the children on the Koeye River, speaks out against tankers, assembles and runs a library and coordinates local emergency cleanup services of shipwrecks, like the *Nathan E. Stewart*, when the inevitable accidents happen. Jess's family act as strong leaders in the Qqs Projects Society, an organization equivalent to Nanakila dedicated to connecting youth with Elders and their territory. She also represented Cecil at the World Indigenous Network. She is a going concern and Cecil knows a matriarch-lady-in-training when he sees one. She has been selected to meet the royal family when they arrive this fall in Waglisla. Cecil's books are the kind of publications that attracted the royals to the region in the first place. The Queen's Commonwealth Canopy Initiative, launched in 2015, selected the Great Bear as part of the commonwealth network of conservation areas supported by this initiative.

Earlier this year, a fire ripped through Jess's library of books. She put out the call to friends far and wide to send books to replace the losses. Cecil decided to pack up his books and send them to help Jess replace her library. His ties to Bella Bella are strong. The Heiltsuk name for Bella Bella is Waglisla. Waglisla is a four-day paddle down Douglas Channel, then left down Finlayson Channel. Cecil's brother Douglas married a Heiltsuk woman. The Haisla and Heiltsuk languages share words, structures, stories, songs, clans and now books.

His two boxes of books weighed in at over 50 pounds. It was going to be a steep postal bill, so we foraged for Coca-Cola cans to get some cash. Cecil's relationship to sugared water and aluminum cans is about as long, tortuous and paradoxical as that to the royals.

When George Vancouver's deputy, Joseph Whidbey, first arrived in Gardner Canal, he commented that the Haisla chief at the time "appeared very fond of bread and sugar; he preferred the latter, and seemed greatly astonished at the taste of it; he gave some to several of his attendants who seemed to be equally surprised."[303] Given that the Europeans had traded 70-pound chinook salmon for sugared water, the Haisla did very poorly out of the exchange.

Chinook salmon is one of the perfect food sources of the world. It is a large fish that forages in the ocean for over five years, packing on essential omega-3 oils and vitamins B3 and D before returning to the river of its birth. Chinook start returning to Gardner Canal at the end of June, peaking in the Kitlope around July 16, when they swim straight by Cecil's cabin on the river. The introduction of sugared water – in particular, Coca-Cola with the added drug of caffeine – left many Haisla with an addiction, debt and diabetes, while the gift of the chinook enabled the Europeans to grab a free resource packed full of life-giving oils that generated an international market for 100 years. As for aluminum cans, packaging the addictive sugared and caffeinated water in a material that requires the destruction of fish habitat – the alternative food source – ensures constant demand and destroys the competition – a Machiavellian exchange.

For the perfect Cecil paradox, one of the big donors of the Kitlope campaign to the Nanakila Society was Glenn Candler Fuller, heiress to part of the Coca-Cola fortune. She spent a month up in the Kitlope with Cecil when she was dying of cancer. Glenn set up the Sweetgrass Foundation in the spring of 1992 to support ecological health and Indigenous cultures throughout the world. She kicked it off with a million-dollar endowment that had come down the line to her from her great-grandfather, Asa Candler Sr., founder of Coca-Cola. When she died in 2006 from cancer, friends and family doubled the foundation endowment, so Sweetgrass now annually disperses millions to mitigate the impacts of its own globalization.

KITAMAAT, MAY 23, 2016
Cecil and I gathered several hundred Coke cans, loaded them up and took them to the bottle recycling depot in Kitimat on an unseasonably hot

355

day in May. After picking them up and sorting them, we were as red and sticky as the cans. The final tally bought those books a boat ride to Bella Bella by surface post. To cool off, we went farther down to the only accessible public beach in Kitimat, Hospital Beach. The view from the beach is Alcan, now Rio Tinto. It is smokestacks, vast buildings and big ships moving bauxite in and aluminum out. A young, enthusiastic teacher had brought down the school kids from Kitimat to give them some beach time. The kids found a handful of clamshells and a few shore crabs. Cecil sat and watched the children exclaim at low tide their fascination with a small pink clam – a drastically changed baseline from the fecund "monster" of an oolichan spawn, injecting their omega oils into the system.

When the books arrived, Jess sent a note to her social network, telling us about it. She photographed the books as they came out of the boxes. Title for title, they were similar to the books given to her by Ed Martin, a Heiltsuk Elder who fulfilled the same role for the kids of Koeye as Cecil did for the Kitlope. Ed too had been at Alberni, didn't read and was a loving presence in those young people's lives. The queen still hasn't apologized. Someone will one day; if Jessie doesn't succeed, she will find someone to pick up the torch. Most people underestimate the resilience of the coastal network.

Lä g̈ølä's: *Put Our Canoe Ashore and Rest*

I told Gerald a few years ago, "Gerald I can't pull anymore. I am tired and sick. *Lä g̈ølä's.* Put our canoe ashore and rest. Build a fire; we'll have a meeting. Discuss. I will go back in the canoe, everybody again, and that was good. Take a look at us now. We must not forget: our gift of love is to protect. The protectors. It is a good journey."

I think that Magic Canoe, it was the beginning of a momentum of how we could paddle all in harmony. Okay, one more trip. Let's sit down and talk about how to put words in this Magic Canoe – the tree. Emphasize the love of all the people that came aboard of the canoe. One thing alone: it was the love of the environment. There should be no hard words to the ones who are fighting. Gotta talk in a soft voice and make them come aboard.

It's my son's turn, my daughter's turn. Cecelia fights for the same thing, whether adopted, it's what she's doing now, so she's helping other people. This journey really helps a lot of people, the Kitlope, the pole itself, brought people from around the universe. All these things could have never happened alone, without beautiful friends who came aboard the Magic Canoe.[304]

KITLOPE, SEPTEMBER 30, 2018

It is dawn, and we are heading out from the Watchman cabin on the Kitlope River for the final leg up to the lake, Cecil's cathedral. Trevor, Gerald's son, is playing the role of Dla la xii la yewx for his dad. Gerald is rising in energy and strength visibly by the minute, every bend his son takes expertly on the river. Even his speech is clearing with the weather. Cecil Jr. is holding the fort back in the village. Cecil is pointing things out to Cecelia, showing her her ancestral lands for the first time. Where he was born, the oolichan spawning grounds, the place of the survey markers. Cecelia comments on her arrival at the river:

> Sitting at the Watchman's cabin – and the river is right here – I keep visualizing my ancestors paddling past the cabin, as if they knew I was here. Sitting there in a quiet moment, I'm thinking my granny would have travelled by here. To go to the Kitlope, to be on the land is more powerful to me today than when I first returned to Kitamaat. I couldn't grasp it back then, the importance and significance of the land. Growing, learning and understanding the culture isn't something that is intuitive all the time. I had heard about the Kitlope ever since I met Cecil, but to be there for the first time in my life at the lake and to walk the land was so moving. I don't think I could appreciate it until I had been there, that connection.[305]

P'ä nii Qwiid: *The Sun Is Kissing the Mountains Good Night*

When it was almost her time, my mother called Sister Louisa to her bed and said, "*Hadii Cecil giilxowd wax mass.* When Cecil goes to sleep, he is the one who is going to turn out all the lights [of Kitlope]." That was how many years before? I sit here and ponder.

So each day now, when I wake up and I see daylight, I say, "Great Spirit, let me walk softly today and not to hurt another human fellow traveller along my path." Tell your children and your grandchildren about this place and enjoy what you see. It is a garden, and we must protect it. I remember my granny and my mum having a chair like this, sitting in the Kitlope, enjoying this time as evening come. I hear my granny singing about the Kitlope. *P'ä nii qwiid.* The sun is kissing the mountains good night. Come, the Creator tells us, we are not alone. This is the Kitlope talking. I want to thank all of you who have left a footprint. I'm glad. Perhaps one day you will come here. Whatever the cause may be, whatever the journey is for us, we'll leave this place and hope that you'll carry the peace of Kitlope in your heart and pass it on to people. Your children, grandchildren. It is not impossible – always there is hope. Thank you for coming to my home.

KITLOPE, SEPTEMBER 30, 2018

It is dawn in the Kitlope and almost excruciating in its beauty. As we wash our eyes and ears in the water one last time, we are all humbled by this new day. I think of Cecil's parting words to his audience back at the Round Up meeting: "My people have a saying, that when we have a parting from our company, when we go our separate ways this afternoon, to return to our loved ones, we ask the Great Spirit that the warm winds of Kitlope will blow softly upon each one of you. Thank you."

MATRILINEAL LINEAGES[306]

Legend: = union/marriage; > child; – grandchild; {} grandchildren

Annie Morrison, Wii'deałh, Salmon Clan (1870 – 1966)
(When Wa'xaid mentions his granny, it is Annie, Wii'deałh. Her play name was
Muk'waxdi – "constantly following closely behind.")
= #1 Samuel Wilson (? – 1917?) (died of influenza)
  > Lizzie (? – 1947?) (died of internal complications)
  > Agnes (1898 – 1947) (died of tuberculosis)
  > Charlie, Wä wii no yew wa (1900 – 80)
    (When Wa'xaid mentions Uncle Charlie, it is this Charlie, aka Dad.)
  > Thomas (Tom), Gwä nax nood (1906 – 47)
    (Tom is Wa'xaid's father. Tom was adopted by his aunt, Esther Wilson,
    Samuel Wilson's sister. Her family tree is below. She married Charles Paul
    of Kitkatla. Tom died of tuberculosis.)
= #2 Johnnie (also Johnny) Paul, Chief Humzeed of Raven Clan (1887 – 1947)
(Annie lost her second husband, and three of her children by her first marriage,
in one year during the epidemics of 1947.)
  > Minnie (1909 – 98) = Guy Ronald Williams (Kitamaat)
  > Louisa (1913 – ?) = Edmond Smith (Kitamaat) {children including Crosby,
    who took Wa'xaid's father, Thomas Paul's, name, Gwä nax nood.}

Clara Thompson, Hay xʷäks, Eagle Clan (1901 – 80)
(Agwii was her play name.)
= Thomas (Tom) Paul, Gwä nax nood (1906 – 47) (see notes on Thomas Paul below)
  > Emily, Gwalask (1922 – 2005) = Joe Daniels (Kitwanga)
  > Joe (1923 – 48) = Edith Wilson (drowned in Kemano)

> Jimmy (1925 – ?) = Ruth

> Leonard (1927 – 47) (died in Miller Bay Hospital from TB)

> Cecil Donald, Wa'xaid, adopted into Killer Whale Clan (November 28, 1931)

= #1 Marguerite Demers (1947) (no marriage, Butedale)

   – Cecelia, Nuyem dzeets 'iksduqʷia (June 4, 1963) (adopted by John and Sharon Cashore) = Dave Reekie {Dave and Chris}

= #2 (Mamie) Patricia Williams (1947 – 99)

   – Rhoda Sheila (May 5, 1967 – July 24, 2002) = Earlin Bolton {Sophia}

   – Maudie Darlene, Gwiiyms Moodzill (June 12, 1968 – August 2, 2017) = James De Kleine (no marriage) {Christopher}

         = Dave Koenders

   – Joyce Cecilia (July 4, 1969 – September 29, 2016) = Pete Smith {Chelsea, Thomas}

   – Cecil Charles, Jr. (December 4, 1970) = Karen Smith

> Douglas (1933 – 2006) = Nora Hunt

> Daniel Thomas, G'psgolox (1934 – 2014) = Edith Cross

> Vincent Harry (1936 – 62) (drowned at Port Edward)

> Florence (1938 – 2000) = Robert Fowler (Kitwanga)

> Louisa, Amalaxa (1939) = Murray Smith (Port Simpson)

> Vietta Linda (1944) = Bernard Wilson

Esther Wilson (? – 1917) (sister of Samuel Wilson)
= Charles Paul, Gwä nax nood (c. 1878 – 1918)
(Both Esther and Charles died during the influenza epidemic of 1917 – 18.)

Thomas (Tom) Paul (1906 – 47)
(Tom was adopted by his aunt and uncle. He was the natural son of Annie, Wii'deałh, and Samuel Wilson, brother of Esther Wilson. The reason Charles Paul adopted Tom was to continue the name Gwä nax nood. Tom was paid the Wä xoxʷ river (Kemano) by Johnnie Livingston in return for a deed.)

Sara (??) Kitlope (possible lineage based on Johnny Paul's death certificate)
= Abraham (Abel) Paul, Wa'xaid, Killer Whale Clan (? – 1925)
(Abel is Charles Paul's brother and Wa'xaid's uncle by adoption. The name Wa'xaid that was passed on to Cecil Paul came from Abel. He and Charles Paul are whom Wa'xaid refers to as "the mysterious brothers from Kitkatla." It is thought that Chief Paul [Sheaks] could be their father, also believed to be a name brought from Kitkatla.)

Johnnie (also Johnny) Paul, Chief Humzeed of Raven Clan (1889 – 1947)

ACKNOWLEDGEMENTS

To the entire Paul family, especially Louisa and Murray Smith, Cecil Jr., Cecelia Cashore Reekie, Sue Lizotte, Sophia, Chelsea and Thomas for their time, generosity, friendship and hospitality; John and Sharon Cashore; Marguerite Wood; the Amos family; the Hill family; the Beebe, Margolis and Ecotrust family; Brian Falconer and the Raincoast family; the Housty family; Donnie Wesley; Kevin Smith, Maureen Gordon, Greg Shea and the Maple Leaf family; Louise Avery and the Kitimat Museum and Archive; Reverend Grant Bracewell, Reverend Brian Thorpe, Blair Galston and the United Church Pacific Mountain region family; Roy Henry Vickers; Sarah Lax; Ian Gill; Erin Nyhan; Sherry Kirkvold; Keith Moore; Andy MacKinnon; Jay Powell; Jay Sherwood; John Pritchard; Bob Peart; Sharon Keen; Charles Menzies and the Gamble family; Mark Hobson; Robert Bateman; Hank Ketcham; Bruce Downie; Wesley Clark; Walter Meyer zu Erpen; Rod Smith; Chris Cook; Jim and Eva Manly; the Kinman family; the Swanky family; Gwen and Harry Underwood; Robin June Hood and Nikki Sanchez-Hood; Eric (Ric) Young; Sage Birchwater; Sabina Leader-Mense; Callum and Ronan Gunn; Alex Harris.

To Don Gorman, Meaghan Craven, Kirsten Craven, Chyla Cardinal, Jillian van der Geest and everyone at Rocky Mountain Books for their support.

To the Canada Council for the Arts, BC Arts Council and Fran Sloan Sainas for their enduring financial support.

Finally, to my mother and matriarch, Rosemary Penn, who wrote a children's book when she was a teenager in the 1940s called "The Magic Canoe" for her two little sisters. It was about a canoe that was only visible to children after being made enchanted by Eagle, Chief of the Birds.

The magic canoe tells her little sisters, "I've been waiting to show children the lovely land they live in, only they're far too busy rushing around with their parents." I discovered her illustrated manuscript days before I finished my own notes for Cecil. She didn't teach us to listen to our elders but to question them. I suspect she thought the adults of her generation had lost their way to beauty and wisdom. It was her great-grandfather, Justice Tyrwhitt-Drake, who was one of the first Supreme Court justices of British Columbia, part of a system that failed to protect Indigenous children and the gifts of the coast. She never finished the story. Perhaps she left it for me to pick up and finish with Cecil.

NOTES

1 It wasn't until June 26, 2014, that the Supreme Court of Canada finally recognized the existence of Aboriginal title – not just rights but title. In *Tsilhqot'in Nation v British Columbia*, 2014 SCC 44, [2014] 2 SCR 257 at para. 69, the judges ruled that "the doctrine of *terra nullius*... never applied in Canada, as confirmed by the Royal Proclamation of 1763" [proclamation reprinted in R.S.C. 1985, App. II, No. 1.]

2 W. Kaye Lamb, ed., *George Vancouver: A Voyage of Discovery to the North Pacific Ocean and Round the World, 1791 – 1795* (London: Hakluyt Society, 1984), 961 – 62.

3 Louise Barbetti, ed., *Haisla! We Are Our History: Our Lands, Nuyem and Stories as Told by Our Chiefs and Elders* (Kitamaat: Kitamaat Village Council, 2005), ii.

4 Elizabeth Anderson Varley, *Kitimat, My Valley* (Terrace, BC: Northern Times Press, 1981), 14 – 15.

5 *The Skeena Pacific Railway: A History*, www.skeenapacific.ca/railway/History/skeena_pacific_railway.htm#_Toc46222629.

6 Gordon Robinson, *Tales of the Kitamaat* (Kitimat: Northern Sentinel Press, 1956).

7 *Coastal Temperate Rain Forests: Ecological Characteristics, Status and Distribution Worldwide* (Portland, OR: Ecotrust and Conservation International, 1992), http://archive.ecotrust.org/publications/ctrf.html.

8 E. A. H. Smithwick et al., "Potential Upper Bounds of Carbon Stores in Forests of the Pacific Northwest," *Ecological Applications* 12 (2002): 1303 – 17.

9 Tom Swanky, *The True Story of Canada's "War" of Extermination on the Pacific* (Burnaby, BC: Dragon Heart, 2002).

10 Tom Swanky, interview, January 5, 2017.

11 William Henry McNeill, *Fort Simpson Journal Commencing 15th day of Sept. 1859 to December 31 1862*, Hudson's Bay Company Fonds [Kept by William Henry McNeill, October 1, 1861 to December 31, 1862], A/C/20/Si B.C.A.

12 "A Trip along the Nor-West Coast," *Victoria Daily Chronicle*, September 2, 1862, p. 3, as cited in Swanky, *The True Story of Canada's "War,"* 486.

13 Swanky, 486.

14 Swanky, 486.

15 Swanky, 486.

16 Haisla Totem Pole Committee, *Chronology of the G'psgolox [sic] Totem Pole Journey* (Kitamaat: Na na kila Institute, 2005), http://www.turtleisland.org/culture/haisla.pdf.

17 Peter O'Reilly to Deputy Superintendent General of Indian Affairs, May 5, 1890, in Peter O'Reilly, *Minutes of Decision Correspondence and Sketches*, Collection of Indian Reserve Letterbooks, Department of Indian Affairs and Northern Development Fonds, file 29858-5, vol. 6 L.A.C., http://jirc.ubcic.bc.ca/sites/jirc.ubcic.bc.ca/files/Volume%2012.pdf.

18 McNeill, *Fort Simpson Journal*.

19 C.O. 306/1, Vancouver Island Acts, pp. 27 – 8, Minutes of the Council of Vancouver Island, 1851 – 61 (Victoria: Archives of BC Memoir No. 2, 1918), cited in Barry M. Gough, *Gunboat Frontier: British Maritime Authority and Northwest Coast Indians* (Vancouver: UBC Press, 1984), 25.

20 George Henry Raley, "Titles to Property on Indian Districts," 1905, George Henry Raley Fonds, 1863 – 1958, H/D/R13/R13.11, B.C.A.

21 Cited in Varley, *Kitimat, My Valley*, 14 – 15.

22 Varley, 15.

23 Peter O'Reilly to Deputy Superintendent General of Indian Affairs, 167.

24 Peter O'Reilly to Deputy Superintendent General of Indian Affairs, 167.

25 The Rev. Arthur D. Price, "The Children's Corner: A Year's Work among North-American Indians," in *Mission Field: A Monthly Record of the Proceedings of the Society for the Propagation of the Gospel in Foreign Parts*, [The Reverend Arthur D. Price of the Kitlope Mission, Gardner's Inlet, In the Diocese of Caledonia, British Columbia], vol. 37 (January 1, 1892), 390.

26 Eliza Scidmore, *Appletons' Guide Book to Alaska and the Northwest Coast* (1893; repr., South Carolina: Nabu Press, 2011), 28 – 29.

27 Truth and Reconciliation Commission of Canada, *Honouring the Truth, Reconciling for the Future: Summary of the Final Report of the Truth and Reconciliation Commission of Canada* (2015), 2, http://www.trc.ca/assets/pdf/Honouring_the_Truth_Reconciling_for_the_Future_July_23_2015.pdf.

28 United Church of Canada Archives, *The Children Remembered: Residential School Archive Project*, http://thechildrenremembered.ca/school-locations/port-simpson/.

29 The history of the five schools operated by the Methodists and Anglicans, and later the United Church (in Port Simpson, Kitamaat, Ahousat, Alberni and Coqualeetza) is called *Living by Bells: A Story of Five Indian Schools 1874 – 1970*, by Isobel McFadden, 1970, unpublished document in UCCBC (United Church of Canada Pacific Mountain Region Archives).

30 *Indian Act*, RSC 1886, C 43 – SC 1894, C 32, S 11.

31 George Henry Raley to Methodist brothers, March 23, 1896, in "Papers Relating to Kitamat and Indians," Rev. George Henry Raley Fonds, 1863-1958 H/D/R13/R13.11, B.C.A. The words "we are willing to help" in the letter refer to building the home and providing dried berries, deer and bear meats, small fish, salmon, canoes and coal oil.

32 Andrew Smith, "Late Chief Paul (Sheaks)," *Nan-na-kwa Newsletter*, July 1900, UCCBC.

33 "Kitimat Souvenir 1898," Archives Reference Collection, Prince Rupert Presbytery, Kitamaat Village, Box 2147.

34 Keryl Mix, "Fire Doomed Former Kitamaat Home," *Northern Sentinel*, October 21, 1976, p. 1.

35 McFadden, *Living by Bells.*

36 Correspondence, May 18, 1919, Margaret Butcher Fonds, B.C.A. See also Mary-Ellen Kelm, ed., *The Letters of Margaret Butcher: Missionary-Imperialism on the North Pacific Coast* (University of Calgary Press, 2006), 195 – 97.

37 Evidence of D.C. Scott to the Special Committee of the House of Commons Investigating the Indian Act amendments of 1920 (L-2)(N-3), cited in T.R.C, 2015 vol. 1, p. 3 RG 10, vol. 6810, table 470-2-3, vol. 7, L.A.C.

38 Evidence of D.C. Scott, p. 46.

39 *Indian Act*, RSC 1906, c 81, amended through SC 1919 – 1920, c 50, s 1.

40 "Vital Statistics, 1919," British Columbia Sessional Papers, 1920 vol. 853-096, 1 May 1919, RG 29, National Health and Welfare/L.A.C., cited in Mary-Ellen Kelm, "British Columbia First Nations and the Influenza Pandemic of 1918 – 19," *BC Studies*, no. 122 (1999): 23 – 47.

41 Maureen Lux, *Medicine That Walks 1880 – 1940* (University of Toronto Press, 2001), 219, cited in Carol Harrison, *Miller Bay Hospital: Life and Work in a TB Sanatorium* (Victoria: First Choice Books, 2016).

42 "M.P.'s Plead for Indians," *The Province*, April 10, 1937.

43 Cited in *The Awakening of Elizabeth Shaw*, directed by Eva Manly, video produced by Eva Manly and Paul Manly (Nanaimo, BC: Manly Media, 1996). Also cited in United Church of Canada Archives, *The Children Remembered*, http://thechildrenremembered.ca/school-locations/port-simpson/#ftn29.

44 Laurie Meijer Drees, *Healing Histories: Stories from Canada's Indian Hospitals* (Edmonton: University of Alberta Press, 2013).

45 J. Coleman, Inspector of Indian Agencies, Inspection of Bella Coola Agency, Kitimat Indian Reserve No. 2 Trespass, October 1941, RG 10, vol. 8213, file 972/1-1, pt. 1, Indian Affairs/L.A.C.

46 Kitlope and Kemano Amalgamation Agreement with Kitamaat, March 10, 1948, RG 10, vol. 8213, file 972/1-1, pt. 1 Indian Affairs/L.A.C.

47 John Kendrick, *People of the Snow: The Story of Kitimat* (Toronto: NC Press, 1987), 2.

48 "Aluminum Industry Project Assailed," *Vancouver Sun*, March 21, 1949. The BCSCA "went on record Saturday as censuring alleged provincial government alienation of the province's natural resources for the development of an aluminum industry."

49 "Aluminum Bill in Rough Ride," *Vancouver News*, March 24, 1949.

50 *Industrial Development Act*, RSBC 1996, c 220.

51 Journals of the Legislative Assembly of the Province of BC from 20th February to 18th April, Second Session of 22nd Parliament, 1951, vol. 80, p. 1.

52 Kendrick, *People of the Snow*, 54.

53 Bev Christensen, *Too Good to be True: Alcan's Kemano Completion Project* (Vancouver: Talonbooks, 1995), 25.

54 Charles Horetzky, Appendix G, November 15, 1874, Letter to Sandford Fleming in *Report on Surveys and Preliminary Operations on the Canadian Pacific Railway up to January 1877*, Sandford Fleming, Chief Engineer (Ottawa: Mclean, Roger and Co., 1877), 137.

55 Horetzky, 178 – 79.

56 *Royal Commission to Inquire into Matters Connected with the Canadian Pacific Railway*, Ottawa, Tuesday, 28 June 1881, p. 1720.

57 Marcus Smith to Sandford Fleming, June 22, 1874, RG 12, vol. 1997, file 3562-9, L.A.C.

58 Marcus Smith to Sandford Fleming.

59 Marcus Smith, Appendix I, 1875, Letter to Sandford Fleming in *Report on Surveys and Preliminary Operations on the Canadian Pacific Railway up to January 1877*, Sandford Fleming, Chief Engineer (Ottawa: Mclean, Roger and Co., 1877), 176, https://open. library.ubc.ca/collections/chung/chungpub/items/1.0056599#p207z-5rof:.

60 Peter O'Reilly to Deputy Superintendent General of Indian Affairs, 156 – 59.

61 Frank Cyril Swannell, "Surveyors Diary," June 1921, in Frank Cyril Swannell Fonds, MS-0392, box 10, file 2, B.C.A.

62 Swannell.

63 Swannell.

64 F.C. Swannell and W. Blane, *British Columbia Forest Service, Kitlope River and Lake* (B.C.L.S., 1921). Forest Survey File #807, pp. 3 – 4.

65 John Pritchard, "Economic Development and the Disintegration of Traditional Culture among the Haisla" (Ph.D. diss., University of British Columbia, 1977), 125.

66 Pritchard, 159.

67 Richard A. Rajala, *Up-Coast: Forests and Industry on British Columbia's North Coast, 1870 – 2005* (Victoria: Royal BC Museum, 2006).

68 Rajala, 174.

69 "Kitimat Mill Once Again Under Study," *Victoria Daily Times*, June 12, 1965, p. 12; "Crown Zellerbach to Compete for North Coast Area Timber," *The Province*, August 3, 1965, p. 2; "Kitimat Quay Goes to Work," *The Province*, December 22, 1970, p. 17.

70 Cecil Paul, interview, June 4, 2016.

71 Reed, FLC & Associates, 1974, Development Strategy for the Eurocan Pulp and Paper Co. Ltd., GR-1002, B.C.A.

72 Kitlope was appraised at 100,178 acres of mature timber, with 7,728,000 cunits (one cunit = around 3 cubic metres).

73 Cecil Paul, interview, September 21, 2016.

74 Brian Downie, interview, September 30, 2017.

75 Ian Gill, "An Easy Million," *Georgia Straight*, August 19, 1994. Archived by Ecotrust, http://archive.ecotrust.org/news/news_archive/Kitlope_EasyMillion.html.

76 Rajala, *Up-Coast*, 215.

77 Cited in Rajala, 215.

78 Brian Downie, interview, September 30, 2017.

79 Rosalina Cordeira, "Clock Running Out, Premier Warned," *Northern Sentinel*, March 14, 1990.

80 John Pritchard, interview, September 18, 2017; Bruce Downie, interview, September 30, 2017.

81 Bart Robinson, "Earthly Treasure," *Equinox*, September/October 1994, p. 45.

82 Barbetti, *Haisla!*, 75.

83 Rev. Thomas Crosby, "Kitamaat," in *Up and Down the North Pacific Coast* (Toronto: The Missionary Society of the Methodist Church, 1914), 259.

84 Smith, "Late Chief Paul (Sheaks)."

85 Haisla Nation, 013, *Final Argument*, May 31, 2013, Northern Gateway Pipeline Project, submitted to Canadian Environmental Assessment Agency, http://www.ceaa. gc.ca/050/documents/p21799/89711E.pdf. Also "Reeve Promises Full Study of Village Protest," *Northern Sentinel*, May 14, 1964.

86 Carol Goddard, "Eurocan and Haisla Work to Address Pollution Concerns," *Northern Sentinel*, April 1, 1992. Also John Pritchard, interview, September 18, 2017.

87 Rosalind Cordeiro, "Clock Running Out, Premier Warned," *Northern Sentinel*, March 14, 1990.

88 Peter O'Reilly to Deputy Superintendent General of Indian Affairs, 167.

89 Rosalind Cordeiro, "Haisla Defiant," *Northern Sentinel*, May 5, 1990.

90 Spencer Beebe, interview, February 27, 2017.

91 Spencer B. Beebe, *Cache: Creating Natural Economies* (Portland, OR: Ecotrust, 2010), 80.

92 Spencer Beebe, interview, February 27, 2017.

93 Spencer Beebe, interview, February 27, 2017; Keith Moore, interview, February 5, 2018.

94 Spencer Beebe, interview, February 27, 2017.

95 Keith Moore, interview, February 5, 2018.

96 Keith Moore, interview, February 5, 2018.

97 Keith Moore, interview, February 5, 2018.

98 BC Ministry of Parks, "Kitlope Basin," *Parks Plan for the 90s*, Information Fact Sheet (Victoria: BC Government, February 1991).

99 John Pritchard, interview, September 18, 2017.

100 Eric Wolfhard, "Historical and Documentary Corroboration Regarding the Haisla Nation's Occupation of Its Traditional Territory: Expert Report." Prepared for Haisla Nation Council, December 19, 2011.

101 John Pritchard, interview, September 18, 2017.

102 Bruce Hill, interview, October 3, 2015.

103 Bruce Hill, interview, July 16, 2016.

104 Yvon Chouinard, *Let My People Go Surfing: Education of a Reluctant Businessman*, rev. ed. (London: Penguin Books, 2016), 205 – 06.

105 Chouinard, 240.

106 Dan Ebenal, "Preserving Kitlope," *Northern Sentinel*, June 1, 1991.

107 Glenn Bohn, "Finnish MP Considers Valley 'Wonderful,'" *Vancouver Sun*, September 3, 1991, pp. A1, 14.

108 H. Roemer, "Kitlope Reconnaissance," internal memo, BC Parks, October 1991, Haisla Kitlope Fonds, Kitimat Museum and Archives.

109 O. R. Travers, project coordinator, *Cultural and Scientific Reconnaissance of the Greater Kitlope Ecosystem* (Kitamaat: Haisla Nation and Ecotrust, September, 1991).

110 Travers, *Cultural and Scientific Reconnaissance*; Grant Copeland, Wayne McCrory, and Ray Travers, *The Greater Kitlope Ecosystem: A Wilderness Planning Framework* (Kitamaat: Haisla Nation, July 1992), http://archive.ecotrust.org/publications/Greater_ Kitlope.html.

111 Travers, *Cultural and Scientific Reconnaissance*; Copeland, McCrory, and Travers, *The Greater Kitlope Ecosystem*.

112 "Chief Councillor Travels to Finland," *Northern Sentinel*, November 20, 1991.

113 Glenn Bohn, "Groups Seek to Preserve Unlogged Kitlope Jewel," *Vancouver Sun*, September 3, 1991, pp. A1, 14.

114 Bruce Hill, interview, October 3, 2015, and August 1, 2017.

115 "Meeting Called to Probe New Options for Kitlope," *Terrace Review*, January 8, 1992, p. 3.

116 Bruce Hill, interview, October 3, 2015, and August 1, 2017.

117 "Decision on Kitlope Deferred until 1995," *Northern Sentinel*, October 10, 1992.

118 Beebe, *Cache*, 127.

119 Bruce Hill, interview, October 3, 2015, and August 1, 2017.

120 Brian Falconer, interview, January 10, 2017.

121 Brian Falconer, interview, January 10, 2017.

122 See the stories "Return of the G'psgolox Pole," "Kemano Completion Project: What Damage Is Going to Come of It?" and "She Is Your Queen" in *Stories from the Magic Canoe of Wa'xaid* (Victoria: Rocky Mountain Books, 2019) about the plans for the Northern Gateway bitumen pipeline.

123 Lamb, *George Vancouver*, 961.

124 Lamb, 962 – 63.

125 Lamb, 963.

126 "How They Say It in Haisla," *Northern Sentinel*, January 12, 1956.

127 Kelm, *The Letters of Margaret Butcher*, 239.

128 "1952 Surrender of Kildala Arm, IR #10," British Columbia (522), in *Status Report on Specific Claims in Canada* (Department of Northern Affairs Canada, 2009), 38, http://treatyandaboriginalrights.ca/index.php/bc-settlement-report-on-specific-claims/.

129 Nanakila Institute brochure, c. 1994.

130 Ken Margolis, interview, February 27, 2017.

131 Bruce Hill, interview, October 3, 2015.

132 Ken Margolis, interview, February 27, 2017.

133 Ian Gill, interview, September 13, 2015.

134 Ian Gill, interview, September 13, 2015.

135 *Watery Visions: Is the Future Potable?*, written by Henning Hesse (Deutsche Welle TV, 2003), https://www.films.com/id/6334/Watery_Visions_Is_the_Future_Potable.

136 Ruth Loomis with Merv Wilkinson, *Wildwood: A Forest for the Future* (Gabriola Island, BC: Reflections, 1990), 5.

137 Ruth Loomis with Merv Wilkinson, 9.

138 Ruth Loomis with Merv Wilkinson, 10.

139 Ruth Loomis with Merv Wilkinson, 21.

140 Ruth Loomis with Merv Wilkinson, 23.

141 "Camps Permitted in Kitlope," *Northern Sentinel*, March 2, 1991.

142 *Coastal Old Growth Dynamics Project*, Coast Forest Region Research Section, https://www.for.gov.bc.ca/rco/research/eco/oldgrowthforests/oldgrowthdynamics/index.htm#second.

143 Andy MacKinnon, interview, November 1, 2017.

144 Sid Tafler, "People of the Kitlope," *Monday Magazine*, September 17 – 22, 1992, pp. 1 – 4.

145 Tafler, 1.

146 Bart Robinson, "Earthly Treasure," *Equinox*, September/October 1994, p. 42.

147 Robinson, 45.

148 Yvette Brend, "Ancient BC Tsunamis Etched Stories into Vancouver Island's Sediment," *CBC News*, July 13, 2016, http://www.cbc.ca/news/canada/british-columbia/paleotsunami-b-c-tofino-prince-rupert-peter-bobrowsky-1.3677842.

149 J. T. Kirby et al., "The 27 April 1975 Kitimat, British Columbia, Submarine Landslide Tsunami," *Landslides* 13 (2016): 1421, https://doi.org/10.1007/s10346-016-0682.

150 "From Coast to Coast," *Missionary Monthly*, January 1938, pp. 21 – 27, UCCBC.

151 Eric Jamieson, *The Native Voice: The Story of How Maisie Hurley and Canada's First Aboriginal Newspaper Changed a Nation* (Halfmoon Bay, BC: Caitlin Press, 2016), 43.

152 Paul Tennant, *Aboriginal Peoples and Politics: The Indian Land Question in BC* (Vancouver: UBC Press, 1990), 95.

153 "Alberni, B.C.," *Indian Residential School Quarterly Returns*, School Files Series, 1879 – 1953 (RG 10), Department of Indian Affairs and Northern Development Fonds, file 877-2 L.A.C. [MIKAN # 157505 Microform c-8759-01985], http://www.collectionscanada.gc.ca/microform-digitization/006003-119.02-e.php?PHPSESSID=ojsjo5d8dob8mdhrq7l4h55hv5&sqn=17&q2=2&q3=348&tt=1715.

154 United Church of Canada Archives, *The Children Remembered*, http://thechildren-remembered.ca/school-locations/alberni/.

155 "Extract from letter from P. Phillipps Harrison, Barrister and Solicitor, Notary Public, etc., Cumberland, B.C., dated January 15, 1918," RG 10, vol. 6431, file 877-1, pt. 1, L.A.C.; Paull to Ditchburn, Aug. 21, 1922. Cited in United Church of Canada Archives, *The Children Remembered*, http://thechildrenremembered.ca/school-locations/alberni/#ftn31.

156 G.H. Barry, "Report on Ahousaht Indian Residential School," [Mar. 24, 1936], RG 10, vol. 6430, file 876-6, pt. 1, Department of Indian Affairs and Northern Development Fonds, file 877-2 L.A.C.

157 [Graham?] to R.C. Scott, February 15, 1941, United Church of Canada Archives, *The Children Remembered*, http://thechildrenremembered.ca/school-locations/alberni/#ftn31.

158 H.M. Morrison, "Inspector's Report, Alberni Residential Indian School, January 16, 1945," Inspector of Schools, Indian Affairs, RG 10, vol. 6431, file 877-1, pt. 4, Department of Indian Affairs and Northern Development Fonds, file 877-2, L.A.C.

159 D.M. MacKay, "Report on Alberni Residential School," Indian Commissioner for BC to R.A. Hoey, Acting Director of Indian Affairs, Department of Mines and Resources, Ottawa, Canada, March 31, 1945, School Files Series 1879 – 1953, RG 10, Department of Indian Affairs and Northern Development Fonds, file 877-2, L.A.C. [MIKAN # 157505 Microform c-8759-01849 to 01856].

160 R.C. Scott, *My Captain Oliver: A Story of Two Missionaries on the British Columbia Coast* (United Church of Canada, Committee on Missionary Education, 1947).

161 Scott, 180.

162 Scott, 182.

163 The word "still" is typed in such a way that the letters slope to the right bottom corner of the page with no period.

164 R.C. Scott Fonds, R. C. Scott Papers, 2006 – EX 573 10 UCCBC.

165 Minutes of the Victoria Presbytery, 1939 – 1944, UCCBC.

166 McFadden, *Living by Bells*, 37.

167 Reverend Grant Bracewell, interview, November 29, 2016.

168 "Pedophile Punishment," *Maclean's*, April 3, 1995, p. 25.

169 Brian Thorpe, interview, January 17, 2017.

170 Brian Thorpe, interview, January 17, 2017.

171 Brian Thorpe, interview, January 17, 2017.

172 "New Deal for Indians Will Cost $12,000,000," *Daily Province*, Ottawa Bureau, October 25, 1945.

173 McFadden, *Living by Bells*, 37.

174 Kay How, 1936 Photo Album of Alberni Indian Residential School, Kathleen How Fonds, box P-35, file 6, item 13, UCCBC.

175 David Wilson, "Not Liable but Still Responsible," *UC Observer*, January 2004, http://www.ucobserver.org/justice/2004/01/not_liable_but_still_responsible/.

176 Brian Thorpe, interview, January 17, 2017.

177 Brian Thorpe, interview, January 17, 2017.

178 *The Western Eagle* 3, no. 1 (1948), RG 10, vol. 6431, file 877-1, pt. 4, Indian Affairs/L.A.C.

179 "End of an Era at A.I.R.S.," *Twin City Times*, June 23, 1965.

180 W.P. Bunt, "President and Superintendent Tours Indian Missions," *Western Recorder* 21 (February 1946): 2.

181 Hubert and Ann Evans, Correspondence to Rev. W.P. Bunt, May 10, 1945, Missions – Superintendent Bunt Fonds, UCCBC.

182 Haisla Nation Final Argument, May 31, 2013, Northern Gateway Pipeline Project, File-OF-Fac-Oil-N304-2010-01, National Energy Board, https://apps.neb-one.gc.ca/REGDOCS/Item/View/960020.

183 Jamieson, *The Native Voice*, 81.

184 Guy Williams, *The Native Voice Newsletter*, May 1947, p. 11.

185 Tennant, *Aboriginal Peoples and Politics*, 116.

186 Guy Williams, *The Native Voice Newsletter*, February 1960, 5.

187 Williams, 5.

188 Philip Mills, "Ship Indians to Reserve," *The Province*, June 17, 1978, p. 4.

189 Heber Maitland, correspondence to Hon. L. Allan Williams, Minister of Labour, June 20, 1978, Iona Campagnolo Fonds, 2009.6.13.17.063 Indian and Northern Affairs/Indian Bands, Councils and Reserves/Kitamaat, UNBC Archives.

190 Heber Maitland, report presented to NDP Caucus, April 22, 1978, Iona Campagnolo Fonds, 2009.6.13.17.063 Indian and Northern Affairs/Indian Bands, Councils and Reserves/Kitamaat, UNBC Archives.

191 "Northwest Coast Canoes," Bill Reid Centre, Simon Fraser Centre, http://www.sfu.ca/brc/art_architecture/canoes.html November 9, 2017.

192 "First Step towards Preservation of Mackenzie Grease Trail," No. 83-10 News Release,

Province of British Columbia, Minister of Lands, Parks and Housing, January 27, 1983.

193 Elizabeth Hardy, ed., *Kemano: Valley of Memories*, Kemano Community Association Book Committee (Kitimat: Ultratech Printing, c. 2001), Kitimat Museum and Archive.

194 R. Geddes Large, *History of the Prince Rupert General Hospital* (n.p., 1971).

195 Robert Bringhurst, *A Story as Sharp as a Knife: The Classic Haida Mythtellers and Their World* (Vancouver: Douglas & McIntyre, 1999), 447.

196 Gary Holland, "The Story of the Davis Raft," *The Nauticapedia*, http://www.nauticapedia.ca/Gallery/Davis_Rafts.php.

197 Hibby Gren, *Book of Poems* (Queen Charlotte Islands: Hecate Press, 1982), 14.

198 *Hansard*, May 7, 1952, https://www.lipad.ca/full/1952/05/07/5/.

199 Milton Weber, correspondence to Iona Campagnolo, February 1, 1977, Iona Campagnolo Fonds, Energy, Mines and Resources/Pipeline/Kitimat-Edmonton Pipeline, 2009.6.13.12.28, 2009.6.13.12.29, 2009.6.13.12.31, 2009.6.13.12.32, UNBC Archives.

200 D. Septer, *Flooding and Landslide Events Northern British Columbia 1820 – 2006* (BC Ministry of Environment, 2006), http://www.env.gov.bc.ca/wsd/public_safety/flood/pdfs_word/floods_landslides_north.pdf.

201 Rainforest Action Network, Mission Statement, https://www.ran.org/mission-and-values/.

202 Gordon Robertson, as told to Emmon Bach, in Appendix 8 in Brian Douglas Compton, "Upper Wakashan and Southern Tsimshian Ethnobotany: The Knowledge and Usage of Plants and Fungi amongst the Oweekeno, Hanaksiala (Kitlope and Kemano), Haisla (Kitimaat) and Kitasoo Peoples of the Central and North Coasts of British Columbia" (Ph.D. diss., University of British Columbia, 1993), 529.

203 Compton, 529.

204 "Oxford Group Connection," *History of Alcoholics Anonymous*, http://silkworth.net/aahistory/oxford_group_connection.html.

205 Bob Stewart, "Radiant Smiles in the Dirty Thirties: History and Ideology of the Oxford Group Movement in Canada 1932 – 1936" (M.A. thesis in Divinity, Vancouver School of Theology, 1974), 341.

206 Stewart, 341.

207 Compton, "Upper Wakashan and Southern Tsimshian Ethnobotany," 31.

208 Kathleen (Kay) Boas obituary, *Times-Colonist*, December 7, 2007, http://www.legacy.com/obituaries/timescolonist/obituary.aspx?n=kathleen-boas-kay&pid=99170078#sthash.Rpgcg03E.dpuf.

209 Lisa M. O'Connell, K. Ritland, and Stacey Lee Thompson, "Patterns of Post-Glacial Colonization by Western Redcedar (*Thuja plicata, Cupressaceae*) as Revealed by Microsatellite Markers," *Botany* 86 (2008): 194 – 203, http://www.genetics.forestry.ubc.ca/ritland/reprints/2008_Botany_Lisa_CwrPhylogeography.pdf.

210 *Annual Report of the Minister of Mines of the Province of British Columbia for the Year Ended 31st of December, 1930* (Victoria: Printer to the King's Most Excellent Majesty, 1931), http://cmscontent.nrs.gov.bc.ca/geoscience/PublicationCatalogue/AnnualReport/BCGS_AR1920.pdf.

211 Hank Ketcham, interview, April 10, 2017.

212 Cecelia Cashore Reekie, interview, June 29, 2015.

213 Heber Maitland to Minister Hugh Faulkner, cc. Minister Iona Campagnolo, May 18, 1978, Iona Campagnolo Fonds, 2009.6.13.17.063 Indian and Northern Affairs/Indian Bands, Councils and Reserves/Kitamaat, UNBC Archives.

214 Stephen Hume, "Canada 150: Campagnolo Was First Female President of Federal Liberal Party," *Vancouver Sun*, March 20, 2017, http://vancouversun.com/news/local-news/canada-150-campagnolo-was-first-female-president-of-federal-liberal-party.

215 Cecelia Cashore Reekie, interview, June 29, 2015.

216 Chris Cook, interview, January 12, 2018.

217 Lorna R. Barr, Peter A. Larkin, and J. Alistair McVey, *Kemano Completion Project Review*, BC Utilities Commission, December 16, 1994.

218 Barr, Larkin, and McVey, 217.

219 Envirocon Ltd., *Environmental Studies Associated with the Proposed Kemano Completion Hydroelectric Development*, vol. 22, 1984, 74 – 90.

220 Dan Gilmore, "Village Prepares for Kemano Injunction," *Northern Sentinel*, May 11, 1989.

221 Barr, Larkin, and McVey, *Kemano Completion Project Review* (Bruce Hill 3.99).

222 John Kelson, "Eulachon – BC's Giant Panda," *Watershed Sentinel*, June 3, 2013, https://watershedsentinel.ca/articles/eulachon-bcs-giant-panda/.

223 A.F. J. Lewis, M.D. McGurk, and M.G. Galesloot, *Alcan's Kemano River Eulachon (Thaleichthys pacificus) Monitoring Program 1988 – 1998*, consultant's report prepared by Ecofish Research Ltd. for Alcan Primary Metal Ltd. (Kitimat, BC, 2002), 136; A.F.J. Lewis and K. Ganshorn, *Alcan's Kemano River Eulachon (Thaleichthys pacificus) Monitoring Program: Haisla Fishery Monitoring*, consultant's report prepared by Ecofish Research Ltd. for Alcan Primary Metal Ltd. (Kitimat, BC, 2004), cited in Megan Felicity Moody, "Eulachon Past and Present" (M.Sc. thesis, University of British Columbia, 2008).

224 COSEWIC, *COSEWIC Assessment and Status Report on the Eulachon* Thaleichthys pacificus *Nass/Skeena Population Central Pacific Coast Population Fraser River Population in Canada*, 2011, http://www.registrelep.gc.ca/default.asp?lang=En&n=C2D0CBF6-1#_tech_sum02.

225 John Pritchard, interview, September 18, 2017.

226 Dan Gilmore, "Haisla Totem Soon to Grace Kemano," *Northern Sentinel*, October 25, 1989.

227 Cecelia Cashore Reekie, interview, June 29, 2015.

228 Report of the Native Affairs Consultant BC Conference, United Church of Canada August 1969 – February 1970, Native Affairs Consultants Reports Folder 21, Native Affairs Consultant (John Cashore) Fonds, box 1354, United Church, Pacific Mountain Region Archives.

229 Report of the Native Affairs Consultant BC Conference.

230 John Cashore to Hon. Jack Davis, February 18, 1971, Native Affairs Consultation – General Correspondence Folder 1, Native Affairs Consultant (John Cashore) Fonds, box 1354, United Church, Pacific Mountain Region Archives.

231 Prince Rupert Presbytery of the United Church of Canada Report on the Visitation to Kitamaat Village, March 19 – 23, 1971, Native Affairs Consultants Reports Folder 21, Native Affairs Consultant (John Cashore) Fonds, box 1354, Bob Stewart Archive.

232 John Cashore to Hon. M. Lalonde, May 29, 1973, Native Affairs Consultation – General Correspondence Folder 1, Native Affairs Consultant (John Cashore) Fonds, box 1354, Bob Stewart Archive.

233 John Cashore, interview, September 15, 2016.

234 John Cashore, interview, September 15, 2016.

235 John Cashore, interview, September 15, 2016.

236 Ron Thiele, "Haisla Put Spotlight on Kitlope," *Northern Sentinel*, March 3, 1994.

237 Hank Ketcham, interview, April 10, 2017.

238 John Cashore, interview, September 15, 2015.

239 John Cashore, interview, September 15, 2015.

240 *Huchsduwachsdu Nuyem Jees/Kitlope Heritage Conservancy Area Management Plan*, Haisla Nation/BC Parks, Draft 2007; Final, 2012, http://www.env.gov.bc.ca/bcparks/explore/cnsrvncy/kitlope/kitlope-mp.pdf.

241 John Cashore, interview, September 15, 2015.

242 Cecelia Cashore Reekie, interview, June 29, 2015.

243 Marguerite Wood, interview, January 17, 2017.

244 Douglas M. Swenerton, *A History of Pacific Fisheries Policy*, Program Planning and Economics Branch, Department of Fisheries and Oceans, 1993, http://www.dfo-mpo.gc.ca/Library/165966.pdf.

245 The Hon. Corky Evans, testifying at Fish Committee Meeting, Standing Committee for the House of Commons, January 20, 1998, http://www.ourcommons.ca/DocumentViewer/en/36-1/FISH/meeting-17/evidence.

246 "Guno Slams Socred Fish Farm Policies," *Northern Sentinel*, November 26, 1987, p. 2.

247 Cited in Stuart M. Leggatt, *Clear Choices, Clean Waters: The Leggatt Inquiry into Salmon Farming in British Columbia*, 2001, p. 9, http://www.farmedanddangerous.org/wpcontent/uploads/2011/04/Leggatt_reportfinal.pdf.

248 Standing Senate Committee on Fisheries, *Aquaculture in Canada's Atlantic and Pacific Regions*, Interim Report, June 2001, 73, https://sencanada.ca/Content/SEN/Committee/371/fish/rep/interim-fish-e.pdf.

249 Auditor General of Canada, *The Effects of Salmon Farming in British Columbia on the Management of Wild Salmon Stocks*, December 2000, 30 – 5, http://publications.gc.ca/collections/Collection/FA1-2000-3-15E.pdf.

250 "Austin Questions Fish Farm Ban," *Northern Sentinel*, April 2, 2008, p. 10.

251 Amy Smart, "BC Fish Farms, a Tangled Net," *Vancouver Courier*, December 3, 2017, http://www.vancourier.com/news/b-c-fish-farms-a-tangled-net-1.23112273.

252 Randy Shore, "First Nations Fish Farm Deal Sets the Table for Aquaculture Expansion," *Vancouver Sun*, December 14, 2018, https://vancouversun.com/news/local-news/broughton-area-first-nations-reach-deal-with-b-c-government-on-fish-farms.

253 National Film Board, *Totem: Return of the G'psgolox Pole*, synopsis, directed by Gil Cardinal (Montreal: NFB, 2003), https://www.nfb.ca/film/totem_the_return_of_the_gpsgolox_pole/.

254 Nanakila Institute, *G'psgolox Pole: Return and Renewal*, pamphlet, 2006.

255 National Film Board, *Totem: Return and Renewal*, synopsis, directed by Gil Cardinal (Montreal: NFB, 2003), https://www.nfb.ca/film/totem_return_and_renewal/.

256 Stacey R. Jessiman, "The Repatriation of the G'psgolox Totem Pole: A Study of Its Context, Process, and Outcome," *International Journal of Cultural Property* 18 (2011): 365 – 91.

257 Marius Barbeau, *Totem Poles*, 2 vols., Anthropology Series 30, National Museum of Canada Bulletin 119 (Ottawa: National Museum of Canada, 1950; repr., Hull, QC: Canadian Museum of Civilization, 1990).

258 Arthur Conan Doyle, *The Land of Mist* (London: Hutchison, 1926), https://www.arthur-conan-doyle.com/index.php?title=The_Land_of_Mist#II._Which_describes_an_evening_in_strange_company.

259 Cited in Nanakila Institute, *G'psgolox Pole: Return and Renewal.*

260 Cited in Nanakila Institute.

261 Cited in Nanakila Institute.

262 John Pritchard, interview, September 18, 2017.

263 Jessiman, "The Repatriation of the G'psgolox Totem Pole," 373.

264 John Pritchard, interview, September 18, 2017.

265 Jessiman, "The Repatriation of the G'psgolox Totem Pole," 374.

266 Trans Mountain Pipe Line Co. to Iona Campagnolo, correspondence, December 15, 1976, Iona Campagnolo Fonds, 2009.6.13.30.53 part 1 and 2 1975 – 1978, Transport/Marine Transportation/Ports, Harbour and Wharves/Kitimat, UNBC Archives.

267 Philippe Kirsch, West Coast Tankers Policy Co-ordination Group Department of External Affairs, July 20, 1976, Iona Campagnolo Fonds, 2009.6.13.30.53 part 1 and 2 1975 – 1978, Transport/Marine Transportation/Ports, Harbour and Wharves/Kitimat, UNBC Archives.

268 Arthur Anderson, United Church of Canada, to Hon. Allistair Gillespie, Minister of Fisheries, Energy Mines and Resources, correspondence, December 28, 1976, Iona Campagnolo Fonds, 2009.6.13.30.53 part 1 and 2 1975 – 1978, Transport/Marine Transportation/Ports, Harbour and Wharves/Kitimat, UNBC Archives.

269 Andrew Thompson, *West Coast Oil Port Inquiry: Statement of Proceedings*, February 1978, http://www.empr.gov.bc.ca/Mining/Geoscience/MapPlace/thematicmaps/Offshore-MapGallery/Documents/West-Coast-Oil-Port-Inquiry-Statement-of-Proceedings.pdf.

270 Liberal Party of Canada, secret briefing document, February 4, 1978, Iona Campagnolo Fonds, 2009.6.13.30.54 1975 – 1978, Transport/Marine Transportation/Ports, Harbour and Wharves/Kitimat, UNBC Archives.

271 Iona Campagnolo to Hugh Faulkner correspondence, May 12, 1978, Iona Campagnolo Fonds, 2009.6.13.30.54 1975 – 1978, Transport/Marine Transportation/Ports, Harbour and Wharves/Kitimat, UNBC Archives.

272 Merv Ritchie, "Hereditary Chiefs Stand United Opposed to Enbridge at JRP," *Kitimat Daily Online*, January 20, 2012, http://www.kitimatdaily.ca/go5571a/HEREDITARY_CHIEFS_STAND_UNITED_OPPOSED_TO_ENBRIDGE_AT_JRP.

273 Joe Oliver, "Open Letter from Natural Resource Minister Joe Oliver," *Globe and Mail*, January 9, 2012; Debates of Nov. 22, 2011, https://openparliament.ca/debates/2011/11/22/joe-oliver-2/.

274 Terry Glavin, "Canada Sells the Oil Sands to China Then Complains about Foreign Influence," *National Post*, January 13, 2012.

275 "Vivian Krause," Center for Media and Democracy, https://www.sourcewatch.org/index.php/Vivian_Krause.

276 Gerald Amos, "The Enbridge Pipeline: The 'Largest and Most Insidious Threat to Our Culture,'" *HuffPost*, January 11, 2012, https://www.huffingtonpost.ca/gerald-amos/ northern-gateway-pipeline_b_1199956.html?ref=canada.

277 Cited in Dave Johnson, "Respect the Rules," *Industrial Safety and Hygene Rules*, https:// www.ishn.com/articles/95315-respect-the-rules-it-helps-to-keep-them-simple.

278 Andrew Nikiforuk, "Three Wacky Accounting Numbers for LNG and Shale Gas," *The Tyee*, February 29, 2016, https://thetyee.ca/Opinion/2016/02/29/ Wacky-Accounting-Shale-Gas.

279 James Wilt, "Claudia Cattaneo," *DesmogCanada*, July 27, 2016, https://www. desmog.ca/directory/vocabulary/21625; Markham Hyslop, "Claudia Cattaneo and the Sad State of 'Team Energy' Journalism," *North American Energy News*, May 24, 2017, http://theamericanenergynews.com/markham-on-energy/ claudia-cattaneo-sad-state-team-energy-journalism.

280 Claudia Cattaneo, "'Sickening': First Nations Left Empty-Handed as Environmentalist Pressure Kills BC Energy Projects," *Financial Post*, November 16, 2017, http:// business.financialpost.com/commodities/energy/sickening-first-nations-left-empty-handed-as-environmentalist-pressure-kills-b-c-energy-projects.

281 Matt Meuse, "LNG Canada Investment Delay Frustrates Kitimat, Haisla Nation," *CBC News*, July 13, 2016, http://www.cbc.ca/news/canada/british-columbia/ lng-delay-frustration-1.3678397.

282 Rob Shaw, "LNG Canada Project in Kitimat Given Green Light to Build by Shareholders," *Vancouver Sun*, October 2, 2018, https://vancouversun.com/news/politics/ lng-canada-green-light.

283 Barbetti, *Haisla!*, 22.

284 Robin Rowland, "Special Report: Clio Bay Cleanup: Controversial, Complicated and Costly," *NW Coast Energy News*, September 29, 2017, http://nwcoastenergynews. com/2013/09/29/4839/special-report-clio-bay-cleanup-controversial-complicated -costly/.

285 Lelu Island Declaration, http://friendsofwildsalmon.ca/campaigns/detail/ liquefied_natural_gas_lng_development/the_lelu_island_declaration/.

286 http://www.cftktv.com/News/Story.aspx?ID=2191430.

287 Dirk Meissner, "B.C. Premier Christy Clark Strikes Back at LNG Opponents," *CBC News*, January 26, 2016, http://www.cbc.ca/news/canada/british-columbia/b-c-premier-christy-clark-strikes-back-at-lng-opponents-1.3419993.

288 Eagle Spirit Energy Holdings, "Game Changing First Nations Energy Company Announced," *CISION*, September 26, 2012, http://www.newswire.ca/news-releases/ game-changing-first-nations-energy-company-announced-510830771.html.

289 Calvin Helin, http://www.calvinhelin.com/about-2/projects.

290 Eagle Spirit Energy Holdings, "Game Changing First Nations Energy Company Announced."

291 Ash Kelly and Brielle Morgan, "Divide and Conquer," *Discourse Media*, June 23, 2016, http://discoursemedia.org/toward-reconciliation/divide-and-conquer.

292 Ian Gill, "Power Struggle in Northern B.C. Deepens as Pressure to Approve LNG Builds," *Discourse Media*, June 27, 2016, https://www.thediscourse.ca/reconciliation/ power-struggle-northern-b-c-deepens-pressure-approve-lng-builds.

293 Statement by Algmxaa (Murray Smith), one of the House Leaders of the Gitwilgyoots Tribes – one of the Nine Allied Tribes of Lax Kw'alaams, Terrace, July 14, 2016.

294 Cattaneo, "'Sickening.'"

295 Nick Eagland, "Petronas Cancels $11.4 Billion LNG Project near Prince Rupert," *Vancouver Sun*, July 26, 2017, http://vancouversun.com/news/local-news/petronas-cancels-11-4-billion-lng-project-near-prince-rupert.

296 Sarah Berman, "Coastal First Nations Call Out 'Eagle Spirit' Pipeline," *The Tyee*, February 13, 2015, https://thetyee.ca/News/2015/02/13/Eagle-Spirit-Pipeline/.

297 Donnie Wesley, interview, January 21, 2018.

298 Carnation Creek Watershed Experiment, Government of British Columbia, https://www2.gov.bc.ca/gov/content/environment/plants-animals-ecosystems/fish/fish-forestry/carnation-creek.

299 Cecelia Cashore Reekie, interview, June 29, 2015.

300 Cecelia Cashore Reekie, interview, June 29, 2015.

301 Terry Allen, "At-Risk Native Talk," *UMassMag Online*, Summer 2003, https://web.archive.org/web/20160213231730/http://www.umassmag.com/Summer_2003/At_risk_Native_Talk_510.html.

302 J. R. (Jim) Miller, "Petitioning the Great White Mother: First Nations' Organizations and Lobbying in London," in *Canada and the End of Empire*, ed. Phillip A. Buckner (Vancouver: UBC Press, 2005), citing "Indians' Petition to King Edward," *Victoria Daily Colonist*, July 6, 1906.

303 For the full account of June 1793, see Lamb, *George Vancouver*.

304 In the long, slow, perpetual cycle of stories coming from the Magic Canoe of Wa'xaid, the one that returns most frequently is that of the Magic Canoe itself. That story reached an international audience in May 2013. The World Indigenous Network Conference was being held in Darwin, Australia, and 1,400 Indigenous leaders were gathering. Ric Young took Wa'xaid's message of the Magic Canoe along with Jessie Housty to deliver it to the gathering.

   Ian Gill reported on the event in *The Tyee* on June 15, 2013, writing about the Indigenous leaders gathered there:

   Among them were a number of Canadians, three of whom – perhaps unknown to many in their own country – offered one of the most moving and important lessons of the entire gathering. They appeared on stage together – Jessie Housty, a young indigenous leader from the central coast of British Columbia, holding a canoe paddle in her hands; Ric Young, the Toronto-based founder of The Social Projects Studio and a world-leading architect of social change initiatives; and, looking down on the huge stage and lighting it with a smile every bit as radiant as Nelson Mandela's, indigenous elder Cecil Paul.

   Every Indigenous group represented there decorated a paddle with their own art – they assembled the 50-plus paddles for a colourful banner under which Wa'xaid's quote is written: "I was alone in a canoe. But it was a magical canoe because there was room for everyone who wanted to paddle together. The currents against us were very strong. But I believed we could reach our destination and that we had to for our survival."

305 Cecelia Cashore Reekie, interview, September 30, 2018.

306 With assistance from Cecil Paul Sr., Louisa Smith, Jay Powell and Charles Menzies. All mistakes are the author's own.

INDEX OF NAMES

Williams, Mae 173, 186, 339
Williams, Maudie 186, 202, 223, 236, 255, 300, 302, 342, 343
Williams, Minnie. *See* Paul, Minnie
Williams, Rhoda 186, 236, 343
Williams, Sadie 186
Williams, Viv 172
Williston, R.G. 64
Wilson, Barry 320
Wilson, Charlie 15, 169, 188, 189, 190, 192
Wilson, Derek 320
Wilson, Elder Bea 92, 103, 110, 111, 256, 339
Wilson, Esther 15, 45, 46. *See also* Paul, Esther
Wilson, Johnny 14, 101, 103, 104, 110, 111, 127, 164, 192, 222, 256, 339
Wilson, Reggie 147, 148
Wilson, Samuel 15, 36, 45
Wilson, Vietta 213, 215, 217. *See also* Paul, Vietta
Wilson, William Griffith 183
Winch, Ernest 50
Winchester, Neville 126
Winch, Harold 50
Windsor, Evelyn 322
Women's Missionary Society 44, 134

Wood, Marguerite 176–178, 224, 285, 300–301. *See also* Demers, Marguerite
Wood, Peter 300
World Indigenous Network Conference 112, 244
Wow'kst River 88
Wuikinuxv/Oweekeno (people) 24
X̌enaksialak̓ala. *See* Xenaksiala (language)
X̌a'islak̓ala. *See* Haisla (language)
Xais-Xais (people) 107
Xenaksiala (language) 7, 11, 24, 35, 71, 138, 139, 180, 322, 348–349, 351
Xenaksiala (people) 11, 13, 14, 19, 24, 27, 28, 29, 30, 49–51, 51, 63, 64, 69, 108, 131, 265
Xesdu'wäxw (grease trail) 11, 166. *See also* Kitlope, The (region)
Xwechtáal. *See* Paull, Chief Andrew
Yahaan. *See* Wesley, Donnie
Yamacisa-Kemaninuxw (mountain) 51. *See also* Mount DuBose
Yorktown Clipper (vessel) 309
Young, Ric 109, 112
Yu, Peter 174
Zentilliwo, Bernardo 81
Zola Spirit. *See* Chief G'psgolox

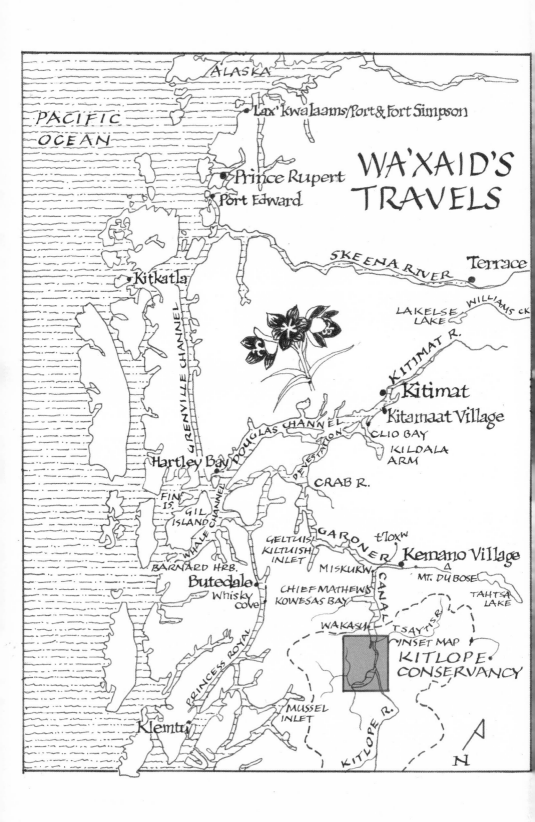

ALASKA

PACIFIC
OCEAN

Lax'kwalaams/Port & Fort Simpson

Prince Rupert
Port Edward

WA'XAID'S
TRAVELS

Kitkatla

SKEENA RIVER   Terrace

LAKELSE
LAKE   WILLIAMS CK.

KITIMAT R.

Kitimat

Kitamaat Village

CLIO BAY
KILDALA
ARM

GRENVILLE CHANNEL

DOUGLAS CHANNEL

DEY. STATION

Hartley Bay

CRAB R.

FIN
IS.
GIL
ISLAND

WHALE CHANNEL

GARDNER CANAL   t'loxw

Kemano Village

GELTUIS/
KILTUISH
INLET

MISKUKW

MT. DUBOSE

BARNARD HRB.

Butedale

Whisky
Cove

CHIEF MATHEWS
KOWESAS BAY

TAHTSA
LAKE

WAKASU

TSAYTIS

INSET MAP

KITLOPE
CONSERVANCY

PRINCESS ROYAL

MUSSEL
INLET

Klemtu

KITLOPE R.

N